Western Culture in Gospel Context

Western Culture in Gospel Context

Towards the Conversion of the West—
Theological Bearings for Mission and Spirituality

DAVID J. KETTLE

CASCADE *Books* · Eugene, Oregon

Cascade Books
An Imprint of Wipf and Stock Publishers
199 W. 8th Ave., Suite 3
Eugene, OR 97401

www. wipfandstock.com

ISBN 13: 978-1-61097-184-3

Cataloging-in-Publication data

Kettle, David J.

  Western culture in gospel context : towards the conversion of the West—
theological bearings for mission and spirituality / David J. Kettle ; with a foreword by
Tim Dakin.

  xvi + 380 p. ; 23 cm. —Includes bibliographical references and index.

  ISBN 13: 978-1-61097-184-3

  1. Mission of the church. 2. Christianity and culture. 3. Knowledge—Theory of
(Religion). 4. Apologetics. 5. Missions. I. Dakin, Tim. II. Title.

BR115.C8 Z95 2011

Manufactured in the U.S.A.

Dedicated to my favorite childhood uncle,
Rex Kettle, 1928–1979

Were you not as Christians taught the truth as it is in Jesus?
Renouncing your former way of life,
you must lay aside the old human nature which, deluded by its desires,
is in process of decay.
You must be renewed in mind and spirit,
and put on the new nature created in God's likeness, which shows itself
in the upright and devout life called for by the truth.
—Ephesians 4:21–24

It is impossible that God should ever be the end, if he is not the
beginning.
We lift our eyes on high, but lean upon the sand.
—Blaise Pascal

Contents

Foreword

KNOWN BY GOD

"IT IS NOT FOR you to know them but for them to know you." So said our guide as we walked around an African animal park and came to the crocodile enclosure. As Westerners reviewing the exhibits of our culture we may come across the God enclosure. Some guides might question whether there's anything there apart from cultural and religious arte-facts. But with David Kettle as our guide we are challenged to realize that it is God's knowledge of us, and not ours of him, which is the basis for human understanding. David reminds us of what P. T. Forsyth once wrote: "Religion turns not on knowing but being known." We discover God's knowledge of us in the reconciling love of Jesus. We participate in God's mission as we spread the knowledge that we are known and loved by God, and that he has good purposes for us and for those to whom he sends us.

It is God's reconciliation of us to himself that shapes his knowledge of us and our knowledge of him. Thus it is our conversion to this way of understanding knowledge—with all the wider transformation that such conversion brings to the whole of life—that this book explores. David is our guide to what it means to be known and to know this God-in-Christ within Western culture.

THE CALL TO CONVERSION

In *Beyond Tragic Spirituality*[1] David Kettle explored the fundamental malaise of Western culture—the lack of hope. Now, in this long-awaited book, he looks at how conversion to the gospel of hope can be the basis for a reconstruction of culture in the West. David proposes a total re-construction, starting with our understanding of knowledge and then

---

1. Kettle, *Beyond Tragic Spirituality*.

considering ten key aspects of life. Finally he discusses how we could
begin to plot out the mission that is now needed.

David has long been an advocate for the work of Lesslie Newbigin.
Here he sets out some of the implications of Newbigin's prophetic call
to the Western church to recognize its need for a new conversion to the
gospel of Jesus Christ. As the coordinator of The Gospel and Our Culture
Network, David has faithfully held Newbigin's prophetic teaching before
the church. But this book is more than a commentary on Newbigin; it
is the distillation of many years of reflection on what it might mean for
Western culture to be newly and thoroughly converted to the gospel.

In Lesslie Newbigin's little book on the challenges of Christian faith
in Western culture, *Truth and Authority in Modernity*, he says, "We seem
to be nearing the end of a period in which it was believed that modern science could provide a corpus of universal truth that would be the possession of all human beings, whatever their cultural differences."[2] Newbigin
points out that this claim, with its idea of self-authenticating logical
foundations, is no longer valid and sits uncomfortably with the multi-
culturalism that brands any claim to universal truth as imperialistic.

For David Kettle the end of the modernistic era is a new opportunity for Christians in Western culture. It is the start of a new period, as
Newbigin foresaw, in which to explore what it means to be known by
God. First, it implies a change in our understanding of knowledge itself
and, second, it requires a deep ongoing conversion of ourselves and of
our culture in all its aspects.

CONVERSION AND CULTURE

David's book is divided into two main parts, with an extended introduction that helpfully reviews the argument. Conversion is the heart of the
matter. Some use the word conversion to refer to those who join another
denomination or another religion. For David conversion is not about
joining a denomination or religion; rather it is about a whole way of
seeing and being human as a follower of Jesus Christ in God's world. It
is about turning towards the God who knows us in Jesus Christ. This reorientation, being located by God-in-Christ, characterizes faith and locates us in the world that has been reconciled to God. As Dalferth says:

---

2. Newbigin, *Truth and Authority in Modernity*, 36.

> On the basis of God's revelation in Jesus Christ Christians hold
> that faith provides that access to the divine knowledge which
> alone enables us to locate ourselves absolutely. But they cannot
> establish the truth of this claim or show that in fact we are ab-
> solutely located, for it is an intrinsic part of their claim that only
> God himself can assure us of the truth of it. They can only testify
> to it, make it cognitively accessible by propagating the Gospel; and
> outline how it may become intelligible and credible to others.[3]

Getting a new understanding of knowledge is the project of Part
One: Conversion as Knowing. Knowledge is a form of indwelling: the
Christian understanding of knowledge is, first of all, a realization that
we indwell a world in which we have been reconciled to God as host.
His reconciling hospitality grounds all our knowledge of the world in
which we live. All avoidance of such knowledge is evidence of the sin
that separates us from God. We only come to know the true depth of this
separation when we accept God's reconciliation of the world to himself.
With this acceptance we enter the Christian way of knowing: the way of
life that is an ongoing conversion.

David's argument in Part Two could be summed up as an exploration of what it means to understand the Christian worldview as the
"social imaginary" of those converted to Christian faith in Western culture. David outlines and then explores the implications of what it means
for people to become believers, converted, in a culture that has been
influenced by Enlightenment rationality: a self-referential and culturally
isolated project. David asks us to reconsider, in depth, what it means
to have the mind of Christ: to have the mind of Christ expressed in all
aspects of social and cultural life. Faith is not a private or personal matter; it requires a full-orbed "worldview" that is lived and expressed in the
whole of life—a social imaginary where values and facts are integrated.

Paul Hiebert, the social anthropologist of mission, defines worldviews as follows: "Worldviews are what people in a community take as
given realities, the maps they have of reality they are using for living."[4]
David would share Paul Hiebert's concerns about the limitation of the
term worldview, i.e., it implies a cognitive basis for faith, it is a term dominated by the language of one sense (i.e., sight), and it can be understood
too individualistically. To these criticisms we may also add that the term

---

3. Dalferth, *Theology and Philosophy*, 210.

4. Hiebert, *Transforming Worldviews*, 15.

"worldview" could be seen as an attempt to get an external universal perspective on faith that questions the singularity of the gospel, i.e., it is just one among many worldviews. As Christians we do not locate, understand, ourselves in this world by selecting the Christian worldview, having compared it with others. Rather, we have been located in the world by God's absolute knowledge of us in Christ. In conversion we discover that we are known absolutely by the one true God in Christ.

Nevertheless worldview is a strong term to use in connection with the kind of change that conversion implies, i.e., requiring of us a transformation of how we view the world and live in it (Rom 12:2). Western Christians have been conformed to Enlightenment rationality for so long that we are hardly aware of what we take for granted. David peels back the implications of being converted anew to the Christian faith, to have a transformed and transforming worldview.

So conversion is about a transforming worldview. This goes to the heart of what happened to Paul. Paul was not only converted within his Jewish worldview to view the world anew through Jesus, he was also converted to see other worldviews from the perspective of Christ. It was out of this deep conversion, "of Christ revealed in me" (Gal 1:6), that he experienced his vocational call: to become the apostle to the Gentiles. Terrance Donaldson writes of the three levels of Paul's conversion:[5]

1.   Our everyday language, symbols, and action

2.   In the structures or systems of our thought

3.   Within our core convictions and beliefs

This kind of conversion provides us with a way of knowing in which all other forms of knowing are evaluated. So, if we only really know when we know that we are known by God, then all knowledge must begin again here. From this position David proposes ten conversions in Western culture:

1.   *From* secular and sacred in contemporary understanding: *to* creation and new creation by God.

2.   *From* the trajectory of individualism and totalitarianism: *to* community under God.

---

5. Donaldson, *Paul and the Gentiles*, 42ff.

3. *From* the modern betrayal of enquiry: *to* attentiveness towards God.

4. *From* contemporary demonization and polarization: *to* divine bearings.

5. *From* the needy consumer: *to* the abundance of God.

6. *From* the tragic sense of life: *to* the gospel of hope.

7. *From* personal fulfillment and contemporary spirituality: *to* eternal life.

8. *From* the ideology of rights and political correctness: *to* God-given dignity.

9. *From* Neoliberal capitalist ideology: *to* the "commonweal" of God.

10. *From* public facts and private values: *to* the sovereignty of God.

If conversion is to become a way of life in Western culture today there must be a conversion of the whole of life. These ten conversions express the singularity of the one gospel as it engages with Western culture. They are specific to the Western context but could provide a framework for comparing conversion in other cultures, worldviews, and a basis for sharing the gospel anew.

RESPONSIBLE MISSION

A final word about the importance of this book. John Drane argues that what Christians do in the West to re-evangelize their culture will have a big impact on the rest of the world.

> Christians sometimes take comfort from the fact that the Church is growing through much of the non-western world, and that is of course something to be aware of. But the idea that this will eventually work in reverse, and the West will be re-evangelized by that route, is almost certainly wishful thinking. We may not like it (and there are many reasons not to), but this is not how the future will be determined, especially not in a post 9/11 world that has seen the rise of a new imperialism among Western powers.[6]

Drane's warning highlights the interconnection between the local and the global. It suggests that what we do in local mission in the West

---

6. Drane, *Do Christians Know How to Be Spiritual?*, 157f.

may have a profound impact on world mission, depending on whether we are strategic about our intentions and commitments. The subtitle of David's book leaves us in no doubt about what is required: "towards the conversion of the West."

Conscious of the fact that the evangelization of the West was a major challenge, a former head of the Church Mission Society (CMS) once called CMS members to rededicate themselves to "a life in God to be discovered, lived, and shared with all the world."[7] In this thoughtful and profound book David Kettle challenges those of us in the West to a deeper conversion: to indwell and share the reconciling love of God in Jesus Christ. Only with that as our hope can we expect to lead a transforming mission in the West.

Tim Dakin
Community Leader, Church Mission Society

7. Cash, *Responsibility of Success*, 66.

Acknowledgments

I AM GRATEFUL TO the following who have, in the middle of busy lives, read and commented upon all or part of the text of this book: Jeremy Begbie, Tim Dakin, Gavin Drew, John Inge, J. Andrew Kirk, Douglas Knight, Andrew Lim, Elizabeth Newman, Sue Patterson, Philip Sampson, Alan Storkey, Paul Weston, and Carver T. Yu.

I am grateful to those who have served on the Management Council of the Gospel and Our Culture Network in Great Britain during its time as a charitable trust and offered me valued collegial support as Network Coordinator. My opportunities to reflect with them have sustained the ministry of which this book is a fruit. They are Craig Bartholomew, Matthew Baynham, Peter Forster, Tom Foust, Stephen May, Murray Rae, Brian Stanley, Jenny Taylor, Carol Walker, Heather Ward, and (once again) J. Andrew Kirk and Paul Weston.

Part One of this book is a "popularized" version of material from an earlier manuscript that I submitted to many publishers for consideration without success in 1990; Part Two engages vital issues in contemporary Western culture brought to light by, and seen in the light of, these earlier proposals. This engagement was hammered out in the course of ministry in the Anglican Church in New Zealand, 1991–1997. For the opportunity for this ministry, I am enormously grateful to Archbishop Brian Davis (in whose diocese I served); to Bishop Brian Carrell who, with his wife, May, regularly hosted a Gospel & Culture group that I convened throughout those years, and which provided excellent opportunity for discussion in an ecumenical group of Christians involved in the ministry of the church, in academia, and in the lay professions); and to Harold Turner, Secretary of the Gospel & Cultures Trust (later DeepSight), whose own work, and whose warm hospitality together with his wife, Maud, were a great encouragement to me.

I am grateful to others with whom theological discussion has, at one point or another, been a stimulus to my thinking: David Brown,

John Flett, Barbara Tyler, Peter Lineham, and members of the "Worth North" group of the Lay Community of St. Benedict.

During parish ministry prior to New Zealand, I found deeply valued opportunities for reflection (bringing some key breakthroughs) while enjoying the hospitality of the Anglican Franciscans at Alnmouth, Hilfield, and Glasshampton Friaries.

I am grateful to two dear mentors (both now deceased) for formative Christian encouragement at an earlier stage of my life, and who acted as referees when I offered myself for ordained ministry: Peter Coleman (my university chaplain) and Frances Van Der Schot (a friend of many years since I served on V.S.O. in Uganda).

Especially, I am grateful to my wife, Anne, for her loyal and unreserved support. As a hard-working G.P. and the mother of our four children she provided most of the family income during the periods 1984–1990 and 1997–2010 in order that I might pursue the ministry of writing and reflection on the gospel and Western culture.

I can hardly imagine having written this book without the resources of the Cambridge University Library and its generous policy towards those wishing to read and borrow its books. My thanks to those who guard this vision, and to the library staff who implement it day by day.

Finally I am grateful to Wipf & Stock for their vision and commitment to publishing Christian theology, for the clarity of their guidance to authors, and for their efficiency in bringing this book to publication.

INTRODUCTION

"OF COURSE, THE NUMBER one question is 'Can the West be converted?'" So murmured General Simatoupong of Indonesia as he returned to his seat next to Lesslie Newbigin. The occasion was a conference of the World Council of Churches, "Salvation Today," in Bangkok in 1973. A decade or so later, when Newbigin turned his attention more fully upon Western culture as a mission field, he recalled this remark often.

Can the West be converted? What might it mean, indeed, to conceive of "the conversion of the West"? Is this to conceive of something that God wills, and Christians are right to seek? To Western Christians, these questions may be perplexing. There is a fairly common tendency to see, on the one hand, conversion as a private affair, a choice made by the autonomous individual. "The West," on the other hand, tends to be seen as a broad cultural phenomenon identified with geographical, historical, social, and intellectual commonalities or affinities. While "the West" may happen to be the broad cultural context in which individuals live, think, and act—and perhaps convert to Christ—it will surely be wrongheaded to seek something called "the conversion of the West" itself?

However this way of seeing conversion, individuals, and their contexts in their relation to each other is seriously wrong. No doubt, if it is set within a deeper understanding, it points to important truths; but taken by itself it offers a false, reductionist understanding of persons, contexts, and conversion alike. In reality individuals and the contexts in which they live are integrally related, while God is their deepest context of all. When the Western individual is converted to Christ, this is at once a conversion of them *from* their culture and a conversion within them *of* their culture. This paradox lies at the heart of this book, in relation to the cultural context of "the West."

For Western Christians this invites reflection both upon their own culture and upon their own faith: are they converted faithfully *from*

1

Western culture, and is Western culture properly *converted within them*? Or is it rather the case that, unawares, their faith is domesticated to Western culture? Are they unable to see this culture, and their domestication to it, for what they are in the light of Christ?

Introducing my topic, I shall first recall what it means to be converted to Christ. For a start, if we profess faith in Christ this does not, in itself, show we are converted: professing Christians may in practice refuse to be responsive to God and allow God to change the way they think, behave, and feel—their whole way of seeing others, themselves, and the world—in ways that God desires. As part of this, they may remain or become captive to cultural beliefs, passions, and worldviews at odds with conversion to Christ. The temptation of cultural captivity to modern Western culture is pervasive among professing Christians in the West today. This, of course, subverts authentic *mission*. I shall indicate briefly the form taken by such cultural captivity as it has been recognized by Lesslie Newbigin. I shall then consider four models for mission that, seen in the light of this, appear in themselves inadequately and ambiguously to define the shape of mission today. Authentic mission must rise above cultural captivity; it integrally embraces the conversion of culture, and this conversion begins within the church. However, some readers will have basic doubts about the very project of "the conversion of the West" in the first place: I shall discuss four such doubts. Finally I shall introduce the arguments and themes presented in this book.

CONVERSION AS LIBERATION, AND THE CULTURAL CAPTIVITY OF THE WESTERN CHURCH

To be converted to Christ is to be turned from the world as one has known it and to see everything anew in the context of Christ. It is to be radically reoriented; it is to find new bearings from Christ. In this new orientation, the gospel of Jesus Christ engages us to our personal depths, permeating our imaginative world in a quite comprehensive way. Jesus Christ—in words and actions culminating in his embrace of execution and his resurrection—reveals and embodies the approach of God in sovereignty as our ultimate context. In Christ, God engages our familiar contexts comprised of our habitual practices and assumptions, worldviews, and personal commitments, and breaks them open, animating them as signs pointing to the deeper context of his approaching kingdom and liberating us for participation in it. In Part One of this book we shall explore what this means; in Part Two we shall examine the shape it gives to the vocations of mission and spiritual life in Western culture today.

In this way the gospel speaks at once *to* and *within* the context of our personal life-world: paradoxically it is always at once *transcendent* and *contextual*. In this same encounter it at once discloses God's *fulfill- ment of* and God's *judgment upon* the context that makes up our personal life-world with its beliefs, practices, and commitments.

Conversion is a matter of unending renewal. It is a matter of an endlessly renewed orientation, both as new insight and implications of conversion dawn upon us calling for faithful response, and as we meet new temptations to fall away from faith. This is the "logic of evangelism."[1] Correspondingly, the call of conversion is a call to a conscious declara- tion of faith—an explicit religious acknowledgement of God's unquali- fied self-revealing action in Jesus Christ.

Although the profession of religious faith is properly central to a converted life, in practice Christian profession shows itself to be nei- ther sufficient for the transforming work of God's grace, nor for that matter immediately necessary to it: evangelization, as the tacit working of God's grace within persons, typically both succeeds and precedes the explicit confession of faith. On the one hand, a person who declares Christian faith may interpret this in practice in ways quite unrespon- sive to the transforming demands of the gospel; we may describe such faith as *domesticated* to the context made up by their unregenerate personal life-world. On the other hand, a person who is not religiously committed in any formal, intentional way may show themselves by their wisdom and virtue to be very open to the transforming grace of God. However, these considerations offer no reason whatsoever for the church to turn away from seeking to bring people to explicit, public profession of Christian faith.

This has implications for our life within any culture, whether cul- ture of a more traditional, premodern kind to which we belong in a single, comprehensive way, or of a more differentiated, fluid, multiple, overlapping or nested kind. As with persons, so with cultures made up of the lives of persons: just as the gospel speaks at once *to* and *within* the

1. William Abraham's *The Logic of Evangelism* is a valuable study of conversion as a continuing event of transformation.

context of a personal life-world, so it speaks *to* and *within* the context of a culture, and in this same encounter it at once discloses God's *fulfillment of* and *judgment upon* that culture. Once again, a prevalent Christian confession is central in a culture whose inhabitants are nourished in openness to Christian transformation; but it does not guarantee such continuing conversion, nor is it immediately necessary to it. A formally "Christian" culture may be domesticated to unregenerate aspects within it. It is the calling of the church to overcome this by its preaching of the gospel in word and deed. However, the church may be vulnerable to the same cultural domestication. The gospel is then robbed—not only in the wider culture but in the church itself—of the sovereign freedom of God *to address* the culture in question so as to mediate God's fulfillment and judgment of the culture. The transcendence of the gospel is betrayed: there is no genuine proclamation of the gospel and there is no authentic Christian conversion.

The domestication of Christian faith to Western culture—within as well as beyond the church—is a major issue today. To ask, "Can the West be converted?" is therefore to ask first of all, "Can the church be converted?" It is to ask whether the people who form the church itself can be converted from a culturally captive form of faith to that endlessly renewed reorientation towards God that is conversion. And it is to ask whether *we ourselves* can be converted in this way.

The domestication of Christian faith to Western culture is a matter of great significance today not only for the West but also for the rest of the world, and for many reasons. Western nations have unprecedented power and wealth to promote what they favor in non-Western countries; Western culture has an unprecedented power of penetration and attraction through the global spread of the mass media; the West retains, despite guilt over past imperial acts of oppression, a vision of shaping other societies to conform with its own tenets (e.g., regarding individual rights and economic restructuring). For the sake of the world as well as for its own sake, the West needs in its use of power and wealth to draw guidance and nourishment from the gospel. But it cannot find this from a domesticated church.

Again, in recent generations trends have accentuated in Western culture that are deeply ambivalent vis-à-vis human flourishing,[2] but yet

2. On "human flourishing" in Christian understanding as God's good purpose for humanity, see Newbigin, "Human Flourishing in Faith, Fact, and Fantasy."

do not obviously connect with or invite judgment by reference to "conventional" Christian virtues and vices. Among these are individualism, consumerism, and the public ideological programs associated with neoliberal global capitalism and with the excesses of "political correctness." These trends cause concern among Christians and others; however, Christian responses to them are often *ad hoc* and a matter of contention. Sufficient guidance is not forthcoming from conventional Christianity, which fails to engage with a cultural trajectory that diverges increasingly from orientation towards God's coming kingdom. In its failure to engage, however, it by default accommodates itself uncritically to this culture. Such engagement is vital, however, guided and nourished by a deeper theological conversation between the gospel and Western culture than is generated by such conventional religion.

The fact of their cultural captivity easily eludes Christians because cultural assumptions lie hidden deep below the surface of everyday life. Christians belonging to a particular culture can quite thoughtlessly assimilate the gospel to that culture. Church life can model confusion as churchgoers sit on the fence between a life shaped and nourished by the gospel and a life ignorant or neglectful of the gospel. This is true for Christians living in any culture in the world; however, in Western culture there is an added barrier to a Christian cultural self-awareness in that Western culture presents to its members a particular, explicit vision and view of itself, especially in its public life. This gives distinctive form to the cultural captivity of the church in Western culture today.

Firstly, Western culture takes a particular view of itself *vis-à-vis Christianity*. The fact of Western culture's own history of engagement with the gospel allows the view that this culture has *moved on*: progress has (supposedly) brought wider, secular horizons for life within which faith is seen as a private choice and no longer a guide for public and private life alike. Christians have tended to go along with this, rather than urging that faith embraces deeper and more trustworthy horizons for life than modern secular culture.

Secondly, Western culture upholds a particular view and vision of itself *vis-à-vis "culture" as a genre* that hinders it from recognizing its true nature. This self-understanding comprises two claims for itself, each at odds with the other. On the one hand, it sees itself as *rising above* cultural customs and assumptions in general: it sees itself as entrusting itself to wherever the individual exercise of universal reasoning powers and autonomous choice may lead. On the other hand, it regards itself as *defining* culture: it sets out to cultivate and civilize its citizens through education and surveillance. In this matter, and despite rhetoric from some quarters claiming "the end of ideology," Western culture is increasingly shaped today by ideology and the programs of "rationalization" that it spawns.

The cultural captivity of the church has taken divergent forms in the United States, continental Europe, and Britain corresponding to their respective ideological trends and their attitudes to the relation between religion and the secular state.[3] In Britain these forms of cultural captivity converge today as the power of the United States and of the European Union impact at once upon British life.

Western indifference to, and domestication of, the gospel reflects a fundamental modern *worldview and way of life* that legitimizes this and is embodied in plausibility structures and loci of power. Involved in this process is the power of personal attachments, sentiment, and—integrally—of certain *fundamental habits of thought and imagination* regarding our human identity. These habits lead even people of deep faith to misrepresent their faith both to themselves and to others. Together these features of Western culture at once reflect and legitimize the sway of principalities and powers.

To understand this we have to recall the origins of modern Western culture in the vision formulated in medieval Europe of a continuing program of state-organized "civilization" replacing and reforming traditional culture, beliefs, and customs. Philosophers associated with the European Enlightenment played a vital part in the formulation of this vision.

The setting for this novel vision was a European society informed in its institutions of power, its social norms, and its imaginative world by Christian religion. Medieval Christendom had sponsored freedom in many respects from domination by sacral authority, opening the way for dynamic social change. When that society became ravaged by what are usually referred to (simplistically) as the "religious wars," however, a secure basis was sought for the future of this society elsewhere than in Christian religion. This "modern" future was sought in the innately good and rational individual and in the state as trustworthy legislator, educator, and enforcer of a program of civil-ization among such individuals.

3. For an illuminating study of these differences, see Martin Marty, *The Modern Schism: Three Paths to the Secular*. We shall explore this further in chapter 10.

Fundamental to this modern vision was the conception of the individual human "self" as autonomous agent and knowing subject. While this conception drew upon a Western classical heritage, it was substantially informed initially by a Christian imagination. However, this imagination has since been eroded in modern Western culture, and the conception has become more absolute and more distorted. Today our cultural imagination is dominated by false conceptions of the human "self," of "knowledge," and of the "contexts" we inhabit as knowing subjects.

This gives rise to the distinctive modern cultural form of blindness and evasion towards God (and thus towards ourselves and the world). Dominated by our modern imagination, when we find ourselves encountered by God, our thinking about this gets distorted to the point of failure. Our thinking betrays, rather than faithfully testifies to, our encounter with God. Modern thinking also tends to pre-empt recognition of God as encountering us in the first place. Moreover, it also colludes practically with the evasion of God in general, by concealing this for what it is and indeed legitimizing it. All of this finds expression not only in modern discourse (especially the discourse of those who seek to manage public social and political life) but also in the social "plausibility structures" of the modern world.

The dominance of the modern imagination, increasingly severed from its roots in Christian faith, is associated today with both a striking decline of church life, and with the distortion both of Western culture in general and of Christian religion itself by contemporary ideologies and consumerism. These tendencies and their history are explored in this book.

The gospel engages human blindness and evasion in this characteristic modern cultural form. Thus it integrally discloses us, our knowledge, and the context of our knowledge in the light of God's self-disclosing approach. The task of theological reflection upon this is vital for authentic mission in the Western church.

Among those who have offered a lead in this task, Lesslie Newbigin is a key figure. He questioned much that goes by the name of mission. At one point he even counseled his friend Dan Beeby, who had submitted to him a draft book for scrutiny, to avoid using the word "mission": "the word 'mission' has been worn so threadbare with misuse that it really ceases to communicate."[4] Authentic mission requires that Western Christians become aware of the pervasive tendency among them towards captivity by the presuppositions of modern culture.

Newbigin grasped that a key problem is epistemology—the theory of knowledge. The living God may draw persons into encounter with himself, but modern habits of imagination then prompt them to think about this encounter (in a second-order, theoretical way) in terms that fail to refer to the reality of this knowledge (or indeed of knowledge in general) and so effectively dismiss it or accuse believers of self-deception.

Correspondingly, the mission task involves challenging the hegemony of these habits of imagination in the course of commending a truer understanding of the act of knowing. This is to be understood as Newbigin's attempt to engage modern Western culture with the contextual and transcendent gospel.[5]

This challenge, which Newbigin raised, calls for a fundamental conversion of thought and he is always at risk of being heard and misunderstood by reference to the very assumptions that he challenges. Thus Newbigin may be heard as proposing that a false theory of knowledge is responsible for the modern loss of faith and that a correct theory will reverse this. His argument is rather, of course, that modern Enlightenment thinkers forsook faith and placed their trust instead in a theory of "sure" knowledge and what it could provide. Again, he may be heard as counting elite philosophical ideas about knowledge more formative than they have actually been historically in modern society. However, the ideas with which he is concerned have far wider currency than academia. They have permeated increasingly the public or "secondary" culture of those who manage society *en masse* within, or under the constraints of registration within, state or private enterprise. From here they have implicitly penetrated daily life among the general population, especially through education and the mass media (we shall explore this at length in Part 2).

---

4. Lesslie Newbigin, in a personal letter to Dan Beeby, September 17, 1996.

5. Newbigin's writing on mission in Western culture is thus to be understood as seamless with his wider, lifelong concern to preach a gospel at once contextual and transcendent. On Newbigin's wider ministry see especially Wainwright, *Lesslie Newbigin: A Theological Life*, and Weston, *Lesslie Newbigin: Missionary Theologian*. Much, of course, has been written on the contextualization of the gospel and much of this has been useful where it leaves room (which is not always clear) to resist cultural domestication, and to uphold the transcendence of the gospel.

Nor is this to subscribe to a view of history as "the history of ideas": it matters little to Newbigin's basic thesis whether intellectuals have themselves originated the ideas in question, or whether they have rationalized and so sought to preserve the vested interests of a ruling class, or whether they have done little more than formulate in a coherent way the prevalent direction of new thinking in their age. Finally, Newbigin's challenge takes account of the sociology of knowledge: he understands that the power of ideas operates not only through debate but also through being embedded in social institutions that constitute their "plausibility structure." Once again, he is not talking about simply theoretical ideas, but practical commitments that may mediate either responsiveness or evasion towards God. There are grounds for seeing Newbigin's concern over false epistemology as also a concern over false ontology.

Newbigin, then, identified the pervasive tendency among Western Christians of domestication to cultural habits of imagination regarding the nature of knowledge. In so doing he opens the eyes of Christians to see and reflect theologically upon the task of mission in Western culture—which is to seek the conversion of the West.

In this book I shall develop critically his key insights into this task. In this I shall not, of course, be speaking into silence: much has been said and written on the topic of mission in recent years. It may therefore be helpful, by way of further preparation for what follows, if I now acknowledge some familiar ideas about mission and offer comment upon them. I shall not differentiate here between evangelism, witness, and mission, but I shall give consideration only to models for witness that explicitly speak the name of Christ, and not to implicit forms of witness through, e.g., advocacy, aid, and service.

MODELS FOR CHRISTIAN WITNESS

What shape does the gospel give for authentic Christian witness in modern Western culture? Let us appraise briefly five visions that currently inform reflection on this.

1. The Witness of Traditional Religious Conformity

There is a conventional form of Christianity defined first and foremost by conformity in certain religious beliefs, moral norms, and attendance at Sunday worship. It is symbolized in parish churches by the display behind the altar of the Apostles' Creed to one side and of the Ten Commandments to the other, and the expectation of going to church on Sundays. Historically this has been associated with respect for a way of life marked on the one hand by Christian principle and on the other by generosity in service and forgiveness, and finds expression in the commendation of "a good Christian person" or "a good Christian family," and also (indirectly!) in the assertion that "you don't have to go to church to be a Christian."

This conformity is undoubtedly an important element in Christian witness. However, it typically fails to provide adequate guidance and nourishment for Christian witness in Western culture today, when wider society is shaped not by Christian-informed reason but more by the ideological thinking of those who manage mass society, its public institutions and private enterprise. These cultivate tacit "religious" allegiance today, defining the end or *telos* of society and aspiring to integrate all its elements within this. Accordingly, the meaning of Christian faith and witness has to be worked out in engagement with these tacit "religious" allegiances. There is no escaping this task. This calls for a readiness to immerse oneself deeply in the Christian "worldview" as a whole and participate imaginatively in the Christian story, in a responsiveness to God that shapes the whole of life in unpredictable ways.

2. The Witness of Traditional Religious Symbolism and Art

In the mainstream denominations, church worship and witness typically draw upon visual and linguistic symbols and music from Christian tradition. The Western Christian cultural heritage is rich indeed, including a heritage of high culture in architecture, music, literature, sculpture, and art.

Now some elements in this heritage still speak in an immediate and eloquent way of the gospel today. Other elements come alive once people are made familiar with the conventions and intentions of their creators living in a very different culture and age from our own. Thus the great brass eagle upon which the Bible is placed in many older churches is quite opaque in meaning until it is explained as being the Word of God perched upon a small globe signifying the earth, while its direct gaze speaks of the fourth evangelist whose Gospel starts, "In the beginning was the Word" and whose symbol is the eagle, which was legendary among creatures as able to look directly at the sun (signifying the evangelist's gaze upon the divine Son). Once this is explained, however, it can "come alive" as a powerful symbol.

Other elements from past cultures that brought alive the gospel in those cultures but are opaque to people in Western culture today may be an unnecessary hindrance to Christian witness today. Among such elements in Christian heritage that arguably hinder witness today are the continuing use in worship of Tudor English (originally a breakthrough adoption of the vernacular language of the people), the use of candles in an age of electricity, the use of Victorian hymnody accompanied by an organ, and the requirement to sit on wooden benches in order to worship God.

Even when elements of Christian cultural heritage have a recognizable beauty, this is not enough for them to witness to Christian faith if they are *only* entertained aesthetically, with disregard towards their message and its truthfulness. Indeed as Harry Blamires points out,

> Historically speaking, the environment is covered with the marks of past efforts to Christianize our culture and our civilization . . . [However,] the atheist . . . thinks that the great works of Christian culture are great *in spite of* their Christian substance and inspiration and in no degree *because of* their Christian substance and inspiration . . . You will certainly not hear our secularized contemporaries say of you or me: "Oh Yes, he's a Christian. Like Bach and Milton, like Leonardo and Raphael, like the people who built our cathedrals and gave us our first schools: he's one of those."[6]

There is, of course, much from past ages that it is right for Christians to continue using (with care being taken over induction into its meaning as necessary), but Christians must not adopt a disposition of blanket allegiance towards established forms of church life, which is likely to obscure the gospel and hinder its coming alive for newcomers. It is especially important that Christians recognize how the living gospel engages with the language, music, and visual symbols that nourish the imaginative world of our own age and culture, whether it engages them by owning them as a medium of celebration and revelation or by challenging and transforming them.

It is also important to recognize that both traditional religious conformity and traditional religious symbols and art relied, as living witnesses to Christian faith in their day, upon something no longer available:

---

6. Blamires, *Meat Not Milk*, 172.

the dissemination of Christian teaching and imagination throughout the wider culture through the mediums of widespread church participation, deference to Christian values in social institutions, and Christian worship and teaching in schools. To be Christian in that environment—for it was a taken-for-granted environment—involved little awareness of having a distinct religious allegiance or vocation. And there was little expectation of talking or being able to talk in a personal way about religious experience; this was a most private affair.

This Christian cultural environment has been fading for a century and more, and in an accelerated way during the past fifty years. Like wallpaper, Christian belief has come to be registered not as bearing a living meaning and message, but simply to be deferred to as something inherited. More recently this wallpaper and deference to it have faded; it has become something to paint over. The church has been slow to reckon properly with this, as if wandering in the haze of Christendom, and has shown a serious a failure of imagination.[7] In our new situation, the witness of Christian art past and present may function in a new ways in intentional tasks of witness.

3. The Witness of an Appeal to Cultural Identity

Modern Western culture has been deeply informed historically by Christian faith. As T. S. Eliot remarked, "It is in Christianity that our arts have developed; it is in Christianity that the laws of Europe have been rooted. It is against a background of Christianity that all our thought has significance. An individual European may not believe that the Christian Faith is true, and yet what he says, and makes, and does, will all spring out of his heritage of Christian culture and depend upon that culture for its meaning."[8]

Today people in general have little awareness of this; indeed year by year ignorance spreads of Christian faith itself. Correspondingly, one model for Christian witness is that of awakening people to cultural self-awareness, reminding them of the fact that much in their taken-for-granted way of seeing and thinking about the world has roots historically in Christianity, and reminding of the content of this.

---

7. On this see Wickham, *Church and People in an Industrial City,* chapters 5 and 6.
8. Eliot, "Notes Towards a Definition of Culture," 121.

The logic of this witness is apparent especially to Christians who come to Britain from beyond Europe. Thus John Sentamu, Archbishop of York, says "For me, the vital issue facing the Church in England and the nation is the loss of this country's long tradition of Christian wisdom which brought to birth the English nation: the loss of wonder and amazement that Jesus Christ has authority over every aspect of our lives and our nation."[9]

How shall we appraise this model for witness? Pursued in its own right, cultural self-awareness can distort into an exercise in identity-politics, and foster the growth of nationalism of an unhealthy and prejudiced kind. On the other hand, it can assist the exercise of discernment towards new situations and the challenges they bring. Joyce Macmillan writes:

> if we feel we have no culture of our own, or that we have lost touch with it over two generations of breakneck social change, then we are bound to feel threatened by others who seem more certain of who they are . . . But if we can begin to see the powerful moral connections between the tradition in which we were raised and the way we live now, and to pass that story on to our children and grandchildren, then we may find ourselves more confident of who we are and where we came from; and therefore better able to enter into a real conversation with people of other faiths and traditions.[10]

In order that new self-awareness regarding one's Christian cultural heritage may witness faithfully to God, two barriers must be overcome. The first is a contemporary dismissal of the old in favor of the new as a trustworthy source of guidance for the future. Madeleine Bunting writes, "It becomes harder and harder to explain how two millennia of meditation and reasoning on the human condition may be worthy of consideration. There is an extraordinary arrogance to the modernity that tosses aside so contemptuously the traditions that have sustained generations of our forebears. Are we so different? Are we so superior?"

The second and contrasting barrier is precisely the adoption and defense of elements of our cultural heritage, but merely as a matter of convention. Here people rehearse elements of tradition as a matter

9. John Sentamu, Enthronement Sermon as Archbishop of York, 30th November 2005.

10. McMillan, "Christian Evolution Holds Key to Tolerance."

of allegiance, without entering into their original meaning as ways of exploring and celebrating the truth; the *point* of them, if you like, is bracketed out.

To overcome these barriers it is necessary to induct people into an exploration of their cultural heritage that brings alive its meaning as an enquiry into and celebration of truth, and which invites people to enter into and take personal responsibility for continuing this project today. The appeal to cultural identity must be embedded in this context if it is to be an authentic Christian witness.

4. The Witness of a Parallel Christian Culture

The growing distance of Western society from Christianity today is not simply from traditional cultural forms of Christian life, but from Christian faith itself. Society—especially the managed society of public life and mass private consumption—is drifting away from Christian religion and values. It is increasingly disinterested in, ignorant of, and prejudiced against Christian faith. This presents a more serious challenge to the church than the challenge of appropriate "modernization"; society needs to repent of cultural attitudes, in renewed understanding of and deference to God. The gap so evident between church and culture today merely brings into the open what has often been concealed and confused in our Christendom past: faith is a distinct personal choice bringing distinctive commitments in belief, action, and social allegiance. Here is a call to the church to stand over against culture, a distinctive and prophetic community. The dominant note here may be one of reform or of retrenchment.

However, pursuit of a deliberately "radical" countercultural stance does not guarantee that as Christians we are not culturally domesticated. The rhetoric of counterculture does not guarantee the Christ-inspired reality. However counter-cultural we may see ourselves, the problem always remains that of discerning the hidden ways in which we remain domesticated to our culture: we may merely be, as some have accused American evangelical constituencies of being, a parallel culture—"of but not in the world."[11] Alternatively, we may simply go the way of retrenchment, giving allegiance without discernment to that which, while it is counter-cultural in the sense of differing from prevailing cultural

11. Two evangelical authors who have notably criticized their own tradition in these terms are Os Guinness and David Wells.

norms, is not counter-cultural in the deeper sense of engaging and challenging the culture; it is largely irrelevant to faith with power to nourish
within and witness to culture. Either way faith tends to be reduced to
explicit norms of belief and practice that endow a self-conscious, sectarian identity in the face of a wider culture that has been dismissed. Faith
tends to be minimalized as the nurturing source of individual character
for deeply attentive, enquiring spiritual engagement with God's grace at
work in the wider culture.

To be countercultural in a truly Christ-like way is rather to *engage*
culture, with discernment, taking bearings from a gospel that will sometimes judge and sometimes fulfill the culture.

5. *The Witness of Consumer Religion*

Another "progressive" model for the church takes its lead from contemporary consumerism and the management ideology and marketing industry associated with this. The need for Christians, if they are to "reach
people where they are" *en masse*, in the imaginative world they inhabit
today, is interpreted in these terms. Donald McGavran's "homogeneous
unit" principle for church life is one strategy suggested by this approach,
identifying and working with cultural niche markets for the church;
what has been called the "Macdonaldization" of the church would appear to be another.

Most commonly, consumer religion takes the form of corporate
mass participation in a "product." "Seeker-friendly" churches court this
temptation. However, it also takes the form of *individual* mass participation in a product. A plethora of books on spirituality and on religion-
informed self-help strategies court this distortion of faith. Commending
themselves in this setting to church leaders are the shamans[12] of mission
consultancy, offering practical strategies informed by consumerist, management, and marketing models for the purveying of religion.

Sociologist of religion Grace Davie sees in northern Europe a general shift from an understanding of religion as a form of obligation to an
increasing emphasis on consumption. Increasingly, she says, people go to
church to fulfill a particular need that arises for them, and not to fulfill
an obligation.[13] In American church culture, Eugene Peterson sees this

12. I owe the term "shaman" in this context to Richard Stivers, *Technology as Magic:
The Triumph of the Irrational.*

13. Davie, "From Obligation to Consumption."

as reproducing the Baal culture of Canaan: "Baal religion is about what makes you feel good. Baal worship is about what I can get out of it. And, of course, it was incredibly successful."[14]

The point is that as a *model* for Christian witness, consumer Christianity is a betrayal of the gospel insofar as it leaves no room for Christian *challenge* to people's beliefs, appetites, and practices. It betrays the transcendence of the gospel. While pursuing engagement, it actually fails to achieve this because, while adopting the elements of a culture, it does not use them so as to *address* this culture itself; it simply defers to it. By simply adopting as given people's beliefs, appetites, and practices, it betrays the power of the gospel to nurture a deeper, more coherent personal identity than their agglomeration represents, and to foster a more coherent worldview than that already inhabited.

The vocation of Christian witness will be guided and nourished by an ever fresh theological engagement between gospel and culture that begins by acknowledging the world-renewing and life-renewing character of the gospel as it engages worldviews, ideologies, and other cultural and personal attachments, breaking them open to the transcendent horizons of God and judging and transforming them by divine grace. This reveals where the gospel comes alive in engagement with culture, in a disclosure that reveals both the living gospel and the culture to which it speaks. We begin with attention to the gospel, allowing its light to shine upon us and upon our culture; we do not begin by assuming what the culture is and then ask how the gospel engages it.

In recent decades, a range of social developments have arisen that, for many thoughtful Christians, awaken Christian concern. Among them are the modern ideologies and consumerism of modern mass society, changes in the pattern of family and community life, and the need to manage responsibly the increasing human impact upon global resources and the global environment. Such Christians find their concerns shared by many other thoughtful people—a fact often but not always due to the generally unacknowledged cultural residue of a Christian imagination.

The gospel comes alive in such concerns, yet those who find this can nevertheless find it hard to say why this is so; they can find it hard to frame their concern in explicit Christian terms. The traditional formulations of Christian faith seem not to address their concerns in any direct way. In the experience of many thoughtful Christians, the church's

14. Peterson, "Spirituality for All the Wrong Reasons," 45.

teaching and preaching seems not to "scratch where they itch." And where connections are explicated for them between the gospel and one concern or another of theirs, there is often little indication of how one concern and another relate to each other in the context of the gospel— of how they may hope to "join up the dots" in a coherent picture of the gospel and the lineaments of its message to their culture.

In this book I indicate some key points where the gospel engages modern Western culture in a deep and lively way, and show how these are embedded in a coherent picture of the gospel in its engagement with the West as a whole. But first let me pause to acknowledge that the entire project of "the conversion of the West" may attract misgivings and hesitations that, unless they are addressed, may subvert the keen attention that this project so urgently calls for.

ON ASKING "CAN THE WEST BE CONVERTED?": SOME DOUBTS AND CLARIFICATIONS

In Western churches in the early twenty-first century there is much acknowledgement of the need for "mission." Within such acknowledgement I have identified some prevalent models for mission. However, a deeper question lies to hand. Among readers my very intention to explore "the conversion of the West" in the first place may produce fundamental doubts of one kind or another. Four such doubts come to mind.

First, some may doubt whether it is *right* to seek the conversion of society itself into a "Christian" society. Surely conversion is properly a free choice made by autonomous individuals, a freedom that is properly upheld in a liberal democratic society, and is not something to be imposed upon individuals by society?

Second, and in a related but even more basic way, some may doubt whether it is appropriate to *conceive* of the Christian conversion of a society or culture in the first place. Surely conversion is about the recognition of a truth that can only be recognized for oneself personally, and not a matter of social conformity? Surely only *persons* can undergo such conversion?

Third, some who rejoice in the vision of a Christian society may doubt whether it is appropriate *to seek* this in any deliberate way. The forces that shape society are, some may stress, beyond the control of the church; let the church be true to itself, and entrust to the Spirit the response of society in general.

Fourth, some who rejoice in the vision of a Christian society may see the vital task as seeking and defending a Christian contribution to public life, and they may think that the church and Christian organizations *have this well in hand*. Nothing of significance is missing from current efforts, that might prompt new attention to what the "conversion of the West" *means*, and what therefore needs to be done.

Let me address each of these questions more closely. Each raises a valid concern; however, each also has the potential to subvert vital attention to the meaning and task of mission and conversion in Western culture today, with which I am concerned in this book. By acknowledging and exploring these doubts, I hope to clarify and commend my intentions.

1. Faith as Choice

Can the West be converted? One response to this question is moral discomfort with the idea of seeking any such "conversion of the West" in the first place.[15] Would this not be to impose upon individuals an allegiance that is properly left to their own choice? Christianity has surely been right to break with the older idea of "territorial" religion that allowed the individual no freedom of choice in the matter of religion allegiance. Does not the decision to embrace a faith lie within that private realm that society is right to assign to and uphold on behalf of individuals? It is not for society to require religious allegiance, or to dictate one religious allegiance rather than another, from individuals. Even the effort to persuade individuals to adopt a religious allegiance may be seen as violating this freedom if it involves offering rewards or even if it offers the promise of rewards from God. Indeed even truth-claims on behalf of religion may be ruled as illegitimate.[16] By all means let the church seek custom as a voluntary association within a secular liberal democracy.

15. "[A]t the same time Newbigin was calling for the pursuit of a Christian society, Douglas John Hall stated that 'It is a wicked thing to seek a Christian society.'" Goheen, "Missional Calling of Believers," 40.

16. Thus the British Committee of Advertising Practice, in its Television Advertising Code, Section 10 (concerned with religion, faith, and systems of belief) rules that "Advertising must not be used to expound doctrinal beliefs nor suggest that viewers should change their behaviour or beliefs" (10.8), adding a note to the effect that references to doctrine *must not be expressed in ways which suggest they are other than the advertiser's belief. The code also states that* "Testimonials and references to individual experiences or personal benefits associated with a doctrine are not acceptable" (10.10).

But to seek the conversion of Western society itself is something very different . . . and wrong.

This hesitation over seeking "the conversion of the West" has roots in a proper Christian concern for freedom. However, it fails to honor Christian insight into freedom or to pay due attention to the nature of Christian conversion. It tends to reduce it to a matter of consumer choice embodying "values" private to the individual. But conversion is about an act of freedom, and an orientation towards freedom, far deeper and more comprehensive than this. It is about choice as a response not only to products on offer but to the world we find given to us and in which we are called responsibly to participate: it is about the responsibility of choosing what is right and good and most worthy of honor. And this carries with it the responsibility of upholding and commending among other people what is worthy of honor; it is an act of responsibility "with universal intent." The deepest resources for freedom and its pursuit— including individual freedom to make "consumer" choices rather than have them made for us effectively by others—lie precisely here.

Nor can freedom be defined as freedom of the individual from oppression by others. This is only one aspect of freedom. The individual, in order to experience freedom, also needs to be affirmed, addressed, and incorporated by others into the human family and with them to be offered entry into participation in the freedom of life under God. This deeper freedom, which individual conversion is about, has cultural dimensions.

The idea that Christian faith is a private choice and the church a voluntary association derives not from Christianity but from late-modern liberalism for which "the detached, pre-social individual becomes the basic unit out of which society is then constructed." Accordingly it has "followed the path of devaluing natural communities in favour of those created by acts of will . . . It ceases to be a point in their favour that we can see something of ourselves in our natural communities and so embrace them 'as our own.'"[17]

But is not Christian faith a decision? It is indeed an act freely of taking responsibility. Moreover, contemporary culture does demand from Christian individuals a new degree of awareness of, and readiness to take new responsibility for, their Christian faith. Louis Dupré writes that for the Christian to survive as a genuine religious believer today

17. O'Donovan, *Desire of the Nations*, 276.

"he or she must now personally integrate what tradition did in the past. Nothing in our culture today compels our contemporaries to embrace a religious faith. If they do, they alone are responsible for allowing their faith to incorporate all aspects of their existence."[18] At the same time he acknowledges that, for the Christian, faith is not a choice but a summons in which one belongs to a community and in which one takes responsibility for the culture or civilization in which one lives. Of vital importance in all this is one's personal spiritual life.

The secularist vision of individual freedom is a distortion. The vision of secular society itself is rooted in a Christian understanding of life within the *saeculum*, the provisional order of creation. Secular freedom is given and upheld by God. This is reflected historically in, for example, the roots of freedom in modern secular democracies that lie in the doctrine of religious freedom forged in England in the eighteenth century.[19] To be sure, this includes freedom from the kind of religious control represented by the theocracies of sacral societies. However, unless secular society is informed and nourished by openness to the God who in Christ liberates human life in an ultimate and comprehensive way, it is prone to capture by totalitarian or nihilistic tendencies that precisely subvert freedom, sliding into hidden forms of paganism and idolatry. A "Christian society" is one that sponsors "godly secularity," resisting theocracy on the one hand and ideological secularism on the other.

2. Faith as Personal Knowledge

Can the West be converted? Another related response is to protest that the question does not arise because conversion is about conversion to the truth of the gospel and that this truth is by its nature a matter of personal discovery and conscious recognition: it is something one has to "see for oneself." To be sure, relevant teaching may have been culturally transmitted, and this teaching may be part of a recognizable context in which an individual has come to personal conviction; but no matter what the context of the verdict of faith, the verdict is one's own alone. "The West" refers to one such general context of conversion; but the question of this context being itself "converted" simply does not arise.

18. Dupré, "Seeking Christian interiority," 655.
19. See Polanyi, "The English and the Continent."

This hesitation about seeking "the conversion of the West" has roots in a Christian understanding of faith as a matter of knowing God in loving response to his personal approach in Christ—a knowledge that shares ultimately in the Son's knowledge of the Father through the Holy Spirit. However, it fails to acknowledge adequately the role of culture and tradition in mediating this knowledge, not least in its rich tacit dimension. Our tacit knowledge is vitally part of our personal responsiveness or otherwise to God; in it we live integrally in relation to God, to other people, and to our culture. God is properly to be understood not as standing apart from our cultural and other contexts, but as our deeper, ultimate context, relative to which our other contexts are provisional. These provisional contexts can themselves be either part of a personal life resistant to God, or part of a personal life open towards or converted to God.

These considerations bear not only upon knowledge of God, but already upon enquiry into God. This too is an essentially personal matter. One has to seek God for oneself, to acknowledge and pursue one's own questions; but these questions are raised for us by God, in the context of culture and tradition.

Secular society, of course, sees itself as sponsoring free enquiry into the truth. However, it tends to neglect the fact that both regard for the truth and enquiry into the truth (which is part of such regard) have tacit cultural and traditional dimensions. This leaves it vulnerable to narrow, explicit, ideological forms of rationality, and inclined to dismiss, trivialize, distract from, or seduce away from the demands of religious enquiry.

Faith as a conscious personal belief is thus only part of the meaning of conversion. Individual conversion involves orientation, within the individual, of the culture(s) they inhabit at the deepest level—that is, at the level of largely unconscious assumptions where it bears closely upon questions of personal meaning and hope, responsibility, and freedom. Harold Turner called for the conversion of such "deep culture," which he distinguished from expressive or surface culture of the sort celebrated in cultural festivals, maintained by cultural centers, and associated with social customs.[20]

---

20. See especially Turner, *Frames of Mind*. Harold Turner pioneered new frameworks for understanding both new religious movements and (as in the above book) the field of religion and culture in general, but whereas the former has been widely acclaimed, the latter has not become widely known or acclaimed.

Andrew Walls, once a young colleague of Harold Turner, has similarly considered the matter of cultural Christianization. Extrapolating from Kenneth Scott Latourette's *A History of the Expansion of Christianity*, he identifies three measures of this expansion that he finds to be *theological* in foundation.[21] The first he calls the "church" test: it asks whether the hearing of the gospel has brought individuals together in Christian community in the formation of a church. The second measure he calls the "kingdom" test: this asks whether the presence of Christian faith has brought tangible blessings, signs of the kingdom, as it takes root among the people. The third he calls the "gospel" test: this asks whether the Christian faith has had an effect upon the whole of the society into which it has been introduced, engaging with the shaping role of principalities and powers, and transforming the "grammar" of its beliefs and practices.

Both of these layered accounts of the conversion of a culture point to elements in conversion that challenge its equation with self-conscious personal allegiance. Indeed they point to levels of culture in which other "religions" operate if Christianity does not. Maurice Cowling seems to go so far as to rate cultural conversion above individual conversion when he writes: "A religion ought to be habitual and ought not to involve the self-consciousness inseparable from conversion. What Christianity requires is a second-generation sensibility in which the oddness and arbitrariness of Christianity's doctrines are so much taken for granted that struggle has ceased to be of Christianity's essence. This is not a situation which can easily be achieved in the contemporary world; indeed, the religions which can most easily avoid self-consciousness in the contemporary world are the secular religions which are absorbed at the mother's knee or from the mother's television."[22] A key point here is that the supposed neutral secular context of religious commitment today is actually itself a religious context, with respect to which the question of conversion does indeed arise.

3. *The Seasons of Faith*

Can the West be converted? A third response is to say, in effect, "God knows. There are huge forces at work in culture and society that are

---

21. Walls, "'A History of the Expansion of Christianity' *Reconsidered.*"
22. Cowling, *Religion and Public Doctrine*, vol. 3.

beyond the control of the church and that determine to a great degree the responsiveness or otherwise of the population to the gospel. All the church can do is faithfully to worship and serve God. It must accept that the cultural context in which this takes place may be more or less receptive to faith, and entrust this receptivity to the work of the Spirit."

This would seem to be the position advocated by Nico ter Linden in a short reflection called "In the Middle of Winter."[23] He recalls Karl Rahner's observation that in Western society today it is "the Season of Winter in Christianity": the light of faith is dim; the voice of God is faint; spiritual life is at a low ebb. Nico ter Linden reflects: "So, this is the way it is. You must not get too worked up about it. You must not become aggressive, neither become depressed about it. You must not try with all your might to turn the tide. Neither should you look around in anger over everything that has gone wrong; neither should you look back with homesickness to all the fine things that have been lost. It is the season of Winter, and why should you not accept that? . . . It is not the first time in history that things were like this. Meanwhile the church will have to burn with a low wick. All right; that is possible. The less bitter we feel about it the more is possible."

If we take this to heart, it may seem to us that our task is patiently to wait for God. New light, new life will come in God's own time. As Dietrich Bonhoeffer wrote, "It is not for us to prophesy the day (though the day will come) when men will once more be called so to utter the word of God that the world will be changed and renewed by it."[24] But for now, it is winter, and we must wait.

Should this be our response to the question "Can the West be converted?" Certainly we have to reckon seriously with a huge, seemingly irreversible drift in Western culture from faith and its imaginative resources. For a start, whereas in medieval Christendom it was virtually impossible for an individual not to believe in God, today in the West belief in God is a choice that individuals opt into. This was the theme of Peter Berger's book *The Heretical Imperative*.[25] To be a "heretic" traditionally meant to "have a mind of one's own"; today, Berger points out, by contrast it is a social imperative that each one of us has a mind of our own in religious matters. Moreover our culture and society offers—

23. Linden, "In the Middle of Winter."

24. Bonhoeffer, *Letters and Papers from Prison*, 160.

25. Berger, *Heretical Imperative*.

indeed widely promotes—"secular" alternatives to belief. Charles Taylor has more recently explored this at length in *A Secular Age*,[26] tracing the changes in cultural sensibilities and the "social imaginary" associated with this profound shift.

Consider also, beyond the modern West, the pattern of Christian history down two millennia: the ascendancy and decline of Christianity in one culture and region and another, with successive centers (as surveyed memorably by Andrew Walls[27]) in Jerusalem, Rome, medieval Europe, and today in the lands evangelized by the modern missionary movement. Does this not suggest that faith has its "seasons," and that the church must trim to this its project of cultural conversion?

There is wisdom here to check two perverse tendencies. The first is refusal to face how bleak is the landscape for Christian faith today and try to carry on inherited patterns of church life and ministry as if nothing had changed; to bury our heads in face of the statistics of decline and the huge ignorance and apathy regarding Christianity. The second is a premature, rash announcement of God's "springtime." Both are acts of denial, and a hindrance to responsible faithfulness. As Nico ter Linden writes in "The Middle of Winter," the more we can accept and be at peace with the present state of affairs, "the more we shall be able to be meaningful to people."

And yet the vital truth stands, that in Jesus Christ God has acted to overcome everything that stands between ourselves and God's good purposes for us all: what can have happened that the sea of faith is today so strongly in ebb? Our bleak situation may lie within the providence of God, but does it not have causes that can be identified and addressed, causes working against God's will in Christ? While Winter is such a *natural* thing, are we not confronted today with an *unnatural* blindness and torpor? We might recall here another Winter—the perpetual Winter of the land of Narnia in C. S. Lewis's *The Lion, the Witch and the Wardrobe,* an effect of Narnia's domination by the White Witch. Are we not bound to ask: what principalities and powers, what great configurations of human sin, cast a spell on human life today making us blind to the light of Christ, asleep to participation in the infinite life of God?

This is not necessarily inconsistent with the history of the rise of secularism as described by Charles Taylor and the history of Christianity's

26. Taylor, *Secular Age.*

27. Walls, "Culture and Coherence in Christian History."

shifting centers globally described by Andrew Walls. Only idealist assumptions drive us to see history as fundamentally an unfolding process with its natural seasons. When Saint Paul, led by the Spirit, preached the gospel around the gentile Mediterranean, he was not simply "going with the flow" of progress: his obedience to Christ was a much more demanding, self-sacrificial life of initiative and proclamation than this. The history of the shift of the centre of Christianity from Jerusalem to Rome was fraught with conflict with local Jews and with imperial Roman persecution. Later, the decline of Christian faith in North Africa, Arabia, and Asia Minor was not a "seasonal decay"; it was a result of the advance of political Islam. And so on. The "seasons" of Christianity, upon inspection, involved intentional close encounter with new cultures, bringing the possibilities of new inculturations of Christianity, of false assimilations of the gospel to traditional cultures, and of resistance and sometimes persecution of Christians—not only upon first encounter, but also in subsequent generations. Central to this was intentional proclamation of the gospel and the modeling of a Christian life.

Faithfulness in the Western Winter of Christianity requires more than waiting quietly for God's voice to be heard afresh. Rather it requires that with renewed vigor we immerse ourselves in the reality of what God has done in Christ, while bringing with us all that modern life has revealed to us, and seeking to discover afresh from God bearings from which to understand our situation and our responsibilities before God. This may bring new insights. In this book I want to suggest some key "moments of illumination" that arise in close Christian encounter with Western culture. It also requires us to grasp with renewed vitality what God has already entrusted to us, to recapitulate afresh our Christian cultural heritage, and to become more intentional, imaginative stewards of this. As Louis Dupré has remarked, since assent is no longer given to the Christian tradition as mediated in its institutions, it falls upon Christians individually and together to "personally integrate what tradition did in the past."[28] Christians in general have hardly begun to reckon with what this will mean.

The gospel cannot be "located" within the seasons of culture as the living world of nature is located within the natural seasons of the year. Culture cannot be a prior "given" for Christianity in this way; if you like, the gospel changes the seasons of culture. To be sure, the living gospel is

28. Dupré, "Seeking Christian interiority," 655.

always inculturated; but as such it mediates precisely the approach of the One who is our ultimate context, in light of which culture is revealed for the provisional culture it is—not least by its openness to transformation by, rather than resistance to, the gospel itself. The church is called faithfully and responsibly to mediate this encounter; whether it happens and whether the gospel is embraced is the work of the Spirit.

4. Mission—A Task in Hand?

Can the West be converted? A fourth response may come from some for whom Christian faith is of great importance; who would rejoice to see others come to the same faith, and to see their churches grow; who would rejoice to see Christian values honored in their wider culture; and who think it right that a Christian contribution to public life should be allowed and indeed valued. Such Christians may understand that the possibility of each of these is beset by special difficulties today, and it is therefore important that these difficulties somehow be addressed. Fortunately, the church is "on to it": there is a new focus on mission. Things are in hand. There is no need for new insight into what is the nature of the mission task in the first place.

The problem is that this kind of confidence is misplaced where there has been—as I submit is generally the case—inadequate attention to the task of theological discernment in mission. To be sure, without this discernment there may still be a sense of the urgency of mission in face of declining church life, increasingly widespread ignorance of the gospel, abandonment of Christian values, and prejudicial misrepresentation of Christianity; but there is not enough here to give proper direction to mission.

The temptation of overlooking the theological task is particularly strong for churches whose life is shaped strongly by an established ministry of a civic or pastoral kind—a vision of chaplaincy to national life and to society; for Christians led by a passionate vision for social transformation through participation in campaigns for justice and peace with wide secular support; and for evangelical and charismatic churches adopting pragmatic mission strategies that place unrealistic confidence in the tools offered by business models of management and marketing and related tools of mass social engineering.

Mission must be rooted in discernment of the message of the tran-scendent and inculturated gospel in the particular setting that is Western culture today.

In conclusion, the mission task was quite well expressed by E. R. Wickham over half a century ago. He writes of the mode of relation-ship to the world that is appropriate to the church though in a period of recession, if it is to witness in a secular society:

> It is the situation where the church is acutely conscious of be-longing to the world, subject to the conditions of the world, yet a catalyst within the world which is its only sphere of obedience. It seeks neither to manipulate nor dominate the world, nor to escape from it, but to understand it, prophesy within it, interpret it, and stain it . . . [This] defines the church in its relation with the world neither as a monolithic rock unmoved by the currents of history, nor as an ark for the saved, nor as flotsam and jetsam floating on the surface, but as a deep current itself running in the seas. The imagery brings to mind Kierkegaard's definition of faith, not as fair-weather sailing in the ship, not as clinging to the rock, but as swimming in the deep with 70,000 fathoms below![29]

This imagery also points forward to the basic imagery in Part One of this book, of our human immersion in and participation in God's hos-pitality—God who is our ultimate context, a mystery deep beyond the provisional contexts which constitute the world we inhabit.

THE BOOK: ARGUMENTS AND THEMES

In this book I build upon the basic insight of Lesslie Newbigin that the Western church is today widely domesticated to the assump-tions of modern Western culture, and that authentic mission requires that Christians recognize and challenge this in the name of Christ. As Newbigin discerned, central among these modern cultural assumptions is a particular way of understanding knowledge. I shall propose that this reflects the prevalence of certain Cartesian habits of imagination by which we misrepresent to ourselves our personal knowing and acting. These not only divert us from openness to God's approach to us in Jesus Christ, but also validate—and thereby pervert by concealing the truth of—what is actually our evasion of God. Even when we come person-ally to know God, when we *think about* this knowledge we are prone

---

29. Wickham, *Church and People*, 230.

to betray it, for we tend to conceive it in terms captive to the same false habits of imagination.

So what is needed? In Part One of this book I shall sketch a theory of knowing and acting that identifies and corrects these distortions by reference to knowledge of God as the paradigm for all knowledge. I shall frame the gospel of God's self-disclosure in Jesus Christ in terms that engage with and radically challenge modern assumptions about our selves as knowing subjects. When we bring these modern assumptions to the gospel, this represents failure on our part to engage the gospel for what it is.

To enlarge: the reflections in Part One on the act of knowing God (taken as paradigmatic for all knowing) are meant to offer a hermeneutical key to faithful mission and spirituality in Western culture today, as follows. During the modern period, social theory and practice has taken bearings—explicitly or implicitly—from an epistemology underlying the formulations of Enlightenment thinkers and their successors. Whereas this initially had significant roots in, and drew nourishment from, a tacit Christian imagination, this link with Christian faith has gradually been severed or eroded (especially in the course of the twentieth century) leading to an increasing narrow and oppressive epistemology. This has both constricted the vision of public life, and tacitly fostered an attenuated and perverse vision of personal life, diverting the modern trajectory from the path of human flourishing in openness towards the kingdom of God. Meanwhile the advance of technology and mass media has allowed this deeply ambiguous vision to penetrate human life in a more comprehensive way than ever before.

In order to bring to light these distortions, I shall set them within our paradigmatic knowledge of God through the gospel of Jesus Christ. For this purpose, in Part One I shall frame the gospel in the following terms:

The Approach of God as Our Ultimate Context:
Transforming Hospitality

Jesus of Nazareth disclosed in word and action the approach of God as our ultimate context. This is introduced here via the biblical theme of divine hospitality. Jesus' message addressed to their depths the human contexts comprising people's lives and worlds, assumptions, and personal attachments, inviting people to yield all wholeheartedly to receive new and eternal life in which God would reign as host. These contexts are revealed as provisional in the deeper context of their creator and redeemer as they are broken open for transformation and judgment. They become signs in and through which God reveals himself in his creation. In this way God's self-revelation in the gospel is at once transcendent and contextual. Also, as God reveals himself, he reveals our selves and our world as they really are, and as God sees them.

The Paradox of Grace

Our encounter with God through signs is immediate and firsthand. It is for us a matter of attention at once "from" God and "towards" God—of relying upon and reaching for, of giving oneself in receptivity and of taking responsibility for oneself before, God. In this radical responsiveness we receive God's self-giving in the fullest personal way. However, we do not receive passively: by the paradox of grace, the act in which we receive him is a most lively personal one, as we entrust ourselves in the fullest personal way to knowing him. God in his grace draws us into participation in the mystery of knowledge of himself, which always remains greater than our present knowledge of him.

Sin as Evasion: Pride and Despair

In our fallen humanity we find God's call to such radical responsiveness to be demanding, and may show ourselves blind and evasive. Such evasion takes two basic forms. We either dismiss the demands of responsiveness upon us, imagining to step back from them in denial and rebellion, or we yield to disorientation, captured and overwhelmed by the demands of responsiveness while being secretly complicit with our overwhelming. In each case we sustain an evasive stance in which—although we conceal this and our evasion from ourselves—we construct an illusory world. In a dismissive stance we construct a world in which we are self-conceived autonomous masters, while in a disoriented stance we construct a world in which we act as haunted, paralyzed victims of our fate either in needy passivity or inconsolable rage. Such evasion may take culturally shared forms.

The Mystery of Redemption in Jesus Christ

The crucifixion and resurrection of Jesus Christ represent the ultimate encounter between God and the power of human evasion. Faced with the prospect of his killing, Jesus enters the ultimate temptation to dismiss or be overwhelmed by the demands of responsiveness to God, but he remains faithful in entrusting himself to God. To know Jesus in his death and resurrection is to be drawn into the unfathomable mystery of encounter between God and our own sinful evasion.

Knowing of God as the Paradigm for All Knowing

The character of knowledge of God is reflected partially in our knowledge of persons and of ourselves; for example, we know a person only insofar as they reveal themselves, and in knowing them we at once appraise them and entrust ourselves to knowing with them, or seeing the world through their eyes. By contrast, our knowledge of the impersonal world slips often towards a matter of registering the world in a routine way by reference to established frameworks represented by cultural assumptions, habitual practices, and theoretical concepts. God cannot be known in such knowledge, for his self-disclosure breaks open and transforms all such frameworks.

As with God, so with knowledge of God: this cannot itself be understood either by reference to any established concepts; rather it is the paradigm by reference to which all knowing may be understood. It can only be known itself through reflective participation.

Cartesian Habits of Imagination
and the Paradox of Divine Self-disclosure

In "modern" society a theory of knowledge has established itself that turns *theoretical* knowledge into a paradigm for *all* knowing, including—in an act of "logical inversion"—knowledge of God. Relying upon Cartesian habits of imagination, this theory explicitly misrepresents and implicitly conceals the realities of God and knowledge of God, including the features of knowledge of God presented above: transcendence, grace, receptivity, and mystery. God engages this misrepresentation, disclosing himself through paradoxical challenges to modern thinking. The odd logic of such disclosure is here described with support drawn critically from the writings of Ian Ramsey and others.

These considerations, set out in Part One, arise from attention to the gospel that, at once transcendent and contextual, engages modern Western culture. They adumbrate a coherent picture of the gospel in its living engagement with this culture. Within this picture can be understood many features of Western culture that press for Christian attention, and call for a conversion in thinking. In Part Two I shall explore ten of these conversions.

The nature of the gospel as integrally transcendent and contextual raises for me the question how to display the relation between Part One and Part Two of this book. My presentation of the gospel in Part One arises from Christian engagement with modern Western culture, and points forward to the analysis in Part Two; however, I have wanted to avoid frequent references in Part One to Part Two, because this might suggest this presentation of the gospel is merely a *reaction to* modern Western culture (understood in some prior way). I have offered, therefore, only the occasional explicit pointer forward to Part Two. I am aware that in doing so, I run the opposite risk of obscuring the unity of Parts One and Two, and concealing the fact that the presentation of the gospel in Part One both transcends modern Western culture and integrally *engages it contextually*.

The ten conversions I describe in Part Two are as follows:

1. Secular and Sacred in Contemporary Understanding: Conversion to Creation and New Creation by God

Modern society envisions itself as "secular" in contrast with "enchanted," traditional religious societies. In secular society—as modern society conceives itself—"nothing is sacred." In contrast, religious societies are held to believe in an overarching sacred cosmos within which certain features of nature and culture have a special sacred status. The vision of a Christian society is understood in these terms. However, this view misrepresents both the sacred and the secular as they are understood properly in Christian faith. In reality, Christian faith sponsors a de-sacralization of the world first begun in Hebrew religion. The truly sacred is found in God alone and in God's purposes, which are for the whole of creation and not just for certain distinctively "sacred" elements within it. Christian faith precisely undergirds, guides, and nourishes the secular realm, and where secular society ignores this it generates all sorts of hidden and distorting sacred totems of its own.

2. The Trajectory of Western Culture, Individualism, and
Totalitarianism: Conversion to Community under God

Modernity connotes a cultural trajectory that derives historically from, but deviates from, orientation towards the dawning kingdom of God. It at once imagines to *define* culture (a development in which the nation-state changes "from gamekeeper to gardener") and aspires to *transcend* it (seeking to advance by the autonomous exercise of universal reason). As tacit Christian horizons fade, the modern orientation liquefies into a residue of ideology, surrogate science, and consumer choices. The renewal of Christian horizons and kingdom trajectory speaks at once into the modern classroom and the postmodern playground.

3. The Modern Betrayal of Enquiry:
Conversion to Attentiveness towards God

According to modern thinking, "value" can be separated from "fact" and is subjective and private. It is relative to an individual, group, or culture. This idea has subverted the exploration of reality at the level of our deepest and most lively personal engagement with the real. It has sponsored a widespread erosion of traditional canon, subverted the primacy of practitioners and their practical wisdom, exalted the secondary and derivative, and colluded in fostering a distracted, superficial, browsing culture. Christian faith sponsors the renewal of loving, demanding pursuit of the real.

4. Contemporary Demonization and Polarization:
Conversion to Divine Bearings

Modern assumptions underlie the tendency of polarization between liberals and fundamentalists in various settings—religious and otherwise—today. This polarization is driven by secular ideology, but it is found within and threatens the church. Liberals exalt questioning, understood as doubting; fundamentalists respond by exalting faithfulness, understood as allegiance. Each tacitly retains secular assumptions; each defines itself negatively over against the other, in mutual demonization. Christian faith is called to start elsewhere, taking positive bearings from God's self-revelation. When this calling is followed, a task of discernment arises in the place of stereotyping and demonization.

5. *The Needy Consumer:*
Conversion to the Abundance of God

Modern consumerism fosters and exploits needy, narcissistic person-alities. It displaces "the real" beyond consumers, peddles "identity" and "life" through consumption, and induces bondage to self-displacing mi-rages and specters. A Christian appraisal of this development is offered beginning from the classical Greek myth of Narcissus and Echo. The church must shun consumerism in its own practice, modeling and nur-turing instead the authentic nature of the "real," "personal identity," and "life" as these are encountered within an eschatological and Trinitarian Christian worldview.

6. *The Tragic Sense of Life:*
Conversion to the Gospel of Hope

The modern prevalence of tragic spirituality, sentiment, and escapism, accompanied by an exalted and enraged victim sensibility, reflect a cul-tural loss of hope and the resurgence of a classical "tragic sense of life." The reasons for this invite exploration. The crucifixion and resurrection of Jesus precisely engage cosmic despair with unqualified, cosmic hope. However, Christian religion and spirituality can themselves fall captive to tragic sentiment and the exaltation of victims. The church must be vigilant in resisting this and pointing to authentic hope in Christ.

7. *Personal Fulfillment and Contemporary Spirituality:*
Conversion to Eternal Life

The modern habit is to oppose freedom to duty, autonomy to authority, and personal feelings to public doctrine. This turns God himself into the oppressor of "life." This modern opposition is incorporated in con-temporary spirituality and alternative therapies in a neo-pagan pursuit of "life" that is at the same time postmodern it its opposition to modern rationality. Contending understandings of "life" invite exploration in a Christian context.

8. *The Ideology of Rights, and Political Correctness:*
Conversion to God-given Dignity

In modern thinking, human rights are exalted as securing the basis of human dignity. The ideology associated with rights has its origins in

Christian tradition and in response to issues raised by modernity. In the modern secular liberal tradition, rights have become a kind of absolute property belonging to an individual or group. Rights ideology including its "politically correct" form is a "moralist" program rooted in the vision of shaping the world in greater conformity to the human person or group, abstractly conceived and exalted. The promotion of choice as a right invites discussion. Rights and freedom of choice are to be understood, together with the distortions created by their contemporary exaltation, in the context of a Christian worldview.

9. Neoliberal Capitalist Ideology:
Conversion to the "Common-weal" of God

The modern program of economic rationalization shapes human life to the dictates of the "real" world abstractly conceived in economic terms and exalted. However, this economic "world" is a construct of neoliberal ideology that falsely ascribes to it (and to capital in particular) features distinctive of human persons such as God-given worth, the power of personal agency, and fecundity. Human persons are now displaced and reduced to human resources. A Christian response includes renewal of the place of service, of what are traditionally called "commons," of fair profit, and of the setting of economic considerations within the wider frame of God's intended blessings.

10. Public Facts and Private Values:
Conversion to the Sovereignty of God

Despite the modern vision of a public domain, this is not, nor can it be, an empty space. It was framed historically as a domain imbued with norms and inviting participation. Today public space and public service are being eroded by false programs of liberation: they are both constrained by "illiberal liberalism" and dissipated by a "tolerance" that is indifferent to truth. English political tolerance originates and derives its meaning from a different, Christian religious tolerance. The existence and content of public space no longer reflects Christian hospitality towards a secular or "provisional" domain. Current changes in English secularity invite consideration, and an understanding of their causes. Ultimately there is a choice to be made between Christ-sponsored freedom and secularist dogmas; the church is called to host public space in the name of Christ.

Conversion and Paradox

I see this approach as according with that of Lesslie Newbigin, while introducing an intermediate stage of analysis between his account of modern Western culture in the light of the gospel and his envisioned engagement with the particular, major institutions of that culture: education, health care, economics, scientific enterprise, the media, law, etc. I believe it identifies points of living engagement and conflict between the gospel and culture that span these various institutions and that recur for Christians working in any of them. Having identified the need for cultural conversion at these points, Christians will be in a better position to understand the parameters of Christian engagement with any particular profession.

It is important that I clarify here the force of my reference to these as ten "conversions." These amount to more than a way of modifying a basically unchanged modern Western worldview that supposedly offers a framework within which to view that from which, and to which, conversion is called for; rather, each one of them overturns this worldview itself, exposing its provisionality and holding it up for judgment. Each conversion is a point of entry for the gospel to break through, revealing a new world in all its depth of mystery. It offers new bearings for and an entire reorientation of understanding. For this reason, the term "conversion" as it is here used bears the connotations also of "transformation" and "restoration."

To be sure, these ten conversions therefore stand for one single conversion. However, in order to convey that each of these represents a conversion in its own right and not merely a "tweaking" of our established modern worldview, it is necessary to focus upon each in turn. Otherwise, having commended one conversion, the other nine habits of thought may be overlooked and our commitment to modern cultural assumptions may remain through our continuing reliance upon them, and take repossession of our converted imagination.

Of course, the call to radical conversion is inescapably vulnerable to such misunderstanding or evasion by reference to unchanged habitual assumptions and commitments. In particular, because this call is not merely a call to understand differently the features of a familiar referent, but rather to see the meaning of any referent itself with new eyes, it typically comes to our habitual thinking as a paradox; and our habitual thinking prompts us to sidestep the demands of wrestling with this, and to (mis)interpret it by reference to itself.

Finally, let me warn that three basic theses presented in this book may be especially prone to such misunderstanding. Of vital importance, they each call for conversion from deeply entrenched, largely unreflective assumptions. Their call for conversion applies as much to Christians as to others, insofar as Christians are domesticated to modern Western culture. I would urge the reader to ponder these three theses with special care, so as not to overlook or evade casually their call for a radical conversion in thinking. These three theses concern:

(1) The nature of our knowledge and enquiry into God as *a lively, self-giving personal act of responsiveness*. The very idea of knowing as a personal act is, of course, odd to our usual way of thinking. Michael Polanyi, however, has helped us to think of knowledge in these terms.

(2) The nature of God's self-disclosure in and through creation, as consistently through *signs*. Signs extend in scope from highly specific prophetic acts, through human experiences of seemingly universal religious significance (light, life) and the formal sacraments of the church, to the incarnation of Jesus Christ. The nature of God's self-disclosure through signs radically shapes the meaning of "creation," "the sacred," and "the secular."

(3) The nature of God as *mystery*. Although mystery is popularly seen as ruling out positive understanding, and contemplation of a mystery as precluding decisive action, these are false oppositions.

The task of elucidating these three themes is a major task in its own right. This is the subject of another book in hand.

Theological Resources

Where are theological resources to be found for exploring mission and spirituality in terms such as these? I find them among a disparate group of writers ranging from academic theologians to lay Christians, and ranging from early church theologians, through medieval "mystics" (notably Julian of Norwich), to twentieth-century Christian writers. Among the last of these groups I find vital insight especially in the work of C. S. Lewis, J. H. Oldham, Dorothy L. Sayers, Jacques Ellul, and Lesslie Newbigin.

My appreciation of this last group perhaps calls for further comment. It seems a dogma of our age sometimes that new insight must be pursued by reference to the latest, "cutting-edge" thinking of others, as if insight were strictly cumulative. Past insights may be disparaged as exhausted of their relevant content, or simply irrelevant. This seems especially true regarding "yesterday's" insights—those of the previous few generations.

However, in the deep matters of God, the truth is captured rather in the saying that "the history of theology is the history of forgetting." The history of theology is like a litter trail that, when inspected closely, is found to be full of treasures. Thus I believe we can continue to draw vital insight into our missionary and spiritual vocations today from twentieth-century Christian writers, especially those concerned to engage the social and cultural developments of that century.

In particular, my thinking has been influenced by three figures who, at the very outset of the twentieth century, showed prophetic insight into the vocation of Christian witness in the emergent setting of a secularist society and culture. The first is the English Congregationalist theologian P. T. Forsyth; the second is G. K. Chesterton;[30] the third is the Dutch Reformed theologian and politician Abraham Kuyper (drawing from Scottish theologian James Orr,[31] and taken up creatively by Herman Dooyeweerd). Each of these, I believe, still has much to teach us today, and they will receive at least passing references in the pages that follow.

30. For a valuable anthology of Chesterton's religious writings, see Morris, *Truest Fairy Tale.*

31. For a helpful introduction to Orr, see Packer, *On from Orr.*

KNOWING THE GOSPEL

*Bearings for All Human Knowledge
and Enquiry*

PEOPLE WHO LIVE IN Western culture today are mostly blind to the living, liberating gospel of Jesus Christ. Western culture blinds its inhabitants to the gospel and to the vital light it sheds upon themselves, their lives, and their world. It provides no constant reminders of the gospel that was so vital to its own emergence. More than this, however, it hinders its inhabitants from ever encountering this gospel. And when the gospel does confront people in word and deed, it is typically captured and distorted by the imperious, imaginative world of Western culture into something else, blinding them to the gospel.

And there is more: Western Christians are themselves commonly captive in their assumptions to the culture around them. Real though their personal encounter with God in Jesus Christ may be, they regularly interpret what they believe in terms dependent upon ambiguous modern[1] cultural[2] assumptions. Typically they are not aware of these assumptions; they have not learned to recognize them for what they are in the light of the gospel—a gospel that engages, judges, and transforms these assumptions.

In particular, as Lesslie Newbigin discerned, those who profess the Christian faith often think about what they believe by reference funda-

1. I shall use the term "modern" consistently to refer to the theoretical vision and practical trajectory of Western culture from the European Enlightenment up to today, incorporating the reactions within it known commonly as Romanticism and postmodernism.

2. I shall use the expression "cultural assumptions" to refer to the fundamental "worldview" commitments and social imaginary shared, often unconsciously, by the inhabitants of a culture—including a highly differentiated modern culture. This use incorporates the anthropological understanding of "culture," but includes equally the ideological commitments prevalent in the framework and practice of public life in Western culture. For further discussion, see Part 2, chapter 2.

mentally to a false way of thinking about *knowledge*—about what it is to know (or for that matter to enquire) and about what may be known.[3] Put simply, this way of thinking sets knowledge in defining opposition to subjective ideas. It sees knowledge as about the attainment of objective information stripped of gratuitous subjective elements. This way of thinking about knowledge misrepresents and subverts in practice the claim to know God, and with this—ultimately—the claim to know anything at all. As an authorized, public view of knowledge, taken to be self-evident, this way of thinking has major historical origins in the European Enlightenment. From it has grown, importantly, a misrepresentation of the relation between Christian faith and the modern world of scientific/utilitarian public investigation and of mass management and marketing. This does not do justice to knowing at its most vital and personal. It does not reflect the reality of knowing God, or ourselves, or anything else at all in God's creation.

I believe Newbigin was essentially right, and that what he discerned is of vital significance today for all in the world who live in or are influenced by modern culture: it is vital for understanding the gospel, our culture, and the engagement of the gospel with our culture. Let us grant that there may be much scope for discussion both regarding Newbigin's account of the Enlightenment and regarding what features of contemporary life may properly be attributed to it in retrospect. Nevertheless, I believe that he was fundamentally right in identifying and describing the cultural captivity that today subverts joyful reception and proclamation of the gospel as it engages people living in Western culture, and which subverts self-awareness regarding this culture for what it is in the light of the gospel.

What then is this gospel? In what terms shall we find it speaking to us, liberating us from blinding cultural assumptions (rather than being domesticated to them)? What is this gospel that opens our eyes to God and to our culture alike?

To ask this is not to ask for a different gospel from that proclaimed by Jesus of Nazareth. To be sure, the good news proclaimed by Jesus of Nazareth does find many expressions as it engages the diverse contexts and commitments of human life. These are not different gospels but one gospel disclosed in living engagement with diverse contexts. However,

3. Newbigin wrote frequently on this topic in the late 1980s and in the 1990s. See especially his *Foolishness to the Greeks*.

when we ask today what the gospel is, we concede that we may have been blind in significant ways to the gospel, and there are ways in which the gospel has yet to come alive for us and liberate us.

In what follows, I shall answer the question "What is the gospel?" in seven summary statements. No doubt much that I write here will appear initially to the reader largely a restatement of what is familiar and a matter of common agreement among Christians. However, as I hope will become apparent, the terms in which I state this and in which I unfold the relation between my statements constitutes an illuminating new and coherent presentation of the gospel as it engages us in modern Western culture.

1. GOD'S SOVEREIGNTY IS AT HAND: GOD, OUR ULTIMATE CONTEXT, IS BREAKING IN

Jesus of Nazareth disclosed in word and action the approach of God as our ultimate context and the host of eternal life. Jesus' message addresses to their depths the human contexts comprising people's lives and worlds, assumptions, and personal attachments, inviting people to yield all wholeheartedly to receive new life in which God would reign as host. These contexts are revealed as provisional in the deeper context of their creator and redeemer as they are broken open for transformation and judgment. They become signs in and through which God reveals himself in his creation. In this way God's self-revelation in the gospel is at once transcendent and contextual. Also, as God reveals himself he reveals our selves and our world as they really are and as God sees them—as secular (i.e., provisional) signs pointing to, and called to transformation through participation in, the sacred self-giving of God.

Commentary

Through Jesus Christ in his life, death, and resurrection, God brings us to know himself.[4] This "knowledge" is a quite wonderful thing—the gift

---

4. Throughout this book, when I refer to "knowing God" I refer at once to knowing God for who he is, and knowing his will as he discloses this to us in the particularities of our situation. Sometimes a false dichotomy is predicated between these two. In general, traditional mainstream Christian churches tend to emphasize knowledge of God as a matter of contemplating who he is, whereas Pentecostal and charismatic churches tend to emphasize an active God who calls Christians to discern—through prayer and providence—what he wants to do, and wants them to do, in quite specific ways. These are, I would argue, aspects of one irreducible act of knowing God.

and possibility of eternal life. Knowing God is about participating in this new life; it is this life enacted, lived. This is our fullest, self-giving personal action, alive at the heart of all the acts in which we know people and things in the world. As such this knowledge sheds radiant light upon ourselves and the world: C. S. Lewis said, "I believe in Christianity as I believe that the sun has risen: not because I see it, but because by it I see everything else."[5] Knowledge of God is of this special kind.

It is necessary to emphasize this because "knowing" means many different things in different contexts and in relation to different things, but this is often poorly understood in modern thinking. In particular, knowledge of God is not understood; instead, knowledge of God is conceived in terms that stand for no such thing but an imaginary "knowledge" and its fictional object. The error of modern thinking in this matter must be addressed in order that God and knowledge of God may be understood and embraced for what they are.

Importantly, we must challenge the routine modern way of thinking about God and knowledge of God summarized as follows: "To know God is something additional to knowing ourselves and the world as generally known. This familiar knowledge of ourselves and the world is supplemented, but not changed, by knowledge of God. However, unlike our knowledge of ourselves and the world, knowledge of God is by its nature always open to doubt—doubt that extends to God's very existence—and is therefore contested by people in general."

We shall challenge this misrepresentation of knowing God, testifying rather to the truth that C. S. Lewis succinctly conveys above: that to know God is integrally to *know ourselves and the world in the light of God*. This testimony may be framed in various ways. Below, I shall frame it by averring that God is *the One who hosts us and the world, whom to know is also to know ourselves and the world in the context of God's hospitality.*

The Hospitality of God

The hospitality of God[6] is integral to the biblical witness to God. It is associated most obviously with the themes of creation, covenant and

---

5. Lewis, *Poetry*, 165.

6. A valuable study of the hospitality of God and the distorted forms of hospitality found in contemporary culture is Elizabeth Newman, *Untamed Hospitality: Welcoming God and Other Strangers*. Another fine study—less theological and more focused upon

belonging, stewardship, and with participation in God's work as apprentices and heirs.

The opening chapters of the book of Genesis tell of a universe created and hosted by God, and of Adam and Eve hosted by God in the Garden of Eden. Adam and Eve turn away from this hospitality, however, distrusting God's injunction not to eat fruit from of the tree in the middle of the garden. They evade the demands of the hospitality of God, and place themselves outside of Eden. The plight of humankind may now be characterized as that of living between two contradictory worlds, each informed by evasion of the hospitality of God. In the first world, God's hospitality is experienced as absent in a final, mocking way. Humankind lives in a desert of disorientation and despair, lacking fundamental personal identity or purpose, like flotsam washed up on a beach, or like aliens trespassing in a world from which they have been excluded. Here "hospitality" tends towards a private haven of (ultimately futile) escape from a mocking, inhospitable world. In the second world, the hospitality of God is endlessly dismissed in favor of a life of personal autonomy. Who needs hospitality? Hope is sought here in mastery of a world now reduced to resources available to be used and managed to one's own ends. "Hospitality" itself becomes one tool among others, as one or other form of private patronage (perhaps offered by the state under the label, ironically, of a "public" realm) that again serves our own ends. Fallen humankind thus lives between despair and pride, rather than delighting in the hospitality of God.

In this fallen human setting, God seeks to restore humankind to his hospitality. God chooses the descendants of Abraham, Isaac, and Jacob, hosting them as his own, inaugurating a covenant with them and granting them the land of Israel to inhabit under his sovereign rule. They are to be his chosen servant, extending his hospitality to all nations as they are brought to worship God in his holy city of Jerusalem.

In the life and teaching of Jesus of Nazareth, God approaches as the sovereign host: the kingdom of God will be like a wedding feast hosted by God for all who would come to it. Jesus extended, in meal fellowship, the hospitality of God to guests who had been counted unfit for such

Christian hospitality and its history—is Christine Pohl, *Making Room: Recovering Hospitality as a Christian Tradition.* Luke Bretherton, in *Hospitality as Holiness: Christian Witness amid Moral Diversity,* approaches the theme of Christian hospitality in dialogue with the writings of Oliver O'Donovan, Alasdair MacIntyre, and Germain Grisez.

hospitality by religious leaders of his day. He also likened the approach of God to the return of a master who has entrusted his property and purposes to the responsibility of stewards, in a setting ultimately hosted by the master. Jesus also spoke of God's hospitality in more intimate terms, describing his followers as his own family. The hospitality of God is at once public (that is, open to all) and personal.

Such hospitality sets us free to live. It is hospitality of the kind that nurtures, teaches, empowers, and provides opportunities.[7] It helps us to discover for ourselves a world in which we are welcome and have a dignified place in which to find our bearings, confidently to exercise our own judgment, and freely to commit ourselves in love to God and to one another.

It is part of the freedom for which God's hospitality liberates us, that when he approaches us in Jesus Christ he neither imposes upon the world the fact of his hospitality, nor leaves the world ignorant of his welcoming invitation. He would have us recognize freely the hospitality that sets us free.

Receptivity and Responsibility

In the Bible, the hospitality of God is experienced first as a gift to be received: it is the initiative of God who creates and calls a people to be his own. Foremost here is the theme of *belonging*. The Jewish Scriptures witness to God calling Abraham and his descendants to be God's own chosen people, belonging to him and bound to him in covenant. In the New Testament Christians are described as "a chosen race . . . a people claimed by God for his own . . . once you were not a people at all; but now you are God's people" (1 Pet 2:9–10). They are not "aliens" but "members of God's household" (Eph 2:19). They belong to God not as slaves but as sons and daughters, adopted into the sonship of Christ, inspired by the Spirit and taught by Jesus to address God as "Father" (Rom 8:14–17). Belonging to God is even compared to the way parts of the body belong to and function within the body as a whole (1 Cor 12:12–31) , and to the way branches belong to a grapevine (John 15:1–5). Talk of being "in

7. The sculptor Rodin conveys the contrast between this and the hospitality of Satan strikingly in his sculptures "The Hand of God" and "The Hand of the Devil" (each is found in more than one version; I refer to the versions on display in the Rodin Museum in Paris). In the former, two little human figures, male and female, emerge into life and freedom from the great, molding hand of God; in one of the latter, the hand of the Devil reaches out to snatch two human figures gaily dancing.

Christ" (as in Saint Paul's letters) and of "dwelling in Christ" (as in Saint John's gospel) indicate the closest possible personal union between the Christian, Christ, and God.

Let us emphasize that "belonging" is a matter here of belonging *to God* and not merely to one human institution among others. This is "belonging" of a radical kind. To belong authentically to, say, God's chosen people or to the church, is at root about being among those who belong to God.

The hospitality of God is *nurturing*. It is like the hospitality of the shepherd who feeds, waters, and protects his sheep, or that of the vine-grower who plants and tends his vines with care. It is comparable to a nurturing environment, like a rock in the desert that, protecting from the scorching sun and wind, nurtures an ecological niche in its shelter (Isa 32:2). It is also about refuge or sanctuary (as in many Psalms). Psalm 91 in particular is replete with images of God's hospitality.

The hospitality of God is, then, a gift to be received. To accept it, however, is integrally to embrace responsibility. It is, most obviously, to embrace *stewardship of God's gifts*. In many of his parables Jesus invoked, as we have already noted, the image of stewards entrusted with property by a master for the moment absent—a practice commonplace in Jesus' culture. Christians have been entrusted with stewardship of knowledge of God, and of ourselves and all creation as belonging to God's good purposes.

The responsibility entailed in the hospitality of God extends beyond that of stewardship of property, material and otherwise. It extends to active *participation in the work of* God. Stewardship of property already entails the responsibility of caring for property with the same concern as its owner; but God lays upon us the responsibility of working with him as apprentices, learning to share in his practical, purposive activity. This is indeed part of the meaning of sonship in Jesus' culture: a son would learn from and work alongside his father in the family business, as Jesus will have worked with his father Joseph the carpenter.

To be called to such apprenticeship is to be called beyond autonomous activity on the one hand, and beyond conformity to rules totally dictating action on the other. We may describe it as the calling to see with our own eyes as God sees—like an apprentice, to pay the same practical attention, and to participate in the same intention, as the one with whom we work.

Such participation extends beyond doing the work of God. It extends to the "responsibility" of delighting in God's creation as God delights in it, knowing the whole world as our inheritance. This is a major theme of Thomas Traherne.[8]

Is it pretentious to speak in this way of seeing with God's eyes? It would certainly be so, were this not a matter of high vocation in which we are mercifully upheld and restored by God's grace. It is no different from the vocation to attend to, and know, God: both attending "to" and attending "from" God are a matter of being drawn into knowledge of a mystery beyond our comprehension—of knowing that which is beyond knowledge.

Our embrace of responsibility as we receive the hospitality of God extends to being a channel of God's hospitality to others. This is indeed fundamental to the mission of the church. We are called at once to receptivity and responsibility, in the very act itself of responsiveness to God. This takes the form both of "centripetal" and "centrifugal" mission: the hospitality we extend in the name of God both invites people to join us in worshipping and serving God, and also enters into the world of others as a sign bearing the presence and promise of the hospitality of God.

By recalling briefly our knowledge of God as our host, we have prepared ourselves to entertain the following claim: *in Jesus Christ, God approaches us as our ultimate context.*[9]

Context and Knowledge: The Act of "Inhabiting a World"

The ideas of God as our "host" and as our "context" clearly have features in common. However, the latter does not immediately display the rich texture of meaning of the former as we have just sketched this as a matter of being personally embraced by, and personally embracing, the hospitality of God. We tend to think of context in impersonal terms, a setting in which we as persons think and act. We also tend to think of context as like a location—more precisely, as a determinate location in

---

8. Traherne, *Centuries.*

9. This is the key disclosure pursued in this book. I realize that "context" is "thin" language compared with the biblical language of hospitality, belonging, etc. However, there is strongly prevalent today in modern culture a distorted, Cartesian way of picturing "context" (at the same time as assuming often that we ourselves do our thinking "free of context") that, as a deeply entrenched habit, subverts in theory and practice personal attention to God, ourselves, and creation. And it is urgent for Christian witness in Western culture today that we challenge this distortion wholeheartedly.

space and time that can in principle be viewed from outside of itself. We see this context as being no part of our knowing itself, although it may condition this knowledge as its prior, irreducible "given." This way of thinking about knowledge and context now contributes to the conception of context-free, objective universal knowledge on the one hand, and limited perspectival knowledge or a particular viewpoint upon the world as a whole on the other.

Now with regard to certain cases of knowledge, this way of thinking about context captures reasonably the relation between knowledge on the one hand and its context on the other. However, it does not reflect the fundamental relation between knowledge and context. With respect to our most fundamental, lively, personal knowledge, our context denotes the world that we actively, practically inhabit in our knowing, and *this act of inhabiting a world-context is integrally part of the act of knowing itself.*

Wolfhart Pannenberg associates what I have called "inhabiting a world-context" with that unique freedom that characterizes human beings and constitutes human "openness to the world." This leads on the one hand to the emergence, for humankind, of a "world" as such: "One can say that man has a world, while each species of animal is limited to an environment that is fixed by heredity and that is typical of the species." On the other hand, "this cannot involve only openness to 'the world.' Rather, openness to the world must mean that man is completely directed into the 'open' . . . beyond the world . . . beyond every possible picture of the world . . . Such openness beyond the world is even the condition for man's experience of the world."[10] We might put it that human beings are directed towards inhabiting ever-deeper contexts and that this is the condition of human habitation of any context whatsoever.

What is it that drives human beings into the open in this way? Something different, says Pannnberg, from "the compulsion associated with animal instinct. The compulsive instinct in animals goes into action only when the triggering object is present. In contrast, the pressure of human drives is directed towards something undefined . . . it drives man into the open, apparently without a goal."[11]

This "pressure of human drives" is fundamentally a matter of human response to an unfolding "world." It is about human *responsiveness to* the

10. Pannenberg, *What Is Man?* 8.
11. Ibid., 9.

indeterminate real as it discloses itself to us. It is through this we come to inhabit a world in the first place, in an act of integration. Through it we go on, during our lives, to integrate at a deeper level the many contexts in which we have come to live and move, and which are each themselves originally a matter of integration. We also inhabit multiple contexts. Some of these we move between—for example, between home, work, and leisure; some we inhabit simultaneously. Some contexts are relatively "local"; others are wider; some may even be humanly universal. Some such contexts are "nested," as when we belong within a family that itself belongs within a local community that belongs in turn to a certain ethnic group. Some contexts may remain influential upon our imagination throughout our lifetime; these may change with time, involving re-integration on our part. Other contexts may appear and fade as we move from one workplace or set of relationships to another as the years go by. Today participation in the internet provides a variety of new contexts for individuals to inhabit. The relations between the multiple and changing contexts that together form the context of our lives is complex, and we are constantly busy trying to integrate them into a single world—an effort that may be sometimes more, sometimes less fruitful.

The Approach of God as Our Ultimate Context

God who calls us in Jesus Christ calls us to be open to finding our belonging beyond all such contexts, in the deeper context of God's sovereign rule. This is in fact the "openness to every possible world" of which Pannenberg writes. In the setting of such openness, human contexts acquire a provisional character.

The approach of God in Jesus Christ addresses to their depths the human contexts comprising our cultural assumptions and personal attachments, calling us to yield all wholeheartedly to receive new and eternal life in which God would reign as host. We must offer up ourselves and our entire world in order to enter into this life. Jesus teaches that one who would gain life must lose it. The language of Christian baptism is of dying with Christ in order that we may receive new life with him. That this involves entrusting ourselves to a new world, a lived offering of ourselves and the world we know, is urged by Paul in the words, "offer your very selves to him: a living sacrifice, dedicated and fit for acceptance, the worship offered by heart and mind. Conform no longer to this present world, but be transformed by the renewal of your minds" (Rom 12:1–2; see also Eph 4:22–24).

The gospel thus addresses us in our human contexts, beckoning us to inhabit the world in a deeper way, indwelling the ultimate context of God. The gospel is at once *contextual* and *transcendent*. It is essentially in contextual form; the gospel does not present itself in timeless, universal terms apart from particular, historical contexts, but presents itself precisely in terms of the latter. This is highlighted in the situation of the cross-cultural evangelist when presented by his hearers with the question, "Who is Jesus?" Lesslie Newbigin observes that the missionary can only begin by using words that have some meaning for his hearers:

> [He has to] begin by assuming a common framework of language, of experience, of inherited tradition, of axioms and assumptions embodied in the forms of speech. He can only introduce what is new by provisionally accepting what is already there in the minds of his hearers.
>
> But what if the new thing he wants to introduce is so radically new that it calls into question all previous axioms and assumptions, all inherited tradition, and all human experience, so that even language itself cannot serve to communicate it? What if the new thing is in fact the primal truth by which all else has to be confronted and questioned? How do you begin to explain that which must in the end be accepted as the beginning of all explanation? That is the problem of the evangelist.[12]

Newbigin also reminds us in this passage that the gospel is also essentially *transcendent*. Contextualization does not mean that the gospel *conforms to* cultural assumptions, but that it *engages* them: it enters into and transforms our cultural assumptions as we see the world anew in the light of the gospel. The issue of inculturation has been a topical one in mission circles in recent decades. It has been argued that if the gospel is to be intelligible and persuasive to the people of a certain culture, it must be framed in terms of the beliefs and practices, the underlying worldview assumptions, of that culture.[13] There is of course an important insight here. However, there is an equally important complementary

---

12. Newbigin, *Light Has Come*, 2.

13. Much has been written by missiologists on the contextualization (inculturation, indigenization) of the gospel in recent decades. Well known is Bevans, *Models*. Within a wider, historical frame, Pelikan, *Jesus*, is a memorable study. On Christology, seen Greene, *Christology*. A classic typology is offered by Niebuhr, *Christ and Culture*.

aspect to the gospel: the gospel *addresses* these underlying worldview assumptions. It does not simply mould itself to them, or speak out of fundamental commitment to them. If it did so, it would no longer be the gospel. It would have nothing to say to them; it would be domesticated to, or captive to, them. This would not amount to an engagement between gospel and culture, but a culture-bound soliloquy that has commandeered the language of the gospel.

In summary: when God reveals himself to us in our context, he does so not simply within our context, but as our *ultimate* context. He engages our habitation of human contexts, breaking them open for us to find our context more deeply in him. Context is never irreducible, but is itself always to be understood in the deeper context of God. God himself, meanwhile, cannot be known from some other context than himself, but only by opening up to him as our ultimate context. Engaging our *context*, the gospel is contextual; *engaging* our context, the gospel is transcendent.

In such terms the gospel calls Christians to be *in* but *not of* the world: "resident aliens," as the second-century writer Diognetus put it. This is not a call to be a separated people, living in a parallel "world" apart from non-Christians (although in some matters and on some occasions there may be good reason for Christians to live this way). It is rather a call to inhabit the world in a such a way as to inhabit more deeply the purposes of God. It is to see and serve God at work in the world in signs.

As citizens of heaven, our lives are "hid with Christ in God" (Col 3:3). Our hospitality lies ultimately in God, and not in any human context. Inhabiting all that has emerged for us as our human context, we are fundamentally open to the essentially emergent context of God's kingdom.

God's Self-disclosure in Signs

In the Synoptic Gospels, Jesus' miracles of healing and exorcism are, for those with eyes to see it, signs disclosing the in-breaking sovereignty of God in his Messiah. In John's Gospel this is formalized: the first sign (turning water into wine at the wedding in Cana) discloses the fact itself that Jesus discloses himself through "signs" transforming established religious custom. Signs then follow that testify to the arrival of God's Messiah bringing sight to the blind, making the lame walk, the deaf hear, lepers cleansed, and raising the dead to life. The final, climactic sign is the crucifixion and resurrection of Jesus. Thus the central sign of God's in-breaking sovereignty is not any particular miracle but the person of Jesus, the incarnate Son of God, now crucified and risen.

The "sign" character of divine self-disclosure is not limited to Christ's miracles and teaching, but is integral to all such disclosure. The sacraments of the Christian church are signs, in turn, embodying the action of God, although their formal nature may rather conceal from immediate view the sovereign freedom in which God approaches his creation in signs. More widely, and more apparently in freedom, God also reveals himself through the ordinary, familiar things of our world, making them come alive at once for what they are and as vehicles or occasions of divine self-disclosure. Another word for such disclosing things is "icon." The contemporary loss of our capacity to see creation in this way is the subject of Rowan William's book *Lost Icons*.

When God speaks to us through signs in this way, this does not leave our world intact; rather, it opens up a new context in which to see this world itself. Aelred Squire writes that a proper spirituality encourages us to "allow our immediate experience constantly to break in upon our preconceived notions with such fresh news that we find ourselves suddenly where we actually are, in a world quite different from the one we supposed it to be, and with many a burning bush among what we always thought to be a waste of dry shrubbery."[14]

The word "sign" is, of course, used in a particular way here. In modern thinking, a sign (or symbol) is commonly regarded as something pointing to something else: we imagine to look at a sign, on the one hand, and at that to which it points, on the other. The latter is the "real thing," while the former is only a pointer to it. Smoke is a sign of fire, but it is not fire; even less so is a conventional sign (such as a road signpost or a food label identifying the ingredients in a jar) the thing it signifies. Now this way of thinking reasonably matches some circumstances where "the real thing" is something familiar to us conceptually, providing a framework of conceptual meaning within which we now set a sign and the thing signified side by side before us. But when God discloses himself in a sign, there is no such wider and more "direct" conceptual encounter with God to be set alongside knowledge of him through the sign. There is no such wider conceptual framework; rather, God himself

14. Squire, *Asking the Fathers*, 4.

is our deepest horizon, into which he leads us as he discloses himself to us in the most direct way.

John Baillie has coined the paradoxical expression "mediated immediacy" to describe this knowledge of God through signs. This is a feature even of that which, of all things in creation, is opaque to the self-disclosure of God: the crucifixion of Jesus of Nazareth. Baillie writes: "it is in Christ that we see God. We see him veiled and humiliated, but it is nevertheless God that we see. The kind of directness for which we have contended in our knowledge of God is thus not at all interfered with, but is rather implemented, by the fact of Christ's mediatorship. This is what I have tried to express in the conception of a mediated immediacy. In Christ we know God not by argument but by personal acquaintance. In Christ God comes to us directly."[15]

When God comes to us we are in a new situation different from where we were before his approach. We have to respond or evade him. This is for us a *krisis*, a moment when we are judged by our response. When our familiar world comes alive as a sign disclosing God, we have either to embrace the demands of letting go our attachment to our familiar world and of opening to inhabit a new and deeper context, or to evade these demands. Such evasion takes two basic forms. On the one hand, we may cling to our familiar context and dismiss God's approach by framing it (supposedly) within, rather than allowing it to challenge, this context. This may be characterized as the way of false, proud integration, in which our manner of habitation of a context turns into a stubborn habit. On the other hand, we may be overcome by the demands of new integration, and allow to collapse the effort of integration in which we inhabit any meaningful world. This may be characterized as the way of personal disintegration, dissolution, and despair.

Restated in terms of the world we inhabit, we are brought back here to our earlier characterization of humanity following the Fall. When God approaches, our world is changed. If we embrace God's approach, the world is restored. It comes alive with signs disclosing God and disclosing the world and our selves as they truly are. If we evade God's approach, our habitation of the world is divided. On one side lies habitation of a world that has our idolatrous "self" at its centre, vaunting its proud but false freedom over against God; on the other side lies habitation of a world in which we are mocked by the idols of despair,

15. Baillie, *Our Knowledge of God,* 196–97.

and are bound in spiritual defeat and captivity. We live caught between these two false worlds.

Krisis: The Uniqueness of Christ

We shall consider later how, in the death and resurrection of Jesus Christ, the above evasion of God is both manifest and addressed in a final way. This is not to dismiss the biblical witness that in a fundamental sense God approaches his creation in life-giving self-disclosure from the act of creation onwards. The Word of God is the life and light of humankind (John 1:4). Humankind's fallen state concerns the blind evasion of God's approach, in pride and despair. Throughout human history, human beliefs and actions have embodied responsiveness towards, or evasion of, God's self-disclosure. To be sure, God approaches in a final, decisive way in the incarnation, death, and resurrection of Jesus Christ. But when he does so, he is not met with neutral personal and cultural dispositions, but with dispositions that already reflect to varying degrees responsiveness to or evasion of God. These predispositions are engaged by the gospel of repentance, forgiveness, and the rewarding of faith.

Does it follow that we may equate the preaching of the gospel to an individual with the moment of *krisis* when God comes to them, calling for response? Does it follow that when someone has heard the gospel preached, and they have not then been converted to Christian faith, that they have evaded God's self-disclosure? We may not pass this judgment. The preaching of the gospel is, of course, vital to God's self-disclosure. But the gospel may not come alive for those listening for reasons that may be hidden from our view. It is a largely secret affair when God speaks (or does not speak) to the human heart. It is not for Christians to judge but rather to seek and recognize ever anew how to bring alive the gospel for what it is. This involves a lively effort to identify, in the light of the gospel, with those among whom mission is pursued: a discovery of the gospel as it engages their context, and a recognition of the signs that disclose the gospel in this context. Such recognition is a work of the Spirit, as is conversion itself.

Where Are We Met with the Truly Sacred?

Our account of God as our ultimate context prompts us to state afresh where it is that we meet the truly sacred. We are prompted to do so because contemporary ideas of the sacred (and of what is not sacred) are

diverse. On the one hand, there remain pre-modern, traditional societies, and religious minorities within secular societies, for whom certain
things within the world have sacred status: sacred rituals, sacred objects,
sacred laws and doctrines, sacred offices and institutions. On the other
hand, there are people who claim that nothing is sacred; that sacredness
is a subjective construct—a claim integral to the secularist vision of the
world and society.

The Christian understanding of the sacred is different from either
of these. True sacredness lies not in particular things in the world, but
in God who discloses himself, in the context of creation, precisely as
himself our deepest context. The sacred is not to be found in the world
in itself; rather, the world is to be found, as God's creation, within the
sacred purposes of God. This means, on the one hand, that the world is
secular in the original Christian sense of being the *saeculum* or provisional world; it is not enchanted in the sense of having irreducible, direct
points of contact with God. On the other hand, the world is God's good
creation and the medium of his self-disclosure, pointing both to God
and to its own true self in new creation. We shall explore further this
vital truth in Part 2, chapter 1.

2. KNOWING GOD: THE PARADOX OF GRACE

*Our encounter with God through signs is a lively, immediate, personal en-
counter in radical responsiveness. Through it we receive God's self-giving,
in the fullest personal way. However, we do not receive passively: by the
paradox of grace, the act in which we receive God is a most lively personal
one, as we entrust ourselves personally in an unqualified way to knowing
him. This is for us a matter of attention at once "from" God and "towards"
God—of relying upon and reaching for, of giving ourselves in receptivity
and of taking responsibility for ourselves. This knowledge is paradoxical
to our normal thinking about knowledge. Knowledge of God is a mystery
into which God in his grace draws us. It is participation in the mystery
of knowledge of himself, which always remains greater than our present
knowledge of him.*

Commentary

When God—who is our ultimate context—approaches, bringing knowledge of himself in Jesus Christ, what is this knowledge like? There are

differences between what it is like to know a person, a good action, a
beautiful work of art, and a medical statistic. There is also a difference
between "know-how" and conceptual knowledge. We have particular
reason to ask what knowledge of God is like because modern ways of
thinking assume a wrong answer, and Christians may unwittingly defer
to and collude with this error. This leads them to betray the reality of
knowledge of God. It also tends to deflect them from knowing God and
deflect others from coming to know God through them.

The theme of knowing God is, of course, a recurrent one in the
Bible. Knowing God also lies at the heart of truly knowing both ourselves and the world. Indeed *what it means to know God is paradigmatic
for understanding all our knowing.*

In asking what kind of knowing this is, we need not assume that
knowledge of God is one kind of knowledge among others, classifiable
by reference to some wider, comprehensive account of knowledge in its
variety. Indeed, as God our ultimate context stands in unique relation
to all that we know from within provisional contexts, so what it means
to know God stands in unique relation to all our knowing within these
contexts. In fact the latter is ultimately to be understood by reference to
what it means to know God. The converse of this is that knowledge of
God presents paradoxes to our normal understanding of knowledge, as
we shall explore below.

To enlarge upon this vital matter of knowing God, we shall explore
some of the paradoxes that knowledge of God presents to our normal
understanding of knowledge. There is no logical sequence in which these
are rightly to be expounded; each paradox is informed by every other,
although in the moment of apprehension of any one paradox the others
that inform it cannot at the same time be made explicit as paradoxes.

Let us begin by acknowledging the paradox that knowing God is
essentially *a first-hand affair*—something true also of our questioning
into or exploration of God and his will. This paradox is related to the
fact that we encounter God as a mystery beyond our fathoming: paradoxically, to know God is to know the unknowable. Such knowledge
is at once entirely the work of God, and entirely our own work. This
is the paradox of grace. This uniquely lively personal, self-giving act is
vectorial, directional or *from-to* in character. This is associated with the
paradoxes that to know God is to *know with* God, and to know ourselves
known by God, and that to know God is inseparably to commune in his

faith, hope, and love. In each case it is the inseparability of knowing God from other seemingly distinct concepts that presents us with paradox: these concepts intimate not only what we know when we know God, but also, in their paradoxical conjunction with such knowing, precisely what this knowing means in the first place.

Seeking and Knowing God for Ourselves

A defining feature of knowing God is that to know God is inescapably to know God *for ourselves*. Knowledge of God is first-hand, personal knowledge. Now our provisional knowledge in general is knowledge of that which we may also, to varying degrees, know second-hand because we have been informed of it, and this second-hand knowledge is more or less the same as first-hand knowledge. Knowledge of God, however, is not only first-hand; paradoxically it *is essentially so*. If we do not know God for ourselves, we simply do not know him.

The same applies to our *searching for* God and his will, or our questioning after God: the question of God is one that we have to *ask for ourselves*, and *ask ourselves* as we attend towards God, or else it is no such thing. We know God through first-hand enquiry. "Knowing by acquaintance" is how John Baillie, as we have seen, describes knowing God; but we must add to this that already when we enquire after God, we respond to One who beckons us personally. We encounter the God we know by acquaintance as much in hope-inspired, loving, attentive searching for God as in finding God.

The paradox that our questioning and our knowing God are essentially first-hand is the subject of the saying attributed to Martin Buber, "You cannot talk about God; you can only address Him." Whereas this might seem to state that we cannot know God, it is in fact a testimony that points us to God by directing us to address God for ourselves. Rather than denying the possibility of talking about God, it models authentic "talk about God" as that which directs us to address—in attentive receptivity—the reality of God for ourselves. Such talk about God is itself directed *towards* God, rather than third-party talk; it stands before God in prayerful address, directed towards first-hand enquiry and knowledge of God, inviting and inducting others into the same address.

Indeed with respect to knowledge of God, we can hardly separate the acts of seeking and finding, asking questions and recognizing answers. The lively act in which we know God is as much about confronting

questions as about knowing answers, and as much about finding oneself
beckoned by clues as about finding clues fall into place as their meaning
is revealed. And *this is essentially so* with regard to knowing God.

This is, of course, paradoxical to our normal way of thinking, in
which we conceive asking a question as strictly alternative to stating a
truth. We direct questions precisely towards what we do not know—
such as the truth of a statement that has been made (as when we doubt
a claim) or the discovery of where the truth lies among a range of
potential claims. With knowledge of God, however, it is different: to
know God is precisely for us to find that questions about God come
alive for us, engaging us (or more truly, find ourselves alive ourselves
to these questions), while to ask questions about God is already to be
born into knowledge of God. Bonhoeffer writes, "There is no general
blind seeking after God. Here a man can only seek what has already
been found," and he quotes Blaise Pascal: "You would not seek me had
you not already found me."[16] The fourteenth-century anchoress Julian
of Norwich wrote that, "we can never seek God until the time when
he in his goodness shows himself to us ... So I saw him and sought
him, and I had him and lacked him; and this should be our ordinary
undertaking in this life, as I see it."[17]

The paradoxical conjunction of seeking and finding, enquiring
and knowing may be presented by bringing together two avowals by P.
T. Forsyth and Gerhard Ebeling. On the one hand, our knowledge of
God is sure beyond all doubt. P. T. Forsyth quotes the testimony that
"a thousand difficulties do not make for one doubt," writing that, "our
certainty is, by the Holy Spirit, a most incredible thing—it is a function
of the certainty which God always has of himself."[18] On the other hand,
God remains for us a matter of profound, attentive enquiry. Gerhard
Ebeling approaches this from a linguistic viewpoint, writing that, "the
understanding of what the word 'God' means has its place within the
sphere of radical questionableness."[19] The mystery of God is such that
whatever we say about him is subject to further fathoming in which we

16. Bonhoeffer, *Christ the Center*, 32.

17. Julian, *Showings*, 193. The inseparability of seeking and seeing God is woven closely into Julian's revelation. See especially the Second Revelation (long text),
93–196.

18. Forsyth, *Principle of Authority*, 44.

19. Ebeling, *Word and Faith*, 347.

re-enter into the probing and searching that gave rise to everything we say about God in the first place.

These and other paradoxes presented by knowledge of God arise as we encounter the *mystery* of God, to which we now turn.

Knowing the Unknowable: Knowledge of God and the Mystery of God

The Bible witnesses to God as one who is encountered in mystery. In the Old Testament, wisdom probes the unfathomable ways of God. Jesus refers repeatedly to the kingdom of God as coming in secret, a secret to which God opens peoples' eyes through Jesus' own acts of healing and liberation, and through his parables. In Saint John's Gospel, Jesus' disciples struggle to understand as he speaks enigmatically of the mystery of God and his purposes at work in himself. Saint Paul writes of God's "secret purpose," declaring that "only the Spirit of God knows what God is. And we have received this Spirit from God" (1 Cor 2:7, 11–12). The Letters to the Ephesians and to the Colossians speak of the mystery of God now revealed in Christ through the Spirit. What is revealed and known in each case is a mystery deeper than we know or can ever know. Regarding Christ's love, the prayer is offered that Christians may "know it though it is beyond all knowledge." (Eph 3:19)

The encounter with mystery is thus integral to our knowing God. However, this needs careful clarification because of the way that knowledge and mystery have usually been understood in the modern period. Typically they have been seen as mutually exclusive: mystery connotes lack of knowledge, while to attain knowledge is to dispel mystery. Knowledge is a positive acquisition; mystery connotes absence of this. To seek knowledge is to eliminate mystery. Michael Foster describes this as the dominant tradition in both science and European philosophy since the Renaissance. "The two following principles," he writes, "seem especially characteristic: 'Thinking consists in answering questions.' 'If you want clear thinking, formulate your questions precisely.' This two-fold principle is one of its chief engines for the expulsion of mystery."[20]

However, as we have just seen, knowing God is irreducibly a matter at once of lively enquiry and of lively knowing. Questioning and knowing are not mutually exclusive alternatives. Indeed to insist that they are is to subvert enquiry itself at its most lively. We shall explore this subver-

---

20. Foster, "Mystery and the Philosophy of Analysis," 22.

sion further, as a fundamental error of modern thinking and practice, in chapter 3.

What has P. T. Forsyth to say about God and mystery? I have quoted him as writing that "our certainty is, by the Holy Spirit, a most incredible thing—it is a function of the certainty which God always has of himself." Does this leave any room for mystery? Indeed it does. He warns, however, against both mysticism understood as "sporadic visions and revelations of the Lord" and against that kind of "practical mysticism" in which the Christian's "centre of gravity is removed from the conscience to the consciousness, from the soul to the heart, and he subsides in a gorgeous cloud of sunset dust."[21] Rather he centers mystery in the moral miracle of regeneration. The contact of God with the soul is in its nature such a miracle. And since miracle belongs to revelation, "it has uppermost the element not of dark but of light, and the movement not of mere emergence but creation. If religion is not mystic, indeed, it is not religion; and it is truly intelligible only to its initiates and regenerates. But in Christianity the mysticism is not psychological but historic, not temperamental but moral."[22] "Religion," he writes, "is not a mystical union with the divine independent of historic mediation . . . Christ . . . is the Creator of the possibility of that mysticism which keeps at its heart the moral crisis of the [human] race, the mystery of sin, the miracle of its conquest . . . It is the mystery and miracle of the cross, where all of Christ was gathered up in one eternal, effective, inexplicable act that meant and means more for the world than its creation. It is quite true that the essence of Christianity is mystery. It is not merely sane and rational. But it is such a mystery as this."[23]

Thus, in its fundamental sense, the mystery of God is not negative. Indeed, as Gabriel Marcel writes, "the recognition of mystery . . . is an essentially positive act of the mind, the supremely positive act in virtue of which all positivity may perhaps be strictly defined."[24]

21. Forsyth, *Principle of Authority*, 464.

22. Ibid., 465.

23. Ibid., 470.

24. Marcel, "Metaphysical Diary," 118. Note also Rowan Williams' insistence that the "positive" and the "negative" in spirituality are not mutually exclusive as assumed in modern thinking (Williams, "Against Anxiety, beyond Triumphalism"). Denys Turner, in turn, argues that apophatic (i.e., negative) theology "is intelligible only as being a moment of negativity within an overall theological strategy which is at every moment both apophatic and cataphatic." He writes "We can, of course, know that God is present

To summarize, in our encounter with the mystery of God, the act of knowing is precisely one of probing participation in that which is deep beyond our comprehension. Our knowledge of God is not knowledge of God who has been a mystery to us but is no longer so. Rather, it is true knowledge of the irreducible mystery that is God, granted to us by God as he encounters us at once as presence and promise. Thus, to encounter God's *love* is not to dispel the mystery of what God is like; it is to be drawn into *the mystery of God's love*; just as to encounter God as our *hope* is not to dispel the mystery of what it means to find God, but to be born into *the mystery of hope in God* (1 Pet 1:3).

Every Christian is called to be such a "mystic," properly understood. The mystery of God remains forever new: we never come into possession of the truth of God as we think of ourselves as doing in other matters; rather the truth of God always beckons us to new encounter.

The mystery of God who is our ultimate context is the very starting-point of all knowledge. G. K. Chesterton contrasts this with the dogma that sure knowledge is grounded ultimately upon clear logical axioms: "The whole secret of mysticism is this: that man can understand every-thing by the help of what he does not understand. The morbid logician seeks to make everything lucid, and succeeds in making everything mys-terious. The mystic allows one thing to be mysterious, and everything else becomes lucid . . . The Christian puts the seed of dogma in a central darkness; but it branches forth in all directions with abounding natural health."[25]

God's Gift and Our Self-giving: The Paradox of Grace

Knowledge of God is, then, knowledge of a mystery: it is not knowledge that we can possess, but rather knowledge through which God possesses us and leads us by bringing us alive to questions and nurturing appre-

---

to us. We can struggle to say what we mean by this. We can live a life centred upon that knowledge. We can experience the world in all sorts of ways consequent upon that knowledge, which would not be available to our experience if we lacked the knowledge of God. And so we can, in a sense, be aware of God, even be 'conscious' of God; but only in that sense in which we can be conscious of the *failure* of our knowledge, not knowing what it is that our knowledge fails to reach. This is not the same thing as being conscious of the absence of God in any sense that we are conscious of what it is that is absent" (Turner, *Darkness of God*, 265).

25. Chesterton, *Orthodoxy*, 47–48.

hension of the truth. It is our own act—indeed our defining act—and entirely the act of God.

Our knowledge of God is firstly, and always remains, entirely the work of God. When God gives us knowledge of himself, he gives himself; he invests his own his life in us. Correspondingly to receive the knowledge that God gives us of himself is to receive him; it is to receive life from him. This is reflected in *how* God has revealed himself: in Jesus of Nazareth, who in radical sacrifice entrusts his life to God and us that we might have life.

Knowing God always remains the occasion of God giving himself to us. To know God is to feed upon his self-giving. This is our daily bread. Knowledge of God is sustained in us by God, nourishing us.

Julian of Norwich wrote that God declared himself the very foundation of our beseeching.[26] It is he who wills some good thing, who makes us wish for it, and makes us ask for it. P. T. Forsyth wrote that our life is fully immersed in God's: "We are rooted and grounded *in Him* . . . The reality in religion is not something to stand on, but something to live from. It does not simply hold, it helps and feeds . . . It is more than ground that will not give way; it is a source that will not fail or dry. We draw life from it, and it a medium in which we live."

God's gift of himself in his holiness enjoins our absolute self-committal, "a surrender to holiness and to communion with the holy. And even that self-surrender is created by Him."[27]

And yet at the same time, paradoxically, our knowledge of God is entirely our own work. Our fullest receiving is at once our fullest self-giving. This is the paradox of grace. Donald Baillie described this as the central paradox of Christian faith, lying at the very heart of Christian faith and vitally affecting every part of it. He writes:

> Its essence lies in the conviction which a Christian man possesses, that every good thing in him, every good thing he does, is somehow not wrought by himself but by God. This is a highly paradoxical conviction, for in ascribing all to God it does not abrogate human personality nor disclaim personal responsibility. Never is human action more truly and fully personal, never does the agent feel more personally free, than in those moments of

26. Julian, *Showings*, 157.

27. Forsyth, *Principle of Authority*, 41, 47.

which he can say as a Christian that whatever good was in them was not his but God's.[28]

As our own act in response to God, knowing God is an act of entrusting ourselves in radical responsiveness towards whatever rightly summons our wholehearted response. It is our most lively personal act, in which we entrust ourselves and the world we inhabit—that is, the provisional context we know as our world—in openness towards the radically new, in order that we may enter into and participate in that deeper context that is the gift of God's kingdom. This is indeed our defining act as persons. It is the act to which and in which we give ourselves without reserve as persons.

The radical responsibility for such knowledge is expressed by Gerhard Ebeling when he writes, "the man who makes a statement about God thereby—in spite of his dependence on tradition, in spite of the support he has in the fellowship of the faithful—stands entirely on his own feet as one who ventures to defend the cause of God, to stand surely with his own reality for the reality of God, with his own existence for the existence of God."[29]

The knowledge in which God gives himself to us and we give ourselves to him is true to the words of Ruysbroek: "All that He has, all that He is, He gives; all that we have, all that we are, He takes."

To summarize: the paradox of grace is integral to the act of knowing God. This act is about more than possessing knowledge of the kind that can be used by people to "inflate" themselves. It is about knowing God through Jesus Christ who is the *way*, the *truth*, and the *life*. To be sure, it is about knowing the *truth*, about getting God "right." But it is just as much about following the *way* of God, turned in the direction of God who beckons us to search ever more deeply into his ways. And it is, most deeply of all, about discovering new *life* from God as, in lively enquiry, we entrust our lives to him.

The meaning of the terms "way," "truth," and "life" needs careful enlargement here, of course. The meaning of each has quite atrophied today and grown away from the others. George MacDonald describes life from God as our participation in the self-willed life of God himself:

28. Donald Baillie, *God Was in Christ,* 114.

29. Ebeling, *Word and Faith,* 346. Ebeling acknowledges that this "sounds paradoxical, indeed downright impious, since the relation would surely really have to be expressed the other way round."

"God is life, and the will-source of life. In the outflowing of that life, I know him."[30] When we are "weary of life," it is not life but death that we are weary of; and we are called to "wake up" and to "keep awake" by God who is our life and our light.[31] We shall explore the meaning of "life" in chapter 7.

Now to our usual way of thinking it is odd to speak of *knowing* as an *act*. We routinely speak, on the other hand, of asking questions, pursuing clues, and searching, as acts. But we think of knowledge as a kind of residue of such activity. To be sure, we may actively *apply* our knowledge in one way or another, but such action appears distinct from the knowledge we bring to bear in it. In the case of knowledge of God, however, *knowing is essentially, irreducibly an act*. Indeed it is action without reserve: it is our most lively personal act of self-giving in unending enquiry and discovery, searching and finding.

Let us explore further the nature of this act. And here we come to the heart of what I propose in this book, regarding what it means to know God. First, it is an act in which we give ourselves in *unqualified attentiveness* and with *wholehearted intention*. This involves more than the kind of knowing in which we perceive things in the world, or act in the world, unreflectively out of habitual knowledge. To know God is to be *radically attentive*. It involves more than turning our full attention upon one thing among others; it involves giving ourselves in the fullest personal way in attending without reserve to the world and to whatever God shows us as rightly commanding this attention. To know God is at the same time to *intend* something *wholeheartedly*. This involves more than pursuing passionately some prior intention towards one thing among others; it means investing ourselves with unqualified intent towards the world, and to what God shows us as inviting such wholehearted intention. Such unqualified attentiveness and wholehearted intention, which characterize the act of knowing God, are primary; they are paradigmatic for understanding the act of knowing in general.[32]

---

30. MacDonald, "Life", 141.

31. "When most inclined to sleep, let us rouse ourselves to live. Of all things let us refuse the false refuge of a weary collapse, a hopeless yielding to things as they are. It is the life in us that is discontented; we need more of what is discontented, not more of the cause of its discontent." MacDonald, "Life," 146.

32. I use the terms "attention" and "intention" where it might be argued that more appropriate terms for what I mean would be "attentiveness" and "intentionality." This argument is not unreasonable, but I shall not address it here.

Our unqualified attention and wholehearted intention towards God are directed towards, and constitutes our participation in, the mystery of God. Gabriel Marcel rightly notes that contemplation—the practice of *attending wholly* to the mystery of God—is by no means a passive affair, but is rather our highest form of *activity*[33] (he observes that unbelief takes the form of inattention[34]). The goal of our *wholehearted intention* lying in the mystery of God is famously explored in the medieval *The Cloud of Unknowing*.

Secondly, and equally important, knowing God has a *dual character*: it is an active disposition at once *receptive* and *responsible*. This underlies the unqualified *liveliness* of the act of knowing God: these two elements interanimate each other in a most lively way. They are indeed mutually constitutive within the disposition of radical responsiveness towards God. On the one hand, through God's self-disclosing gift of himself, our ultimate context, we are drawn into personal unity with him, entrusting ourselves to him in wholehearted receptivity; on the other hand, rising to responsible personal judgment, our knowing God is a matter of critical discernment. This will prove later to be of crucial importance for understanding the origins of, and the way of liberation from, false modern ways of thinking about knowledge.

The lively, dual disposition of being at once radically receptive to, and of responsibly judging, whatever presents itself to us in the world may be described as a matter at once of being *receptive to the value of*, and of *responsibly evaluating the worth of*, what we encounter; as a matter at once of relying on or *entrusting ourselves to* the truth and trustworthiness of, and of *appraising* the truthfulness of, what we encounter; a matter of at once *trying to* put something to use, or to "own" it, and of *testing* something in the sense of putting it on trial to see whether it can be relied upon; and as a matter of *giving weight to*, and of *weighing*, whatever we encounter.[35]

This dual disposition sheds light upon what may be called the lively "from-to," directional, participatory character of the act of knowing God.

---

33. Marcel, *Being and Having,* 191.

34. Ibid., 212.

35. Here, then, are a number of connotations with my chosen designation of the dual poles of responsiveness as dispositions of *receptivity* and *responsibility*. There are many other such connotations. In this book, I shall also connote receptivity with *commitment* and *allegiance,* and responsibility with *discernment, critical appraisal,* and *judgment*.

Receptive to God as our ultimate context, our attention is directed *from* God, through our provisional context; in responsible judgment, our attention is directed *towards* God through that which we encounter in this context. To know God is to attend *both to and from* God while inhabiting our world—our provisional context—as a sign. A sign is the occasion of seeing through creation *to* God and *from* God who is our deepest context, in "mediated immediacy." At the same time we see creation for what it is when we see it as such a sign.[36]

We acknowledge that we know *from* God when we speak of God as our ultimate context. This has also been acknowledged traditionally in various ways. Some of them we have considered: seeing with God's eyes, living as those who have been created by, and belong to, God as his children, enjoying his hospitality. We *rely upon* the Bible, doctrines, and Christian tradition and appraise the world from these. But this reliance is inseparable from responsible judgment, in which we discern how these disclose God to us.

The *from-to* character of knowing God sheds defining light upon the character of all knowing. Valuable insight into the *from-to* character of all knowing is offered by the philosopher Michael Polanyi. He de-

36. This truth is absolutely key to knowledge as I describe it here in Part One of this book, and build upon it in Part 2. The *irreducible directionality* of knowing, seeking, and serving God discloses their *liveliness*. However, this disclosure tends to be blocked by the Cartesian assumption that directionality is *not* irreducible, and that we can always step back from "looking along" a line of view and look *at* what is looked *from* and *to* (see the section on Cartesian habits of imagination, below; see also Kettle, "Cartesian Habits"). A concrete model for the irreducible directionality of lively knowing is afforded by the skillful performance of sailing, skiing, and even walking, in which we invest ourselves in an orientation towards at once seeking and maintaining a form of dynamic equilibrium. However, this model does not yet capture the features of *wholehearted personal responsiveness to*, and *participation in communion with*, another person as in the paradigmatic case of knowing God.

The Cartesian tendency to reduce this irreducible directionality may be checked by insisting that it is not merely about orientation in one direction rather than another with some pre-established framework, but rather about an orientation towards directionality which seeks at once to *rise above disorientation* and also to *find true orientation* (and not rely upon false bearings).

The irreducible, lively directionality of knowing God has to do with the theological themes of *telos* or purpose, and eschatology. This is an essential theme within theology if a proper account is to be given not only of the *continuity* between knowing God and all knowing, but also the *distinctiveness* of the former, so as to avoid lapsing into a Christian ideology. It is an important virtue of Newbigin's theology that he keeps hold of this central theme better than some who have used his work. On Newbigin's insight here, see Schuster, *Christian Mission*.

scribes all knowing as constituted by a dual awareness: we attend *from* that which lies in our "subsidiary awareness" *to* that which lies in our "focal awareness." We shall return to this later.

The vitality of knowing varies according to the degree of personal, self-giving and indwelling involved in lively receptivity and responsible discernment. As Polanyi remarks, knowledge of persons or works of art involves deeper indwelling than knowledge of a star.

Knowing God and Knowing with God

Knowing God involves a number of other paradoxes, which we note briefly here.

We have acknowledged that knowing God entails knowing from God. Another way of approaching this is to say that our knowing God is inseparably a matter of our knowing *with* God, in communion with him.

This extends to both conceptual and practical knowledge—bringing us back to the theme of our being called by God's grace to be apprentices in his work, obeying his will not merely slavishly but learning to see with his own eyes as we work with him. To know God is to seek and do his will, while to obey God is to grow in knowledge of him. George MacDonald wrote: "Would you know God? Then do his will."

To know God is to participate in God's knowledge of himself, God's knowledge of the world as his creation, and God's knowledge of us.

Knowing God and Being Known

P. T. Forsyth writes, "In religious knowledge the object is God . . . and that object differs from every other in being for us far more than an object of knowledge. He is the absolute subject of it . . . We find him because he first finds us. That is to say, the *main thing, the unique thing, in religion is not a God whom we know but a God who knows us.* Religion turns not on knowing but on being known."[37]

This fact is not only about what it is we know when we know God; it belongs to the very meaning of such knowing. To know God is insepa- rably a matter of *knowing ourselves as known* by God—indeed known before and more deeply than we know ourselves. If we do not acknowl- edge God's knowledge of us, then we do not know God.

---

37. Forsyth, *Principle of Authority*, 167.

Knowing God, we have seen, always remains inseparable from seeking God and his will; the two interanimate each other. We may now add that our seeking God is always embedded in God's seeking ourselves; our questioning God, always embedded in his questioning of us in Christ.[38]

Knowing God: Faith, Hope, and Love

Saint Paul writes that earthly knowledge will pass away, but three things last forever: faith, hope, and love (1 Cor 13:13). Knowledge of God, however—unlike "earthly knowledge" as Paul means it—is inseparable from faith, hope, and love, as it is inseparable from seeking God. Julian of Norwich expressed the matter succinctly: "[the soul] can do no more than seek, suffer, and trust ... And illumination by finding is of the Spirit's special grace, when it is his will. Seeking with faith, hope, and love pleases our Lord, and finding pleases the soul and fills it full of joy."[39]

Regarding our *faith* or *trust* in God, it is as true that we know God as we entrust ourselves to him, as it is that our knowledge of him brings us to have faith in him. Faith or trust in God is not blind; rather it is in faith that we apprehend him. Jesus of Nazareth sought, both through his acts of healing and liberation and through the parables he told, to open people's eyes to the mystery of God's approach in sovereignty: he sought for God to give them this knowledge. The "faith" that he sought in people was precisely God's gift of responsiveness, to see in Jesus' words and actions the approach of God's kingdom. Such faith involves more than trusting for some specifiable outcome (as faith is often understood); it involves entrusting our very selves and our world—everything—to God. And it is for us a continuing, lively act—a "living sacrifice" of ourselves, in the words of Saint Paul. Moreover it is embedded inseparably in God's act of entrusting himself to us in Jesus Christ. To entrust ourselves to God is to know him as entrusting himself to us.

It is similar with our *hope in God*. Hoping in God, we come to know him; knowing God, we see in him hope for all humankind. Hope is not blind, wishful thinking on our part; rather, it is in hope that we apprehend him. Moreover our hope is embedded in God's unreserved hope in us, forever forgiving, forbearing as he gives himself to us in a costly way.

---

38. On Jesus Christ as the one who truly questions—questions God and ourselves—see Torrance, "Questioning in Jesus."

39. Julian, *Showings*, 195.

To hope in God is to know God's hope in us. As it has been said, "God created the world with finality; he created man in hope."

Similarly again with our *love of God*. To love is, in modern thinking, to "value." But love of God cannot be understood as a matter merely of subjective valuing. To know God is to find one's eyes opened to that which is of infinite value—an ultimate treasure, to recall Jesus' imagery. We aver that God is infinitely worthy, calling for unqualified worship by all humankind.[40] To love God is at once to know God and, knowing him, to love him, and to love God and, loving him, grow in knowledge of him. As it has been said, "love is not blind: love is the only thing that sees." We do not blindly ascribe value to God, or submit blindly to him, but do so in the act of apprehending him for who he is. And this is embedded in God's love for us. To love God is to know ourselves loved by God. Paul writes, "Knowledge inflates a man, whereas love builds him up. If anyone fancies that he has some kind of knowledge, he does not yet know in the true sense of knowing. But if anyone loves God, he is known by God." (1 Cor 8:1b–3).

Knowing God in His Presence and Absence

We have reflected above upon what it means to know God who approaches us in sovereignty, acknowledging some of the paradoxes into which such reflection draws us. Now such reflection may be seen as reflection upon what it is to know God in his presence to us. But this raises the question of the absence of God. What does it mean to encounter the absence of God? This question penetrates Christian faith to its very core in Jesus' cry of dereliction on the cross.

With respect to our knowing in general, to be met with the absence of something is precisely not to encounter it first-hand: absence of the known issues in the occasion of absence of knowing. But with respect to knowing the mystery of God, the picture is more paradoxical. To know God is to know him in both his presence and his absence, in the following way.

To know God, we have averred, is a matter of radical responsiveness in which we give ourselves fully in unqualified attention and wholeheart-

---

40. Although talk of "values" has come to the fore only in recent decades, early in the twentieth century P. T. Forsyth was already concerned to distinguish between the idea of a God who is "of value to us" and the Christian idea of a God who rightly deserves our worship. See *The Principle of Authority*, chapter 20.

ed intention, and in a dual disposition of receptivity and responsibility, valuing and evaluating, appreciating and appraising. To know God in his *presence* is to be upheld by the grace of God in this disposition as God reveals himself and his will through signs in creation, intimating the in-breaking kingdom. We are given a foretaste and pledge of what is to come. Such knowledge is lively and this liveliness shows itself in the interaction of question and answer, searching and finding, as we move forward into ever-deeper orientation and integration of the world as we know it in the ultimate context and hospitality of God.

To know God is also, however, to know him in his absence. Here we are upheld by the grace of God in exactly the same disposition, a similar lively act of personal self-giving, while finding that no such movement arises leading us into the deeper orientation and integration of our world. Rather, our questions are problematic and unresolved; the act of searching is elusive. Our personal self-giving immerses us in an indeterminate state, in which we cry out to God and for his presence, neither of which we can, in this moment, imagine. Ours is a stance of waiting, but of the most lively kind—waiting in radical trust for a resolution beyond our reach, but waiting still, without losing hope. We thus refuse on the one hand to turn away from God and look for our own answers, and on the other hand to resign ourselves to the view that there *is* no answer. These evasions are prompted by the felt demands of knowing God, felt most acutely in his acute absence. We shall consider them now.

3. PRIDE AND DESPAIR: SINFUL EVASION OF GOD

In our fallen humanity we find God's call to such radical responsiveness to be demanding, and may show ourselves blind and evasive. Such evasion takes two basic forms. We either dismiss the demands of responsiveness upon us, imagining to step back from them in denial and rebellion, or we become despairing, captured, and overwhelmed by the demands of responsiveness while being secretly complicit with our overwhelming. In each case we sustain an evasive stance in which—although we conceal this and our evasion from ourselves—we construct an illusory world. In a dismissive stance we construct a world in which we are self-conceived autonomous masters, while in a despairing stance we construct a world in which we act as haunted, paralyzed victims of our fate either in needy passivity or inconsolable rage. Such evasion may take culturally shared forms.

Commentary

Our knowledge of God is, we have averred, a matter of personal encounter initiated by God; it concerns that which holds our deepest attention, that which we seek and know for ourselves as a matter of God's self-disclosure to us. Thus, as P. T. Forsyth remarked, our knowledge of God is self-evident in the strict sense of the word.

However, despite God's self-disclosure, God is not necessarily known for who he is in reverent joy. His approach does not necessarily evoke that radical responsiveness in which people entrust themselves personally to him in an unqualified way. The question why this should be so forever defies answer. It is a defiant, mocking, unresolved question that presents itself throughout the Bible. Jesus himself finds the question pressing upon him. He is himself surprised by those who show faith, and by those who do not (see for example Mark 6:6; Mark 9:19; Luke 7:9) For them, faith—as the recognition of God's approach in himself—is a gift from God himself lying beyond Jesus' own control. When it becomes apparent to his disciples that Jesus' teaching and miracles are not bringing universal acclaim of God's self-disclosure, the old puzzle presents itself. One of Jesus' disciples asks, "How has it come about (or, what can have happened) that you mean to disclose yourself to us and not to the world?" (John 14:22). Jesus does not offer an answer but points to those who love him and heed his words and those who do not; he points simply to the heart of the issue. Jesus himself cries out with the central question on occasion: why cannot people recognize the truth of God at work in himself? (as in Luke 12.54–57). He weeps over Jerusalem, that the way of peace he brings is "hidden from her sight" (Luke 19:41–42). People have eyes; how vital that they see with them!

The fortunes and misfortunes that beset God's self-disclosure and that defy comprehension suggest compellingly that God's purposes are doomed to failure. However, accordingly to both the prophets and Jesus himself, this—and this may be equally beyond our comprehension too—is not so. In the first of Jesus' parables recounted by Saint Mark—the parable of the sower—Jesus presents the varied misfortunes that beset God's self-disclosure, only to conclude the story with a rich harvest. Now according to Jesus, failure to understand this parable portends failure to understand any of his parables at all (Mark 4:13). It not only exemplifies Jesus' teaching; it testifies to it, a parable shedding light on parables. Failure to understand this parable is a fulfillment of the words of the prophet Isaiah: "they may look and look, but see nothing; they may listen and listen, but understand nothing; otherwise they might turn to God and be forgiven" (Mark 4:12). The same passage from Isaiah is invoked by Saint John the Evangelist at the end of his account of Jesus' public ministry, before turning to the final Passover. Immediately before, Jesus has called his disciples to trust in the light; immediately following, Jesus declares that it is he himself who brings light to the world (John 12:34–46). The endless failure of God's self-disclosure, prophesied by Isaiah, will somehow be embraced by God within his purposes.

The failure of God's self-disclosure is depicted often in the Old and New Testaments—as it is in Isaiah—as a matter of blindness, deafness, or closed minds (Isa 6:10, 42:16–19; Ezek 12:2; Mark 4:12; John 12:40; Rom 11:8, 9). It is also depicted as a matter of human rebellion, stubbornness, hardness of heart, and ignorance. New Testament authors add further images of sinners as those who hide in the dark (John 3:19–21) and those who "sleep" (1 Thess 5:5–7).

The failure of God's self-disclosure is a different matter, in principle, from the hypothetical situation where a person has not encountered God. It is also a different matter from the unknowability of the mystery of God, which belongs to the very self-revelation of God in radical responsiveness—awaking a knowledge of that which is beyond knowing (see Eph 3:18–19). The last of these concerns that which is always more than God has given us or than we can receive, whereas the first concerns the fact that we fail to receive what God gives us. Let us acknowledge in passing here that when in practice we are confronted with a person's lack of understanding of God, it may be hard for us to tell in a given situation whether this reflects lack of encounter with God or an evasive response to such encounter.

Now in whatever terms it is pictured, the failure of God's self-disclosure reflects human sin. Sin is more truly defined by reference to this than as any matter of disobeying rules of conduct laid down by God. Fundamentally sin concerns a response to God for who he is—an evasive response. It represents an evasion of the demands of God made in radical responsiveness, which are experienced as great. This is not to say that knowing God is in itself a demanding affair; in truth the yoke of life in Christ is a light and easy burden. However, because humanity is blinded by sin, we can find it demanding.

Let us acknowledge in passing that these demands arise as much with respect to questioning or seeking God as with respect to knowing God. They are the demands made upon us by unqualified attention and wholehearted intention towards God in faith, hope, and love. They are the trial or testing of our faith (*peirasmos*), which is the fundamental meaning of the temptation to sin. Indeed the demanding character of faith defines our very fallen condition: to be fallen is to lack a pure and true will, responsive to our maker.

Sinful evasion forms into many different kinds of behavior. In the Bible, two sides of sin may be discerned. One is the way of chosen rebellion against God—the enactment of a false autonomy in which the demands upon us of the reality of God are dismissed. This side of sin is about a disposition of false "freedom from God." The other side of sin is rather about an experienced *loss* of freedom—it is about being overcome and held in bondage to idols and ultimately to Satan. Although it may not be immediately apparent, both of these sides to sin are a matter of evasion.

The medieval English anchorite Julian of Norwich identifies and distinguishes between these two sides of sin when she points out "two secrets sins, extremely busy in tempting us." "One is impatience, because we bear our labour and pain heavily. The other is despair, coming from doubtful fear ... it is these two which most belabour and assail us."[41] These two prevalent sins are each in their own way, for Julian, evasions of the demands made by hope in God.

In the twentieth century, Joseph Pieper described the forms taken by hopelessness in terms that identify and distinguish between these two faces of sinful evasion: "hopelessness can take two forms: it can be presumption, *praesumptio*, and it can be despair, desperation. Both are forms of the sin against hope. Presumption is a premature, self-willed anticipation of the fulfillment of what we hope for from God. Despair is the premature, arbitrary anticipation of the non-fulfillment of what we hope for in God ... Both rebel against the patience in which hope trusts in the God of the promise."[42]

Pieper recognizes the evasive character of each. In the first case the disposition of "premature anticipation" is evasive towards the demands

41. Julian, *Showings*, 167–68.

42. Pieper, *Über die Hoffnung*, 51. As quoted in English translation in Moltmann, *Theology of Hope*, 23.

of maintaining hope that arise when there appear no immediate signs of its fulfillment. It is a *dismissal* of the requirement to live within creaturely limits, to live with the tragic, to live with human perversity, while remaining hopeful. Refusing this demand, we presume to exalt as the fulfillment of our hope that which we ourselves can define and pursue, investing it with cosmic meaning. In the second case, Pieper identifies the disposition of despair also as involving rebellion. He does so even though the despairing person normally registers their experience as one of being *overwhelmed by* the world rather than *acting upon* it at all. In despair we actively collude with that which overwhelms us. We take the present non-fulfillment of our hope in God and invest this with cosmic meaning as the last word upon such hope.

Now in Christian tradition more attention has been paid in general to the former side of sin (I shall call this a *dismissive* stance) than to the latter (I shall call this a *despairing* stance). Sin has been more recognized in the proud oppressor than in the despairing oppressed, and more recognized in those who treat victims dismissively than in those who are overwhelmed by their victimhood. The latter side of sin has been recently noted by Alister McFadyen when he suggests that we need to take seriously the sinfulness of inner personal defeat. He proposes that such "self-loss" is a sin—the deadly sin of sloth.[43] Karl Barth had earlier noted that "sin has not merely the heroic form of pride but also, in complete antithesis yet profound correspondence, the quite unheroic and trivial form of sloth. In other words, it has the form not only of evil action, but of evil inaction."[44] To consider sin only in the form of pride, he says, is to fail to "recognize the real man whose whole heart, according to Luther's rendering of Jeremiah 17:9, is not merely desperate but also despairing."[45] Further light is found as we trace the origins in meaning of the "seven deadly sins" (sloth being one of these) in the teachings of the desert fathers, for whom they represented *"logismo"*—trains of thought that shape how the world is seen and that have an inner momentum of their own towards deepening, enslaving perversity.

43. McFadyen, *Bound to Sin*, 139ff.

44. Barth, *Dogmatics Vol. IV*, 403.

45. Ibid., 404. Whereas Barth emphasizes the banal character of sloth, I shall emphasize a deeper captivity within this, in which we are overwhelmed and spellbound by that which mocks us.

The *"logismoi"* point to a tacit association between sin and a certain communicated logic. This association will come further into light as we now explore further the two sides of sin. I want to examine these in the light of our account of God as the One who approaches in sovereignty as our ultimate context. In this light, we are helped to understand three vital features of both a dismissive and a despairing disposition. Firstly, they each represent a way of seeing God, ourselves, and the whole world. Secondly, they each conceal a fundamental *evasion* of God, ourselves, and the world. Thirdly, they each *construct* their own distinctive "context": that which they register in evasion is an illusory construction of "God," "ourselves," and "the world."

Let us now consider each side of sin in turn.

Evasion as a Dismissive Stance

The biblical story of proud rebellion begins with Adam and Eve disregarding God's injunction not to eat the fruit of the tree in the middle of the garden in which they have been placed. Rebelliousness among God's chosen people confronts Moses, and then the prophets, and comes to final expression in the rejection of Jesus as the Messiah. The whole sorry story is recalled by Stephen when confronted by his accusers; a provocative act that precipitates the story into a new phase with the first Christian martyrdom.

It may not be immediately apparent that proud rebellion against God is an act of evasion. Rather it is commonly thought of as behavior of the sort that is reasonable and natural, but is proud in its disregard for the requirements of God. This is to deny that the question of response to God arises for us always as our most fundamental question. In truth, however, rebellion is fundamentally in the face of, and a denial of, the demands of engagement with God. In the act of rebellion we willfully blind ourselves to this; we imagine to act in freedom. But in truth we act in evasion; indeed it is precisely the demands of freedom that we evade—the demands of responding freely before God. We evade these demands by setting them aside, dismissing their reality and the response to which they call us. Such a stance may reasonably be denoted by the term "dismissive."

A dismissive stance (in this sense) corresponds to what Pieper calls "presumption"—a premature, self-willed anticipation of the fulfillment of what we hope for from God. It is a denial of the demands presented

by the present non-fulfillment of these hopes, in favor of a false, premature resolution of these hopes in our own terms—in terms of a world
of things available to us to be mastered and used. In so doing, we place
(whether openly or secretly) ourselves and the world as we know these at
the centre of our own hope, allowing this now to define hope itself for us.
We take that which is properly a sign pointing to God and to the fulfillment of hope in him, and we invest this sign itself with cosmic meaning
as the ultimate fulfillment of our hope.

Now this is a dismissal not only of the demands of God, but of the
world and ourselves for what they really are. This is because we no longer
see the world and ourselves by reference to God who is our ultimate
hope, but by reference to that presumptuous hope that we have endowed
with ultimate meaning in the place of God.

We may adopt a dismissive stance by paying attention explicitly to
something, but doing so without due regard. In the key instance, we may
explicitly dismiss God, rejecting the reality of God either by rejecting a
true understanding of God or by rejecting belief in his very existence.
We may similarly explicitly dismiss other people, or God's creation, or
indeed ourselves, in ways that are ultimately dismissive towards God.
We may explicitly deny the demands of responsiveness to what is good
and true and reflects God—especially to persons themselves made fundamentally to be responsive towards God. Such dismissal has a long
history associated with the devaluation of victims of disease, deformity,
and handicap, and of those beyond one's tribe. It is also associated with
the exploitation of the material world in a manner dismissive of the
demands of stewardship of creation under God. This may involve taking and using natural resources irresponsibly, or claiming and enacting
absolute rights of disposal over private property.

We may also adopt a dismissive stance by simply *disregarding*
something—by ignoring, or refusing to pay any attention whatsoever to,
that which rightly demands our attention. Again, a dismissive stance towards something—whether in the form of explicit dismissal or of simple
disregard—may be based explicitly upon, or rooted tacitly in, that which
is held to be importantly right or of value. It may even claim legitimization from God: the religious offense taken at Jesus by many scribes and
Pharisees—especially their charge of blasphemy—is the ultimate example of this. Insofar as the legitimization is believed in—and not merely
a matter of rhetorical strategy to defend an action—it may be described

as idolatry. A special case of this is presented by modern ideologies that commend a program of rationalization to be implemented as a dispassionate response to the realities of the world, when in truth they define the purpose or end of such rationalization as absolute and to be exalted without qualification—as the substance of ultimate hope.

When a dismissive stance involves explicit attention to something (rather than simple disregard for it) this attention may take various forms. It may take the form of detached observation and perhaps management or employment of something (or someone) as a means to one's own ends. Here attention is paid of the kind we pay towards an *object*. This is the kind of attention that Martin Buber called "I-It," in contrast to "I-Thou." The demands of critical receptivity are denied, in a stance of active dissociation: we push away the claims of personal regard. We simply manipulate things for our own purposes. Another form taken by dismissal is aggression. Here attention is paid of the kind that sees only an object with which are irreducibly associated feelings that override a response of lively, critical receptivity. This may arise for example when a person or group makes special demands upon our responsiveness by virtue of the challenge they present to us as rivals, or to our norms, or to our vested interests, or to our sense of security. In such cases we may demonize or scapegoat them. A vicious circle is often created when, confronted with a victim, we reject the demands of identifying with them as too frightening and rationalize this by minimizing their plight or justifying it, thus revictimizing them; another is created when, confronted with a victim, we see ourselves implicated in their victimhood and reject this by the same means, again revictimizing them.

I have said that a dismissive stance represents an evasion both of God and of everything else created—especially the human person (including ourselves). How may we understand this as an evasion of God who approaches as our ultimate context? It may be understood as a matter of our clinging to our familiar, established, habitual contexts, and refusing the demands of allowing these to be opened up to transformation in a this deeper context. Instead of allowing these to be judged and renewed in the course of our radical responsiveness to a new emergent deeper context, we see the new by reference to them, entrenching ourselves in the position defined by our commitment to them as the source of bearings. However, this destroys our engagement with reality in unqualified attention and wholehearted intention. Instead we register a false abstraction of the new (abstracted from its own context and framed by reference to our established context), and we inhabit a now fictional context that has become the construct of our false commitment and a false integration of the world.

Through this we replace God, creation, and ourselves with a constructed world at our own disposal—at the disposal, that is, of a self that is itself the fictional construct of our evasion. The world becomes *defined* by what has been called instrumental reason—by its potential usefulness to us; it makes no claims upon us personally. It is important to understand this well. It is not the case that we first see the world as it is, as an objective reality available to be used, and then display instrumental reason by identifying how we may put it to use and doing so. Rather, our dismissive stance shapes our apprehension of the world in the first place. Evasion is already, irreducibly built into this. In the course of this we also construct a fictional self: we construct ourselves as those whose identity is as masters of creation, and who are subject to no claims, called to no deference. In all of this we dismiss the demands of radical responsiveness to reality; we refuse the demands of honesty, deceiving ourselves about God, the world, ourselves, and our own evasion and self-deception.

Given this account of a proud, dismissive, and fundamentally evasive stance, what will be involved in conversion? This will involve acknowledging claims upon us—not simply allowing certain things to make claims upon us in a world that remains intact for us, but rather offering up the world as we know it in order to discover and entrust ourselves to a new world with whatever claims it makes upon us. To acknowledge our evasion of claims upon us is already to be set on the path of conversion.

In summary, when we view a dismissive stance in the context of responsiveness to God, we may describe it as about commitment to a false resolution instead of openness to true resolution of the question of hope; commitment to a false integration instead of openness to true integration of the world; commitment to false orientation in place of openness to true orientation for living; and commitment to a false independence instead of openness to true independence in relationship to God and his creation.

Evasion as a Despairing Stance

Although sin is encountered often in the Bible as willful human rebellion against God, it is also often encountered—especially in the New
Testament—as a matter of human enslavement. In the Old Testament,
God is known as the one who leads his people into freedom—the God
who led them out of slavery in Egypt, who promises liberation to those
exiled in Babylon, and who will one day send a Messiah who will restore
the sovereignty of Israel under God. The Messianic hope was for more
than political freedom, however; it was for freedom from disease and
handicap and poverty and all other such personal bondage. The Messianic
hope was also for forgiveness—a hope integrally related to the hope for
freedom since political and personal oppression were commonly taken
to be a punishment for, and consequence of, sin. In the Gospels (notably
Saint Luke's Gospel) Jesus speaks of God as the author of freedom and
Satan as the oppressor (see Luke 4:18–19; 13:16; see also John 8:32–36).
In the course of this, and as part of that comprehensive reconfigura-
tion of meaning awakened by the sovereign approach of God in Christ,
"freedom" and "slavery" now find new and definitive meaning in relation
to God who approaches. These new meanings have an irreducible inner
dimension and reveal a purely "external" account of freedom and slavery
as naive. Already in the Old Testament there is much acknowledgement
of the importance of a person having a faithful heart or right spirit before God (most notably in the Psalms) and the prophets had declared
God's promise of new "heart" and a new "spirit" (Jeremiah 31:33; Ezekiel
36:26). Now, for New Testament authors (notably for Paul), freedom is
the gift of God's Spirit within his people, while sin is a matter of being
led by and ensnared by the "flesh" or unspiritual nature and ultimately
by Satan. Thus Paul can refer to sin as slavery "to passions and pleasures
of every kind" (Titus 3:3) and sees this in common forms of a dissolute
life that he recounts (e.g., Gal 5:19–21). He speaks of sin as a "snare":
people "fall into temptations and snares and into many harmful desires
which plunge people into ruin and destruction" (1 Tim 6:9). Ultimately
this bondage is to Satan, while for a person to know Christ is for them
to "come to their senses and escape from the devil's snare in which they
have been trapped and held at his will" (2 Tim 2:26). In chapters 6 and 7
of his Letter to the Christians of Rome, Paul speaks consistently of sin as
subservience, rather than as proud rebellion: he refers to sin as a "master,"
as "exacting obedience," as that which "held us bound," and as that which

"commands"; and he refers to people as "yielding" to sin, as "seduced by sin," to "sinful passions," and to being "slaves to sin." "With my unspiritual nature," he concludes, "I serve the law of sin."

It may not be apparent that to be overwhelmed and captured in spirit involves active evasion of God. Certainly when we experience being overwhelmed, we register the question of our response as one that simply does not arise for us in this experience itself; we register ourselves as having been overcome without opportunity to respond; the victim of a *fait accompli*. Something has overtaken us; has been done to us. We experience ourselves as entirely in the hands of forces that have their way with us. In truth, however, this experience involves our hidden collusion; it is an evasion of the demands of hope in face of its immediate non-fulfillment. It represents what Pieper calls "the premature, arbitrary anticipation of the non-fulfillment of what we hope for in God." We might say that, faced with what we find unfaceable, we are overcome by this and take the unfaceable into ourselves as an inner contradiction.

Here, then, is a second face of sin that has to do with a captivity of spirit. Like a dismissive stance, it takes many different forms. Importantly, although I characterize this as a despairing stance, it takes many forms in which despair is not obvious. Despair is obvious enough when people are captured by a tragic sense of life, which we shall explore in chapter 6. But it is not so obvious in, for example, the experience of being seduced (in a broad sense). Yet it is hidden in the promiscuous casting around which holds no hope of finding what it seeks, and in sentimental longing, and in compulsive gambling, and in other forms of escapism. Addictive behavior of any kind, which may be described as expressing bondage to mirages of hope, reflects as much a despairing stance as does oppression by specters. Each are in their own way expressions of the human spirit overwhelmed, defeated, and insatiable in its neediness. A key expression of this defeat is narcissism, which is far more a matter of self-despair than of self-love. Here, driven by despair of the world, we either construct and manipulate the world as an extension of our very selves, taking it into ourselves, or we project our "selves" beyond ourselves into a world forever beyond us (like the reflection of Narcissus' face that mocks him) that we pursue and consume in insatiable, needy dependence. We shall explore narcissism in chapter 5.

Adopting a despairing stance, we may on the one hand take the bad into ourselves as somehow "deserved," in a contradictory mix of resignation and resentment, giving rise to self-pity, demoralization, and low self-esteem. Alternatively, we may project the bad outwards. Driven by rage, we may hit out randomly at the world that we see as having betrayed us; or we may frame and focus implacably on a scapegoat. Or again, we may seek to compensate personally for feeling defeated and in the power of "someone" beyond ourselves, by seeking to overwhelm others in turn, and feeding upon their victim-perception of *us* as holding all power over *them*.

Underlying each form taken by a despairing stance is the dissolution of radical responsiveness to the real and its replacement by a different world: one in which we are captured and spellbound in a state at once restless and paralyzed. This may be a matter of anxiety and distraction in face of a faceless, indeterminate nothingness, or it may be a matter of pursuing self-displacing mirages and being pursued by self-displacing specters, each with mocking faces.

How does a despairing stance appear as sinful evasion in the light of our account of God who approaches as our ultimate context? Here, met with the demands of responding to our ultimate context, we are overcome by these demands. We yield up our familiar context of meaning that we inhabit, but not in that lively effort of integration in which meanings come to light or are revised as a new context in which to live. Rather than embracing the demands of achieving a new and deeper integration, we may take these demands into ourselves, *as unfaceable.* The paradox that these present to us becomes a self-contradiction *within us*. We experience the endless personal disorientation and pre-emptive dis-integration of unresolved loss. The world is lost to us and we to the world; we take loss into ourselves as the final, cosmic word upon us.

Through this we replace God, creation, and ourselves with a constructed world at our own disposal—at the disposal, that is, of a self that is itself the fictional construct of our evasion. The world becomes *defined by* our despairing stance towards it. Once again, it is important to understand this well. It is not the case that we first see the world as it is—as an objective reality before us—and react to it in despair. Rather, our despairing stance shapes our apprehension of the world in the first place. Evasion is already, irreducibly built into this. Moreover it is, in its own distinctive way, *active*; it is a despair*ing* stance; in despair we *actively engage* the world in a particular way. Despair is not an endpoint we have reached at which we have run out of hope; it is a turning from active hope to active despair. It is a way of attending to the world in which we are held fast by the summons to despair, a message we constantly imbibe, a message that disfigures and reconfigures our world—while secretly constructing and collaborating with this message. In the course of this we also construct a fictional self: we construct ourselves as those who have lost hope in God, the world, or ourselves, for whom the possibility of personal, responsible, hopeful action simply does not arise. In all of this we dismiss the demands of radical responsiveness to reality; we refuse the demands of honesty, deceiving ourselves about God, the world, ourselves, and our own evasion and self-deception.

Given this account of despairing evasion, what will be involved in conversion from this? This will be a matter of rising above the spell that binds us—not just breaking free of the spell of certain things in a world that remains intact for us, but breaking free into a new world in which we are endowed inalienably with freedom and responsibility.

Sin as captivity of spirit is, we have noted, a less prominent theme in Christian tradition than sin as proud rebellion. However, it is—in a hidden way—a central theme of modernist art and literature. Here is depicted the existential plight of humanity in thrall to meaninglessness, although with little acknowledgement of this as a matter of despairing evasion. Thus in *Being and Nothingness* Jean Paul Sartre's account of human existence as the "*pour-soi*"—as the "self" that is constituted precisely by its self-projection towards what it is not—resonates closely with the way a despairing stance constructs a self-displacing world of specters and mirages, and itself as paralyzed in its movement relative to these. His account of existential "lack" has affinities with the irresolvable neediness we have noted is a feature of narcissism. Modernist playwrights have explored the dissolution of meaning and story in a variety of ways. In *Six Characters in Search of an Author*—which has been hailed as the first modernist play—Luigi Pirandello (1921) portrays a stand-off between, on the one hand, the play as unfolding story, managed by its director, and, on the other hand, a set of characters who rehearse forever their own distinctive, defining moment in a way that resists incorporation into any coherent wider story, so as to raise the question "which is reality: the coherent story, or the timeless, 'cosmic' existential encounter?"

To summarize: seen in relation to a stance of radical responsiveness before God, a despairing stance is about being captured, rather than liberated, in spirit. It is about being captured and bound by the experience of *non-resolution or dissolution*, in which we are defeated by the demands of taking responsibility to *seek resolution*; being captured by the experience of *disintegration*, in which we are defeated by the demands of taking responsibility to *seek integration*; of being captured by *disorientation*, in which we are defeated by the demands of taking responsibility for *seeking orientation*; and of being captured by a spirit of false *dependence*, in which we are defeated by the demands of taking responsibility independently for our relationship to God and other people. Thus, when comparing the two faces of sinful evasion, we may describe a dismissive stance and a despairing stance as a matter respectively of false resolution and non-resolution, false integration and disintegration, false orientation and disorientation, false independence and false dependence.

Loss of Reality

Let me conclude by emphasizing two things. First, it is not possible to talk faithfully of the real—and of what is involved in engaging the real—without acknowledging what our experience of "reality" is like in general when knowing God, on the one hand, and when evading him, on the other. Second, to know God is to address the real in an unqualified way, while to evade God is to turn from addressing the real in favor of entertaining the illusions of pride and the phantoms of despair.

In both these matters, we are called to shun any idea that the real is defined by what we can know theoretically by reference to a familiar conceptual framework, and that what Christians call knowing and evading God is a subjective interpretation of such an objective world. Rather, the "objective" world is known for what it is when it is known as sign—as pointing to God—while our evasion of this when it presses upon us involves our distorting the world either into material at our disposal (in a dismissive stance) or into a place of anxiety, fear, and seduction. The "objective" world of creation is known by reference to God and the promise of new creation—it is a matter at once of presence and promise—whereas our evasion of this distorts the world into mere presence as fact (bereft of purpose and therefore available for our own purposes) or into mere absence as endlessly deferred encounter with phantoms.

To know God is endlessly to seek, love, and celebrate what is real. It includes the requirement to take responsibility for, and not betray, whatever we know to be real; more than this, it requires us responsibly to seek what is real in the first place. Conversely, it includes the requirement to be receptive and open to new understanding that corrects our grasp of reality; while this extends to receptivity to new understanding that deepens and confirms our existing grasp of reality.

Evasion of God, on the other hand, involves a loss of engagement with and exploration of the real. When we adopt a *dismissive* stance, we reduce what we see to a collection of things that are in principle at our disposal; the only questions raised for us by their reality are instrumental ones of the kind such as, "How do I wish to use this? Of what value is this to me? Can I achieve power of control over this?" Here we stand ultimately alone and alienated in our game of mastery. We acknowledge nothing that faces us as a living presence making claims upon us. We are above the law—any law. The result is an erosion of our encounter with reality altogether. G. K. Chesterton warns an amoral colleague of this. Pointing to a flame, he says: "That flame flowered out of virtues, and it will fade with virtues. Seduce a woman, and that spark will be less bright. Shed blood, and that spark will be less red. Be really bad, and they will be to you like the spots on a wallpaper."[46]

When we adopt a *despairing* stance, we once again turn away from engagement with reality. Here, rather than mastering "reality" (as in a dismissive stance), we are mastered by it. We are spellbound by self-displacing phantoms—mirages and specters—which raise for us no question of response but only act upon us immediately, "performatively" or "preemptively" by way of *fiat*, enacting our endless submission.

Evasion is a temptation to us especially where the demands of God are greatest—faced with tragedy, powerlessness, and human injustice. The temptation is strong either to push away these demands, in a dismissive stance, or to be overcome by them in a despairing stance.

Our account of responsiveness to God and of sinful evasion has begun to open up the deeply personal dimensions of what may seem the relatively abstract matter of the nature of knowledge. These dimensions now come fully alive as we explore the definitive meaning of these manifest in the crucifixion and resurrection of Jesus.

46. Chesterton, *Tremendous Trifles*, 230.

4. ULTIMATE EVASION, ULTIMATE EMBRACE: THE MYSTERY OF REDEMPTION IN JESUS CHRIST

The crucifixion and resurrection of Jesus Christ represent the ultimate encounter between God and the power of human evasion. Faced with the prospect of his killing, Jesus meets the ultimate temptation to dismiss or be overwhelmed by the demands of responsiveness to God, but he remains faithful in entrusting himself to God. To know Jesus in his death and resurrection is to be drawn into the unfathomable mystery of encounter between God and our own sinful evasion.

Commentary

At his baptism by John, Jesus of Nazareth found himself anointed by the Spirit of God to be God's Son, the expected Messiah. Jesus was then driven by the same Spirit out into the wilderness to be responsive to God regarding what this might mean. In the public ministry that followed, Jesus fulfilled prophecies of a coming Messiah who would liberate victims: "then the eyes of the blind will be opened, and ears of the deaf unstopped. Then the lame will leap like deer, and the dumb shout aloud" (Isa 35:5–6). He restored hope to many by extending the hospitality of God to those excluded from participation in social life, and to those whose sins he declared to be forgiven by God. Such acts of liberation pointed to a final liberation from both the material agents of victimhood and the power of victimhood to intimidate people personally into despair and defeat.

Jesus also summoned people to repentance, challenging them to give up personal attachments of any kind that had in effect won their ultimate allegiance in place of God. Where people lived a life turned away from God and dismissive of his will, Jesus called them to turn to God and lose their life in order to gain eternal life.

Both by liberating victims and by summoning people to repentance, Jesus' words and actions were signs at once pointing to and embodying the approach of God in sovereignty. The kingdom of God was at hand.

Jesus' words and actions did not however match popular anticipations of the Messiah. The Messiah was expected to be a leader who would overthrow Roman occupation and restore sovereignty to her victim nation, Israel. The victory of God would be seen in the political liberation of Israel. But this was too simple an equation. After all, time and again those who spoke prophetically with the voice of God had been persecuted in Israel herself. What would happen when the Messiah came? There was a victory to be won by God in Israel herself, as well as beyond.

The sovereignty of God that Jesus proclaimed would indeed bring the final vindication of victims. However, he taught that this was a sovereignty growing secretly in the midst of the conditions of the world, which conditions included the persistence of victimhood. In the Beatitudes Jesus affirmed the promise of the kingdom to people faithful under various conditions of victimhood. The spiritual power of victimhood—its power to overwhelm, in despairing evasion—was even now overcome.

In a radical development, the Messiah himself would now appear *within* the course of human history in which the coming kingdom grows secretly. Doing so, he would take leading place among those who, as victims, look to God for final liberation and vindication. This was the vocation that unfolded for Jesus, and that he came to embrace.

A catastrophe of cosmic proportions was now imminent. The expectation had been, of course, that a Messiah would come amidst great welcome to fulfill God's purposes on earth. The rejection and barbaric execution of the Messiah represented the worst scenario imaginable. The crucifixion of any man was seen as a horrific affair, a specter held by Romans before robbers, insurgents, and disobedient slaves. The prospect of the crucifixion of *the Messiah,* of all people, could only be utterly devastating to the human spirit. This was the prospect that confronted Jesus, and that he shared with his disciples. We can hardly overestimate the force of Peter's response: "Heaven forbid, Lord!"

For Jesus himself, the prospect of his execution compellingly tempted him to despair both of *God* and of *humankind*. It urged him to despair utterly of *God*, because if God now allowed his own Messiah to be killed, this would mean that rather than bringing his purposes to final fulfillment God had betrayed and abandoned them in a final way. Jesus has committed himself utterly to the fulfillment of these purposes; but what hope in God could there remain in these circumstances? Accordingly Jesus' death presented itself to him as obscenely futile—as a final, triumphant mockery of the goodness and faithfulness of God. It confronted Jesus with the great final trial or temptation to lose faith and despair utterly of God.

The prospect of his execution also gave Jesus every reason to despair utterly of *humankind*. Jesus' hope in God involved an implicit hope that God's purposes would be fulfilled among his people. They would be given a new covenant, respond faithfully to God, and participate in this fulfillment. Jesus committed himself wholly to awakening such as response among God's people, his hope hinging upon it. Facing his execution, however, such hope for God's people appeared futile: religious leaders were planning the most outrageous denial of God's good purposes; one of his own disciples would betray him; even Peter who had declared him Messiah would deny knowing him. There had been acts of rebellion, blindness, and betrayal among God's people in the past, of course; but there had also been many stories of repentance and renewed faithfulness. This time it was different. If the Messiah himself was rejected by God's people, what hope could now be placed in them to be faithful? What possible hope could remain for them?

For Jesus, therefore, the prospect of his crucifixion was a trial of ultimate proportions. It had monstrous power spiritually to compel Jesus to betray God—evading the unfaceable demands of faith either by turning away, or being overwhelmed by it.

Jesus however, met this unqualified trial open in an unqualified way to God. He allowed the unthinkable possibility that even this could be a vocation from God—that against seemingly impossible odds, God's good purposes would yet have the last word. In so doing he shunned evasion in a final way. On the one hand, he shunned the temptation of dismissal: in the Garden of Gethsemane he embraced fully the grief of his abandonment by God and by humankind, which intimated the defeat of God's purposes. On the other hand, he shunned the inner, personal defeat of faith: he trusted God that his death would yet prove somehow a baptism (Luke 12:50). And in such extremity he continued impossibly to address God with hope, and in so doing address humankind.

Through this, God addressed not only Jesus; through Jesus he addresses us, and we are raised to participate in Jesus' response to God. For consider: if the prospect of the crucifixion of the Messiah presented *Jesus* with compelling grounds for despair, its execution forever urges the same upon *humankind*. In Jesus' life we see all goodness and justice, all blessing and promise, coming to fulfillment among us. In his crucifixion we see human beings descend to their worst act, and we "own" our complicity in this. We have opposed and utterly betrayed God and ourselves. We have renounced the hope and meaning upon which human life depends. Recognition of this now draws us, with Christ, into trial beyond measure. What conceivable hope remains for us, whose only hope lies in the God whom we have utterly rejected and whose purposes we have finally defeated? The temptation is extreme, either to turn away or be overwhelmed.

Jesus Christ, however, now wins our attention, drawing us to himself. We become attentive to the miracle that, having accepted this as his vocation, Jesus refuses either to dismiss or to be overwhelmed by what we have done to him. He neither dismisses what we have done, denying the message it carries of the ultimate hopelessness of God's purposes, nor is he overwhelmed by what we have done, abandoning hope in us and in God. Rather, in dignity and freedom he addresses God and us: "Father, forgive them, they do not know what they are doing." He addresses us as our outrageous victim, calling us, like himself, neither to dismiss what we have done nor be overwhelmed by it.

Thus, on the one hand, Jesus confronts our temptation to *dismiss* what we have done. Facing us as our victim, he refuses himself to dismiss what we have done; but he forgives us, and in so doing he empowers us in turn to acknowledge what we have done and embrace his forgiveness. On the other hand, Jesus confronts our temptation to *despair*. Jesus presents us with grounds beyond measure for despair and rage; but he himself engages this temptation in a new way. The specter that paralyzes us is something *shown to us personally* by Jesus—Jesus who enters fully and freely into the depths of sorrow and lament, embracing his victimhood without being overcome by despair or rage, and who now invites us to do the same. As Jesus has shares in the immeasurable sorrow of his Father over his faithless servants, he becomes for us a channel of the same graceful forbearance. And he empowers us with the same grace in turn: paradoxically as we are drawn into his own victimhood we find ourselves *liberated* fully and freely to embrace the grief of injustice and tragedy, and *dignified* with the power to confer the gift of forgiveness, like him, without reserve.

In so doing, Jesus raises us into his own dignity and freedom. Precisely because he embraces what we have done to him in forgiveness, we find ourselves free to do the same—on the one hand, free from the great temptation to dismiss the grim reality of what we have done, and, on the other hand, free to acknowledge it without being overwhelmed in spirit. And because the power of the temptation here to do one or the other is unqualified, the power of his forgiveness to set us free, as he is free, is unqualified. Thus liberated, we can acknowledge our guilt with the dignity endowed by his forgiveness.

Similarly where we in turn experience victimhood, Christ frees us from its paralyzing power. He dispels its ultimate claim upon us. He lifts us above its power either to force us into dismissal and denial, or to defeat us and plunge us into despair and rage. Again he bestows upon us his own dignified liberty. The Christian gospel thus urges that no victim who comes to see and understand Christ will find beyond reach the ultimate promise of vindication; no accomplice in tragic victimization will find beyond reach the ultimate hope of forgiveness. Victims will find, like Jesus, the dignity and grace to forgive; oppressors, the humility to confess and ask forgiveness from their victims as from Christ. Jesus has carried the dignity of hope—hope for God and for humankind—into the fathomless depths of victimhood. We shall explore this theme further in chapter 6, when we shall examine Christian hope, victimhood, and "tragic spirituality."

Redemption: The Mystery of Ultimate Encounter

Jesus' death and resurrection represent the ultimate encounter between God and human sin, in which humankind is liberated. In what terms may we further explicate the finality of this encounter?

Jesus, for his part, embraced his passion and death in these final terms, as his inescapable Messianic vocation—a baptism to undergo (Luke 12:52), a cup given him to drink by his Father (Luke 22:42). Correspondingly, Peter's protest at the prospect of his death is for Jesus the voice of Satan. His crucifixion would prove, in a shocking and dramatic way, the way in which God would fulfill his purposes, revealing Jesus for who he was. In the extremities of God's worth and its defeat, we meet the mystery of God's final encounter with all that works against him and his good purposes.

The final significance of Jesus' crucifixion is made manifest in his resurrection. The Risen Christ who addresses us is the same Jesus who has addressed us in his crucifixion; the meaning of them is revealed together. Their relation is one that takes us beyond familiar stories of tension and resolution, pain and relief, loss and recovery. In the story of Jesus' crucifixion and resurrection, paradoxically, defeat and victory are at once *more closely intertwined* and *more radical in their opposition*. We may understand this, and the finality of the event that these together constitute, by reflecting further on the victory they represent for Jesus and ourselves in turn over the ultimate temptation of evasion that presents itself to us here.

Firstly, let us recognize that the meaning of Jesus' resurrection is integrally bound up with that of his crucifixion. Indeed it is simply not possible to think of the former apart from the latter. It is mistaken to think of the resurrection as if it simply put right the wrong of the crucifixion, restoring things to normal, and leaving our world intact. This would be to imagine that we can look past the crucifixion to the resurrection as if we inhabited a wider context from which we could view each of them. Jesus could do no such thing, and neither can we. Jesus could not see his crucifixion as a limited wrong that he might see and accept as a means to an end in a wider context. Nor can we see his crucifixion in these terms, as if with hindsight in the light of the fact that everything worked out alright with the resurrection. There is simply no such wider context that would enable this. Rather, the crucifixion stands for the defeat of all ends and of any meaningful world. This is what is meant for Jesus, and it means no less for us. The meaning of resurrection lies beyond this, through Jesus' embrace of this, and through our imaginative participation in this, upheld by Christ. This brings a new world, no less.

Any idea of resurrection that circumvents this is fundamentally dismissive of the world-shattering reality of the crucifixion and resurrection of Christ. If we have such an idea of resurrection, then the reality of crucifixion will defeat our hope. It presents us with the ultimate violation and defeat of all that is meaningful, hopeful, and good in human life under God. Here we are shown an outrage deeper and darker than any victimhood we have yet faced: here is the ultimate specter of victimhood. We simply cannot fathom the depths of this; it is always more than we can acknowledge, refusing to be dismissed. There remains for us no trace of grounds for optimism about ourselves or the solidity of human life and meaning.

It is precisely this, with its unqualified power to overwhelm us with despair, which Jesus embraces in his passion, and he breaks its power. Thus the huge *meaningfulness* of Jesus' passion cannot be divorced from the spectral *meaninglessness* intimated by his victimhood: we ask ourselves, overcome with awe, what sacred love is this which gives rein to, and suffers, its own final denial? It is only when we hold firmly on to this paradox that we may speak of Jesus' passion as having always been part of God's eternal plan. Otherwise our faith in his resurrection is superficial and ultimately dismissive of his victimhood—and we remain vulnerable to overwhelming by the reality of it. Austin Farrar wrote, "the act of God always overthrows human expectation: the cross defeats our hope; the resurrection terrifies our despair";[47] and this always remains our situation as cross and resurrection encompass us.

If cross and resurrection are more closely bound than we can conceive, as we (supposedly) look on at them side by side, they are also more radically opposed. It is when we see Jesus' unqualified honor that we see his crucifixion as the catastrophe it is for humankind; when we now see Jesus embracing this extremity trusting in God, his honor moves us all the more. But this enhanced honor now enhances in turn the darkness of his victimization. And therefore his embrace of this darkness discloses yet further still his exalted honor. His exalted honor discloses that our condition is worse than that which we had understood as having been addressed by the resurrection of Jesus; and in turn the resurrection is now revealed as beyond what we have understood it to be. In this way the immeasurable power of Jesus' crucifixion as a message conveying the defeat of God's purposes and of faith in God, on the one hand, and the immeasurable power of his resurrection as a message conveying the victory of God's purposes and of faith in God, on the other hand, reinforce each other without limit. In the crucifixion of Jesus, that the command of Satan implicit in every trial—the command to yield to defeat and despair—urges itself with unfathomable power; and it is addressed by the resurrection of Jesus with its own unfathomable power. This is how Jesus is glorified (John 1:14; 17) with the glory of the Messiah (Luke 24:26) and revealed as God's Son (Rom 1:4).

Thus cross and resurrection endlessly open us, in their inseparability and radical opposition, to depths we have not fully fathomed—depths in openness to which, by the grace of God, our souls are enlarged as we are drawn further into the mystery of divine forgiveness.

5. KNOWING GOD: THE PARADIGM FOR ALL KNOWING

Among all our knowing, our knowing of persons shares to a unique degree in the disposition of unqualified receptivity and responsibility in which we know God. To know a person is to attend through them as a unique sign,

47. Farrar, *Glass of Vision*, 139.

*towards and from God; to know a person is to encounter the image of God
in a living sacrament. By comparison, our knowledge of creation in general
slips readily towards routine engagement with the world by reliance upon
established tacit frameworks that take the form of habitual skilful practices, cultural assumptions, and theoretical concepts. God cannot be known
in such knowledge; rather, his self-disclosure breaks open and transforms
all such frameworks.*

*As with God, so with knowledge of God: this cannot itself be under-
stood by reference to any routine know-how or conceptual knowledge;
rather it is the paradigm by reference to which these and all knowing, enquiry, and action may be understood. As for itself, knowing God can only
be known itself in reflective participation.*

Commentary

All knowing has the same fundamental character, which is found paradigmatically in our knowledge of God. Within this, knowing can take a
diversity of forms. The relation between knowing God and such other
knowing is paradoxical. It may be described as a limiting case of knowing: knowing is in general a qualified personal act of response, while
knowing God is an unqualified act, in which a person gives themselves
without reserve.

We have spoken of the uniquely lively act of knowing God as a matter of radical responsiveness, of unqualified attention and wholehearted
intention, and of a dual disposition of receptivity and discernment, of
valuing and evaluating. In it we know that which is of intrinsic worth,
through our readiness to indwell or inhabit it in a probing way so as to
attend as much to the world *from* it (or in its context) as *to* it from the
world.[48]

Such knowledge of God, we have averred, is a matter of knowing God in the "mediated immediacy" of *signs* in creation. Now some
realms of encounter in creation define a more lively participation in that
knowing which is our encounter with God through signs. They may be
thought of as implicit signs, or lively sacramental encounters with God.
Two such realms are those of encounter with goodness and beauty. Our
encounter with *goodness* arises as we are attentive and intentional to-

48. I have elaborated philosophically this account of knowing, seeking, and serving
God as paradigmatic for all human knowing, seeking and action in Kettle, "Knowledge,
Context and Evasion."

wards participating in good action: in discerning appreciation (i.e., in the dual disposition of receptivity and responsibility) we acknowledge an action into which we enter and from which we now address the world. When other people recognize such a good act for what it is, this in turn involves something of the same discerning appreciation: it takes goodness to recognize goodness, and this capacity is awakened by goodness itself. Similarly, our encounter with *beauty* arises as we are attentive and intentional towards entering into the beautiful, in discerning appreciation: this brings to light the artistic act and achievement into which we now enter and from which we now view the world.

Unique among such lively sacramental encounters within creation is our encounter with the human person. Here we encounter—in the dual disposition of receptivity and responsibility—one who stands under the same call of God as we do, to respond in an unqualified way to the call to know God, their creator and redeemer. Through persons we encounter God, and through us they encounter God, in a unique way. Human relationship is characterized by this exploration of giving and receiving, in a shared responsiveness ultimately towards God, in a dual disposition of receptivity and responsibility. We each seek to put ourselves in the other's place, trying to see from them, and they from us, as we each try to see *from* God, and challenging each other when the other seems to turn away from the demands of this in evasion.

The act of knowing persons, then, is uniquely related to knowing God; and other realms of knowing such as the pursuit of goodness and beauty also stand in closer relation to knowing God than do some other kinds of knowing. This threefold realm of knowledge, and the primacy within it of knowing God, is portrayed by the medieval Saint Bonaventure as the threefold realm of knowing God himself, knowing the mirror or image of God in persons, and knowing the footprints of God in creation (a more elaborated account would distinguish between our knowledge of animal life, of life in general, and of inanimate creation).

With regard to knowing creation in general, we meet a relatively basic distinction between two kinds of knowing: of knowledge of things, and our practical know-how. Michael Polanyi calls these "representational" and "skilful" knowing. Let us consider each in turn, in relation to our paradigmatic knowing of God.

Representational Knowledge: Knowing God and Knowing "That"

Consider first our knowledge of objects and their properties, and of the meaning of words and symbols and concepts that refer to them. This is the realm of "knowing what," "knowing that," and "knowing about": the realm of representational knowledge, theoretical knowledge, and conceptual or categorical thought. It is also the realm of knowledge and enquiry with which linguistic (and more widely, symbolic) representation is concerned. Fundamentally it about knowing that which we grasp as existing independently of our knowing it.

How may we understand such knowledge as arising for us out of a disposition of radical, primary responsiveness? Such knowledge emerges when, in this disposition, we find that the demands of radical responsiveness—of a lively dual disposition of receptivity and discernment—subside towards the twin, lesser demands of two distinct elements within this. On one hand, we are now faced with the lesser demands of indwelling a settled meaning, in a *disposition of receptivity*. In this regard we find that the question arises no further of a continuing lively, irreducibly *dual* disposition not only of *receptivity* but equally of *discernment* (with the personal demands of lively self-disposal that this dual disposition makes upon us). On the other hand, we are faced with the lesser demands of appraising a question that arises before us, in an act of *critical discernment*. In this regard, we rely in a routine way upon the settled meaning we have formed and indwell receptively, and in which we find that the question arises no further of a continuing lively, irreducibly *dual* disposition not only of *discernment* but equally of *receptivity* (with the personal demands of lively self-disposal that this makes upon us). In short, representational knowledge is about a kind of knowing in which receptivity and critical appraisal *diverge*.

Polanyi's account of representational knowledge reflects faithfully the from-to character of this and all knowing (he frames this as an act of integration in which we attend from our subsidiary awareness to our focal awareness, or from the "proximal pole" to the "distal pole" of knowing). However, our account goes beyond any simple identification of an object of perception with that to which we attend. Rather, our account of knowing God in the "mediated immediacy" of signs sets knowledge of the object within the fundamental character of that in creation through which we attend at once *to* and *from* God. We know creation for what it is when we attend through it to God; also, knowing an object as existing independently of us involves a tacit self-identification with it as existent like ourselves facing the world, and so in a sense knowing the world *from* it.

Knowing God and Knowing "How To"

Very different, at first sight, from our conceptual knowledge of things is the practical know-how through which we perform a skilful action such as cycling or swimming or using a tool. Whereas conceptual knowledge is distinctive to human beings, many skilful performances that human beings achieve are also achieved by animals. There is a fundamental difference, however: for human beings, the performance of a skilful action may be achieved as a *voluntary* action, and this is constitutive for the meaning of practical, personal knowledge.

We may understand such knowledge as coming about for us when we find that the demands of radical responsiveness—of a lively dual disposition of receptivity and discernment—subside into a settled, practical way of attending to the world. We find that we are faced with the lesser demands of indwelling a particular, practical way of seeing everything, in a disposition of receptivity where the question arises no further of a continuing lively *dual* disposition not only of receptivity but equally of discernment (with the personal demands of lively self-disposal that this dual disposition makes upon us). Whereas in representation knowing receptivity and critical judgment diverge, here they *converge*: one "tries/tests whether" one can perform a skilful act precisely as one "tries to" perform it, and this—within the performance of a skill once mastered—reduces to an act performed in some measure in a routine, automatic or habitual way. Thus when we master the skill of cycling, our primary, full attentiveness to the world subsides into a particular way of seeing the world—that is, seeing the world in a "cycling" way, or from the tacit act of cycling.

Once again, it is in our foregoing insistence that knowing God is paradigmatic for all knowing, enquiry, and action that I go beyond Polanyi's account. Polanyi does not sufficiently distinguish the skilful activity of humans from that of animals, as far as I can see. On the other hand, such skilful human activity is not adequately distinguished from that in animals as the autonomous, voluntary action of an individual with a "free will" animals don't have. Our own account roots skilful human activity in primary, radical responsiveness to God, in receptive, responsible participation in the will of God as we attend to him.

Knowing "Knowledge of God": Two Clarifications

In closing, let me clarify in two respects what it means to speak as we have of knowing God in its paradigmatic relation to all human knowing, enquiry, and action. In both respects we are led back to the mystery of such knowledge, and the paradox into which we are led when we attempt to speak of it faithfully.

First, I am not claiming that knowledge of God has certain particular features by which we may locate it within a more comprehensive account of knowing and its varieties. Rather, I am intimating the mystery of knowledge of God which confronts with paradox all false, narrow, and distorting assumptions or frameworks that we bring—explicitly or tacitly—to our understanding of knowledge, and breaks them open to renewed attention to the mystery of the God whom we know. If you like, our account of knowledge of God works at once positively and apophatically upon our understanding of knowledge.

Second, to speak as we have of what it means to know God is to speak in reflective awareness: we speak out of knowing God. What we say has therefore the character of witness, avowal, or testimony. That is to say, on the one hand, it is not an assertion of truth that asks for understanding, assent, or dispute in detachment from itself. On the other hand, it is not the kind of testimony that merely asserts a private, subjective experience without making any kind of truth-claim. Rather, it is a claim regarding what is real and true, presented with the authority of personal encounter. The testimonial character of what we say about what it means to know God may be explicated as, "Behold the One we know, and the knowing in which we here participate: must we not speak of this so?" This tacit question (or illocutionary force of what we say, if you prefer) always remains a living one in our own reflective awareness, as well as our testimony to other people: for we are driven to speak in paradox when we speak of God, and of knowledge of God, and are compelled to test our strange language against the reality that we would honor: "For all the paradox into which we are here drawn, must we not speak of this so?"

6. BREAKING WITH CARTESIAN ASSUMPTIONS: PARADOX AND THE SELF-DISCLOSURE OF GOD

In modern society a theory of knowledge has become prevalent that turns theoretical knowledge into a paradigm for all knowing, including—in an

act of "logical inversion"—knowledge of God. Relying upon Cartesian
habits of imagination, this theory explicitly misrepresents and implicitly
conceals the realities of God and knowledge of God, including the essential
features of knowing God presented in our own account: transcendence,
grace, receptivity, and mystery. As God brings us to know himself in Jesus
Christ, he engages this misrepresentation, disclosing what it means to know
him. This disclosure, we have seen, presents paradoxical challenges to mod-
ern thinking about what it means to know. The odd logic of such disclosure
is here described with support drawn critically from the writings of Ian
Ramsey and others.

Commentary

The Primacy of Theoretical Thought

Knowledge of God is hindered today in modern societies by a certain
way of thinking about what it means to know something. This way of
thinking corresponds to certain modern philosophical or ideological
beliefs. These beliefs are adhered to particularly by those who aspire to
manage mass society (notably professional workers in politics, the media, and education), but they are widely diffused throughout society. We
shall explore this further in chapters 8 through 10.

This way of thinking about knowledge attracted allegiance in medieval Europe in the setting of sustained social change (sponsored by
Christendom) when the ultimate bearings for such change were fragmented in what are known as the religious wars. New bearings were
now sought in the pursuit of sure truths commanding universal assent,
either because they seemed self-evident to the general population, or
because they were regarded as subject to proof by reason or experiment.
Rene Descartes' "method of doubt" for establishing such truths was influential among those who declared their thinking to be the arrival of
enlightenment.

This way of thinking about knowledge may be described as making
conceptual knowledge the paradigm for understanding all knowledge.
This tendency has had a long history and is reflected in what has been
called the "primacy of theoretical thought" stretching back to the philosophies of classical Greece.[49] It misrepresents knowledge especially

---

49. "The primacy of theoretical thought" is a key theme in the writings of Hermann
Dooyeweerd (Dooyeweerd, *New Critique*). On the relevance of this theme to modern
thought, Colin Gunton writes: "It is not difficult to realize that the Cartesian theory

because it fails to grasp knowledge as a lively personal act, and therefore fails uniquely to grasp knowledge of God. Knowledge of God cannot be understood in the context of theoretical knowledge; rather vice versa, as we have seen. When things are inverted in this way—when it is claimed that knowledge of God is to be understood by reference to conceptual knowledge—we have what may be called an act of "logical inversion." This amounts in practice to a dismissal of "knowledge of God" as no such thing. It also involves inner contradictions—contradictions that upon investigation extend to its account of conceptual knowledge itself.

All of this can be portrayed as a matter of being committed to certain false beliefs or assumptions. More deeply, however, I propose that we may see it as a matter of being dominated in one's imagination by a certain image drawn from visual perception, giving rise to Cartesian habits of imagination.

Cartesian Habits of Imagination

The image that dominates our modern thinking about knowledge is that of looking on at a knowing subject on the one hand and that which is known on the other. When we ask about knowing and about what is there to be known, and about the pursuit of knowledge, we tend to rely upon this picture to understand what we are doing.[50]

---

of the self is the Platonic transposed into a modern key, and its dissolution in recent theories of the loss of self almost entirely parasitic upon it" (Gunton, *The One, the Three and the Many*, 61). For further insightful perspectives on the Classical Greek heritage of Western and Christian philosophy, see Yu, *Being and Relation*, 64–114, and Schindler, "Mystery and Mastery," 188–94.

50. The distorting effect upon modern epistemology of imagery drawn from visual experience has been acknowledged by Gabriel Marcel, John Macmurray, and William Poteat, among others. Marcel writes that Descartes and Kant "made illegitimate borrowings from optics in their epistemology, with effects that can hardly be exaggerated" (Marcel, *Being and Having*, 192). For Macmurray, the distorting effect upon epistemology of a false reliance upon visual experience is a foundational insight. He sees this as underlying dualistic Cartesian philosophy which casts knowledge as purely receptive and action purely active. For his own part, he gives primacy to the self as agent, whose action includes theoretical knowledge as a limiting case. However, while this enables him to frame many vital insights, he seems to retain unwittingly the very dichotomy he has attacked when he misses the *fundamental* role of receptivity (towards God, and towards other people) in action and knowledge (see Macmurray, *The Self as Agent*, 104–7). For Poteat, similarly the hegemony of the visual image of "looking on at" the knowing subject is the key error of Cartesianism in Christian philosophy, and reflects a preoccupation with engaging the static conceptuality of classic Greek philosophy rather than with the aural/oral Hebraic tradition.

Upon examination, this picture rests upon two fundamental elements standing in conceptual opposition with each other. The first is a human self as a subject achieving theoretical knowledge, a subject who is conceived apart from the world that is there to be known, and with whom we identify as the aspiring subject of knowledge. The second element is the world that is there to be known, conceived apart from the act of its being known—conceived, as it were, "directly" by ourselves without our participating in the act of knowing we ascribe to the subject at whom we look on. Behind this way of picturing things lies an assumption of "direct" contact on our part with each—with knower and known—as distinct, determinate entities within our own field of view. From this arises a particular way of understanding the pursuit of knowledge as doubting and questioning the correspondence between an idea and reality.

Now this way of picturing things accords well, up to a point, with our experience of theoretical knowledge. However, it fails to reflect the truth of our knowledge of God or of knowledge that is of a lively personal character. To understand these, we must begin not from a knowing human subject on one side and a "given" world that is there to be known on the other, but from God and the knowledge to which he raises us—knowledge of himself, of each other, and of the world as God's creation.

The mistake of the Cartesian way of picturing knowledge is to assume that, given a knowing human subject, we can step back from them and view them and view what they (claim to) know alongside each other from within wider horizons. Now this assumption corresponds with reality insofar as the knowing subject in question makes a theoretical statement by reference to concepts that are themselves routinely understood, and understood by us. However, insofar as the knowledge in question is of a lively personal kind, this assumption is mistaken. The truth is rather that in order to recognize *either* the knowing subject *or* that which is known we have to enter critically into the context of the knowing subject given precisely by that which is known. We have to allow that what is claimed as knowledge may challenge assumed meanings we have brought to it without realizing we rely upon them. This requires us to explore whether a knowledge-claim can be understood from within our own context (in which case we can indeed look on dispassionately at knower and known), or whether it breaks open our own context and calls us to understand things in a new and deeper context presented by this knowledge-claim itself.

Insofar as knowledge is of a lively personal kind it typically presents us with this question regarding which way round the truth lies: can we locate the act of knowing and what is known within our own horizons, or do these locate our own act of knowing and what we know by presenting new horizons in themselves? In the case of theoretical knowledge, it is not vital that this question be asked, because if we assume unreflectively that our own horizons are wider this does not mislead us. In the case of our own knowing God, however, we meet the other extreme: it is vital that we ask the question which way round, because with respect to everything we know of God it is the other way round: God presents us with deeper horizons in which to understand both our participation in knowledge of himself, and himself whom we know.

Now does this not reflect how we normally behave in conversation: we enter into the claims of the other as much as we step back from them, so as to see the world properly from their horizons as well as from our own, thereby together bringing each of these horizons to light? It is only when we begin *thinking conceptually* about what we do here, that we imagine to step back; it is only in theoretical thought, in the natural sciences and the human sciences and their programs of rationalization, that we impose *a priori* the "critical method" or "method of doubt" to claims seen as theoretical. And when we do so, we fail to recognize that we step back into horizons that we have ourselves posited, and not into some realm of universal rationality conceived by Enlightenment thinkers as a kind of universal space free of context, perspective, or horizon.[51]

My claim, then, is that in general we cannot and do not explore the truth of an assertion by "stepping back" and viewing it in detachment. I call for conversion to the primacy of radical responsiveness, of entering critically into an act of assertion; this is its meaning. The trouble is, not uncommonly this claim is itself understood by reference unreflectively to persisting Cartesian habits of imagination, notwithstanding its challenge to abandon these. This misunderstanding plays out in the supposed replacement of absolutism by relativism: having conceded that there is no

---

51. Hans-Georg Gadamer notably challenged such Enlightenment assumptions in his *Truth and Method*, proposing that conversation represents a meeting of "horizons of questionableness," oriented towards communion. However, his account of this meeting of horizons and its outcome fails to do justice to conversation properly attentive to the most lively questions of truth and of God and including mutual challenge. For a detailed critique of Gadamer's proposals by reference to the account of knowledge I have presented in this book, see Kettle, "Truth and Dialogue."

such thing as a "view from nowhere" (or "from everywhere"), it is averred that every knowledge-claim is located somewhere in particular. But, of course, this avowal itself relies upon an illusory "view from nowhere": "everything is relative" becomes the new absolute truth. Cartesian habits of imagination are self-referentially inconsistent, and the turn to relativism generates in principle an infinite regress of "steps back in detachment" that threatens to collapse into nihilism. To understand rightly both knowing and context requires an imaginative conversion and liberation from these habits of imagination.[52] Divine self-disclosure effects this in an implicit, practical way; but I shall now explicate this conversion, engaging—with the help especially of Ian Ramsey—Cartesian habits of imagination as they informed British Empiricism and its lingering and highly influential heritage in public thinking.

The Paradoxical Logic of God's Self-disclosure

When God approaches in sovereignty, revealing himself and the world in this light, he does so as we have acknowledged through signs in creation. In so doing he engages that which we know, at once bringing it alive so as to reveal himself through it, and bringing ourselves alive to him through it. In so doing the approach of God lifts our knowing—what we know, and our knowing of it—out of the realm of routine skilful and conceptual knowledge into lively knowledge of his self-revelation.

This fact defies understanding in terms of Cartesian habits of imagination, however, since these rely upon conceptual knowledge as the paradigm for all knowledge. This defiance of Cartesian habits by God and by our knowledge of God confronts our conceptual thought as the occasion of paradox—paradox that refuses to be eliminated.

This paradox confronts us in particular when we try to speak about signs that point to God, *as* signs: as—using once again John Baillie's paradoxical terminology—mediums of immediate encounter with God. In this concluding section I shall consider briefly our attempt to speak about *the language in which we speak of* God. What is involved in the encounter with God when the language of our conceptual knowledge comes alive as a sign disclosing him? How shall we describe linguistic signs that point to God, and describe them *in this capacity*?

---

52. Although Polanyi's theory of knowledge opens the way, I believe, to such a conversion from Cartesian habits of imagination, it is often interpreted by reference to these habits that persist. On this see Kettle, "Cartesian Habits."

Here we have to deal with that which stands in unique relation to language in general. We are not dealing with what can be viewed as one example of language among others, within wider linguistic horizons; we are not dealing with that which can be viewed by "looking on at it" in Cartesian fashion. We cannot "step back" here and view on one side speech about God, and on the other side—in supposedly more direct encounter, apart from such language—the God who is spoken of.

Among those who have studied this question, J. D. Crossan offers some provocative insights. He describes religious language as what happens on the edges of language, with its own odd—sometimes paradoxical—logic in which language open upon that which transcends all language. At one point he compares this odd, limiting location on the edge of self-contradiction with sailing a boat close-hauled—as close to the eye of the wind as possible (total non-sailors may wrongly assume that to sail is to be blown along by the wind, in its own direction, but this far from the truth: in principle it is possible, blown by the wind, to sail in any direction except directly against or into the eye of the wind). Crossan writes:

> The limitation is absolute. One cannot sail into the eye any more, I would argue, than one can get outside language and outside story. But one can sail as close as possible into the wind, and one can tell that you are as close as possible only by constantly testing the wind. Then the boat heels over, strains hard, and one experiences most fully, or at least I do, the thrill of sailing. My suggestion is that the excitement of transcendent experience is found only at the edge of language and the limit of story and that the only way to find that excitement is to test those edges and those limits.[53]

It is illuminating to compare this with another picture offered immediately before this by Crossan, and which is more central for his own thesis. For him, language is like a raft on a sea, where the raft is all we can know, and religious encounter is about the edge of the raft and of language. He writes:

> If there is only language, then God must be either inside language and in that case ... an idol; or he is outside language, and there is nothing out there but silence. There is only one possibility left, and that is what we experience in the movement of the raft, in the breaks in the raft's structure, and, above all,

---

53. Crossan, *Dark Interval*, 45.

what can be experienced on the edges of the raft itself. For we cannot really talk of the sea, we can only talk of the edges of the raft and what happens there.

Now this latter picture surely reflects the continuing hold of Cartesian habits of imagination. Crossan imagines to stand back and look on at language, on the one hand, and at an unknowable reality beyond it, on the other, without acknowledging that his own location looking on at these is problematic. However, his comparison of religious language with sailing close-hauled is more promising. It need not be interpreted by reference to these habits of imagination. It acknowledges implicitly that all linguistic meaning is a dynamic affair analogous to a motion that rests upon pressure from beyond (*viz.* the wind), and collapses without it. But whereas when we "go with the flow" of the wind (i.e., sail with the wind behind us) we are less aware of the source of our motion in the wind, and need less to test it, when we sail close-hauled we are most aware of engaging with and testing it. Here, we should note, we find "the edges" not by looking directly for them but by attending to that which is the source of all our motion from beyond.

We might add here that the starting point of encounter with God is not, as it seems to be for Crossan when employing his "sailing close-hauled" image, a search for "the excitement of transcendent experience" to be found by testing the edges of language. Rather, we are encountered by God who enlivens us, and we respond by entrusting ourselves attentively to his call. Caught up and held in God's own lively movement, when we try to speak of these things we find ourselves driven—despite ourselves—to what Crossan calls the edges of language. These edges are, of course, *growing* edges (so to speak); they are about that most lively encounter with meaning from which all our language arises in the first place. They represent the revival of language to its most vital, in encounter with God. It would be truer to describe them as the deep root of language than as its edge.[54]

Further exploration of the unique logically odd character of religious language is found in the writings of Ian Ramsey. His work is, I suggest, vital for linking what I have written to the concerns of British empiricism and linguistic/conceptual analysis, which, even if it not to the

54. Charles Péguy evokes wonderfully the mystery of the growing edge which sustains that upon which it seems to depend, meditating upon the three and its buds. See Péguy, "Portal of the Mystery of Hope."

fore in philosophy today, reflect concerns that remain so in much public thinking. I shall therefore consider his work in a little more detail.

In his book *Religious Language*, Ramsey characterizes religious language (following John Wisdom) as "logically improper." This is necessary, he writes, in order for it to be currency for the distinctive *odd situation* that religious people claim to speak about. This situation is marked by a distinctive *discernment* and *commitment*. *Discernment* is about "perception and more," which finds parallels in situations that become distinctively different as "the light dawns," "the ice breaks," or "the penny drops." This moment of recognition or realization provokes a *commitment* that is at once total in depth and comprehensive in scope: Ramsey compares it to the commitment we show when in conscience we yield to the claims of duty, and to the devotion that we show to persons, communities, and nations to which we belong.

Ramsey finds the odd logic of religious language most explicit where it takes the form of an everyday "model" qualified in a "logically odd way." For examples of this he takes *first cause, infinitely wise, infinitely good, creation ex nihilo,* and *eternal purpose*. In each case, as he demonstrates, we start with a familiar situation—represented by the "model"—and then qualify this in an odd way that leads us into another situation that lies beyond all such familiar situations and cannot be reduced to them, and that talks about a mysterious situation that is "what's seen, what talked about in familiar language, *and more*."[55]

Ramsey demonstrates however that the same odd logic characterizes all religious language, albeit in more tacit ways. This includes the divine attributes of negative theology, and divine attributes such as "unity," "simplicity," and "perfection" that may easily be (mis)understood casually as simple examples of observational or conceptual language.

Let me clarify what Ramsey means by religious disclosure by taking his first example, that is, the logical behavior of the negative divine attribute "immutable":

> Let us imagine that we are travelling by train in a remote district as darkness falls. Little by little the scene is obliterated; first trees, then houses, slowly disappear from view; then the pylons, then the particular folds of the hills; then the hills themselves. Darkness has fallen: "Fast falls the eventide"; "the darkness deepens." Change (if not decay) in all around I see. Now at every point

55. Ramsey, *Religious Language*, 62.

in this changing scene, "immutability," as an attribute of negative theology, whispers to us: "But not everything changes . . . Is there not something which is unchanged? Do you not apprehend something which remains invariable in the situation despite what is so visibly changing?" . . . Such suggestions are constantly repeated as the scene constantly changes, in the hope that at some point the penny will drop, the ice break, the light dawn; that there will break on us that "discernment" which is a "sense of the unseen," a characteristically religious situation, to which "immutability" has led us.[56]

Ramsey's proposals in this book invite three critical reflections in the light of our reflections so far on knowledge of God.

1. Ramsey's account of religious disclosure offers the same potential challenge to Cartesian habits of imagination as does Crossan's "sailing close-hauled" analogy. However, as we shall see, *it is not clear that Ramsey himself realized this.* This issue comes into focus when we ask about the self-referential consistency of his account of religious language: did he realize that what he says about religious language and its empirical placement is itself consistent with his account? Let us tease out the question.

Ramsey points out how "immutability" discloses itself at the limiting, "boundary" situation towards which we are led as we apprehend increasingly comprehensive change, to the point that all we observe is subject to change. It is at this point on the very edge of self-contradiction—like moving against the source of one's movement, like sailing almost directly into the wind—that "immutable" discloses itself almost directly in the face of universal mutability. This is indeed the nature of paradox—whether explicit or implicit—in religious language, poised on the edge of collapse into meaningless self-contradiction, language stretched beyond limit in unqualified meaningfulness.

Now this means that the very terms in which Ramsey speaks of disclosure share themselves in the same logical impropriety as that of which he speaks as the content of disclosure. To grasp what he means by "what's seen *and more*," or by a "qualified model," or by the very term "logical impropriety" itself, we must see each of these as themselves "logically improper" "qualified models." Ramsey is offering no strictly second-order account of religious language here, but an account that

56. Ibid., 51.

draws us into encounter with God for ourselves.[57] Now there are hints
that Ramsey realizes this—for example, Ramsey acknowledges that
the expression "a sense of the unseen" is itself logically odd[58]—but I do
not see that he addresses anywhere this issue (which is in truth one of
self-referential consistency) as such. If he does not realize this, then his
thinking remains captive to Cartesian habits of imagination.

The extension of Ramsey's account of religious disclosure to this
account itself opens up further the truth to which religious people lay
claim, that, as Ramsey writes, "the 'initiative' in any 'disclosure' or 'revelation' must come from God." Ramsey points to this claim as a way of
interpreting the fact that suitable language is, by itself, no guarantee of
religious disclosure—something that would be, he says, "semantic magic
. . . we should then have a technique which gave us power over God."[59]
We can now add that our very recognition, with Ramsey, of the nature of
religious language (or knowledge, or experience of, God) is itself given
by God, in attentive encounter with God. The "wider empiricism" of
Ramsey's account does not provide a tool in our own hands, apart from
God, but rather the responsibility of testimony.

2. Ramsey is right to add religious commitment to religious discernment
when characterizing the "religious situation." However, did he recognize
the irreducible, primary place of the latter in religious discernment itself? Did he understand that in responsiveness to God, discernment and
commitment interanimate each other in a mutually constitutive way, in
what we have called the dual disposition of receptivity and responsibility? Let us tease out this question.

Ramsey writes that religious language talks of "the discernment
with which is associated, by way of response, a total commitment." Now
this way of expressing the matter might be taken to mean that discernment is something that happens for us—perhaps through the agency
of the Spirit—whereas commitment is our human response. However,
this would not be satisfactory. The paradox of grace is, as we have seen,
such that knowledge of God is entirely the work of God and entirely

57. The same applies to every account of religious language, experience, and knowledge: there is no possible second-order account of these. This needs to be made more
explicit, I believe, in much theological writing, in order to clarify the challenge these
realities pose to Cartesian habits of imagination.

58. Ramsey, *Religious Language*, 46.

59. Ibid., 79.

our own work. Accordingly, discernment is both fully the work of God and fully our own work; our human response does not wait upon any given sense or apprehension given to us, but is already constitutive of it. And our commitment is both fully our own work and the work of God; without it, discernment does not happen in the first place. As John Baillie writes: "The reason why we must not say that faith is based on religious experience is that religious experience, if it is authentic, already contains faith. Faith is the cognitive element in it . . . faith is experience but, like all veridical experience, it is determined for us and produced in us by something not ourselves."[60]

We may put it that commitment is as much the starting-point of religious disclosure as vice-versa. Commitment is already there, by the grace of God, in the attentive searching and waiting of faith that yields, in God's good time, the disclosure of himself. Faith is that commitment— that receptivity—that opens our eyes to God in the first place. As Saint Anselm said, "I do not understand in order to believe, but I believe in order to understand."

This is not to say that discernment comes as the answer to a well-formulated question, rooted in commitment to certain presuppositions. Rather, it comes into focus in the integration of clues that are only in this event confirmed for what they are, *as* clues to something. Discernment or disclosure comes as a gift to the committed waiting that is at once fully attentive and wholeheartedly in its intention to seek and know.

This affects how we understand discernment itself. By drawing a parallel between this and situations where "the penny drops," etc., Ramsey valuably highlights the "living" character of religious knowledge. However, these parallel situations are passing: so to speak, once the penny has dropped, it comes to rest. The moment of recognition fades. This is not so in the case of religious discernment. It is essentially undying. Thus, we might note, religious metaphors are "undying"[61]—unlike other metaphors that continue to refer successfully (the "leg" of a chair, the "eye" of a needle) even when, as metaphors, they have "died," collapsing into simple reference. The undying character of religious discernment is reflected in our sense of quietly "feeding" in contemplation upon the mysteries of God—and of drawing vital life from "sailing close-hauled" in sustained encounter with God transcendent.

60. Baillie, *Sense of the Presence of God,* 65.
61. Thus Alston, *Philosophy of Language.*

3. Ramsey affirms the special character of religious language relative to other (e.g., "observational") language. However, does he understand that religious language is not a phenomenon *additional to* existing language (just as Crossan thinks of existing language as a "raft" of meaning on which our understanding rests)—that rather, religious language is the occasion of language being revived to its primary form, out of which all meaning arises in the first place, in attentive responsiveness towards God? Let us tease out this question.

We may do so by considering further the account Ramsey offers of the word "immutable" as an attribute of God. He writes that this works by leading us beyond all the changes we observe around us, until—although everything we observe is changing—we grasp that something is unchanging, in an apprehension of the "unseen." Now let us describe this further in the light of our own account of knowledge, which finds its paradigm in knowledge of God, we would describe this further as follows: Our routine observation of change rests upon an established framework of meaning, which *is itself unchanged*; more precisely, it *defines for us what counts as unchanged,* in the same way that when we rely upon bearings to orient ourselves we take these to *define* a fixed orientation. However, such routine observation originates in a lively disposition of receptivity and responsibility out of which we come to embrace bearings as trustworthy for their purpose in the first place. Bearings are not simply "given" to our perception; nor are they a relative, even arbitrary choice. When "immutable" leads us beyond all observed change, it does so by bringing us to the point at which, faced with universal change, the idea of "unchanging" is paradoxical, and re-opens the question of very meaning of the framework by which we see change. This question commands our lively response, in a renewed disposition of receptivity and responsibility.

This helps us to understand properly some claims made often about religious language and its forms. Firstly, let us take the distinction employed by, for example, Wolfhart Pannenberg between religious language in the form of doxology and analogy, which he takes from Ninian Smart. *Doxological* language is that which finds its primary referent in God; it is about words whose meaning is offering up to God in worship to him: it is God who gives the words meaning. *Analogical* language is that which takes a referent in creation, and uses it to indicate God by reference to this.

In the light of our own account, we would want to clarify the nature both of doxological and analogical language. Firstly, we should not see *doxological* language about God as providing a distinct conceptual vocabulary about God that distinguishes God from creation *but in so doing places God within some universal conceptual framework as one thing among others.* This would of course, re-open the way for attributing certain "sacred" things within creation to the realm of God, and lapse into pre-modern "sacral" apprehensions of the created order. Rather, doxological language is the language of lively knowledge and of enquiry in its primary disposition towards God, which, taking the things of creation, ascribes their deepest meaning to God, and so animates creation as a sign and foretaste of the kingdom. Thus when Jesus says, "call no man 'father,' for you have only one father, and he is in heaven," he takes a conceptual meaning and offers it to God as its defining referent. He turns "father" into a sign pointing in lively paradox to a God forever *beyond* creation but known *through* creation.

Secondly, regarding *analogical* language about God, we should not see this as locating God in some realm distinct from creation while *leaving creation intact, without God, as the literal referent of all language and concepts.* This would be to open the way to a false secularist apprehension of the created order. Now there have been perceptive accounts of religious metaphor that acknowledge that religious metaphor discloses a new referent through the interanimation of vehicle and tenor (or poles of the *from-to*) in metaphor, refusing reduction to either.[62] However, we would want to emphasize that such a new referent is not simply derivative upon literal language; rather it is the occasion of a reanimation of that lively responsiveness out of which all meaningful language emerges most deeply in the first place.

> This is illustrated in G. K. Chesterton's description of how fairy tales work: when we are very young children we do not need fairy tales: we only need tales. Mere life is interesting enough. A child of seven is excited by being told that Tommy opened a door and saw a dragon. But a child of three is excited by being told that Tommy opened a door ... (nursery tales) say that apples were golden only to refresh the forgotten moment when we found that

---

62. See, for example, Soskice, *Metaphor*.

they were green. They make rivers run with wine only to make us remember, for one wild moment, that they run with water.[63]

This passage reminds us that the liveliness of meaning in which we apprehend God in wonder does not depend upon metaphorical language derivative upon literal language; it lies at the heart of literal language itself, in which creation is animated for what it truly is: a sign that points to its creator. To be sure, metaphors and other odd, paradoxical language plays a vital role awakening us to God in wonder; but this is, as Chesterton's passage suggests, a matter of reawakening to creation for what it most truly is.

63. Chesterton, *Orthodoxy*, 94.

Spreading the Gospel

*Ten Conversions towards the
Christianization of Western Culture*

PART TWO: Introduction

IN RECENT DECADES, A set of trends that are a matter of concern to many thoughtful Christians and others have been accentuated in Western culture. In Part Two I shall address these trends. They are deeply ambivalent vis-à-vis human flourishing, but yet do not obviously connect with or invite judgment by reference to "traditional" Christian virtues and vices. Among them are individualism, consumerism, and the ideologies of neoliberal capitalism and "political correctness." Christian response to these is often *ad hoc* and a matter of contention among Christians themselves.

Despite their seemingly disparate nature, these trends are rooted in basic habits of imagination that are widespread and comprehensive in scope within contemporary Western culture. These habits are at once hidden and influential. I hope to show how these are illumined at new theological depth and in a fresh way when understood within the theological epistemological bearings I have offered in Part One. The result is a coherent Christian framework for understanding and addressing these developments for the vital Christian concern that they are. Of course, it is only possible within the space of this book to give fairly brief treatment to each trend or theme. Other, more specialized works are available for further study in many cases. My purpose here, as I say, is to reveal their nature and significance in the light of a coherent underlying theological account. Readers of the present book will find it helpful to draw, in further study of each trend or theme, from this coherent theological account.

It will be apparent that the relation between Part 1 and Part 2 of this book is not one of linear argument. Rather, Part 1 composes a picture the elements of which are integrally but implicitly related to the whole. My aim in the book as a whole is to intimate a suggestive coherence between the whole sketched in Part 1 and the ten conversions explored in Part 2. Also, let me reiterate that these ten conversions are not a series of conversions adding up to the conversion of the West, but rather a set of gateways each opening out onto the vista of Christian faith in which all the other conversions are implied. The purpose of considering each of these ten conversions in turn is to identify the major points of "singularity" where the gospel engages Western culture in a living way, and where—if these conversion are not acknowledged—there is a danger that unregenerate thinking will render Christianity as a whole captive to its presuppositions.

Let me acknowledge that Part One of this book is ultimately itself of the same character as each of these conversions: it is a gateway opening out upon the vista of Christian faith, through which we may pass. My argument is that it is a uniquely vital gateway for modern Western culture today, because it breaks though the wall of a false epistemology within which this culture is trapped and its trajectory diverted in thought and practice from openness to the vista of God's coming kingdom.

The reflections that I offered in Part One on the act of knowing God (taken as paradigmatic for all knowing) were intended as a vital hermeneutical key to faithful mission and spirituality in Western culture today for the reasons I explained briefly in the Introduction. In the ten chapters of Part Two which now follow, I shall present ten conversions in which a series of false orientations or disorientations in Western culture are challenged and new bearings offered in Christian faith. I shall summarize these ten chapters now. These summaries will necessarily be dense, and sometimes rather cryptic (for example, where I indicate topics that I shall address but that I have not yet explained).

SECULAR AND SACRED IN CONTEMPORARY UNDERSTANDING: CONVERSION TO CREATION AND NEW CREATION BY GOD

Modern society envisions itself as "secular" in contrast with traditional religious societies, which it sees as holding certain features of nature and culture to be sacred. Sociologists have often added to this their belief in an irreversible historical process of "secularization" whereby traditional religious societies turn gradually, under pressure of reasonable enquiry, into societies in which "nothing is sacred." The emergence of modern societies from medieval Christendom is often viewed in these terms as a liberation.

However, this view profoundly misconceives the nature both of Christian faith and of modern "secular" society itself. It is blind to the source of modern liberation in Christian faith itself, and is blind to its own perversion of liberation. For a start, Christian faith, for its own part, has never stood simply for the belief that "sacredness is to be found in the world." Rather, Christian faith in general strips nature and culture of any intrinsic sacred status of the sort endowed upon it in traditional "sacral" societies. It seeks to do the same today in "secular" culture itself wherever this culture, despite its self-understanding, unthinkingly adopts sacred totems and taboos of its own. Christian faith finds the sacred in, and finds "the sacred" defined by reference to, a transcendent creator God. It finds the whole of God's creation—the *saeculum*—good and imbued with worth in his eyes; it is the medium in which God acts to reveal himself and his good purposes for creation through signs, and acts to effect these purposes. This Christian desacralization of the world as the arena of God's purposes is found in ancient biblical faith and finds its consummation in the incarnation: in Jesus Christ, God draws the entire secular, material world into his purposes for transformation in the kingdom of God.

The Christian desacralization of nature and culture was midwife, in medieval Christendom, to unprecedented social dynamism and, in a decisive development, to experimental science. However, conservative sacral tendencies persisted in the church, which now appeared unable to provide secure unified foundations for this emergent world. In response particularly to religious wars, "secular" foundations were sought for the future in place of religious ones.

In truth, the unfolding "secular" modern world has continued tacitly to draw nourishment from Christian faith. In a less welcome development, however, secular ideologies have themselves acquired, unacknowledged, a false "sacred" status; so too have personal features of life in consumer society. Through these the world gets distorted ironically by the secretly religious—even sacral—worldview of "secularism."

Meanwhile it may appear that the recent popular discovery of "spirituality" testifies a renewed openness to Christian affirmation and to discernment of the sacred in a world where "nothing is sacred." However, in truth this may rather indicate a readiness to entertain a pagan re-sacralization of the world.

These considerations shape fundamentally the vocation of Christians in "secular" society today. This vocation is to call for a conversion to the celebration of God who delights in the goodness of the provisional *saeculum*, his creation, which as a sign participates in and points towards its promised fulfillment in new creation by God, in whom alone the mystery of true sacredness is definitively found.

THE TRAJECTORY OF WESTERN CULTURE, INDIVIDUALISM, AND TOTALITARIANISM: CONVERSION TO COMMUNITY UNDER GOD

What we call "modern culture" is not just one culture among others, but stands in its own distinctive relation to all traditional cultures. This relation is captured in its dual self-understanding as at once (1) *defining* culture: its trajectory is that of state-sponsored cultivation or civil-izing of individuals, and (2) *rising above culture*: its trajectory departs from traditional culture in openness to a future arising from the autonomous exercise of critical reason by individuals. Modern culture differs from traditional cultures, accordingly, in constituting itself less as a cultural *state of affairs* than as a cultural *trajectory*—that of "modernization" and "progress." This vision derives historically from, and derives its warrant from, Christian orientation towards the dawning kingdom of God. However, it is less than fully open to God's future insofar as it is committed to the particular "methodology" inherent in its dual self-understanding as above.

This dual self-understanding may be understood by reference to the dual aspects of God's dawning kingdom, which (1) forms a new world, as it (2) breaks open existing cultural and personal norms and assumptions. These two aspects of the coming of God's kingdom arise within, and are known in personal response to, our transcendent God's approach in covenantal love; and they arise in integral relation to each other, within the forming of community grounded in God's love. Their relation to God and to each other opens culture to the possibility of ever further differentiation and integration.

However, these two cultural impulses have with time become increasingly separated from their guiding context in the sovereign approach of God, and exalted as sovereign each in their own right. At this point they come into irreconcilable competition with faith and with each other: each pursues its own absolute claims at the expense of faith and of the other, and in so doing contradicts its own true vocation as pointing to God.

This distortion has marked modern history. It has contributed to an erosion of human community under God in the name of the sovereign "civilizing" state, on the one hand, and of the sovereign individual, on the other. This is reflected today in a harmful breakdown of community and family life and of intermediate social structures.

As the individual and the state continue to be falsely exalted today as irreducible, incommensurate "goods," they each drift further from their proper character in relation to God and each other. The rational individual is dissolving into the managed, impulsive consumer, while the cultivating state is increasingly subservient to a neoliberal global capitalist system. These developments are legitimized in a new ideological vision for the rationalization of society that gives renewed momentum and new direction to the trajectory of "modernization." Meanwhile, advances in technology have given individualism and economic rationalization new penetration into human life, accelerating the polarization of human life between them.

One form of resistance to the dissolution of communal bonds has arisen from time to time with political effect: that which is today associated with the "politics of identity."

Recent cultural developments have been variously characterized as the rise of postmodernity, late modernity, liquid modernity, and consistent modernity.

It is the Christian vocation today to witness to and to embody the richness of community and conviviality under God to which God calls humankind in Jesus Christ. This involves calling for conversion from the modern cultural trajectory insofar as it has become directed towards individualism and totalitarianism in their modern and "postmodern" forms, and seeking to restore the bearings of this trajectory in the dawning kingdom of God.

THE MODERN BETRAYAL OF ENQUIRY: CONVERSION TO ATTENTIVENESS TOWARDS GOD

Modern culture sets out to challenge tradition: it regards every tradition as open in principle to questioning and judgment in the light of innate human rationality and goodness. However, in reality the enquiry into truth and goodness is, at its most deep and lively, mediated in Christian tradition in attentiveness to God. God can be known only in such deep and lively attentiveness; insofar as God's world can be known only in similar attentiveness, enquiry into God's world is nourished by enquiry into God. Modern culture, however, fails to understand lively enquiry. Rather, it sees enquiry into truth as a matter of doubting traditions and propositions, and enquiry into goodness as matter of testing actions in the light of moral principles; and it interprets Christian faith by reference to these. The vision of enquiry (like visions of the secular, of reason, and of cultivation or civilization) drifts here from its moorings in Christian faith, and effectively becomes itself a distorting, secretly "religious" modern framework. It now *misrepresents theoretically* religious enquiry, effectively trivializing it; and it *practically subverts* it. It also (ironically) misrepresents to itself the truth in its own vision and subverts practically its own efforts.

In the course of this, modern culture *inverts God and the human subject* and *subverts the act of enquiry*. This inversion unfolds in two stages. In the first, the secular world is projected in theory and in practice as autonomous and self-sufficient, and trust is directed towards wherever this may lead. This sets the secular world in rivalry with Christian faith, turning the latter into something contested and problematic. In the second stage, faith is itself framed by the secular world as an act in which human subjects ascribe their own private meaning to the world; faith is no longer understood as about deeper attentiveness to the reality of the world.

While these two stages of inversion appear historically in succession, today they face us side by side, with one or another presenting itself to the fore. The first inversion sponsors rationalism, the second relativism; the first is to the fore in modernism, the second in postmodernism.

Importantly, these two stages of inversion apply both to *the act of questioning* and to *the act of valuing* as modes of enquiry. We shall explore these in turn.

The modern inversion of God and human subject, in which questioning and valuing at their most deep and personal are subverted, contributes to some recent cultural developments. These include the erosion of canon and its normative role in the arts and in some science-based professions such as medicine; the pre-eminence in academia of secondary, critical studies over primary studies; the imposition of theory-based strategies, through directives and target-setting, upon reflective practitioners constraining their judgment; and neglect of the responsibility of moral judgment and initiative in favor merely of conformity to legally framed rights and responsibilities. These developments subvert the deepest pursuit of truth and goodness; covertly demanding conformity to diktat, they erode the roots of liberty.

When religion and the humanities are viewed in a rationalist or relativist way, the demands of deep enquiry are dismissed. Incredulity towards such enquiry leads either to denying its subject matter or to domesticating it to the theoretical framework imposed on it. Practical evasion of deep enquiry is also found in a collapse into disorientation and escapism. This is allied to a contemporary culture of distraction, credulity, and anomie.

It is the vocation of Christian faith today to contend with rationalism, relativism, and the culture of distraction. It is to call for conversion to, and to nurture, the recovery of lively, attentive personal questioning and deep valuing, starting with attention to the gospel itself.

CONTEMPORARY DEMONIZATION AND POLARIZATION: CONVERSION TO DIVINE BEARINGS

The church is increasingly marked today by a polarization between postmodern liberal and fundamentalist Christians. Although each of these sees themselves as faithful to the truth regarding Christ and their opponents as unfaithful, the views of each reflect as much the influence of modern ideology and culture as they reflect Christ. In particular, the polarization between them has much to do with the logical inversion just described in Conversion Three.

The liberal Christian tradition, for its part, has long celebrated faith as opposing prejudice in the name of attentive openness towards truth, opposing oppression in pursuit of liberty, and opposing self-delusion in the name of honesty and integrity. The Evangelical Christian tradition, meanwhile, has celebrated faith as opposing betrayal of the truth in honor to the demands of allegiance to the truth, opposing disobedience in honor to the demands of trustworthy obedience, and opposing doubt with confident trust. Both these liberal and evangelical celebrations of faith are right in what they oppose. However, they tend each to be blind to the error that the other opposes, and are each therefore vulnerable themselves to falling into the error in question, calling forth a proper reprimand from the other. Equally, each tends not to recognize when the other properly challenges their own error, assuming instead that any such challenge is a false one arising out of the error that they themselves are intent habitually to oppose.

This lack of discrimination and self-awareness on each side has developed further in more recent postmodern liberalism and fundamentalism. Polarization arises as faith now gets *defined by* reference to what is seen as its opposite. At this point a particular enemy of faith gets demonized as *the* enemy; in effect bearings are taken (negatively) from it and not from God. It becomes, ironically, a hidden, spectral "idol." In the case of liberal Christians this happens when, in a postmodern non-realist development, faith gets *defined as* resistance to commitment to any religious truth-claim; it happens for evangelical Christians when, in a fundamentalist development, faith gets *defined as* resistance to any questioning of certain religious truth-claims. In each case, faith gets defined in a way that betrays the character of attentiveness to God as fully a matter *both* of lively personal questioning *and* of commitment. Their polarization thus reflects as much a (distorted) Cartesian epistemology as it reflects opposing views upon doctrines.

Such polarization is illustrated by (1) an encounter between John Spong and Don Cupitt, and (2) the controversy over "creationism."

When faith is thus defined by that against which it stands in opposition, it changes from radical attentiveness to the truth into an act of self-definition that, cut adrift from such attentiveness, is of a distorted kind. The postmodern liberal lays claim to faith as an act of personal self-construction, while the fundamentalist claims it as bestowing personal identity through allegiance; in either case, the central object of concern is the "self."

This polarization within the church echoes certain polarizations in wider modern society. Two such wider developments are (1) conservative "fundamentalist" reactions against the erosion of traditional cultures such as Naziism and radical Islamic ideology, and (2) progressive fundamentalisms such as the phenomenon of "moral inversion" described by Michael Polanyi. Both reflect ambiguities at the root of modern critical theory that are already discernible in the philosophy of John Locke.

If we turn to consider more widely within Christian history, the pursuit of the truth of God in the face of a recognized enemy of faith, it is vital that we discern between historical responses of two kinds: those where an antithetical stance has arisen as proper to inculturation, and those that conceal a negative form of syncretism ironically captive to that which it demonizes.

The Christian vocation today is to call the protagonists within a polarizing church each to recognize the possibility of their own ideological captivity, and to be converted to a deeper Christian self-awareness before God, which involves integrally both receptivity and critical appraisal. The ensuing readiness to learn from the other—without forsaking responsibility—is not about compromising, but about participation in a shared covenantal stance under God. This call includes a distinctive challenge both to liberal and evangelical Christian thinking, in order that they may each maintain their faithfulness to Christ.

THE NEEDY CONSUMER:
CONVERSION TO THE ABUNDANCE OF GOD

Although the cultural trajectory of "the modern" is informed by explicit principles propounded in the European Enlightenment, it is not adequately described by reference to the dominance of these ideas and of the social structures shaped by them. The application of Enlightenment principles has also affected in a personal and practical way people's openness to deep and lively enquiry—including its paradigmatic form in Christian faith. The modern failure theoretically to grasp either the nature of such deep and lively enquiry, or the nature of evasion, or to take seriously the difference between them, has in practice endorsed evasive personal stances of proud dismissal and despairing disorientation. We have already noted practical consequences of this sort in the loss of deference to God, the erosion of personal life in community, and the slide towards a culture of distraction. Also complicit with these is the contemporary consumerist way of life.

The key practical and personal dimensions of modern life associated with these developments can be explored by reference to David Riesman's account of character formation in his classic *The Lonely Crowd* and Richard Sennett's *The Fall of Public Man*. Central to the practical, personal developments described here is the new cultural prominence of narcissism. Christopher Lasch's writings—especially *The Culture of*

Narcissism—draw attention to the wide-ranging ways in which this distortion of character is reflected in many aspects of life in modern culture.

A Christian appraisal of this development may begin from the classical Greek myth of Narcissus and Echo. These mythical figures may be interpreted as each in their own way representing the person who refuses trusting relationship with God within the limitations and under the demands of creaturely existence. For solitary Narcissus in particular, this refusal leads from proud dismissiveness to despair in which he is overwhelmed with longing for an unattainable "self." Like Echo, his life becomes defined by reference to "the unattainable." Evasive of, and disoriented and defeated by, the demands of living with hope, he enacts a lived contradiction of hope in God, of relatedness, and of personal participation in God's purposes. Correspondingly, the modern Narcissus has given up hope of being affirmed and incorporated within the loving purposes of God, and fixes upon an imagined "self" that alone matters; the whole world is seen merely as an extension of this self and as existing to serve it. This fixation conceals despair; it is driven by, and secretly frames, a radical sense of lack. In effect the normatively "real" is here displaced away from anything in which one may discover oneself to be a personal participant.

The "plausibility structure" for this fiction of finding oneself through union with the unattainable "real" is provided by modern consumerism. For the modern Narcissus the "real" comes to lie today not in that which is personally homemade but in the mass-produced product with a brand name; not in that which can be achieved personally in self-reliance but in the professional job; not in the hero to be emulated personally but in the celebrity to be envied; not in the community that invites personal participation but in the soap opera to be watched. Various critiques of consumerism touch on its complicity with such personal alienation. It is in the fostering of narcissism and neediness that consumerism develops an idolatrous and enslaving character.

The contemporary prominence of narcissism and neediness has roots, we have seen, in features of the Enlightenment vision and in the social structures that these have generated. Today narcissism and neediness are often inflamed and exploited by those wishing to manage and manipulate the public for power or profit.

The Christian vocation today is to call people to live by the abundance of God who has gracefully hosted us and endowed us with life—life as a creature of God who is oriented towards life with God, and may participate now in this promised reality to come.

THE TRAGIC SENSE OF LIFE:
CONVERSION TO THE GOSPEL OF HOPE

Narcissistic tendencies and personal neediness, prominent in Western culture today, reflect an abandonment of hope. This abandonment is not an act merely of "self-expression"; rather it enacts a view *of the world itself,* as a world offering no hope.

This way of seeing the world can be defined as a "tragic sense of life." Evoked with unique power in classical Greek tragedy, this sense of life apprehends the world as a place in which humankind is ultimately mocked by catastrophic and irredeemable loss that sears the human soul.

In the history of drama, a "tragic sense of life" was, according to George Steiner, eclipsed by "Judaeo-Christian optimism." However, signs of its re-emergence in popular Western culture have been noted by researchers. These signs appear in a range of cultural features, but most strikingly in "tragic spirituality" and intense victim sensibility occasioned by extreme circumstances.

"Tragic spirituality" presents itself in mass outpourings of emotion following tragedies such as the death of Diana, The Princess of Wales, and in such practices as the placing of floral bouquets and memorabilia at the scene of fatal traffic accidents. Victim sensibility presents itself in outrage and sometimes in violence in the name of a victim who has been exalted to "sacred" status. Intense victim sensibility also fuels the formulation and enforcement of draconian legislation against certain recognized, recurrent forms of victimization.

Tragic spirituality and victim sensibility have been criticized by Patrick West as "fake." In *Conspicuous Compassion* he draws upon the work of Stjepan Meštrović, who, in *Postemotional Society*, describes the synthesizing and cuing of emotion through mass manipulation. This process exploits and reinforces what John Macmurray called "unreal feeling." It may also be seen as exploiting the fantasy of "corporate personality" that, together with narcissism, marks the "intimate society" described by Richard Sennett.

However, while granting its "fake" aspect, conspicuous compassion—in hand with narcissism—originates in an unbearable loss of hope. This loss is real, and is associated with such features of contemporary modernity as the erosion of family and community life with its personal relationships and roles, the undermining of confidence in progress or even a public vision of goodness and truth, and the fading of Christian faith.

The dissolution of hope informs diverse features of Western culture today. These include narcissism and needy consumerism; credulity and promiscuity; escapism through addictive pleasure and fantasies of control; and a fondness for Hollywood-type stories in which unreal sentimental solutions are offered in a heartless world.

At the centre of all this lies the distinctive contradiction within a tragic sense of life: a world from which personal meaning is absent—the impersonal "secular" world conceived by the secularist vision—confronts us with a mocking personal face that mocks us precisely by the absence of the personal.

The gospel has often been preached, within modernity, as challenging people to give up modern pride in autonomy and self-sufficiency, and hand over control to God. In the context of the contemporary loss of hope, however, the Christian vocation is to preach the gospel that calls people not to be overwhelmed by the bad, but by God. This means taking personal responsibility for living to the glory of a good God who blesses us and reaches out to us in unconditional forgiveness. The crucifixion and resurrection of Jesus manifest this gospel.

PERSONAL FULFILLMENT AND CONTEMPORARY SPIRITUALITY: CONVERSION TO ETERNAL LIFE

Contemporary Western culture is marked by illusory hope, behind which lies the actual loss of personal hope noted above. Prominent is pursuit of the fulfillment of our personal potential for "life." Such fully realized life is held to be something that we must each define for ourselves; it is to be attained by enacting personal choices. However, its pursuit is held generally to incorporate certain elements, notably pursuit of the goals defined by health and beauty, health and fitness, and health and wholeness. The cultivation of life entails self-valuing, self-care, mastery, and faith in "nature."

This contemporary exaltation of "life" may be compared and contrasted with the Christian hope of eternal life in fulfillment of God's promises.

W. Visser 't Hooft remarked upon the exaltation of "life" in 1937. Later he characterized this as "neo-paganism," setting it in the historical context of paganism and contrasting it with Christian faith. His account may be fruitfully updated.

The pursuit of "life" informs much contemporary "spirituality." Paul Heelas and Linda Woodhead in their research report a new popular outlook upon religion and spirituality today. They define this by its opposition to what it turns away from: it exalts freedom in place of domination, choice in place of conformity, self-trust in place of trust in authority, and guidance from feelings in place of guidance from dogmas.

Heelas and Woodhead see this shift in outlook as a change in the focus of value from *God* to *life*. However, for Christians the promise of God is precisely life; it is not an alternative to life. Accordingly, what they describe must be either the pursuit of what God actually promises (albeit unacknowledged), or the pursuit of an illusory substitute for this.

In their account, the "life" to which supreme value is ascribed today is defined by opposition to the same enemy as that which the Enlightenment opposed. Correspondingly, the pursuit of "life" generates the same one-sided distortions as those of the Enlightenment described in conversion 4, framed now in more personal terms. Thus, whereas a true orientation towards life—eternal life—integrates responsible personal judgment, on the one hand, with attentive, receptive regard towards the truth, on the other, the modern vision of "life" simply exalts unlimited individual choice and fulfillment. In so doing, on the one hand, it wrongly scorns regard towards the truth, failing to distinguish this from false subservience to dogma and tradition. On the other hand, it wrongly slips into the bondage of subjective feeling, in blindness to the distinction between this and personal freedom.

However, the shift in outlook identified by Heelas and Woodhead is also as much a "postmodern" reaction against the Enlightenment itself as it is modern. Central to it is the "subjective turn" that constructs a world to inhabit that is more congenial to personal life than the world of Enlightenment rationalism. This involves both abandonment to the romance of nature on the one hand, and the illusory pursuit of mastery on the other: "alternative" therapies employing *simulacrae* of science extend further the scope today of surrogate science which has arisen in response to the latter.

The contemporary exaltation of "life" thus inhabits the same contradiction as modern life in general, driven by despairing echoes of the pagan gods Apollos and Dionysius. The Christian vocation today is to call for conversion to an antithetical hope. Christian hope embraces the limitations and ambiguities of created life, affirms the project of natural science as an account of the natural order, and embraces the Creator's gift and promise of eternal life in Jesus Christ.

THE IDEOLOGY OF RIGHTS AND POLITICAL CORRECTNESS: CONVERSION TO GOD-GIVEN DIGNITY

The modern project of "gardening" culture (Ernst Gellner) by reference to certain explicit principles has intensified in recent decades, facilitated by advances in information and communications technology. Two public ideologies have held central place in this process: the ideology of individual rights and the ideology of free-market capitalism.

The ideology of rights has origins in the Christian tradition of rights, in which the affirmation of rights belonging to the human subject ("subjective rights") derives from a concern to pursue and uphold what is right in the eyes of a good and just God.

In the modern secular liberal tradition, rights have become a kind of property belonging naturally to the individual. They have been promulgated to provide strategic protection against oppression of the individual by others, particularly the state, where the latter claims autonomous power of action rather than acknowledging that it derives legitimation from, and bears responsibility before, a good God. Accordingly the promulgation of rights featured especially at the outset of the modern period (in response to the dissolution of the web of rights and responsibilities characterizing of feudal society), in the 1948 Universal Declaration of Human Rights (in response to the failure of Christian and civilized values to hold Nazis back from "crimes against humanity"), and in recent decades (in response to the threats and requirements imposed by the intensification of global capitalism).

As the liberal understanding of rights has gradually lost tacit roots in Christian faith, it has contributed to a modern cultural trajectory that is increasingly divergent from that of openness to the in-breaking kingdom of God. In particular, its abstraction from a Christian context has generated problematic issues in the following respects:

1. It has diminished, in popular understanding, the scope of morality.

2. It has constructed on its own reductive basis a framework for understanding that which properly constitutes right action, generating the distortions of "political correctness."

3. It has subverted the actual springs of concern for justice, sponsoring rhetoric while failing in general to motivate authentic practical concern for justice.

4. It fails to reach beyond an incoherent moral framework comprising the incommensurate claims of individual rights and an ethic of organizational utility.

5. It lacks any basis for reconciling competing claims between one right and another, and between the rights of one person and another.

6. It leaves rights severed from the religious and social framework within which they are conceived in the first place and by reference to which their claims are corporately acknowledged.

7. Exalting individual choice as a right, it severs human freedom from its true sources in responsiveness to God and to fellow human beings.

Whereas the ideology of individual rights aspires to uphold human dignity, it is often impotent to do so and may even end up subverting it. The Christian vocation today is to expose this, to call for conversion to the true source of human dignity in God, and to uphold the dignity of every human being in the light of this understanding.

NEOLIBERAL CAPITALIST IDEOLOGY: CONVERSION TO THE "COMMON-WEAL" OF GOD

Like the ideology of individual rights, neoliberal capitalist ideology sponsors a program of rationalization; it pursues a social trajectory, seeking to conform society more closely to a particular normative framework. Both in rights ideology and neoliberal ideology, the framework in question can be understood as abstracted from and ambiguously related to the purposes of God for human life in the world. For its part, the program sponsored by rights ideology aims to conform the world more closely to the human—more specifically, to the abstractly conceived autonomous

human individual, conceived in abstraction from concrete human beings related to God and to other human beings. Neoliberal capitalist ideology aims, in a parallel way, to conform human life more closely to the
world—more specifically, to an abstractly conceived economic model
for the world, conceived in abstraction from its relation to God and to
human life. Each of these programs of rationalization is fundamentally
rationalistic; each represents the narrowing of rationality from a richer
rationality open to God's sovereign approach.

Each of these programs of rationalization, or social trajectories,
inclines towards a "religious" exaltation of its method and goal as the
defining good on the stage of world history. Rights ideology exalts the
rights-bearing autonomous individual (abstractly conceived) as absolute agent, subject, and embodiment of worth; neoliberal ideology exalts
autonomously owned private capital in a parallel way. Insofar as they do
so, each is idolatrous. Christian faith rather exalts God as the sovereign
agent, subject, and embodiment of worth.

In Christian tradition, employment and trade have an important
place in the responsible stewardship of God's creation and the maximization of human well-being as an experience of God's blessing. In
neoliberal capitalist ideology, however, commerce is made absolute and
autonomous, invested with defining moral and religious meaning, and
extended in scope so as to provide a framework for all aspects of human
life, shaping them according to its own principles and profit motives.
It is an irony that the new liberty with which this framework shapes
social change today has been declared by some as marking the "end of
ideology" precisely at the moment when the program that Marx called
an ideology—*viz.* capitalism—has become the occasion of intensified
ideological commitment.

Neoliberal capitalist ideology effectively exalts capital as the unqualified, unambiguous agent of good. Capital is made fertile in itself
and the defining source of fertility. Humanity is made to play a role subservient to this, the role of human resources maximally at its disposal.
Debt repayments become the purest expression of the fertility of capital
and of human dependence upon capital.

The worldview of neoliberal ideology has in recent decades been
crafted and promulgated very deliberately. Ideological rhetoric has been
formulated to present as "natural" features of capitalism that in reality
are deliberately constructed and maintained. Examples of such rhetoric

include "wealth creation," "trickle-down," "free market"/deregulation, and "consumer choice." Such principles have, between them, been divorced from and overridden other principles upheld within a richer Christian context such as the vision of service, the place of "commons," market reciprocity between buyer and seller, the principles of fair price, fair profit and fare wage, and the freedoms associated with complex and locally diverse economies. Most fundamentally, they subvert the Christian vision of the substantive good and of responsible service directed towards this good.

The Christian vocation today is to challenge the "totalizing" rhetoric of neoliberal capitalist ideology and relocate its principles within a Christian context. It is to seek a conversion in which the agent of substantive good and wealth is found definitively in God, human indebtedness is found definitively in indebtedness towards God in his graciousness, and the rationalization of society is found definitively in receptivity and responsibility towards God's good purposes.

PUBLIC FACTS AND PRIVATE VALUES: CONVERSION TO THE SOVEREIGNTY OF GOD

Those who manage society today view Christian faith often as a matter of "private" religious beliefs and values that should not be allowed to influence the conduct of secular public life based on reason and free enquiry. In this concluding chapter we draw from insights in previous chapters to appraise this view and to set the vision of public life more adequately in a Christian context.

Christian faith proclaims the sovereignty of God. It seeks to be open towards, and to open the world towards, God's in-breaking, liberating kingdom. Correspondingly, it is called to resist anything that effectively claims sovereignty over, or rivalry towards, God. Sometimes the claims of state, official *cultus*, or ideology call for resistance among Christians. Thus the early church resisted Roman imperial ideology, which venerated the Roman Emperor as divine; the church claimed divinity rather for Christ. Similarly today Christian faith is called to resist contemporary ideology when it dogmatically exalts as sacred certain liberties so as to subvert the true liberty that is realized in grace-filled enquiry and action at its most lively, deep, and personal in openness to the sovereign approach of God.

The contemporary ideological pursuit of liberty is producing a society increasingly constrained by "illiberal liberalism," on the one hand, (one form of this is found in rights ideology and another in neoliberal capitalist ideology), and subverted by a tolerance indifferent to truth, on the other (expressed in the exaltation of "choice"). The former is associated with ideological programs for the rationalization of society; it is fed by a fundamentally dismissive evasion of the demands of receptiveness to God. The latter is associated with disoriented personal life; it is fed by a fundamentally despairing evasion of the demands of personal responsibility under God.

In British society today, these distortions appear to be worsening. They can be described in terms of Martin Marty's characterization, in *The Modern Schism*, of the divergent forms taken by secularity in Britain, the United States, and continental Europe, and the impact of the second and third of these upon British society today. In Britain this brings an accompanying loss of moral bearings as the vision of tolerance drifts increasingly towards indifference to truth, from its root meaning in its historical origins in the eighteenth-century English Christian formulation of religious tolerance.

The claim that the gospel is "public truth" is often rejected today as an attempt to restore political "Constantinianism." It is no such thing. What it does claim, however, is that the very meaning of "public" and "private" are most richly defined and nourished in a Christian context of greater liberty and when the distinction between them is framed relative to this. Such meaning may be discernable in the historical construction in England of the "public domain" as a domain of participation and service. However, Enlightenment secularist assumptions have, from the start, driven a different understanding of public and private as supposedly mutually exclusive, autonomous realms. This distorts our understanding of public and private and indeed of the "secular" realm as such. It prompts us to conceive of and inhabit public space either as a social construction in which the legitimate possibilities for action are formally prescribed (the dominant outlook of continental European political ideology) or as a space in which all "choices" (apart from those prohibited by law) are permitted as a matter of public indifference, being relativistic expressions of individual autonomy (the dominant outlook of consumerism). The former effectively turns public space into a state-owned private domain, while the latter sponsors a moral and social vacuum.

These developments have impoverished the vision and practice of public life and public service today. Faced with this, Christians are called not to settle for a private niche in a society either ideologically multi-faith or secularist. The Christian vocation today is, rather, to call for conversion to, and to host, richer, freer, more lively expressions of public life and public service than those hosted by the secular state. This conversion is to a new hospitality rooted in the ultimate vision of offering the whole of public life to God in his sovereignty.

1

SECULAR AND SACRED IN CONTEMPORARY UNDERSTANDING

Conversion to Creation and New Creation by God

THE "SECULAR" VIEW OF THE SACRED

PEOPLE WITH A MODERN secular education tend to think of religion, including Christian religion, in a particular way. They tend to see it as laying down beliefs and practices, in principle for any area of life whatsoever, that bear divine warrant. These are proclaimed by religion as right, important, and necessary and not to be questioned or violated; they are authoritative and to be trusted. According to the educated secular viewpoint, however, they are no such thing, but this does not matter fundamentally since (it is held) people can do perfectly well without religion; we can live responsibly and organize our society and our world in a reasonable, sensible way without reference to religion. Indeed religion tends to hinder us from freely thinking and acting in a responsible way by its insistence upon "absolute" dogmas and rules. For this reason, religion is therefore best kept out of public debate and policymaking.

This way of thinking about positive or revealed religion is characteristically modern. By "modern" I mean informed by the European Enlightenment; in what follows I shall continue using the word "modern" in this scholarly sense rather than in the casual popular sense of "up to date." This way of thinking extends towards other concepts related to religion including the "sacred," the "spiritual," and the "divine": belief in such things in general is seen as blocking reasonable, critical, responsible thought and action. In what follows we need to hold in mind this range of concepts, while acknowledging the variations in meaning between them.

The modern secular view of religious matters has taken shape and gained ground in a particular historical setting. It originated in medieval Christendom and had in view, first and foremost, medieval Christian belief and practice itself. And this view was not without some justification. Nevertheless, it quite misconceives the living heart of Christian faith while also misunderstanding (or refusing) to examine properly its own secular outlook.

In order more faithfully to understand both Christian faith and the secular outlook, we have to challenge the latter's assumption of two opposed views of the world—the religious and secular. We must see these, together with the opposition that the secular outlook conceives between them, in the wider context suggested by Christian faith itself as it has been explored in the first part of this book. This invites us to understand the sacred and the secular by reference to *three* bearings. I shall call these the sacral worldview, the Christian worldview, and the secularist worldview. Let us consider each of these in turn. As we do so, we shall introduce ideas and topics to be elaborated later under other headings.

THE SACRAL WORLDVIEW

Medieval Christians believed that a certain plant with heart-shaped leaves had been given by God to ease the heart, and so they called it "Heartsease"; they believed that a plant with blotched leaves had been given to heal diseases of the lung, and called it "Lungwort." They believed that the appearance of these plants was given by God as a clue to their human usefulness. This set of beliefs is called the "doctrine of signatures."

Christians today do not regard this as a true Christian doctrine. Not only so: Christians today do not regard it as a true Christian doctrine *that the world and God are like this*. Christian faith does not call us to this fundamental worldview.

The basic view of the world and of God that is reflected in the medieval doctrine of signatures is rooted in what is called a "sacral" worldview. Such a worldview can be traced widely in ancient history. An illustration of this concerns a wild relation of the French Marigold, native to Mexico. This plant was regarded by ancient pre-Inca farmers as sacred to their agricultural gods. They planted it among their root crops to protect them. Today it is known that the plant, *Tagetes minuta*, exudes a natural pesticide effective against eelworms and other root pests.

This ancient belief belongs to a sacral view of the world, of the divine, and of how they connect. In this worldview, the familiar world of both nature and human culture is taken as having features given directly by divine mandate and as such sacred in their own right. The worlds of the divine, of the human, and of nature are united in an enclosed religious cosmology, which is typically unchanging or cyclical in pattern. Within this world, certain places, objects, events, etc., may have a special sacred status and be a special channel of access to the power and authority of the cosmic whole: in nature there may be sacred mountains and springs, and sacred events such as full moon; in human culture, sacred rituals (notably sacrifice) and taboos. There may also be invocation of sacred powers in the practice of magic. And there may also be a vision of mystical possession by the divine. These sacred things command deference. They are not be meddled with or questioned. The price for violating them is imponderable, being a violation of the cosmic upon which human life is utterly dependent.

A sacral society is one in which the sacral worldview reigns among its members. To indwell this worldview is, using Max Weber's terminology, to inhabit an "enchanted" world. Another term used for such society or worldview is "ontocratic." Premodern societies are generally of this kind.

THE CHRISTIAN WORLDVIEW

Archaic sacral societies were many and, for all the cosmic claims of each, they varied according to culture, tribe, and locality. In some regions of the world, wider civilizations later formed that loosely incorporated local religions within a common horizon. These gave rise to what have been called the historical "axial" religions including Hinduism and Buddhism. Such religions have tended to set local religions in the context of a dualistic worldview that devalues the claims of the material world and posits the sacred in another, parallel realm. Such religions have raised no radical challenge to sacral worldviews, but have rather coexisted in unresolved tension with them.

Biblical and Christian religion represent a quite different development. Their story is similarly one of historical engagement with sacral worldviews, opening up each and all to new horizons. But here a radical challenge and transformation is under way. Here the sacred is found not in nature or culture, but in the transcendent personal creator of the world who acts within creation. He acts through signs to reveal, and to bring to effect, his good purposes. These purposes embrace the whole of creation. Central to them is God's will to draw humankind into personal relationship with himself. Here "the sacred" acquires new and unfathomable meaning in God, while nature and culture acquire new meaning as *signs* of God and of God's purposes. In this development, all that has belonged previously to the sacral world is engaged and given new meaning relative to a transcendent God. All creation becomes material for the worship of this God; and all human life is summoned to become a living sacrifice under the sovereign rule of God.

Such desacralization of the world was inaugurated in ancient biblical faith, turning Canaanite sacred fertility rites into celebrations of God's sovereign and saving acts in history. More generally, the Bible can be understood as narrating a recurrent battle by the prophets and others against the resacralization of the gifts that God had given as signs of his purpose in creation: covenants of people and land, monarchy, temple, and law. Such signs found their consummation (and redemption, when they had become resacralized) in Jesus Christ, in whom the entire world is to be transformed into the kingdom of God.

When, in the early centuries of the church, the Christian gospel was taken to non-Jewish cultures, the biblical story of desacralization was echoed in engagement with local religion and culture. This process of "contextualization" or "inculturation" of the gospel—in which, under the guidance of the Spirit, the gospel message re-embodies itself in signs particular to a new culture—involves desacralization of that culture relative to Christian faith. The key elements in the history of this have been depicted succinctly by Andrew Walls.[1] Also echoed, however, was the biblical story of a recurrent tendency of slipping back into a sacral worldview and of the proper battle to resist this. We may put it that "inculturation" is always vulnerable to distorting into syncretism as sacral religion reinterprets the gospel in its own terms. Such domestication of the gospel has always been a threat. This threat takes a special form where Christian faith engaged with civilization-wide worldview features that stand apart from local culture, as did Greek rationalism and Roman

1. See for example Walls, "Culture and Coherence," and other essays in "Part 1: The Transmission of Christian Faith," in *Missionary Movement in Christian History.* On the historical depiction of the figure of Christ himself in diverse cultural terms, see Pelikan, *Jesus.*

imperial ideology.[2] The struggle to transform religion and culture into authentic signs of God has typically been a struggle extending over generations as people's imaginations are formed more deeply and comprehensively by Christian belief and practice. This struggle weaves an ongoing story of success, defeat, and renewal.

It is of vital importance to recognize that the Christian worldview is different both from a sacral and a secularist worldview. It is important to recognize its distinction from a "sacral," "enchanted," or "ontocratic" worldview today at a time when some Christian theologians are responding to secularism by commending a "re-enchantment" of the world in one respect or another, and other world religions stand for the same. In this setting, it is right to emphasize the authentic "desacralizing" character of Christian faith, as does Harold Turner:

> This feature of contingency and openness in the relation between the world and divinity belongs to what we have called the de-sacralized world. There is a whole range of terms to be found in use here. In this new understanding the universe is also called "de-animized," "de-magicized," "disenchanted," de-mystified," "demythologized," and even (in its proper sense) "secularized" or "profane" used as the correlate of "sacred." I shall continue to use the term "desacralized" as indicating this process most clearly.[3]

The contrast between a Christian worldview and a sacral one is expressed from one point of view by C. S. Lewis in popular style. He writes:

> [T]he doctrine of Creation leaves nature full of manifestations which show the presence of God, and created energies which serve Him ... the thunder can be His voice (Psalm 29:3–5) ... this is clearly in one way close to Paganism ... But the difference, though subtle, is momentous, between hearing in the thunder the voice of God and the voice of a god ... the voice of a god is not really a voice from beyond the world, from the uncreated. By taking the god's voice away ... the thunder becomes not less divine but more. By emptying Nature of divinity—or, let us say, of divinities—you may now fill her with Divinity, for she is now the bearer of messages. There is a sense in which nature-worship

---

2. Sherrard, *East and West*.

3. Turner, *Roots of Science*, 62. On sacral or ontocratic society as the context of biblical desacralization, see especially van Leeuwen, *Christianity*.

silences her—as if a child or a savage were so impressed by the postman's uniform that he omitted to take in the letters.[4]

It is equally important today to distinguish a Christian worldview from a secularist one.[5] This is because Christian theology has been distorted in modern history by deism and (less obviously) by theism, both of which posit a world self-sufficient apart from any integral context in God's sacred purposes for creation.[6]

MEDIEVAL CHRISTENDOM

Modern society was born out of medieval Christendom and cannot be understood apart from this. Medieval society itself had come into being in Europe out of the "dark ages" that followed the collapse of the Roman Empire. During this period Christian monasteries had maintained their communal life and they eventually became the centers around which the wider communities of European medieval society developed. Saint Augustine had offered intellectual foundations for such a society in Trinitarian faith. The society that emerged was an officially Christian one, in which the monasteries and the church held much power. However, church authority was not such as to constitute a theocracy; church and

---

4. Lewis, *Reflections on the Psalms*, 70–71.

5. I realize that my terminology may be misunderstood. Terms such as "desacralization" and "secular" get used in differing ways. However, the most important thing, given the Christian understanding of the relation between our self-disclosing God and the creation through which God discloses himself, is that we find the necessary terminology to distinguish this on the one hand in a timeless, sacral worldview, and on the other from in a secularist (or for that matter, deist) worldview. By "desacralization" I most certainly do *not* mean the adoption of a "secularist" worldview, but a Christian understanding of the secular as the provisional or "*saeculum.*" This use of "secular" is fully consistent with the recognition that creation shines with the glory of God. I acknowledge, however, that this claim is paradoxical to those who follow the general usage the term "secular," which has lost virtually all Christian reference. Moreover, I grant that often I myself refer to "secular thinking," "secular professions" etc. without adverting to this issue. In passing, we might note that similar problems of terminology arise when talking about, for example, "contexualization," "liberalism," and "fundamentalism."

6. The continuing recovery of Trinitarian theology during recent decades is important here. On knowledge of God as personal participation in the communion of the Divine Trinity, see Torrance, *Persons in Communion*. On the contribution to this of the Eastern Orthodox doctrine of "deification," see Allchin, *World Is a Wedding*. For an early twentieth-century insistence that Christian theology transcends classical theism, see, for example, Forsyth, *Principle of Authority*, 99. On the origins and current decline of philosophical theism as a modern concept, see Dalferth, "Historical Roots of Theism."

state were not fused together. While its rulers could be challenged by church leaders, medieval society was, under the patronage of Christian faith, free from any sacral blueprint. In the social space opened up in this way, medieval Christendom sponsored a period of uniquely lively and sustained social change.[7]

Alongside this, a sacral view of the world also persisted in Christian guise in medieval society. Medieval people saw themselves as living in a cosmos ordered by God.[8] The relation between God and the earth was understood as the relation between two worlds—the spiritual, eternal, invisible world of heaven and the material, temporary, visible world of earth. These worlds were seen as joined together through sacred places (churches) and sacred people (Jesus above all; then the saints, prophets, bishops, and kings). Time was ordered by sacred religious festivals and seasons. Participation in the sacraments was seen popularly as secur-ing one's personal standing before God; and the general population conformed to the baptism of infants, church weddings, and funerals required by a church exercising territorial authority. Christian faith also entailed conformity in assent to the creed and in obedience to the Ten Commandments.

Of particular influence in this medieval religious culture was its heritage of Roman and Greek civilization. Christian faith had lived in close engagement with these civilizations in the early centuries of the church, and their influence was renewed in the Renaissance. In retro-spect we must ask with regard to both influences whether Christian faith was not captive to them in ways of great consequence for the vision and course of modern history that followed.

In *Roman civilization* the emperor was exalted as a divine figure who subdued chaos and brought universal order to the world. The influ-ence of this ideology upon the Latin church is apparent in the latter's ju-ridical and territorial structures of authority growing especially from the time of Constantine onwards, and again later in the self-understanding of the church in medieval society and the organization of that society in relation to the church.[9] This question arises: do we see, in medieval

7. On the globally unique vitality of culture in Western medieval Christendom, see Dawson, *Religion*, chapter 1.

8. For an illuminating introduction to the medieval Christian worldview, see Lewis, "Imagination and Thought in the Middle Ages."

9. Philip Sherrard cites, in this respect, Henri de Lubac's documentation of the me-dieval "degeneration" of "the idea of the essentially sacramental nature of the Church"

Christianity, a faithful Christian engagement with, and transformation of, Roman imperial ideology? Or do we see Christian faith captured by, and domesticated to, this ideology? Which way should we interpret, for example, the great wooden screen placed by King Henry VIII in the centre of Kings College Chapel, Cambridge, and modeled on a Roman imperial archway? Was "constantinianism" an authentic, inculturated form of Christianity? The question is of import for interpreting, for example, the advent of Christian religious wars in the sixteenth century.

Turning to classical *Greek civilization*, human individuals were held to possess a divine spark within them in a rational and naturally immortal soul. The influence of this belief upon the church is apparent from the Greek apologists onwards. Again early in the medieval period the philosophy of Aristotle acquired new influence as Thomas Aquinas responded to its use by Islamic scholars, providing a Christian interpretation of it. Again, the question arises: do we see in medieval Christianity a faithful engagement with and transformation of Greek rationalism? Or do we see—in, for example, the theoretical separation of natural and supernatural, reason and revelation—the domestication of Christian faith to such rationalism? This question, too, is of import for interpreting the European Enlightenment and the ideas that it promulgated.

THE BIRTH OF EXPERIMENTAL SCIENCE

Turning to the world of nature, again we find elements of a sacral worldview persisting. The classical Greek view of a natural world imbued with divinity and eternal remained largely in place.

Against this background, experimental science arose as a crucial breakthrough in the scope of desacralization. Already in the first millennium AD, however, the seeds of such science had germinated in Christian soil nourished by its doctrine of a created world at once rational and contingent. Where nature had been taken as a sacral order

---

(Lubac, *Corpus Mysticum*). According to Sherrard, this nature becomes "veiled" "by the conception of a visible Church as—to use Ciceronian terms—a great *civitas*, or constitution, or corporation, modelled on the pattern of the city of God, the invisible Church, under the government of a single, divinely appointed authority, the supreme pontiff who, like Moses, or the Roman Pontifex Maximus, is the chief guardian of that pattern on earth." Sherrard, *Greek East and the Latin West*, 86.

given by direct warrant of God, now the question arose of its deeper investigation as the creation of God.[10]

However, the pivotal role of Christian faith in sponsoring and nourishing experimental science was not well understood theoretically. Francis Bacon's characterization of science as "man putting nature to the question" was far from adequate. It described reasonably the experimental testing of hypotheses, but it gave no adequate account of how one arrives at a fruitful hypothesis in the first place. Fundamentally, the questions posed by scientists are raised for them by God's creation. These questions are raised as scientists attend deeply (in what we have called "radical responsiveness") to possible clues and their integration in the disclosure of a fruitful hypothesis, coherent entity, or heuristic framework. This is the deeper exploration upon which experimental science rests. The idea that it is the "scientific-minded" human agent who creates questions misrepresents alike God, creation, and human agents themselves. The baleful legacy of this misrepresentation remains today not only in sterile conflicts between science and religion but also in many wider ramifications for modern culture.

For its part, the church showed a continuing attachment to elements of a conservative, sacral worldview and this could lead it to interpret claims for the authority of science as contradicting its own authority— especially when propagandists for science imagined themselves presenting precisely such a challenge to religion. In the face of bold new ideas, the church tended too often to defend traditional beliefs and a "God" who lingered in the gaps of ignorance not yet closed by science.

Accordingly, there were questionable claims for authority to be found both in the church and among those who sought foundations for the emergent world elsewhere than in religion. Let us turn now to the latter.

ENLIGHTENMENT

Another feature of the medieval context in which modern society was born was religious conflict among Christians. Church reformers had

10. For discussion of the emergence of experimental science and its dependence upon elements within the Christian worldview, see Michael Foster's seminal article "The Christian Doctrine of Creation and the Rise of Modern Natural Science," 446–68. See also Hooykaas, *Religion and the Rise of Modern Science*; Jaki, *Road to Science and the Ways to God*; and Hodgson, *Theology and Modern Physics*, chapter 2.

protested against beliefs and practices in the Western church, contesting the church's authority in these matters and forming their own Protestant churches. The divided churches had then become party to religious wars. No longer did Christian faith appear a secure basis for social order and direction in the emergent world. Wolfhart Pannenberg writes: "The mutually conflicting positions of belief among the Christian confessional parties were bracketed off, and in place of religion based on traditional authority, that which is common to all human beings, human 'nature,' became the basis of public order and social peace. That became the starting point for a secular culture in Europe." [11]

Pannenberg argues that this should not be seen as a rebellion against faith, but as a largely pragmatic decision. The ensuing social and political program, led by thinkers who championed the diffusion of their ideas as enlightenment, was ambiguously related to Christian faith. Many leading thinkers of the day continued to profess Christian faith, as did the vast majority of the population. Also, their reasoning and understanding were deeply imbued with Christian beliefs and values, as will be apparent to a reader of their works today whether from any non-European culture or from contemporary Western secular culture. This was true, importantly, of precisely those elements in their thinking that guided the vision of enlightenment itself. For example, belief in progress drew nourishment from faith in the dawning of God's kingdom; altruism in pursuing the public good drew inspiration from the vocation of Christian service; and the affirmation of personal dignity and freedom was nourished by the doctrine that Christians are sons and daughters of God endowed with God's Spirit.

Conversely, those who professed Christian faith could precisely *ignore* the resources of faith when theorizing about the secular world in general. Thus Rene Descartes, searching for reliable guidance for managing change and new knowledge, had famously reasoned that the foundations for sure knowledge lay in the thinking self. Although Descartes affirmed belief in God, he did not allow this properly to shape the foundations of his philosophy of enquiry. Accordingly the complaint could be laid against him, attributed to his near contemporary Blaise Pascal, "I cannot forgive Descartes: in his whole philosophy he would like to do without God; but he could not help allowing him a flick of the fingers to set the world in motion; after that he had no more use for God."

11. Pannenberg, *Christianity in a Secularized World,* 13.

The issue of such betrayal of faith by Christian thinkers arose also in connection with ideas about knowledge. The Greek-influenced idea that human beings were, as individuals, endowed naturally with the power of universal, autonomous reason had affected how Christian revelation as such was understood. In particular it contributed to the idea that human knowledge had two distinct sources in reason and revelation. The former was seen as first-hand and sure; the latter was something to be taken, in trust, on authority.

THE SECULARIST OUTLOOK

For Enlightenment thinkers in general, the personal exercise of creative, responsible exploration and judgment was identified with the use of natural reason by innately good human beings. They were confident that this would provide a sound basis for the future of society. Their confidence was enhanced by the promise of experimental science to contribute to a growing body of universal and sure public knowledge.

The light of reason was seen generally as upholding familiar religious truths such as the existence of a good God who is our creator and judge. Thus far, "within the limits of reason," Christian faith might make a contribution to public life. Revealed Christian doctrine, by contrast, was seen as lying beyond the evidence of reason, a matter rather of propositions to be accepted on authority as true. Such acceptance was, as philosopher John Locke expressed it, "belief short of knowledge." Faith operated to the exclusion of reason, and reason to the exclusion of faith.

The resulting position was profoundly ambiguous vis-à-vis Christian faith. On the one hand, reasoning remained informed tacitly by Christian belief and practice. Even the opposition of modern thinkers to a continuing public role for church authority can be seen as directed rightly against sacral religion—not against faith itself—and as picking up the mantle of Christian desacralization of the world. The very secularization of society was in part driven, tacitly, by Christian faith.

On the other hand, the explicit prohibition of any public appeal to the authority of revealed religion pointed society in the direction of a public world shaped by and imbued with practical agnosticism or atheism. By the middle of the nineteenth century, when for the first time in England "secularism" drew attention as an explicit philosophy, broad swathes of the population—especially in the new industrial cities—

tacitly inhabited such a world even though few would ever join the elite circle of explicitly secularist thinkers.[12]

I shall use the term "secularist" for a viewpoint involving the explicit dismissal not only revealed doctrines about God, but of belief in God's very existence. I shall also use it for the outlook that treats faith in God *practically* in the same way, as no more than a private choice among religious believers. The term "secular*ist*" is preferable to "secular" here because the latter obscures the fact that the secular realm is itself grounded intrinsically in, and upheld for what it is, by Christian faith and its program of desacralization.

By definition, secularism fails to understand its Christian grounding. Believing in the autonomous goodness and rationality of human beings, it typically equates Christian faith with sacral religion, and sees itself (rather than Christian faith) as the sponsor of desacralization. Accordingly it wrongly envisions secularization and desacralization as each meaning the progressive elimination of Christianity and all religion. And it celebrates this.

Secularists, then, misrepresent the secular in their thinking. As a consequence they also, ironically, distort the path of modernization, secularization, and desacralization in practice. As G. K. Chesterton wrote, "[they] do not succeed in pulling up the roots of Christianity; but they do succeed in pulling up the roots of every man's ordinary vine and fig tree, of every man's kitchen garden. Secularists have not succeeded in wrecking divine things; but Secularists have succeeded in wrecking secular things."[13]

Such destruction and distortion comes about gradually. It comes about firstly as explicit secularism, even while remaining tacitly informed—without acknowledgement—by Christian faith, disparages such faith, and as implicit secularism ignores such faith in practice. It comes about, secondly, as reasoning itself loses its tacit bearings in Christian imagination and the stories that nourish it. The guiding principles of the modern vision such as human goodness and rationality, liberty, equality, progress, and tolerance, drift away from their moorings in Christian faith. They now assume for themselves, unacknowledged,

12. See for example, Wickham, *Church and People in an Industrial City*, chapters 4 and 5.

13. Chesterton, in the *Illustrated London News*, April 26, 1924.

autonomous status as religious doctrines rival to Christian faith and its doctrines.

While it is true that this has led today to a form of public life that might have surprised Enlightenment thinkers, this is nevertheless a result of their confidence in certain ideas—ideas they regarded as universal and immutable truths of reason—as guides to the future of society. Accordingly Oliver O'Donovan writes:

> The flowering of an idea comes when it assumes a structural role that determines what else may be thought. Its origin is never contemporary with its flowering, nor are its organizational implications apparent to the minds that first conceived it. And so, as historians may point out with perfect justice, the eighteenth century was actually formed far less by the "Enlightenment" ideas that we associate with it than by the older tradition of religion ideas common to Christendom ... It is we who find the Enlightenment ideas particularly important, because it is we who have seen them grow to form a matrix within which everything that is to be thought must be thought.[14]

Meanwhile the popular Christian imagination continues to be eroded, exposing to view secular humanism's Christian roots. Non-Christian author John Gray can recognize in various forms of secular humanism "hollowed-out versions of Christian myth." "Humanism," he writes, "is not an alternative to religious belief, but a degenerate and unwitting version of it."[15]

What is more, the humanist vision itself is losing depth in a landscape depleted, humanly speaking, by global capitalist ideology on the one hand and "politically correct" ideology on the other. In this landscape, a traditional liberal humanist can appear before a Christian like a familiar, if quarrelsome, partner with whom one has many intimately shared common concerns.

This continuing drift in the vision and principles guiding public life has too often gone unrecognized or engaged by the churches. Adrian Hastings writes of twentieth-century Christianity: "It could seem as if the churches themselves had been but the Trojan horse enabling their most subtle enemy to take possession of their dearest heartlands ... the massive decline of Christian influence within European society in this

---

14. Oliver O'Donovan, *Desire of the Nations*, 272.
15. Gray, *Myth of Secularism*.

period is not, then, due simply to an alien attacking from without, but at least as much to a formation of mind fostered by Christianity, and with many friends within its walls."[16]

SECULARIST RELIGION

Secularism has then effectively acquired an unacknowledged "religious" character of its own. On the one hand, it continues secretly to draw nourishment from Christian faith; on the other hand, it enacts unawares its own rival religiosity. In both respects, of course, it contradicts its own explicit account of itself and of the world. Secularist religiosity extends beyond its unacknowledged religious exaltation of its own stated principles. Jacques Ellul wrote in 1975: "[F]or nearly half a century we have witnessed a massive invasion by the sacred into our western world. Rational man has not been able to adhere to his rationality . . . The more man penetrates into himself the more he is led to question the systematic certitudes so painfully acquired during the nineteenth century . . . Man is forced to create something to serve as a sacred . . . the sacred is proliferating all around us."[17]

Too often, once again, the church has failed to recognize this or has acclaimed it uncritically and sought to patronize it. The church needs rather to recognize and engage wisely that which is rival to faith. Thus Lesslie Newbigin remarks upon the "pictures of the good life which are being ceaselessly pumped into every living room in the country, the advertisements and the soap operas which provide an image of the good life more powerful than anything Islam or mediaeval Christendom every managed to fasten on an entire population. Ours," he writes, "is not a secular society, but a society which worships false gods."[18]

Of course, secularists will not readily acknowledge that they inhabit their own "religious" world with its own "sacred" features, etc. Less still will they readily accept that their own ultimate symbols of liberty are in reality symbols of bondage. Nevertheless, as Henri de Lubac writes, "There have been tyrannical gods—and there is the God who makes us

16. Hastings, "The Twentieth Century," 229.

17. Ellul, *The New Demons*. For a discussion of the sacred hidden within modern secular culture, see "The Sacred Today," in ibid., 64–87.

18. Newbigin, *Foolishness to the Greeks*, 118.

free. Tyrant gods, nowadays, do not, as a rule, assume the names of gods. They prefer pseudonyms. But their tyranny remains the same."[19]

Newbigin perceives false gods in "pictures of the good life." Idolatry takes varied forms as it echoes in a distorted way various features of worship, religion, spirituality, and the sacred as these are defined by Christian faith and practice.

Idolatry can take the form of dogmatic allegiance to an ideology. Here a set of ideas is taken to define what counts as human advancement; Christian faith is excluded from this definition or domesticated to it; and a program of ideological rationalization is imposed upon society. Secularist, atheist philosophy is itself an example of this. Other examples of dogmatic allegiance to ideology arise with reference to the ideology of global capitalism and the ideology that seeks to construct society on the basis of comprehensively formulated human rights. We shall give further attention to these ideologies in chapters 8 and 9.

An idolatrous stance also arises wherever a practice or methodology is taken, explicitly or implicitly, to be all-sufficient: that is, to provide trustworthy means to achieve even the greatest of human ends. An important example of this arises in attitudes to technology. When technology is seen as a tool to be used responsibly to good human ends, it is imbued with no religious status. However, once it is seen, in however confused a way, as promising unlimited possibilities to those who use it, it has attracted "religious" deference. Thus technology may, as a tool, appear an intrinsically good means to any end such that it cannot be morally questioned but becomes, as a means, precisely an end in itself. Approached from the other end: it may appear to have the power to disclose ends—even unqualified power to disclose ultimate ends—and not just to provide the means to previously defined ends. At such points, technology begins in effect to offer "salvation"; it becomes the occasion of a "religious" faith.

Jacques Ellul has described how the awe once inspired among people by the natural world is in our own age inspired rather by *techne* or technology widely conceived. Today technology is, as Richard Stivers writes, "that which is the means of life and the greatest threat to life, that which is most immediate to us, and that which mediates all our relation-

---

19. de Lubac, *Discovery of God*, 193.

ships." He finds the sacred or magical powers irrationally ascribed to the *techne* of mass media, therapy, and management.[20]

Another example of secular religiosity arises in the organization of secular professional life today. Bruce Wilshire depicts practices within the academic profession in the U.S. today as priestly or shamanistic activities concerned with maintaining the purity of roles and disciplines. He writes that "a presumptive connection between contemporary professionalism and archaic purification ritual runs across the entire face of the university."[21]

Secular religiosity today often echoes the worship of one or other Greek divinity. For example, the figure of Apollos speaks today of mastery or power of control as the way of participation in the divine. The religious meaning of contemporary ideologies and programs of ideological rationalization is of this kind. Such idolatry represents the proud evasion of God that we have characterized in Part 1 of this book as dismissiveness; it involves the construction of false purpose in, and a false integration of, the world.

Another secular religiosity concerns rather *loss* of responsible control, in the despairing evasion of God that we have characterized as disorientation. Here the figure of another Greek god, Dionysius, is heard sponsoring a personal surrender to ecstasy as the way of participation the divine. This may be echoed in a personal life dominated by the pursuit of excitement and ecstasy, or by the search for "reality" through participation in the prescribed "life-giving" experiences. Such religiosity is associated with, for example:

- *shopping and the ownership of products:* shopping malls reminiscent of cathedrals are places of sanctuary and social gathering for the young, the rituals of which are policed by private security staff. Their shop windows display products as if they were sacred treasures for veneration. The purchase and sporting of "label" products endows upon the purchaser identity and validation that is of "religious" stature. Products are marketed as the way to ecstasy and the fulfillment of ones deepest dreams.

- *entertainment:* the viewing of television "soaps" and news bulletins has for many the status of religious ritual. Figures in the entertain-

20. Stivers, *Technology as Magic.*
21. Wilshire, *Moral Collapse of the University,* 152.

ment industry such as TV and film celebrities and Radio DJs hold a religious place in the imaginations of their dedicated "followers." Talk of "cult" figures and pop "idols" has foundation.

- *sport*: football matches (for example) have the aura of religious festivals in which huge crowds exult together. The fortunes of a sports team may have enormous significance for its supporters. A dean of Liverpool Cathedral recalls that the day when Liverpool United won the F.A. Cup gave him a unique image of the return of Christ as people poured out of their homes and hugged each other, tears of joy streaming down their faces.

- *therapy*: in a culture where affliction of the human spirit is seen often as a medical condition, the orthodox doctor is like a priest who dispenses sacramental tokens in the form of placebo pills. The practitioners of "alternative therapies" meanwhile offer true anointing through massage with aromatic oils, or invoke the sacred power of crystals.

- *health and beauty*, and *health and fitness*: beauty and fitness can each acquire "religious" status for those who seek them. Like therapies they can be associated in the popular imagination with a spiritual sense of wellbeing, and be seen as presenting an image of divine "perfection." Naomi Wolf wrote in *The Beauty Myth* that the pursuit of beauty can be a pursuit of "perfection" involving experiences of guilt and salvation.

Corresponding to these secular forms of religion there are, of course, religious specters: powerlessness, anonymity and boredom, illness and death are the unfaceable faces of perdition today.

SECULARISM AND CONTEMPORARY "SPIRITUALITY"

In practice, then, secularism contains its own hidden elements of religiosity. The very terms in which it conceives the world and the manner in which it inhabits the world are imbued with religious meaning. The world of the secularist is by no means disenchanted or devoid of sacred totems and taboos. Secularists, of course, do not acknowledge this.

Meanwhile there might appear to be signs of a new openness to God in secular Britain and Europe at the turn of the third millennium. There has been a remarkable growth of popular interest in "spirituality." This has opened up a new market for goods and services, and has also been incorporated sometimes by managers into the stated goals, work practices, and support systems of public and private institutions.

Should Christians celebrate the new popular interest in spirituality as a sign of spiritual life inspired by God's Spirit? To ask this is to ask whether such interest involves a concern to recognize and honor that which is truly sacred as it reveals itself in the world and whether it resists that which is a denial of God-given liberation from all false sacral worlds. Is contemporary spirituality open to God, or does it reinstate pagan sacral elements in the world? Does it reach out towards a deeper integration of the world, or does it rehearse an illusion of escape from a secular world left untouched by such spirituality?

The answer to these questions is, I suggest, profoundly ambiguous. We shall reflect at greater length on contemporary spirituality in chapter conversion 7.

IN CONCLUSION

So what is the Christian vocation today? Jacques Ellul stresses the need to address the "veiled, hidden, and secret gods, who besiege and seduce all the more effectively because they do not openly declare themselves as gods." He comments:

> It is clear that the task facing Christians and the church differs entirely according to whether we think of ourselves as being in a secularized, social, lay, and grown-up world which is ready to hear a demythologized, rationalized, explicated, and humanized gospel—the world and the gospel being in full and spontaneous harmony because both want to be religionless—or whether we think of ourselves as being in a world inhabited by hidden gods, a world haunted by myths and dreams, throbbing with irrational impulses, swaying from mystique to mystique, a world to which the Christian revelation has once again to play the role of liberator and destroyer of the sacred obsessions in order to liberate man and bring him, not to the self his demons are making him want to be, but to the self his Father wills him to be.[22]

There remains for Christians today, then, a continuing task of desacralization. Today its task is to "desacralize secularism," revealing and judging its hidden gods in the setting of faith. To do this is not to rob them of meaning, but to open them up as signs pointing God. The test in each

22. Ellul, *The New Demons*, 227.

case is whether they will yield to such conversion and transformation; insofar as they resist this, they show themselves to be idols, destined to dissolution.

In summary, Christians are called by God today to live converted to creation and new creation by God. They are called faithfully to witness to these, and to seek the conversion of others to them, through their own practice and thought. They have a vocation today to:

1. contend against the prevalent theoretical opposition between "secular" and "religious" views of the world in favor of a three-way encounter between "sacral," "Christian," and "secularist" tendencies.

2. discern and distinguish between each of these tendencies. This involves cultivating openness to God, self-awareness, and attentive conversation in which we learn from and challenge other people regarding these tendencies. This includes learning to recognize and repent of our own complicity in "sacral" and "secularist" worldviews, and calling other to the same repentance.

3. pursue publicly desacralization through conversion from false forms of the sacred, whether explicit or implicit.

4. celebrate publicly the truly sacred, found in the transcendent God and revealed through his good creation in the mediated immediacy of signs, and revealed above all through Jesus Christ incarnate—signs that bear the presence and promise of new creation.

2 THE TRAJECTORY OF WESTERN CULTURE, INDIVIDUALISM, AND TOTALITARIANISM

Conversion to Community under God

"THE KINGDOM OF GOD is upon you," Jesus of Nazareth proclaimed. The approach of God in sovereignty was the constant focus of his teaching, and his acts of healing and liberation were signs of its approach in fulfillment of God's promises:

> Then will the eyes of the blind be opened,
> and the ears of the deaf unstopped.
> Then the lame will leap like the deer,
> and the dumb shout aloud,
> for water will spring up in the wilderness
> and torrents flow in the desert.
> (Isa 35:5–6; cf. Luke 7:22)

> He has sent me to announce good news to the humble,
> to bind up the broken-hearted,
> to proclaim liberty to captives,
> release to those in prison
> (Isa 61:1; cf. Luke 4:1–13)

When we turn from the Christian vision of God's sovereign rule to the vision inspiring modern culture, we find here also a vision of liberation. The emergence of modern culture from the medieval world was envisioned as the pursuit of freedom and truth, liberated from traditional sacral authorities and beliefs. Is the vision of liberation that inspires modern culture fundamentally that of the coming of God's kingdom? Is the unfolding history of modern culture an outworking of openness to God's good purposes for the world? Does this capture the trajectory of modern culture?

In what follows, we shall ask this question with regard one particular issue: that of *community*. We shall reflect on the changing nature of, and relations between, individual life, family life, varieties of association, the state, and diverse traditions in the setting of modern culture. Are these changes guided by openness (however unacknowledged by those concerned to the approach of God's kingdom)? Let us begin by recalling our description, in Part One, of the approach of this kingdom.

THE TRAJECTORY OF GOD'S KINGDOM

The proclamation of the gospel, we have seen, challenges our cultural assumptions and personal attachments, confronting them in a paradoxical way. It breaks them open, judges and transforms them in the new light and new context of God's approaching sovereignty. And it brings new life to us as we entrust ourselves to it in an unqualified, lively personal way.

In a corresponding sense we may speak of the *trajectory* of God's kingdom. By this we shall mean the call, and the direction of calling, of God's gracious action upon people in their particular, provisional, historical context, relative to that deeper context. The trajectory of God's kingdom is the direction in which God would move people, individually[1] or corporately, in their particular situation, given where they are.

The approach of God's kingdom has, we have seen, two aspects:

1. On the one hand the gospel *breaks open* every personal and cultural context, opening us to the sovereign approach of God. It relativizes our familiar world. In so doing it *enlivens us to question and discern,*

---

1. I shall use the terms "individuals" and "persons" more or less interchangeably in this chapter, depending on the setting. I do not intend by this to equate the Christian understanding of the person with "individual*ism*" whether of a modern or any other kind. I do, however, want to affirm that true "individuality" is fostered by Christian faith. On the Christian sources of this, see for example Zizoulas, "Persons in Communion." Historically, we might note the tradition, attested from the beginnings of the church, of giving a new Christian name to those who made their individual public confession at baptism. A new cultural acknowledgement of the individual arose later under the aegis of early medieval Christianity (see Morris, *The Discovery of the Individual*, 1–25). This represents a different understanding of the individual (one which associates the individual more with a unique personal integration of multiple social contexts) than that which the individual in irreducibly defined by their belonging to a fixed, often hierarchical, nesting of family, tribal, and wider contexts. On the non-Christian philosophical sources of Western individualism, see Yu, "Concept of Being."

with new self-awareness, a world we have taken for granted, bringing a radical new dynamism into our world.

2. On the other hand the gospel discloses *a new shared context we are called to inhabit*. And in so doing it *elicits our commitment*: we entrust ourselves wholly to this context as the real world in which we live and in which we will find ourselves given sure hope, purpose, and responsibility. The gospel is *world-forming*.

These two elements of response—questioning and trusting, appraisal and receptivity, discernment and commitment—arise firstly *in the context of God's sovereign approach*, and are elicited by it through God's grace. Secondly, they arise *inseparably together*, each animating the other in a single disposition of responsiveness towards God. That is, they are integrally related to God and to each other. Moreover, such responsiveness belongs constitutively to our very life in Christ, in filial relation to the Father.

In what terms should we think of the approach of God addressing and opening up to his sovereign rule our historical forms of individual and social life? What guidance will this offer for the life that is our own unique calling as an individual made in the image of God? What guidance will it offer for the communal life that is the calling of all who share this image?

Let us begin from the fact that our knowledge of ourselves and of each other as persons arises in the context of, and shares in the character of, our knowledge of God as we respond to his approach. Both our individual and communal life inherently entail relation to God and relation among persons.

Lesslie Newbigin writes of this relatedness as follows:

> I believe that the Christian view of God's purpose for the human family ... arises from a distinct belief about what human nature is. From its first page to its last, the Bible is informed by a vision of human nature for which ... what is fundamental is relatedness. Man—male and female—is made for God in such a way that being in the image of God involves being bound together in this most profound of all mutual relations ... Human beings reach their true end in such relatedness, in bonds of mutual love and obedience that reflect the mutual relatedness in love that is the being of the Triune God himself.[2]

---

2. Newbigin, *Foolishness to the Greeks*, 118.

This relatedness is embodied in our mutual love when we each attend fully to, and put ourselves in the place of, the other person "as ourselves," in the context of God. This giving of ourselves to other people is rooted in God's giving of himself to us in Jesus Christ, and our giving of ourselves to God in response. It constitutes our deepest and fullest personal participation in human life under God. All aspects of human relation to the world are to be understood by reference to this, our richest, most lively, relationship with God and with other people.

What does this imply for our particular, historical experience of individual and communal life? With what message does the sovereign approach of God address this experience? God's approach, we have seen, confronts our taken-for-granted personal identity and communal belonging with paradox so as to open them up and locate them within, and relative to, its own deeper context. In this confrontation, one of a variety of possible directions may appear as the direction in which God's kingdom leads and in which its liberation lies.

Thus on the one hand, the gospel may call the individual to a life less dictated by certain communal bonds and more personally distinctive than the life they have so far lived. Individuals may be called to discover that there is more to themselves than they had understood, and that their belonging lies at a newly recognized deeper level "elsewhere" in the purposes of a transcendent God. In the course of this they may discover a new common life with other people or in other circumstances than those familiar to them, as they learn to inhabit new horizons that are at once given by, and point to, God. As they become part of such a wider community that God is raising up, this will speak of the unifying of all things in Christ in God's coming kingdom. In this way Christian history has sponsored (to take two fundamental examples) the emergence of a multicultural church out of the Jewish religious community, and the emergence of each individual human being as a unique named person known by God.

However, it does not follow that the approach of God always portends the dissolution of any particular concrete community for the sake of either greater individual autonomy, on the one hand, or wider and more "inclusive" community on the other. Rather, the approach of God may lead the individual to re-enter his or her familiar relations with a deeper personal freedom and sense of personal responsibility before God. Such an individual may find that God is disclosing himself in new ways precisely through what is familiar, in a way that renews the meaning of familiar figures and groups, structures, and traditions of wisdom. It may be that belonging to a familiar community deepens for an individual as, with the approach of God, this intimates more deeply what it means to belong to God.

Briefly, then, communal bonds sometimes represent a bondage from which God liberates; other times they are a corporate source of life before God, and their dissolution is to the detriment both of individual and community life. Sometimes the call of relatedness to God and to other persons lifts us out of a particular form of corporate life; at other times it immerses us more deeply in it. For example, sometimes it lifts us out of a culture of unduly promoting one's family, mutual interest group, or "old boys" network at the expense of others; while, at other times, it immerses us more deeply in personal, collaborative relationships where there had been only relatively detached and formal association. Human relatedness under God generates new patterns of life in untold and unanticipated, richly diverse and complex ways as God's will for human life in society is discerned.

THE TRAJECTORY OF MODERN CULTURE

The approach of God's kingdom, then, on the one hand, breaks open existing bonds of allegiance, enhancing individuality, and, on the other, deepens the bonds of community. This may either loosen existing communal bonds or deepen and renew them. When we turn from the approach of God's kingdom to the vision of modern society, how does this compare? We notice that modern society has envisaged itself from the start in a *dual* way, the two elements of which may be seen as continuous with the two elements above in the dawning kingdom. Between them, these have deeply shaped the trajectory of modern society.

On the one hand, modern society has envisioned itself as *rising above culture*: modern society would be open to a future arising from the autonomous exercise of universal, critical reason by individuals. On the other hand, it envisioned itself as *defining* culture: modern society would be shaped by the nation state which would cultivate or civil-ize the population through education. The trajectory of modern culture may then be explored by asking how far these two elements together serve the coming of God's kingdom. Let us consider each of them in turn.

1. Modern society envisions itself as *rising above* culture: In continuity with the radical, critical thrust of the gospel that breaks open established culture, modern thinkers sought to break with the unquestioned assumptions of culture and tradition and the authorities upholding them. These were now to be questioned and critiqued in the light of universal reason—a light that was natural, it was believed, to all individuals and that could (and would) be exercised by them autonomously. The vision was that individuals would responsibly question familiar habits of ignorance and superstition and, in the later words of Kant's famous injunction, "Dare to know." They would rise above, and question, "culture" in the sense of traditional belief and custom (the term "culture" is often used in this sense today, although it was not so in early modernity).

2. Modern society envisions itself as *defining culture*: In continuity with the responsibility that the gospel lays upon people for inhabiting the deep horizons of God's kingdom, modern thinkers envisioned their efforts as *defining* culture. Modern culture was to be an experiment in deliberate, planned "cultivation," in which the state would "civil-ize" its citizens for participation in civil society. Ernst Gellner described this as a "garden" culture, contrasting it with "wild" culture. Zygmunt Bauman quotes him as follows: "Wild cultures, says Ernst Gellner, 're-produce themselves from generation to generation without conscious design, supervision, surveillance or special nutrition. "Cultivated" or "garden" cultures, on the contrary, can only be sustained by literary and specialized personnel. To reproduce, they need design and supervision; without them, garden cultures would be overwhelmed by wilderness' ... The emergence of modernity was such a process of transformation of wild cultures into garden cultures."[3] It is perhaps hard for those of us who live in modern societies to recognize the novelty of this aspiration.

In his book *Legislators and Interpreters* Bauman describes the setting for this "civilizing" and "cultivating" vision of early modernity. Following land enclosure, peasants were forced to migrate in search of opportunities to sell their labor to others. This raised a new threat of lawlessness, since they were no longer constrained by the mutual surveillance of traditional village life. The challenge facing the rulers of the

3. Bauman, *Legislators and Interpreters*, 51.

nation-state was to cultivate and educate this new, mobile population to be "civil" participants in a new, "civil" society.

This involved a greatly extended exercise of power and control by the state in pursuit of the vision of constructing civil society *ex nihilo* (as we might put it) and maintaining it for each new generation—through state education. The modern state penetrated society in a way quite different from the aristocrats of pre-modern society who behaved more like gamekeepers. Modern thinking also fostered processes of *rationalization* that would find expression in guiding ideologies, professionalization, and the development of structures of management and bureaucracy. In passing, it also opened the way for another entirely new concept: that of *revolution*.[4]

MODERN SOCIAL STRUCTURE
SEEN IN CHRISTIAN CONTEXT

The two elements in modern vision described above are, each in their own way, continuous with the vision of God's coming kingdom: the modern vision of a culture guided by the exercise of individual reason (rather than by tradition and convention) is continuous with the approach of God's kingdom breaking open cultural commitments; the modern vision of civilizing or cultivating a population is continuous with the approach of God's kingdom forming a new world to inhabit. In the approach of God's kingdom, these are not in opposition to each other, but integrally related.

When this modern vision is pursued therefore, will the resulting cultural trajectory will be towards the coming of God's kingdom? Two major considerations bear upon the answer to this question. Firstly, what understanding of the individual and of the state informs this vision? Is this a Christian one? According to a Christian understanding, the individual derives existence and meaning in relation to God and in relation to other human persons and groups of persons; similarly the state derives its existence and meaning in relation to God and in relation to the persons and groups of persons of which it is comprised and the wider groupings of which it part. How far is the modern vision of individual and state informed by such a Christian understanding?

---

4. See Schouls, *Revolution and Postmodernism*.

The second major consideration is as follows. Even though the modern vision may be thus guided, there is a potential for distortion lying in (1) the reduction of its understanding of human relatedness to the relation between the two elements of individual and state, and (2) the equation of "breaking open" with the former and "world-forming" with the latter. In the complex reality of life, however, openness to the coming kingdom of God brings growth in individuality and in community in a far richer variety of ways than this reduction can capture. Certainly the individual and the state will feature within this richer picture. But so will many other groupings more or less unique and more or less formal compared to the state with its uniquely assigned powers of legislation and coercion. These groupings include families, local communities, and communities of common purpose or common interest, sometimes called "mediating social structures" or structures "intermediate" between the individual and the state. It is unfortunate if this terminology implies that these structures arise in relation to an already existent framework of individual and state; in reality, individual and state have each acquired their meaning from more informal expressions of human relatedness. I shall therefore prefer to call these structures "informal communities" (although I acknowledge that there are degrees and kinds of formality involved in them.) We are now left with the second question: how far does the modern vision of individual and state honor the richness of human relatedness arising from God and expressed in informal communities?

THE SOVEREIGN INDIVIDUAL,
THE SOVEREIGN STATE, AND GOD

Let us turn to the first consideration: in the modern period, do we find the modern vision of individual and state informed by Christian understanding? Certainly in its early period the modern vision in general was influenced tacitly by Christian faith, as we saw in the previous chapter. *Individuals* on the one hand were seen as existing in relation to God, their creator and judge; as endowed with conscience and with a faculty of reason extending into the realms of religion and morality; and as bound in relation to others, bearing responsibilities under God towards their family, local community, and country. The *state*, in the same way, was seen as accountable before God (a fact of which state rulers were reminded by church leaders when they saw fit); and as entrusted by God with responsibility for the common good of its people.

Nevertheless, as we also noted in the previous chapter, the modern vision was framed explicitly without reference to revealed Christian faith. Accordingly, as the tacit Christian imagination faded this vision could drift from Christian faith, and this would itself further subvert tacit Christian imagination.

Contributing ambiguously to this situation, we have already seen, was an inherited Greek rationalist understanding of the individual and Roman imperial understanding of the state. These had been held together up to a point by the Christian vision of the sovereign approach of God with its corresponding, inseparable elements of "breaking open" and "world-formation." In the modern vision, however, the separation of these elements was reinforced by their assignment respectively to the different social entities of the rational individual and the cultivating state. With each element deriving its own mandate from the vision of God's approaching kingdom, the tendency was now reinforced that each of these would be falsely endowed with an absolute or sacred status of its own. Each, once severed from relation to God, could now usurp the place of God and, severed from relation to the other, could confront the other with ultimate, and incommensurate, claims.

Thus the state, on the one hand, could become falsely endowed with an absolute sovereignty of its own. At this point the state could claim for itself absolute authority in its own right, apart from God and apart from its populace. Such claims have sometimes been made for the state in the modern period. Sometimes they have been invoked in revolution; in the twentieth century they led to the claims of the totalitarian state. At this point the cultivating state could—in addition to challenging the chaos of uncivilized, unformed, individual life—without proper discrimination challenge also that liberty of individuals and of informal communities that is willed by God.

Equally, the individual could become falsely endowed with an absolute sovereignty of his or her own. The sources of liberty and security that individuals had found in their traditional rights had been removed and the new "civilian" populace was potentially at the mercy of the state. In response, the English philosopher John Locke asserted basic rights that pertained to the individual simply by virtue of being a citizen. However, insofar as such rights were shaped by reference to the threat from the state that they opposed, they could themselves mirror its tendency towards absolute autonomy. They could lead to ultimate claims for the individual apart from God and apart from other people. Thus, Tim Jenkins writes that, "In the period of the English revolution, defenders of the king's authority borrowed the Continental theory of absolute sovereignty; this was not a description of a previously existing state of affairs, but an ideological weapon forged in battle. It was adopted by the opponents of royal power and applied to the emergent individual, in the claim that every person is a divine king with absolute rights of disposal of the objects in his sway."[5]

At this point, the claims of individual sovereignty become more than the challenge posed by the rational individual to arbitrary convention and tradition; they challenge and resist not only these but also, indiscriminately, traditions of rationality that are properly open to God and to God-given individual life. Again, they represent more than the challenge posed by the autonomous individual to the false demands of an oppressive state; they challenge and resist not only these but *also*, indiscriminately, the proper demands of communal life including the life of the democratic state.

Thus, despite the tacit influence of Christian imagination, the modern vision has been associated with tendencies falsely to grant incommensurate, absolute sovereignty to the state, on the one hand, or to the individual, on the other.

INDIVIDUAL, STATE, AND INFORMAL COMMUNITY UNDER GOD

This same picture is evident when we turn to our second consideration. In the course of the modern period there has been, by and large, a marked decline in informal communities. Has this flowed from openness to the sovereign approach of God? Certainly, the modern vision gave new impetus to the Christian subversion of "sacral" forms of belonging, bringing new individual liberties, new social differentiation, and new forms of community. It might seem therefore that lament over the loss of informal communities is driven merely by undiscerning cultural conservatism.

However, there has also been a false exaltation of the individual and the state, and both of these have falsely eroded the vitality of informal communities. As each make their rival claims for sovereignty over the other, the intermediate structures of society find themselves subverted

5. Jenkins, "Sacred Persons," 65.

from both directions, by both the sovereignty of the individual and the sovereignty of the state.

Many have noted the erosion of informal community within modernity. Daniel Hardy writes: "most social practice in the modern West has drifted towards a polarization of the formal (the civil state or the large-scale religious organization) and the fragmented (the individual, whether as citizen or as faithful), with a correlative de-emphasis of units more informal and local."[6] He argues that these movements are not theologically neutral, but that rather, "conceptually they require the marginalization of God as Christians understand him; to suppose [that they are normal] undercuts the presence in human social structures of the social coherence which is embedded in God's very being and work, together with the deeper and more varied form of human rationality which that presence implies."[7]

John Milbank depicts this marginalization of God as the displacement of "complex," "sacred" space, and the destruction of its intermediate associations, which "variegate the monotonous harmony of sovereign state and sovereign individual." Such space is displaced by what he calls "enlightenment simple space." He compares "enlightenment simple space" with "complex" or "sacred" space as follows: "The former is 'secular,' the latter is 'sacred.' In the first case religious authorization or providential intervention is moved to the margins: God commands the absolute sovereign . . . or else God/Nature co-ordinates our desires behind our backs, through the operation of the capitalist market. But in the second . . . case, every act of association, every act of economic exchange, involves a mutual judgment about what is right, true, and beautiful, about the order we are to have in common."[8]

By the late twentieth century, sociologist Peter Berger could see the disintegration of mediating structures as a crisis of our time. He writes:

> Modernization brings about a novel dichotomization of social life. The dichotomy is between the huge and immensely powerful institutions of the public sphere . . . and the private sphere . . . The (ensuing) progressive disintegration of mediating structures constitutes a double crisis, on the level of individual life and also on a political level. Without mediating structures, private life

6. Hardy, "God and the Form of Society," 132.

7. Ibid., 35.

8. Milbank, "On Complex Space," 271, 279.

comes to be engulfed in a deepening anomie. Without mediating structures, the political order is drawn into the same anomie by being deprived of the moral foundation upon which it rests ... it is confronted with the necessity of substituting coercion for moral consent.[9]

The suppression of mediating structures has sometimes been a quite deliberate policy pursued with totalitarian aims. Michael Polanyi noted this regarding Nazi rule in Germany. Drusilla Scott comments:

> A state that has this rich variety of independent associations has a strength to its freedom ... It is significant that the beginning of the Nazi domination of Germany was the destruction of such association. Society was atomized, social structure destroyed, and trust between people broken down. "There was no more social life, you couldn't even have a bowling club." Men had to choose between solitude and the mass relationship of a national organization. "It was a failure of perception that let this happen ... There is a test," Polanyi says, "which proves that all such groups effectively foster the intrinsic power of thought: ... these circles ... are feared and hated by modern totalitarian rulers."[10]

"You couldn't even have a bowling club," Polanyi writes. More often when such organizations disappear today, however, this is not a matter of deliberate suppression. Rather, they appear simply to have withered away under the conditions of modern society. In *Bowling Alone*, Robert Putnam writes of this development in the United States.[11]

These conditions of modern society themselves reflect, we have seen, the tacit assumptions of modern thinking, setting modernization upon a particular trajectory. Moreover these assumptions give rise to explicit ideologies of the state and the individual that, while they do not set out deliberately to suppress informal communities, have the effect of assaulting them. Nicholas Boyle writes of recent British society:

> [We] have seen a sustained assault on all the intermediate social organizations, the autonomous and semi-autonomous institutions, the constitutional checks and balances, that lies between central government and individual citizens, that protect them from direct, and always potentially arbitrary, central interfer-

---

9. Berger, "In Praise of Particularity," 170, 173–74.

10. Scott, *Everyman Revived*, 86.

11. Putnam, "Bowling Alone."

ence, that give shape and substance and continuity to their lives, a focus for loyalty, and a place of engagement with other citizens that is not simply an extension of the market-place—the fabric of society, in short ... British society is thus at once polarized and homogenized. The great institutions that gave it depth and complexity fade away. Instead we have on the one hand the un-differentiated mass of individual "consumers," and on the other hand the legislative and executive power of central government organizing those same masses, but as workers, into employment and unemployment and enforcing its will, in the last analysis, by the power of the police.[12]

A DEEPENING POLARIZATION

Individual rights were promulgated, we have seen, in face of the new power of the modern state in the seventeenth century. But now, in recent decades, this response to state power has seen dramatic further development. The Second World War brought home the horrifying potential of the totalitarian state and the vulnerability of individuals within it. In response to this, the wide-ranging Universal Declaration on Human Rights was promulgated. Since then, human rights have been incorporated increasingly into state legislation. The current effect of this upon intermediate associations is mixed. On the one hand, it is helping to lessen abuses. On the other hand, it is subverting intermediate associations by imposing sometimes unreasonable and hard to fulfill criteria regarding such matters as individual health and safety, privacy, freedom from discrimination, and security. We shall assess these ambiguities more closely in chapter 8.

Meanwhile advances in technology in recent decades are making it possible for the state to "garden" its population (using Gellner's image) much more intensively. These advances enable new degrees of state control through the formulation of new legislation and the implementation of this through new surveillance techniques, including computerized data collection and storage.

We have so far focused on polarization between the individual citizen and the legislating state. However, other forms of polarization between the individual and the agents of mass culture have also marked the modern period, and these too have intensified with recent techno-

12. Boyle, "Thatcherism," 18, 21.

logical advances. In recent decades many small independent businesses have been replaced by chain stores and multinational companies with their own distribution networks and retail outlets. Independent employers have been replaced by large corporations with their mass-imposed employment policies and terms of service. And they have been replaced as providers of goods and services. Although large corporations claim to offer consumers more choice, they have often driven out of business the small, local manufacturers who between them once provided a richer "gene-pool" of choices. Instead they use their power of control to shape consumption by acting directly upon individual consumers through their sophisticated mass advertising which saturates our culture and homogenizes it.

Indeed, as we try to judge what is today shaping the trajectory of modern culture, it is evident that the power of economic theory and practice rivals that of the state. And it is as much the polarization between large private corporations and individual consumers which shapes the modern trajectory as the polarization between the individual citizen and the legislating state.

The polarization between corporate system and individual consumer is quite as destructive of human relatedness to God and to other persons as is the polarization between state and citizen. On the one hand, corporations are, in their pursuit of profit, endowed with freedom from any fundamental accountability either before God or before individuals beyond the constraints of national and international law. Correspondingly they do not have the moral authority of the state before God or before the population. Their rationality is also, of course, narrower than that of the cultivating, civilizing state; it is that of maximizing profit for shareholders. Correspondingly in place of the individual right to vote for a democratically elected government there stands only the (unevenly spread) power of the individual to choose, within the limits of their financial resources, to make purchases from what is for sale. On the other hand, individual consumers are, in the use of their private resources, created similarly free of accountability beyond the law. In their choices they do not carry the moral authority or responsibility of the rational citizen. Their rationality is simply that of private preference. No doubt corporations and consumers alike are today increasingly aware of the challenge to behave ethically in ways beyond the requirements of the law. But these challenges are often in turn engaged only insofar as concerns over them threaten to limit the power of business or of the consumer.

As individual and communal life lose their fundamental bearings here in relation to God and to each other; they also lose their own proper character. As consumer, the individual loses coherence: taking responsibility for oneself is inseparable from showing responsibility towards God and others. The consumer life reduces persons to a "fleeting bundle of appetites" living for the present moment and dismissive of responsibilities arising from past actions or future freedom, e.g., from debt. Corporate life reduces to subservience to market forces. And there is no common framework for these two: together they constitute a perverse symbiosis, not elements woven together within human community.

We have seen the erosion of informal communities in the face of such polarization. However, sometimes there has arisen a passionate resistance to corporate power by those who, alienated, focus their very identity in belonging to a group under attack, to be aggressively asserted in face of opposition. This happened in Germany between the First and Second World Wars. A nation of people humiliated by crippling war reparations and experiencing the subversion of their communal bonds by aggressive capitalism reached for unique claims for their race. Today we can see parallels with the efforts of radical Islamists who, driven by humiliation, similarly conceive Islam anew as a source of personal identity and dignity to be aggressively asserted in the face of opposition.

In Western society generally, there is a widespread recognition of the erosion of informal community and mediating structures, not least among local leaders of the established and mainstream churches who find themselves providing advocacy on behalf of local community interests. Also the churches themselves can add up to the largest mediating structure in a given society.

In Britain, the political setting of such advocacy reflects something of the polarization above. In recent years under New Labor, government has tended towards overcentralizing power through the use of legislation, directives, target-setting, official accreditation and reaccreditation, and surveillance, etc. This is the political context of appeals by Rowan Williams, Archbishop of Canterbury, from time to time that government learn to listen more closely to local religious leaders and "work with the grain." [13] On the other hand, the current attack (at the time of writing)

---

13. See for example Williams, "Archbishop's Address to Faith Leaders in Birmingham."

by Conservatives on "big government" in the name of "big society," and on "welfarism" in the name of a more responsible civil society, calls for just as vigorous a critique. The open door it is offering to large private corporations to move into areas that have been under the management of democratic institutions with their own professional culture and practical canon of wisdom (the most obvious among these being the educational and healthcare professions) is just as threatening to a society richly structured by mediating associations as is an overcentralized state. It is also arguably more dangerous to such associations because its program of mass privatization is often concealed behind the rhetoric precisely of civil society and personal responsibility.[14]

IS THIS TRAJECTORY PROPERLY CALLED THE "MODERN" ONE?

We have sought in this chapter to compare the trajectory of modern society in certain respects with the trajectory of openness to God's coming kingdom. However, before concluding our reflections on this we ought to acknowledge that recent social developments have been designated in a variety of ways other than simply "modern." They have been characterized variously as the advent of "postmodernity"; "late modernity"; "liquid modernity"; and "emergent modernity." Which is appropriate? Our answer to this will reflect our perception of what comprises the "modern vision" in the first place, our assessment of developments during the modern period, and our assessment of current developments. Let us consider briefly these four designations in turn.

1. *Postmodernity*: we may take the view that the modern vision incorporates a vision of corporate cultivation and individual exercise of reason that is normative for this vision but which has not been normative for recent developments. Something else has taken its place. This view may be positive towards recent developments, for example viewing them as a welcome celebration of diversity in place of an oppressive, narrow rationality found in modernity; or it may be nega-

14. In Britain, a recent example at the time of writing is Phillip Blond, *Red Tory*. Internationally, a notable author of such writing in recent decades has been Gertrude Himmelfarb. See for example her *The De-Moralization of Society*. Interesting, Himmelfarb's work was held in high regard by Gordon Brown. For criticism of its use by neo-conservatives, see Hadley, "The Past Is a Foreign Country: The Neo-Conservative Romance with Victorian Liberalism."

tive, for example, viewing them as the disintegration of rationality into relativity and a struggle between competing powers.

2. *Late (or high) modernity*: we may take the view that the modern vision incorporates a vision of corporate rationalization and individual autonomy that is normative for it and which has remained so in recent developments despite dramatic social change. What has been lost is not of the essence of the modern, but indifferent to it, reflecting rather the continuing influence of older social traditions.

3. *Liquid modernity*: more parallel to our own focus on the polarization individual and corporate life is this characterization of recent developments by Zygmunt Bauman. As will be apparent from the passage below, his choice of the term "liquid" is not about a more flexible and open form of rationality than that of past modernity; rather it is about the dissolution of that inner structure of integration and differentiation binding together individual and corporate life, a structure in which informal communities are a vital part. Bauman writes:

> The "melting of solids," the permanent feature of modernity, has ... acquired a new meaning, and above all has been redirected to a new target—one of the paramount effects of that redirection being the dissolution of forces that could keep the question of order and system on the political agenda. The solids whose turn has come to be thrown into the melting pot and which are in the process of being melted at the present time, the time of fluid modernity, are the bonds which interlock individual choices in collective projects and actions—the patterns of communication and co-ordination between individually conducted life policies on the one hand and political actions of human collectivities on the other.[15]

4. *Emergent modernity*: we may take the view that the modern vision is, in recent developments, coming to fuller expression than in the past. We are seeing the emergence of a more consistently and comprehensively modern society. According to this view, what we have seen in the modern period up to this point is a society shaped only *partially* by the modern vision, and partially by other older social

15. Bauman, *Liquid Modernity*, 6.

traditions. This is expressed in the contemporary political rallying cry of "modernization."

CHRISTIAN ENGAGEMENT

Whatever designation Christians may judge appropriate for the polarization of mass society today, their task is to appraise this by reference to the trajectory of openness to the kingdom of God and to the fundamental relatedness within this of persons to God and to each other. Christians have every responsibility before God to contend with a culture that is closed to this trajectory and that shapes instead a world defined by corporate power on the one hand and the individual consumer on the other—a world that is heading for totalitarianism or nihilism.

Various authors have noted this dual trajectory. Lesslie Newbigin noted in 1958 that the reaction against the terrible logic of totalitarianism had "carried many into mere futilitarianism, into mere absorption in the most superficial of momentary satisfactions and the abandonment of any attempt to make sense of life as a whole."[16] Later he warned that "if . . . the drive to a new kind of human society is not informed by the biblical faith concerning the nature of the Kingdom of God it will end in totalitarianism; and that if the secular critique of all established orders is not informed and directed by the knowledge of God it will end in a self-destructive nihilism."[17]

Earlier, at the outset of the Second World War, T. S. Eliot warned of the likely future alternatives to a Christian society:

> We might, of course, merely sink into an apathetic decline: without faith, and therefore without faith in ourselves; without a philosophy of life, either Christian or pagan; and without art. Or me might get a "totalitarian democracy," different but having much in common with other pagan societies, because we shall have changed step by step in order to keep pace with them: a state of affairs in which we shall have regimentation and conformity, without respect for the needs of the individual soul; the Puritanism of hygienic morality in the interest of efficiency; uniformity of opinion through propaganda, and art only encouraged when it flatters the official doctrines of the time.[18]

16. Newbigin, "Summons," 183.

17. Newbigin, *Honest Religion*, 39.

18. Eliot, *Idea*.

The alternatives of totalitarianism or nihilism have perhaps been most memorably characterized by Neil Postman. He sees them respectively in Orwell's *1984* and Huxley's *Brave New World*:

> What Orwell feared were those who would ban books. What Huxley feared was that there would be no reason to ban a book, for there would be no one who wanted to read one. Orwell feared those who would deprive us of information. Huxley feared those who would give us so much that we would be reduced to passivity and egoism . . . In *1984* . . . people are controlled by inflicting pain. In *Brave New World*, they are controlled by inflicting pleasure. In short, Orwell feared that what we hate will ruin us. Huxley feared that what we love will ruin us.[19]

Later in his book, Postman notes that Huxley "believed that it is far more likely that the Western democracies will dance and dream themselves into oblivion than march into it, single file and manacled. Huxley grasped, as Orwell did not, that it is not necessary to conceal anything from a public insensible to contradiction and narcoticized by technological diversions."[20]

It would appear that the responsibility of challenging the erosion of mediating structures is a vocation laid upon Christians in Western nations today—perhaps especially in Britain. Britain has a particularly rich heritage of informal associations nourished, in part, by its distinctive religious heritage. However, in recent decades its participation in the global capitalist market has opened the country to socially formative pressure from two directions. On the one hand, participation in the European Union has brought pressure to conform to a continental European Enlightenment vision that pursues a more aggressively secularist program of rationalization. This is associated with further polarization between the rights-bearing individual and the legislating state (through membership of the European Union). On the other hand, participation in a global market for trade in which the United States plays a dominant role has brought pressure to conform to a model of economic rationalization associated with further polarization between the individual (increasingly constructed as consumer) and the large private corporation. I shall have more to say about these ideological drivers of social change in chapters 8 and 9.

19. Postman, *Amusing Ourselves to Death*, vii–viii.
20. Ibid., 113.

Having come to England from Hungary, Michael Polanyi observed that in England during the modern period, social change and advance was influenced by Christian faith in a distinctive way. Whereas in continental Europe social progress has been associated with anti-clericalism and Enlightenment, in Britain it has been prompted, on the whole, more by religious sentiment and the influence of Puritanism.[21] Its heritage of religion has helped maintain the rich complexity of institutions and informal associations in England, whereas polarization has long been at work in continental Europe. Nicholas Boyle notes another factor: in England globalization has, until recently, been kept at bay largely by the country's preoccupation with running an empire. Another factor again, perhaps, is the traditional English distaste for grand ideas such as those inspiring the European Enlightenment.

Insofar as explicit principles can be employed effectively to resist ideological distortions, there is one Christian doctrine that offers help against the polarization we have noted. The doctrine of subsidiarity, first formulated in the Roman Catholic Church by Pius XI in 1932, promulgates the principle that corporate life should be organized at the highest level necessary but the lowest level compatible with its purpose.[22]

This principle is an important corrective to the forms of polarization we have been considering. However, we have seen that openness to the approach of God's kingdom can as equally bring the relative dissolution of corporate bonds as their deepening. The principle of subsidiarity tends to conceal this, although on closer examination the provision for whatever is a *necessary* level of organization may turn out to offer room for it.

At a deeper level, the corrective to polarizing structures in society is not to be found in a principle regarding social structures as such, but in something more primary to the practice of life in society itself: the recovery of openness to the trajectory of openness to God's coming kingdom. This is about recovery of the vision of human relatedness to God and to each other, together with recognition that this is denied by the false exaltation of either the individual or the state as entities autonomous of God and external to each other.

Among those well aware of the realities both of totalitarianism and of nihilism was Vaclac Havel. Writing in "post-totalitarian, consumerist"

---

21. See Polanyi, "English and the Continent."

22. Pius XI, *Quadragesimo Anno.*

Czechoslovakia, he articulated the role of the informal literary and artistic community resisting the nihilism of ultimately arbitrary individual life and renewing "truthful" life. Faced with modern political parties that "release the citizen from all forms of concrete and personal responsibility," he declared what was to be done: "Above all, any existential revolution should provide hope of a moral reconstitution of society, which means a radical renewal of the relationship of human beings to what I have called the 'human order,' which no political order can replace. A new experience of being, a new rootedness in the universe, a newly grasped sense of 'higher responsibility,' a new-found inner relationship to other people and to the human community—these factors clearly indicate the direction in which we must go."[23] In such terms the early modern vision might be reclaimed and restored to a trajectory more open to the sovereign approach of God.

In summary: Christians are called by God today to live converted to community under God. They are called to witness to such community, and to seek the conversion of others to this through their own Christian practice and thinking. They are called to acknowledge, and repent of, their own complicity in Western cultural habits of thought and action that pre-empt this, pointing away from it towards individualism and totalitarianism—whether these be of a modern rationalist or postmodern consumerist kind.

Conversion to community under God celebrates, in thought and practice, the relatedness of persons to each other, rooted in the presence and promise of participation in the divine life of the Trinity.

---

23. Vaclac Havel, "The Power of the Powerless," 116–18. See also Habermas, "An Awareness of What Is Missing."

3   The Modern Betrayal of Enquiry

Conversion to Attentiveness towards God

ODERN ENLIGHTENMENT THINKERS BELIEVED in the innate goodness and rationality of humankind confronted with a world open
to exploration. They lived by the hope that, through the exercise of reason and with the help of experimental science, exploration would bring
progress towards a better world. In this world personal liberty would
attain its proper scope and civil life would be grounded upon sure moral
principles and truths self-evident in the light of reason and upon facts
that had been established with confidence.

The foremost enemy to be overcome in the course of this project
was, in the view of modern thinkers in general, sheer prejudice arising
from attachment to habitual beliefs and practices. Often such prejudice
derived from personal identification with the established customs and
conventions of traditional cultures and from deference to the traditional
authorities upholding these (officials, institutions, sacred writings, etc.).

Accordingly, for modern thinkers a better understanding of the
world would be attained by observing beliefs and practices and adopting a critical stance towards them, judging in the light of reason. In the
case of traditional beliefs, these might no longer be taken as trustworthy
now; in the case of newly conceived hypotheses, these stood in need of
testing. Fundamentally here, the act of enquiry was conceived in terms
consistent with Descartes' "method of doubt." "The good" was similarly
now taken as a matter for reason; it was to be found in "self-evident"
moral principles such as liberty and equality, and no longer to be defined
by or derived from God and worship of God.

This way of thinking was a rejection of Christian faith as offering
the deepest roots and most vital nourishment for enquiry into truth and
goodness; it effectively sought these elsewhere, in an imagined autonomous human nature. Modern culture thereby set itself on the path of

a radical logical inversion: instead of seeing the human subject and its world in the context of God, it imagined to see God in the context of the human subject and of a "secular" human world.

Such "inverted" secularist thinking misrepresents not only God but also itself, and subverts, in practice, not only faith but also secular life. To quote Chesterton again, secularists "do not succeed in pulling up the roots of Christianity; but they do succeed in pulling up the roots of every man's ordinary vine and fig tree, of every man's kitchen garden."

INVERSION—IN TWO STAGES

The modern inversion of God and the human subject may be described as coming about in two successive stages, as follows.

In the first stage, the human subject in a secular human world is conceived as autonomous. It is believed that civil life, its vision and its foundations, can be explicitly framed without reference to Christian faith, and trust is placed, practically, in this belief. Christian faith meanwhile is conceived still as making claims for what is good and true; however, the claims of positive revelation are not trusted explicitly to inform public decisions and debate. After all, it is held, these claims have shown themselves to be an untrustworthy foundation for social and political cohesion, having given rise to seemingly irresolvable disputes; and it is believed also that something more trustworthy for the purpose has been found to take its place: human nature. In other words, there are better things to do than seek patiently and painfully a true universal consensus grounded in and nourished by faith. Profound though the matters of goodness and truth might be with which Christian faith is concerned, they can be set aside in the task of ordering life in society.

Here we see a loss of trust in the gospel as the ultimate source of knowledge of what is good and true. Christian faith no longer compels from people an effort of understanding and obedience as if everything hinged upon this for the sake of themselves and the world. Instead they believe that everything hinges on the innate goodness and rationality of human beings. This wrongly dislocates Christian faith from the radical pursuit of what is good and true. Those who do continue to pursue Christian understanding and obedience "as if everything hinged on them" are therefore seen as problematic; they are perceived as being driven, in reality, by something less than the radical pursuit of what is good and true; Christian faith itself comes to be viewed as problematic.

In the second stage, the claims of faith no longer evoke deference towards the possibility of a deeper purpose behind the world. They are no longer seen as concerned with a deeper, more costly personal enquiry than routine questioning; faith is not seen as serious attention to what might be real at all. Religion is taken rather as an expression of what people *bring to* the world, and of the meaning people invest in their lives.

Here Christian faith is no longer seen as addressing questions of truth, even though Christians may see it this way; rather, it is seen as a private affair. As such it can be tolerated, *provided* that it understands itself in the same way. Appropriate is the public response, "Whatever floats your boat." Now this may *seem* a more tolerant attitude than the older disputative or teasing attitude towards religious belief. Nevertheless, the older attitude at least testified implicitly to faith as making truth-claims. The "tolerance" that has replaced it relies entirely upon the assumption that religion is of no consequence for public life. Indeed because religion is (supposedly) a harmless private affair, *criticism* of religion is now seen as the thing that is intolerable: people have a right to their private beliefs! However, if people with private religious beliefs tell others they should accept them as true, then it is they who infringe intolerably the rights of others to hold their private beliefs.

Recent decades have seen a significant shift from the first to the second stage of the above inversion. A minister who has worked for many years with students has described this shift as follows. Years ago, he says, students presented with Christian beliefs would ask him, "But how do you know this is true?"; today they ask rather, "But what about the others: the Buddhists, the Hindus, the Muslims?" Christian truth-claims are seen no longer as offending secular concerns regarding what is true, but as violating the constraints upon Christian faith as one private faith among others.

Lesslie Newbigin describes this shift as it confronts Christians in the context of witness:

> in trying to communicate the gospel to our European contemporaries we are dealing at the same time, and perhaps in the same person, with two different reactions to it. On the one hand, those parts of our society where modernity still reigns will object both that the gospel is not objective truth but only one very subjective way of interpreting human experience. On the other hand, those who are being shaped by the post-modern reaction will tell us

that our "metanarrative" is simply our attempt to recover the kind of power that Christianity once had in Europe ... They will be happy to let us play our games if we want to, so long as we do not try to impose our game on the whole playground.[1]

The shift from first to second stage of inversion connects, as Newbigin indicates, with the shift in recent decades from modernity to "post-modernity." At the same time, however, both first and second stages have historical roots stretching back to early in the modern period. In brief, the first stage is already implied by John Locke's exclusion of positive revelation from religion "within the bounds of reason," and the second by Herder's defense of cultural authenticity.

Now this suggests another way of approaching the modern inversion. Rather than seeing this as the subversion of deep enquiry in two successive stages, we may see these "stages" as deriving from two *alternative* ways in which modern thinkers have always tried to locate Christian faith within their worldview. Initially each of these was understood, tacitly at least, in a Christian context; but each has become dislocated from this and became part of an autonomous "religious" modern framework as a context within which everything—including Christian faith—is to be seen. The first has been about a dislocation of rationality (with associated ideas about questioning and knowing the truth) from the context of Christian knowledge of God; the second has been about a dislocation of valuing (with associated ideas about goodness, beauty, and desire) from the context of Christian worship of God. The first dislocation has given rise to narrow forms of rationalism; the second has given rise to an understanding of value as a merely subjective affair.

These two approaches to religion were illustrated clearly in a primary school assembly in which the author's son participated some years ago, and in which they appeared concurrently. The theme of the assembly was "God," and was approached from two directions. In the first part of the assembly, a succession of children asked "why?" about things we normally take for granted. "Why is the sky blue?" asked one. "Why am I me?" asked another. In the second part, a succession of children reported what they personally valued. "I value my pet rabbit," said one. "I value my stamp collection," said another. The assembly adopted two secularist ways of locating and discussing religion: (1) religion offers answers to questions about what is familiar to us all but to which we find no cause

1. Newbigin, "New Birth into a Living Hope," 5.

routinely to advert and about which no public consensus has been and perhaps can be reached, and (2) religion expresses what is personally valued by an individual or group. The former approach is representative of classical modern rationalism; the latter of postmodern relativism.

These two approaches to religion are not compatible, of course. The first approaches religion through a concern for facts, sees religion as making truth-claims, and seeks to evaluate these claims in the light of reason. The second approaches religion through an interest in values, sees religion as viewing the world relative to certain values it brings to the world, and seeks to clarify these.

These two approaches to religion, which rely on an effectively "religious" secular modern framework, may also be brought to bear upon deep human enquiry other than that of explicit religion. Let us now consider the inversion of God and the human world in terms of each. To do so is to understand this inversion as reflecting an inversion in our understanding both of questioning and of valuing, following their dissociation from the Christian context in which they find their primary meaning.

FAITH, RATIONALISM, AND THE ACT OF QUESTIONING

Fundamental to the emergence of modern society is the vision and practice of critical enquiry into the world. However, the modern understanding of enquiry itself misrepresents enquiry at its most lively.

Let us begin by recalling some of our insights about questioning. Our most lively questioning arises, we have averred, in response to the approach of God. In a deeply personal way we open up our understanding of the world in radical attentiveness to God. Far from choosing to put questions, we find we are impelled to ask ourselves questions, weighty ones; indeed our questioning is, at its deepest level, a matter of God's interrogation of us. In it, we adopt a dual disposition of at once "entrusting ourselves to" (X) and appraising (X), "trying to" (X) and "testing whether" (X), valuing (X) and evaluating (X). Within this disposition, what we attend to focally and what we attend from (i.e., rely on) in a subsidiary way are endlessly renewed in mutual inter-animation.

When other people speak to us of God, we are summoned to the same disposition. Our questioning is properly directed at once *to* what they are saying (critically appraising it from our own position) and *from* what they are saying (entering with them into what they are saying). In the former respect we take responsibility for the possibility that we bring to a conversation wider horizons than those from which the speaker speaks; in the latter, we are receptive to the possibility that that our own horizons may be opened up by the speaker and what they say.

Such lively questioning is, we have seen, paradigmatic for all questioning, in which enquiry generally takes quieter forms. Thus the routine questioning that takes place when a scientific hypothesis, once conceived, is tested, reflects circumstances in which the lively mutual inter-animation of focal and subsidiary have subsided and we have come to rely for understanding upon a settled meaning. The question of receptivity to new meaning has subsided, so that questioning reduces to critical appraisal of the truth. Similarly when someone else makes a scientific claim to us, the questioning to which this summons us reduces to critical evaluation.

Now the modern inversion of God and the human subject can be described in such terms, that is, in terms of the practice of questioning and of how this practice is understood. Inversion begins when the quieter questioning characteristic of experimental science is taken to be an autonomous act of the human subject, understood without reference to the paradigmatic deeper questioning characteristic of Christian faith. Questioning gets equated with doubting an idea. All trust is placed in such questioning, initiated by autonomous human beings, in pursuit of the human good.

Religious questioning, meanwhile, is left aside. Its questions are held to be unresolved, without however necessarily implying that they are essentially beyond resolution or that religious beliefs are false.

As the practice of questioning drifts from its tacit Christian context, however, the quieter questioning represented by doubting a claim is taken increasingly as paradigmatic for all questioning—including religious questioning. The way now opens for the latter to be held to account by the canons of rationalism and empiricism. Since Christian faith eludes rational proof of any routine kind, it is now seen as reflecting precisely a failure to question its own claims. It is seen as a matter of uncritical, dogmatic allegiance to unsubstantiated truth.

Here inversion is complete: questioning in general is no longer seen within the deeper context of religious questioning; instead religious questioning is seen (necessarily in a distorted way) in the context of rationalist interrogation. Christian faith is seen as a reliance upon unwarranted presuppositions when it should be open to rational enquiry. Such reliance is seen typically as a matter of conforming to the demands of authority or tradition.

This inversion amounts to a dismissive stance towards Christian faith. Secular modern thinking simply *assumes* that it inhabits wider horizons than such faith, rather than deferring to the possibility that it is Christian faith that inhabits the wider horizons. The same assumption may be made towards tradition of any kind; once it is believed that reason is encapsulated in the testing of ideas, a dismissive attitude is taken towards tradition, with the practical effect of subverting it.

In truth, of course, this systematically misrepresents religious questioning. Firstly, it misrepresents questioning as the testing of ideas, failing to understand that questioning is necessarily *receptive* when at its most lively. It therefore fails to see that the receptivity of faith is as much about paying attention to God, seeking God, and asking questions about God as it is about holding to claims about God. It also fails to see that such receptivity is about lively personal engagement with God rather than about conformity to authoritative statements.

Despite the way modern thinkers see their critical thinking, then, the dislocation of their questioning from the context of faith does not amount to their stepping back from authority in order to question for themselves; rather it amounts to their stepping back from the demands of enquiring personally into God. The practice of questioning that follows this is a less lively and more theoretical form of questioning, from whose premises modern thinkers are called to conversion by encounter with the question of God.

Indeed, at this point modern thinking shows *itself* (rather than Christian faith) to be based on unwarranted presuppositions, while Christian faith sponsors a radical openness that calls into question these presuppositions. It is modern thought that is conformist, relying upon ideological presuppositions, while Christian faith sponsors radical openness to God and to God's world.

The dogmas of Christian faith do not contradict such openness; rather their character is precisely to draw us more deeply into openness to God. They invite us to indwell tacitly a world of signs and stories that nourish openness to God. Correspondingly, the dislocation of questioning from the context of faith is about more than dismissing certain religious ideas; it is about the subversion of that imaginative activity in which we give ourselves practically, in a deep personal way, to the discovery of God.

FAITH, RELATIVISM AND THE ACT OF VALUING

In recent decades there has been much talk about "values." However, this talk typically misrepresents the act of valuing at its most lively.

Our most lively valuing is our worship of God in deep, reverent attentiveness towards God in his utter goodness. It connotes the tacit dimension of our knowledge of God, whereby we indwell and entrust ourselves to the mystery of God. Here in God, we acclaim the definitive meaning and reality of goodness; this is inseparable from God himself as we here know him to be. The goodness of God awakens in us a desire for, moral appreciation of, and recognized obligation towards, that which is good. Valuing, here, is reverent love for the One who is wholly and beyond all measure good.

Worship of God is paradigmatic for all valuing, which is in general valuing of a quieter kind. Such quieter valuing comes about where indwelling settles into a familiar way of seeing the world such that everything has meaning by reference implicitly to that which we here value. Such valuing includes a wide variety of apprehensions—so varied, indeed, that the word "valuing" seems hardly to have coherent meaning when used for them. They include our moral orientation towards goodness, our apprehension of beauty, our exercise of a practical or mental skill, and our physical appetites. In each of these diverse occasions of "valuing," we are not seized by the deep, lively question, "What in the world is of real value?"; rather we have settled into a certain way of valuing, and so of configuring, the world. In other words we have been left with certain things, familiar in some respects, that routinely awaken in us the act of valuing that, in its most lively form, is directed towards God. It is important for understanding the origins of modern culture, that in such acts of lively valuing are formed moral principles.

Now the modern inversion of God and the human subject may again be described in these terms, that is, in terms of the practice of valuing and how this practice is understood. Inversion begins when such quieter valuing is understood to take place independently of the more lively valuing that is our worship of God. All trust is then placed in such valuing, which is displayed by autonomous moral human beings in pursuit of the human good.

Thus in modern thinking, goodness tends to be identified with universal, immutable moral principles supposedly self-evident to reason. Moral apprehension of these is not seen as part of deeper and more lively apprehension of God. Similarly, beauty is not seen as serving apprehension of God; nor is desire seen as directed most deeply towards God. The experience of goodness, beauty, and pleasure as—each in their own terms—an end in themselves is no longer understood in the context of the apprehension of God as an end in himself and as the end of all things.

In the first stage of inversion, the objective reality of goodness is still affirmed, but its goodness is identified with its apprehension as such by innate moral reason. The idea now becomes problematic of a God who defined goodness in himself, and who inspires all apprehension of goodness. Similar difficulty arises regarding the idea that the desire for goodness is born in attentiveness to the concrete will of God and conceives initiatives freely to undertake.

In effect, worship of God is here left aside. As a practice, such worship is seen as raising unresolved moral questions, without necessarily implying however that worship does not truly involve moral apprehension or that the object of worship does not exist.

As the practice of valuing loses its tacit Christian context, however, the quieter valuing represented by the intuitive (supposedly) deference of reason to moral principles is taken increasingly as paradigmatic for all valuing. "Value" is seen as an entirely subjective act of ascription to that which can be known apart from such valuing. Directed towards intrinsically value-free objects, this ascription orders the world by reference to itself; it *refers back to the agent of valuing.*[2] God is now seen as a construct or projection of such valuing, which configures the world in its own subjective way.

This inversion amounts again to a dismissive stance towards Christian faith. Secular modern thinking simply *assumes* that it pursues greater moral freedom than do people with Christian "values," rather

---

2. Thus, today "the footballer and the choreographer, the painter and the couturier, the writer and the ad-man, the musician and the rocker, are all the same: creators" (Finkielkraut, *Undoing of Thought*, 113). This goes hand in hand with a calculative rationality that "widens its domain, discovering utility in uselessness, making systematic forays into the realm of fancies and pleasurable indulgence ... From now on no transcendental beliefs must be allowed to check or even to modify the economic exploitation of leisure and the growth of consumption" (ibid., 119).

than deferring to the possibility that these values, rooted in worship of God, open upon greater freedom. The same assumption gets made towards traditional cultures, which get patronized in a romantic way as colorful acts of self-expression by historical communities. Such an attitude is fundamentally dismissive towards tradition, and has the practical effect, ironically, of subverting it precisely in the act of "celebrating" it.

In truth, of course, this systematically misrepresents Christian "valuing." Firstly, by misconceiving values as constituting a subjective way of seeing and configuring the world as a whole, it fails to understand that valuing at its most lively, and above all in the worship of God, is an enquiry into the real. It fails to understand that such lively valuing is intrinsic precisely to that enquiry into the world in which the realm of "objective" things come to light for us. The fundamental truth is not that we imbue objective things with subjective value, but that objective things can be signs pointing to the goodness of God: they can come alive as the occasion of that lively valuing that is directed ultimately towards God in worship.

Despite the way that modern thinkers see values as subjective, then, this modern dislocation of valuing from worship of God does not bring personal liberation; rather it amounts to the practice of stepping back from personal enquiry into what is held to be of value—which is whatever happens to be a matter of personal attachment. Such valuing is a matter more of romance, sentiment, or blind appetite than true liberation. Modern relativist thinking is therefore not only dismissive of Christian values; it is about the subversion of that attention in which we give ourselves practically, in a deep personal way, to the discernment and fulfillment of what is good.

In summary, then, logical inversion represents the theoretical dissolution and practical evasion of knowing and enquiring in their most lively, paradigmatic form—that is, in knowing and enquiring into God. The Christian testimony to these presented in Part One of this book is eclipsed, as a matter both of theory and practice, by rationalism and relativism.

It is generally agreed that the earlier, Christian understanding of knowledge and enquiry (guided by knowledge and enquiry into God) was more or less eclipsed by the end of the seventeenth century. It is the eclipse of what Ellen Charry calls "sapiental" truth. She writes: "Sapiental truth is unintelligible to the modern secularized construal of truth . . .

Knowing the truth no longer implied loving it, wanting it, and being transformed by it, because the truth no longer brings the knower to God but to use information to subdue nature."[3] The result is the fragmentation and relocation of "truth" under the domination of what may be called "instrumental," "utilitarian," "strategic," or "functional" rationality.

In the chapters ahead, we shall examine how the resulting split between "facts" and "values" has led to the ideological capture of thought on the one hand and the severance of individual life from spiritual and personal formation in community on the other.

LOGICAL INVERSION AND RECENT CULTURAL TRENDS

The inversion of God and the human subject, entailing the subversion of lively, deep personal enquiry into truth and goodness, can be seen at work in various Western cultural developments that have accelerated in recent decades. These may be labeled as the erosion of canon, the dominance of critique, the direction of practitioners, and the reduction of moral action to legal conformity. Let us consider each of these in turn.

The Erosion of Canon

In matters of deep and lively enquiry, the practice of enquiry is furthered by cultivation. Such cultivation is typically provided by some form of apprenticeship to a tradition that acquaints the learner with guides and resources to nourish and inspire their own enquiry. This implies a certain deference to tradition. This deference may—as commonly in sport—take the form of trusting a program of coaching and competition to develop one's personal skills. In other cases it may take the form of accepting a traditional canon of material as normative: the learner is promised within this the stimulus and guide they will need to pursue enquiry every more deeply. The learner is thus drawn into a community of practitioners who share actively together in a tradition of enquiry.

The paradigmatic example of canon is that of sacred Scripture. In the case of the Christian Bible, as also of the Hebrew Scriptures, the body of texts counted as "canonical" has been a matter of formal decision. An example of a less formally constituted canon is the broader canon of Western literature. In science, too, however, tradition plays a key part; Michael Polanyi describes well how scientists judge new scientific ideas

---

3. Charry, *Renewing of Your Minds*, 236.

and claims by tacit reference to established scientific tradition and its debates. At the same time he can describe scientists as a "community of explorers" and science as a "republic"; in this way the tradition of science functions, practically, as a "canon."

In recent decades, deference to traditional canons has been eroded. There has been a tendency to regard traditions with suspicion: not as offering comprehensive apprenticeship in enquiry but as privileging one set of assumptions or interests. Enquiry itself is now commended as a matter of *surveying and critiquing* traditional canons relative to the assumed wider horizon of a multiplicity of alternative canons. The guiding vision of such enquiry is "inclusiveness"; canons, by contrast, are accused of promoting self-interest, elitism, prejudice, censorship, and oppression.

Now, of course, traditional canons need to be open to critique and self-criticism. However, the need for reform in tradition is itself a matter of discernment through deep enquiry of the sort nurtured precisely by lively tradition. It is not something to be called for casually by those outside a tradition, as is assumed by those who take it for granted that canon is merely a tool of elitism, self-interest, etc. This assumption, which is indiscriminate in its attack upon traditional canon, actually subverts enquiry insofar as this is inspired and nourished precisely by critical participation in a tradition of enquiry.

One significant erosion of deference to canon concerns the practical wisdom that shapes community and family life. We shall consider this further in chapter 5. This erosion has led today to a major loss of parental self-confidence when it comes to bringing up and giving personal guidance to one's children.

Suspicion towards tradition has, of course, always been a mark of modern thinking ever since the Enlightenment. What is new is that this suspicion has been turned in recent decades upon precisely the canons of "reason" belonging to modern thinking itself. Such suspicion has penetrated further in the humanities and human sciences than into the natural sciences, although *science-based professions*—such as medicine—have been significantly affected. Here "alternative" therapies have multiplied, each therapy constructing its own canon of theory supported (supposedly) by research findings and framed in pseudo-scientific language (for more on this see chapter 7).

Uncritical allegiance to such new canons seems to reflect, sometimes, an almost "fundamentalist" reaction against the vacuum opened up by loss of traditional canon and a pursuit of personal meaning and identity through this allegiance. Ironically, however, it can more obviously serve self-interest than the traditional canons that are scorned. Profits are sought from the sale of goods and services based on dubious "science" (as in the provision of some alternative medicine and some forms of consultancy); minority groups seek sometimes to advance their own power by promulgating their own "private" (and thus exclusive) canon of wisdom calling for uncritical allegiance.

The erosion of canonical tradition and its marginalization as merely one private tradition among others is perhaps most evident today where this serves private profit or political interest. It is also most evident in areas of society most subjected to mass management and its guiding ideologies. Participation in established traditions of practical wisdom remains lively in more informal fields of endeavor such as the communities of mountaineers, of gardeners, and of those who cook "slow food."

Of course, such informal communities have themselves declined, as we discussed in the last chapter. This decline represents an erosion in a personal way of life in which people understand themselves as enquirers oriented towards, and participating in, a deeper, purposeful context of truth and goodness. The erosion of canon is indeed an element in that dissolution of modern culture that Bauman calls "liquid modernity," in which common participation in a normative canonical context is dissolved into the mass of individuals competing on behalf of their private interests.

Lively deference to canon reflects something of that lively interrogation of God in which, fundamentally, it is *we* who are interrogated. Thus it is acknowledged that properly to enquire into Scripture is to find oneself interrogated by Scripture. Regarding literary canon, Harold Bloom remarks in *An Elegy for the Canon* that "Freud does not deconstruct Shakespeare; Shakespeare deconstructs Freud." Composer John Tavener says "If music or art is truly sacred, it dissects us . . . We do not dissect it; it dissects us."[4]

---

4. Tavener, "Notes from the Celestial City," 19.

The Hegemony of Critique

The erosion of canon, then, is about the erosion of the normative role of canon and tradition; it is about the fact that, if or when we find ourselves morally impelled to enquiry, we no longer defer to canonical tradition as a model inducting us into such enquiry. Now there is another cultural change related to this, which has more to do with the attitudes of academics and critics of the arts. This is a change in which lively, normative enquiry of the sort inducted by canonical tradition becomes itself the primary *object* of enquiry by reference to supposedly wider horizons of enquiry. That is to say, in the place of that primary enquiry into truth and goodness sponsored by canonical tradition, pride of place is given to (supposed) enquiry into enquiry itself in the form it takes within one tradition or another. The lively and primary, canon-forming enquiry pursued through belief and practice is approached via the secondary business of critiquing belief and practice, which is taken to have the primary claim upon our attention.[5] Here again we see the characteristic modern inversion at work. A result of this is that moral enquiry is now

---

5. This is characteristic of much popular "postmodern" thinking. However, key post-modern theorists may see themselves not as subverting the primary pursuit of truth but rather as refining it. Peter Donovan expresses the matter well: "Suppose there are lessons to learn from the social distortions and injustices unearthed by Foucault, and the new insights into oppression and otherness brought to light by the deconstructions of Derrida. Those lessons will be appropriated not through abandoning notions of rationality and a common quest for truth, but through a greatly enhanced appreciation of the difficulty involved in properly applying such notions, given the inevitability of their being compromised, in subtle and unsuspected ways, by their involvement with economic and political interests and power-struggles. The intent is not to overthrow rational, critical methods, in other words, but to free them up and make them perform far better.

This is not, of course, something that postmodern ironists and radical deconstructionists can ever admit. To do so would be to destroy the power of their rhetoric, the effectiveness of their paradoxes ... As in the old game of out-staring one's partner, in confrontation with conventional epistemic liberals, postmodern radicals cannot afford to blink first" (Donovan, "Intolerance," 223).

A problem remains about this strategy, however, at least insofar as it *assumes* a higher power of critique than that of self-critique in the tradition under examination. This is a relevant issue especially where there is an attempt to deconstruct Christian belief. The truth may be rather that postmodern critique mimics precisely the dynamic of irreducible Christian paradox that breaks open every ideological understanding of faith. For more on such issues, see Kettle, "Three Actors"; see also the section on Spong and Cupitt in chapter 4.

taken to be defined by critique of, and independence from, any particular traditions of enquiry.

The domination of primary enquiry over secondary shows itself today in a turn away from attentiveness to the truth and towards *subjective beliefs about, or claims for, the truth*. Much effort is put into managing people's subjective ideas and attitudes, rather than exploring whether these are right and justified. A striking example of this is the concern expressed constantly by political, financial, and business leaders to build public trust and confidence towards themselves, whereas concern is almost never raised over whether this trust is *deserved*—that is, whether a *trustworthiness* is being displayed that invites such trust.

The domination of primary enquiry by secondary is perhaps most striking in the contemporary treatment of that which is most indisputably primary: in the treatment of those unique acts of enquiry we call art. An autonomous profession of art critics, literary critics, etc. has in recent decades arisen which, far from deferring to the endeavor of art or literature, exalts itself over this endeavor and over its explorers. The work of artists and authors is seen as a private effort to be judged within public horizons of criticism, rather than as potentially opening new horizons. Media commentators proliferate, each with their area of specialization; the dominance given to their views over their subjects serves the self-exaltation of the mass media as *the* medium of enquiry, in place of any traditional canon.

George Steiner laments this "dominance of the secondary and the parasitic" in his book *Real Presences*. He contrasts such secondary comment with the primary endeavor of the "executant": "[U]nlike the reviewer, the literary critics, the academic vivisector and judge, the executant invests his own being in the process of interpretation. His readings, his enactments of chosen meanings and values are not those of external survey. They are a commitment at risk, a response which is, in the root sense, responsible. To what, save pride of intellect or professional peerage, is the reviewer, the critic, the academic expert accountable?"[6] It is this "responsive responsibility" that the practitioners of primary enquiry (Steiner's "executants") exercise, into which apprentices are drawn in a practical way, and into which others are inducted into lively appreciation of the arts: this appreciation, too, participates in the primary artistic or

6. Steiner, *Real Presences*, 8.

literary endeavor of enquiry. All of these stand in contrast to the secondary critic and theorist.

The domination of secondary enquiry over primary has become commonplace in Western university education today. Courses of study are often more occupied with surveying theories than apprenticeship in the field of enquiry that gave rise to these theories in the first place. For example, Religious Studies surveys religions without evidently promoting the enquiry into God that they sponsor; courses such as Sociology, Psychology, and Political Studies focus on the theories of their respective disciplines without inducting students into the task of understanding from which these theories spring.

The loss of the primary, normative context of enquiry often passes unnoted; it is likely to catch our attention, however, when some contemporary matter of concern is made the subject of a new course of study. Take, by way of illustration, concern for the welfare of animals. If a course is organized on this topic, it may survey public sensibility regarding this topic, farming practices that attract public concern, arguments used in debate, the role of legislation, the effect of campaign groups, and implications for the sale of products. And it may do so without ever offering apprenticeship in the primary task of enquiry into animal welfare and asking what actions are indicated by the normative requirement of animal welfare. If students have personal concerns for animal welfare, these concerns will be treated as a private affair that should not intrude upon such studies.

Ironically, here once again what takes the place of canonical tradition tends to be more a source of constraint than such tradition itself. Here, in place of critical participation in tradition, there is uncritical deference to the expert critic or commentator. While such experts claim to serve those who would enquire for themselves into a subject, in reality they tend to subvert the other's power and freedom of judgment by diverting attention from the subject to their own "angle" or framework of interpretation that they bring to it as normative.

The Directing of Practitioners

Another cultural change, of a more political nature, similarly reflects the characteristic modern inversion. This has to do with new levels of control sought by political and business leaders over practitioners engaged in lively enquiry—practitioners who have typically, with experience, acquired discernment and practical wisdom in their field. Forms of such practical wisdom are wide-ranging; they include the wisdom of those in the major professions of medicine and education.

The judgment of such practitioners carries weight and is of special value. In order to fulfill its value, however, it needs cultivation, and needs time and opportunity for this cultivation. It also needs liberty for its exercise in practice. And it needs to be respected in practice as a trustworthy guide for action.

In recent years we have seen many experienced practitioners subject to new controls, both by central government in the public sector and by corporations in private enterprise. In public sectors, including health care and education, such direction has been given by setting targets, with financial rewards and penalties; by directives and legislation; and by consumers' charters and rights. Some controls have been more coercive, others more persuasive; many have been introduced without serious regard for the views of practitioners themselves despite the formalities of consultation.

In part this reflects a concern for accountability: accountability towards the proper goals of practice; accountability towards those people who are served as patients, clients, students, etc., with goals of their own; and accountability towards those who manage funding in an age when, in any given field of practice, the issues to be addressed and the tools for addressing them make new demands upon the resources available.

In private enterprise, meanwhile, a parallel imposition of new levels of control from the "center" or "top" enforces accountability of another kind: accountability towards the maximization of profit for owners and shareholders.

However, good practice is endangered when practitioners are told authoritatively by others that certain goals (e.g., measures of achievement) should hold their attention as they practice. The problem here is that, as it has been said, a measure may be true, but once it becomes a *target*, it is no longer a true measure. As a general principle, practitioners must be allowed to retain primary responsibility for practice. They must be allowed to keep their eye on the ball and not, first, on the numbers. As for those who would direct them, their primary responsibilities lie in the same direction; their first task is to enter imaginatively into, and to serve the proper aims of, practitioners engaged in lively and wise enquiry.

It seems today that, through a modern inversion, experienced and wise practitioners are denied the liberty to exercise their distinctive responsibility. Contemporary political and business leaders have lost their grasp of the primary task of lively enquiry into truth and goodness and the primary role of practitioners to serve this task. Instead, political or business goals have been imposed, by such means as directives and targets, as effectively the ultimate context and purpose of practice.

The resulting regime is often quite brutal to the best of practitioners when they take a moral stand against the subversion of wisdom. Professionals in medical practice, in education, and in other fields find themselves bullied, subject to disciplinary action, or threatened with litigation. Consequently they may be dismissed or resign under great stress. Whistleblowers are similarly badly treated for taking a moral stand.

These impositions are routinely promoted as effecting modernization, improving efficiency, and shaking off outmoded work practices and institutional structures. However, in practice they precisely undermine liberty and truth insofar as these are served by participation in the fruits of wise, experienced practice. Instead they covertly demand conformity to the *diktat* of central political or business authority. But the primary "center" of authority lies in reality in that which is served by the lively enquiry of wise practitioners, not in the centers of politics or business, and its authority is of a different kind than that of *diktat*.

The Reduction of Morality to Legal Conformity

Moral enquiry at its most lively is about deep attentiveness to the will of a good God. Clearly this entails far more than routine conformity to rules of behavior. It seeks in liberty to judge and fulfill the good: it seeks through comprehensive consideration and imagination to conceive and pursue that which will express the goodness of God. Such lively moral enquiry fosters lively moral community among enquirers.

In recent decades in Britain, the formation of personal moral judgment nourished by worship of a good God has diminished in family and community life and in state education. This reflects in part the declining role of faith within British society and it has itself reinforced this decline. It also reflects a post-war perception, following Nazi atrocities, that new ways were needed of securing humane treatment of each other by human beings. The Universal Declaration of Human Rights was promulgated in 1948, and since then human rights legislation has

been used increasingly as a tool to shape civil life. This and other legislation increasingly threatens with public prosecution or private litigation.
Meanwhile public surveillance has been greatly intensified using new
technology for cameras and computerized records. Such mechanisms
have to a considerable degree displaced the formation of lively personal
responsibility as the trusted basis for moral life in public and private.
Meanwhile, in personal life, the formation of moral judgment has been
substantially displaced by the exaltation of private choice and of private
values, omitting any reference to obligation. Taken together, these two
displacements encourage people to take the view that "if its legal, it's my
right, and that makes it moral."

Of course, within the formation of moral life there is indeed place
for both pressure to conform morally in public and for the affirmation
of private liberty. However, the proper role of these is revealed in the
context of lively moral enquiry; and they can never *take the place of* such
enquiry. Any such idea is another example of logical inversion at work,
exalting secondary enquiry over primary, and denying what might be
called the "primacy of the moral practitioner." This inversion appears a
feature of recent political and social life in Britain.

Living on the Surface

We have seen that prevalent modern thinking about the human subject
as the autonomous agent of questioning and valuing misrepresents these
activities at their most lively; that religious questioning and valuing are
thereby misrepresented because God can only be engaged in this most
lively way; and that such misrepresentation has the practical effect of
subverting lively engagement with God and with God's creation.

Now such theoretical misrepresentation may be seen as itself an
evasion of the demands of lively questioning and valuing, as well as
sponsoring such evasion. It adopts and commends a proud, dismissive
stance. This is so whether the misrepresentation of lively questioning
and valuing takes a rationalist or a relativist form. However, it also—by
neglecting to engage responsibly with the demands of lively enquiry—
leaves people vulnerable to the temptation of evasion in its alternative
basic form of despairing, personal disorientation. It becomes complicit
in a turn from attention to inattention, from attraction to distraction,
from conversion to diversion.

Distraction floods Western culture today. Advertisers catch our eye by every possible means, soundbites grab our fleeting attention, and information floods over us. "Vast enterprises described as the communications industry inform, misinform, or dis-inform the public about politics, wars, and revolutions, about religious and racial conflicts, and also about education, law, medicine, books, theatre, music, cookery," writes author Saul Bellow. "To make such lists," however, "gives a misleading impression of order. The truth is that we are in an unbearable state of confusion, or distraction." [7]

A central conduit for distraction today is the entertainment industry. Neil Postman's book *Amusing Ourselves to Death* focuses upon the role of television in this. The very manner in which mass entertainment is used is distracted when, for example, "grazing" between TV channels and surfing the internet. Reveries of consumption are a widely prevalent form of diversion, stimulated by product displays and advertisements. More intense diversionary activities of concern today include gambling, alcohol and drug abuse, and the immediate stimuli of sex and violence pursued for distraction.

The pull of diversion and distraction are not, of course, new in our day. In the seventeenth century, Blaise Pascal noted that diversion "prevents us thinking about ourselves and leads us imperceptibly to destruction. But for it we should be bored, and boredom would drive us to seek some more solid means of escape, but diversion passes our time and brings us imperceptibly to our death." [8]

By the beginning of the twentieth century, a new cultural tendency of distraction had caught the attention of some Christian commentators. In 1906, theologian P. T. Forsyth remarked with regret that people "will not attend, they will not force themselves to attend, gravely to the gravest things . . . they read everything in a vagrant, browsing fashion. They turn on the most serious subjects the holiday, seaside, newspaper habit of mind." [9] G. K. Chesterton, writing in 1909, discerned a prevalent laziness and fatigue: "It is customary to complain of the bustle and strenuousness of our epoch. But in truth the chief mark of our epoch is a

7. Bellow, "The Distracted Public," 155–56.

8. Pascal, *Pensées*, (no. 414), 120. See also his more extended reflections in *Pensées*, VIII: Diversion (nos. 132–39), 37–43.

9. Forsyth, "The Reality of Grace," 152.

profound laziness and fatigue; and the fact is that the real laziness is the cause of the apparent bustle."[10]

While Forsyth's remark was provoked in response to a widespread casual *disregard for* religion, a casual attitude can also give rise to a *cheap embrace of* religion. Here, instead of the *incredulity* found in rationalism we find religious *credulity*. Perhaps Forsyth saw this in the danger of sentiment: "The serious thinkers are discredited as ponderous pedants . . . But religion must be either theological or sentimental, and if it is sentimental its life is brief. It has no depth of earth."[11] More recently Melvyn Matthews has warned of "a sickness of spirit abroad which forces us into cheap or sentimental theological solutions. An avoidance of moral conflict, a ready acceptance of so-called religious experience, whatever its origin or quality, these are the signs of a cheapening of the religious spirit in men and women."[12] Here genuine, lively, religious enquiry dissolves into credulity.

Bellow notes, however, that a state of dispersed attention does seem to offer certain advantages to those involved. "It may be compared to a sport like hang gliding. In distraction we are suspended, we hover, we reserve our options."[13] This can help to maintain a certain illusion of control when we see ourselves as possessing "uncashed" choices. However, this is indeed an illusion; control is lost if we make a choice. Commitment is thus shunned as a bereavement. We shall consider further, in chapter 5, how the rhetoric of choice is used to maintain an illusion of control that is fundamentally evasive and escapist. Authentic power of choice, by contrast, is realized precisely in the exercise of choice itself in the commitment of lively religious enquiry.

Before we turn to consumerism and choice, however, we shall trace further consequences of the modern inversion that appear in a distinctively modern fragmentation and polarization of society—including the church.

To summarize: Christians are called by God today to live converted to attentiveness towards God. They are called to witness to such attentiveness, which is at the heart of enquiry, knowledge, and action at their most deep and lively, and grounds a disposition of radical responsive-

10. Chesterton, *Orthodoxy*, 228.

11. Forsyth, "Cross as the Final Seat of Authority."

12. Matthews, *Delighting in God*, 99.

13. Bellow, "Distracted Public," 161.

ness. And they are called to seek the conversion of others to this through their own Christian practice and reflective thinking. They are called also to acknowledge, and repent of, their own complicity with Western cultural habits of thought and action that subvert this—in particular their complicity with the Cartesian "logical inversion" that understands questioning as doubting, and interprets all questioning (including religious) by reference to this.

Attentiveness towards God does not narrow down the scope of enquiry: rather, it enlarges it. It grounds rationality, moral judgment, valuing, and choice at their most deep and vital. And it also upholds the proper primacy of reflective practice and of canon as inescapable expressions of human participation in the probing wisdom of God, through God's indwelling Spirit, and to the glory of God.

4   Contemporary Demonization and Polarization

Conversion to Divine Bearings

In Western societies today the church has tended to polarize between two groups. One of these groups has arisen from the liberal Christian tradition; the other from the evangelical tradition. Upon investigation they hold opposing views, in practice, of the nature of faith itself. The former holds to faith as a way of life in which all human truth-claims are to be questioned (including truth-claims about God) in the name of God. It is a way that opposes, in the name of a God of inclusive love, prejudice against any part of the human population, its beliefs and practices. The latter holds to faith as a matter of allegiance to Christ and to the gospel that brings membership of the group of all those who have made the same decision of allegiance. The former group opposes the latter group as standing for precisely the kind of human dogmatism and prejudice that faith seeks to overcome; the latter group opposes the former as contradicting in a basic way the commitment of faith itself. The divergence between these groups is thus seen by each not as about a difference of view regarding questions that arise *within* the life of faith, but as about the difference between faith and its contradiction. Accordingly, Christian dialogue between the two groups is seen as inappropriate by each; each denies that there are common foundations for such dialogue. They tend each to go their own way, regardless of the other; when face to face, they are effectively polarized.

To discuss this polarization I shall use the following terminology. Where liberal Christians have fallen into the kind of implicit denial of faith that is habitually and rightly opposed by evangelical Christians, I shall call their position "relativist liberal." Where evangelical Christians have fallen into the kind of implicit denial of faith that is habitually and rightly opposed by liberal Christians, I shall call their position "fundamentalist."

It may be observed that the polarization between relativist liberal and fundamentalist Christians tends to be sharper among Christians for whom *correct views on certain religious matters* are an occupying concern and are seen as a critical test of faith. It tends to be sharper among those who have received some formal theological teaching, including church leaders and teachers. It can also grow sharp between the liberal elite of central church institutions and individual congregations. Polarization is also more noticeable in those cultures such as the United States where a sense of personal identity is formed more by conscious allegiances and affiliations than by unreflective participation in an ancient common cultural heritage.

In past generations church congregations saw themselves as belonging first and foremost to historic denominations that tended each to go their own way. Today it is increasingly common for congregations (especially Protestant ones) to see themselves as belonging to either liberal or conservative/evangelical Christianity—each, again, going their own way.

How shall we understand this polarization? I suggest that its logic may be outlined as follows. I shall then elaborate the two polar positions and appraise them in a Christian context, drawing on what has already been written.

1. Each of the two traditions—liberal and evangelical—has rightly identified, and is concerned to oppose, an enemy of faith.

2. Neither of these traditions would be right simply to identify the other with this enemy; rather, each tradition must exercise discernment towards, and engage in discussion with, the other in order to recognize where the responsibilities of faith lie.

3. Polarization arises where one group (or both groups) identify the other with the enemy opposed by itself. That is, one or more groups deny that the question of discernment arises; a dismissive stance is adopted towards the other.

4. Where one group is dismissive towards the other, it thereby falls precisely into the denial of faith that the other group opposes.

If follows from this outline that when liberal Christians see all evangelical faith without discrimination as fundamentalist, they show themselves to be relativist liberals; and when evangelical Christians see all liberal faith without discrimination as unambiguously relativist liberal, they show themselves to be fundamentalists.

This framework sounds simple enough and even-handed. However, in its application, it is otherwise. We are required to interpret with discernment a diverse range of encounters some of which may by no means invite even-handed treatment. In one case, polarization may arise from a divergence between faithful liberal Christians and (faith-distorting) fundamentalists; in another, between faithful evangelical Christians and (faith-distorting) relativist liberals.

Let us now explore more closely each of the positions referred to here, and consider how each relates to the other and to the gospel.

LIBERAL CHRISTIAN FAITH

The sovereign approach of God breaks our cultural presuppositions and personal attachments open; God judges and transforms such commitments, bringing our lives under his sovereign rule. In so doing, God draws us to share by grace in his own interrogation of our presuppositions and attachments: the gospel summons and empowers us to question for ourselves our assumptions and attachments in its own light.

The faithful liberal tradition within Christianity is impelled by a concern to honor this responsibility. It is especially concerned, on the one hand, to honor the responsibility of self-criticism in matters of faith, allowing God to challenge our understanding precisely of God and of faith; it is concerned, on the other hand, to honor the possibility that people who are not explicitly Christian may show openness to God and may present to us, unacknowledged, this same challenge from God to our understanding of God and of faith.

Standing in contrast with such liberal concern, and neglectful of this dual responsibility, is the attitude of those who claim to possess for themselves an understanding of God and of faith that puts them above any such challenge by God whether through the gospel or, under God's providence, through people who are not professing Christians. Such religious claims attract the censure of liberal faith as incorrigibly closed to the truth of God and of human life under God. Such claims are the enemy of, and a radical distortion of, faith.

However, this liberal sense of responsibility is itself vulnerable to a radical distortion of its own. Having been drawn into God's interrogation of our assumptions and attachments, we may imagine to take over control of such interrogation from the gospel and thereby move beyond any further such interrogation of ourselves.

This is a distortion of faith. To turn to Christ is not to place ourselves beyond further interrogation but to hold ourselves open to, and to take responsibility for, endless further interrogation by God in Christ. This is what it means in effect to "walk in the light" (1 John 1:7). Faithful interrogation arises fundamentally from God and participation in it is through openness to God, bringing to light the subject of interrogation. It always retains this character. To a modern way of thinking, however, interrogation is, by contrast, the autonomous action of an individual who turns their attention upon an idea of their choice, decides what question is to be put regarding it, and puts this question. Once this view of interrogation gets applied to questioning the gospel itself, we effectively take over control of interrogation from the gospel. In this way modern thinking fosters a radical distortion of liberal faith itself.

This modern way of thinking, we have seen, is based on the unwarranted assumption that autonomous, rational human beings always inhabit horizons as wide as or wider than those whose Christian belief they now question in would-be detachment. It fails to allow in principle that such belief may open upon wider horizons than those brought by the would-be modern questioner and subverts, in practice, receptivity to this possibility. Accordingly, when those who are interrogated by the modern questioner defend their beliefs, the latter fails to discriminate between two possibilities: that these beliefs are unwarranted (and exposed as such by interrogation) and that these beliefs point as a sign to God, interrogating the questioner himself and interrogating the imagined wider horizons he brings in his questioning. Instead, the modern interrogator simply assumes that the former is the case.

As we have seen, this assumption of detachment is not misleading where reflection is taking place within a shared theoretical framework; the interrogation it instigates is reasonable enough. In this context, the questioning of a belief and commitment to that belief are indeed mutually exclusive; enquiry into the truth of a belief is incompatible with commitment to its truth. However, the modern way of thinking wrongly carries over into the realm of more lively enquiry this dichotomy between questioning of a belief and commitment to a belief. In so doing it identifies as the enemy of enquiry and turns hostile attention upon commitment to any belief that it itself questions. What is more, it *defines questioning by reference to this enemy.*

Once questioning is defined in these terms, however, the way opens for a further development: the very act of questioning as such may be recognized as itself, of logical necessity, called into question. Questioning may be "deconstructed" as a way of viewing and interrogating the world that reflects entirely the interests and commitments of the originating, autonomous questioner (apart, of course, from the deconstructive questioning of questioning itself, which is taken as free of self-interest). We have already described a similar development in modern (secularist) thinking as the logical inversion of the human subject and of God. Now we see this development arising within faith itself, as liberal Christianity becomes "non-realist" or philosophically constructivist. At this point, self-criticism collapses in Christian faith into self-assertion: one's faith is one's chosen way of seeing the world. At this point, the enemy of truth gets seen as lying not only in commitment to a particular belief as true but already in the assumption that the question of truth arises in the first place with regard to a particular belief. There now remains nothing left to discuss with those who are committed to what they believe as objectively true.

EVANGELICAL CHRISTIAN FAITH

God who approaches us in sovereignty calls us to trust him radically: to entrust ourselves and our world to him without reserve, and draw life and understanding anew from him. God calls us to personal conversion: he calls us to offer up everything in which we have placed our trust, leaving God to grant to these things whatever place they may or may not have in the new life he gives us. And where we have resisted showing necessary trust, he calls us to do so.

Such radical trust in God is a compelling yet freely offered, proper response to God's trustworthiness or faithfulness. As we respond to God in trust, God draws us to participate for ourselves by grace in his own trustworthy faithfulness: he calls forth faithfulness on our part as we take responsibility for what God has shown us, given us, and has promised us.

The faithful evangelical tradition within Christianity is impelled by a concern to honor this responsibility of believing and trusting in God. It is concerned especially, on the one hand, that Christians should be faithful to their calling and not be Christian in name only, but to live converted lives; on the other hand, it is concerned that Christians should be trustworthy witnesses to God, evangelizing and bringing to conversion those who do not believe and trust in God.

Standing in contrast with such evangelical concern, and neglectful of the above responsibilities, are those who, claiming that every belief should be questioned, mean by such questioning an autonomous act of doubting that presumes to approach any belief from wider horizons than those of the believer. Such claims attract the censure of evangelical faith as incorrigibly closed to the trustworthy truth of God and of human life under God. Such claims are the enemy of, and a radical distortion of, faith.

However, this evangelical sense of responsibility is itself vulnerable to a radical distortion of its own. Having been drawn into God's faithfulness, we may imagine that this faithfulness of ours can in effect take the place of God's faithfulness towards us; we may imagine that we need entrust ourselves no further to God because we already have from God everything for which we needed to trust God.

This is a distortion of faith. Our responsibility to believe and trust in God always entails that we remain open to fresh discovery of what this responsibility involves in new circumstances as this is shown to us by God. It can never be reduced to commitment to the truth of certain beliefs formulated within an established theoretical framework of understanding. Unfortunately, however, we may be persuaded to think this way if we adopt modern assumptions about questioning and about faith. We may come to define faith as *commitment to* the truth of certain beliefs in contrast to *questioning of* their truth. Faith gets equated with allegiance in face of questioning; questioning is seen as the great enemy. Faith is now *defined by its opposition to this enemy*. Ironically, however, this definition of faith—by positing the opposition of questioning and commitment—secretly adopts the presuppositions of the enemy it opposes.

In reality, of course, (true) questioning is not the enemy of faith; rather the enemy of faith—*an* enemy of faith, to be precise—is that distorted form of questioning endorsed by modern ideology that exalts the autonomous human subject over what it encounters. True questioning belongs precisely to, and finds its paradigmatic instance in, faithful religious enquiry. Once its defining character is no longer acknowledged to be in such enquiry, the residual form taken by religious allegiance becomes a distorted one. Because of this distortion, all questioning now gets seen as an instance of ideological liberalism, to be opposed. However, this generates opposition not only to such questioning but also, indiscriminately, to true religious enquiry. In effect, religious allegiance distorts here into precisely that kind of false commitment, closed to enquiry into truth, that liberals are concerned rightly to challenge in a spirit of Christian responsibility. Evangelicalism turns into the betrayal of faith that is called fundamentalism.

THE LOGIC OF POLARIZATION

The polarization between relativist liberalism and fundamentalism is between two positions each conscious of themselves and held in conscious opposition to the other. These positions are defined, by those who hold them and those who oppose them, in terms of their own beliefs; and the holding of these positions and beliefs is seen as a matter of absolute personal import. They are, however, both distortions of Christian faith.

This distortion arises insofar as liberal or evangelical Christians *turn their attention from God to that which they rightly oppose as against God, but then effectively grant to this ultimate status such that opposition to it is taken comprehensively to define and prescribe faith itself.*

To help us picture this development, let us use an analogy from what is involved in finding our bearings physically. Let us consider the business of taking bearings when at sea. Suppose that a lighthouse marks dangerous rocks. It is indeed necessary to avoid these; however, it would be quite wrong to adopt this lighthouse as providing all bearings for our journey itself. Were we to do this, we would be in danger of endlessly circling or spirally round the lighthouse as a moth circles a light. Our bearings need to be taken from wider horizons, horizons within which dangerous rocks of the lighthouse are themselves set. Discerning these wider horizons is our primary concern; the rocks we must avoid are of secondary concern, even though at a particular point on our journey, the whole task of pursuing our journey may rightly be focused upon avoiding them. To adopt the rocks as a primary source of bearings for our journey would be wrongly to invert what is primary and what is secondary.

To adopt a relativist liberal or fundamentalist position is analogous to adopting, for all bearings, the rocks to be avoided. Each positions sees the other as spelling "shipwreck" and steers away from it, taking bearings from this picture alone.

This picture may help us to think a little further about relativist liberalism and fundamentalism and the polarization between them. Consider firstly that the act of taking bearings from rocks that must avoided, rather than from the wider horizons within which they and we are set, is mistaken. It is to find our bearings in the wrong place. And thus far it would seem a mistake that can be corrected by argument and demonstration. However, this act of "taking bearings wrongly" may possibly reflect a failure *seriously to attend to the question of* true bearings, and give priority to other things in place of this. This is precisely so in the analogous case of Christian horizons: not only are the bearings wrong; there is something wrong about the act of "taking bearings" in which they are adopted. Here, ignorance of true bearings reflects an ignoring of the question of true bearings and an evasion of the demands of this question.

What are these demands? They are personal demands of an unqualified nature: to give ourselves in radical responsiveness to God. This is where our analogy breaks down. While the business of finding our bearings for a journey makes certain demands upon our perception, we will normally have a certain destination in mind and purpose in hand. Accordingly, there is a sense in which such bearings are a tool in our service: we use such bearings for our own ends. By contrast, in the case of Christian faith, our attention to, and discernment of, true bearings demands that we yield up all such ends, for the bearings we seek are such as to shape our direction and purpose in the first place.

When, in a Christian context, we take bearings from "what spells shipwreck," in effect we reduce the business of finding bearings (with its unqualified demands upon us) to an established procedure at our disposal, instead of entrusting ourselves radically to seeking and responding to true bearings. We rely on a methodology to secure our journey. We take a strategy that is particular to our situation in a given moment and project it forward into the future as if it were absolute. This is rather like—to borrow an image from Marshall McLuhan—"driving by the rear-view mirror." Instead of discerning and responding to the road as it unfolds before us, we rely upon steering away from what is behind us.

There is an inner contradiction hidden here. On the one hand, by making absolute our present strategy to avoid shipwreck, we make absolute our own situation whatever it may be—and in effect make ourselves absolute. In a Christian context, we put ourselves at the centre; the bearings we should seek and serve we reduce to our own service.

On the other hand, by making absolute our present strategy to avoid shipwreck, we make absolute that from which we take bearings, and allow this to define our journey. In a Christian context, we allow that which we have identified as the enemy of faith to define faith itself. We turn it into a kind of negative idol, and come under its control.

Basically in all this we have turned our attention away from God. We have turned our attention upon a strategy (upon the use of bearings we think can rely on) and we have turned out attention upon ourselves (upon we who use these bearings).

Correspondingly, the restoration of faith from its relativist liberal and fundamentalist distortions will have two aspects. On the one hand, it will involve the revision of bearings: the bearings that are falsely assumed *as* bearings are exposed and attention is revived to the question of true bearings. The methodology trusted as absolute is exposed as belonging to particular situations within the wider horizons of faith. On the other hand, it will involve personal conversion: our attention to ourselves rather than to God is exposed—revealing our hidden captivity to false idols—and our attention is turned back upon God who is the source of who we are.

Let us consider these two aspects in turn.

POLARIZATION AND ITS RESOLUTION: ADDRESSING FALSE ASSUMPTIONS

With what argument may we confront relativist liberalist and fundamentalist beliefs in order to persuade those who hold them that they distort Christian faith? We have compared each position to that in which reliance is placed on false bearings, instead of continuing to discern what might constitutes true bearings. Instead of being a matter of lively responsiveness, in discernment and commitment, towards God, bearings have become for us, unacknowledged, a closed matter. The argument must proceed by reawakening this question—that is, by directing the attention of those in the liberal and evangelical traditions to the responsibilities they are concerned respectively to uphold, and to probe with them the meaning of these responsibilities. This can be done by inviting each to explore the question of, and to seek, self-referential consistency in their understanding of these responsibilities.

Let us consider an example from the liberal and evangelical traditions in turn. For the latter, we shall consider a case that poses the question whether the evangelical emphasis upon faithful allegiance to the truth has distorted into an indiscriminate, misguided allegiance. The case in question is allegiance to creationism. First, however, we shall consider, for a liberal example, the slightly more complex case of a liberal theologian (John Spong) who, indiscriminately critical of orthodox Christian belief, finds his own criticisms of orthodoxy levelled *at himself* by a "more liberal," non-realist theologian (Don Cupitt); who defends himself (ironically) against these criticisms precisely with arguments like those by which orthodox Christians defend themselves against his own criticisms; and who therefore faces the challenge, as a matter of consistency, to be more open to orthodoxy in the same way that he calls Cupitt to be more open to his own liberal realist position.

Liberalism Interrogated

We may address those who see themselves as inheriting and developing the liberal sense of responsibility towards the Christian faith, asking to examine with them what this responsibility means. Here we can celebrate the principle upheld by the liberal tradition, that responsibility towards the truth requires every belief to be open to challenge and to rational enquiry; and we can then seek to examine together what this means. After all, what should the liberal make of the fact that the critical principle itself invites our *commitment*? If commitment is seen as the enemy of critical enquiry and therefore of truth, this surely means that we must distance ourselves from and criticize the critical principle itself? However, this would be to subvert critical enquiry. The alternative is to acknowledge that commitment to the principle of critical enquiry does not itself contradict critical enquiry; that is, commitment does not, as such, contradict critical enquiry. Accordingly, in principle commitment *to Christian belief* does not contradict critical enquiry; rather such belief may precisely sponsor and enlarge such enquiry. Will liberalism allow this possibility? If so, it has to acknowledge the need to discriminate, as an integral part of critical enquiry, between (1) occasions when commitment to a belief is rightly to be challenged in rational enquiry, and (2) occasions when commitment to a belief precisely endorses critical enquiry and to withhold commitment from it would be to subvert critical enquiry.

The contours of this argument may be discerned in an exchange between John Spong and Don Cupitt at the British "Sea of Faith" conference in 1995. As is well known, John Spong adopts a critical stance towards those who take orthodox Christian beliefs "literally" rather than "symbolically," accusing them of clinging to false securities. He sees Christian doctrine (including the physical resurrection of Christ) as humanly constructed from our limited cultural experience and not reflecting the objective reality of God. This objective reality, however, he affirms: at the 1995 conference he reaffirmed his belief in "a God who is real beyond my constructs of the divine one and a God who constantly impinges upon me as I open myself to that in-breaking presence and as I walk in the wordless wonder of that reality."[1]

In his opening talk, Don Cupitt had criticized any such position, taking a non-realist stance. To him, this position belonged still within a "very ancient, long-established culture of dependency. People reckon they must have something out there to lean on, however minimally." He challenged "those who cling fiercely to that tiny speck of objectivity, that feeling that there is, there must be, something real out there to which all the symbolism refers, even though we cannot say anything about it. People cling fiercely, desperately to that last sliver of objectivity."[2]

John Spong protested at the pejorative quality of this language. For him the reality of God was "not a sliver but an essence in its pristine beauty." He saw those like himself as "breaking open the symbols and removing the barnacles" and seeking a church that has "scraped itself much cleaner than ever before."[3]

We see here Spong claiming the mantle of the courageous, honest, self-reliant critic, challenging all clinging dependency among Christians; we see Cupitt wrest this mantle to himself from Spong, whom he sees as clinging still to false securities; and we see Spong seize it back again with

---

1. Spong, "Religion as a Human Creation," 12. This and the following quotations are taken from the *Quarterly Magazine of the Sea of Faith Network*, October 1995.

2. Cupitt, "Our Dual Agenda," 5.

3. Spong, "Closing Conference Address," 18.

the implication that Cupitt's challenge is indiscriminate: Cupitt fails to discriminate between false dependency and a position (such as Spong's) that precisely challenges false dependency. As a consequence—from Spong's point of view—when Cupitt imagines to challenge the former, he actually challenges and subverts the latter: his criticism attacks the critical stance itself.

Now this response to Cupitt is ironic because Spong's *own* criticism of orthodox belief is similarly pejorative in tone and indiscriminate in target: it simply assumes that orthodox belief represents false dependency. Thus Spong's own contribution to another, earlier debate drew the comment that his "use of pejorative words . . . and of sweeping generalizations was clearly designed to undermine a biblically-serious stance . . . without the necessity of offering either substantive evidence or logical argument."[4] Spong ought, therefore, to pay new attention to the possibility that, insofar as his own rejection of Cupitt's criticism are well founded, similarly the orthodox rejection of his own criticisms may be well founded. In this way his own critical stance towards orthodoxy might be "scraped clean" of the barnacles that modern thought has attached to critical enquiry!

However, insofar as Spong remains wedded to the confident assumption that he criticizes orthodox belief from a higher, more pristine encounter with God, there is a sense in which he deserves the criticism he receives from Cupitt—not because he affirms the reality of God, but because his affirmation of the reality of God shows itself a source of false security for him precisely as he relies on it to uphold his (false) self-image as a courageous and honest critic. If Spong wishes more faithfully to speak of the reality of God, he must abandon this self-image. Instead he must allow that orthodox belief has things to teach him (and Cupitt) about openness to the reality of God. Their own openness is not authentic; they rely upon false assumptions leading them to an indiscriminate dismissal of Christian belief; and their resistance to facing this reveals that they are less concerned with actually being open to God than with maintaining an image and pretence of openness in the eyes of themselves and of others.

4. Hancock, "Reflections on the Use of Language," 31.

Evangelicalism Interrogated

When we turn to those who see themselves as inheriting and developing the evangelical sense of responsibility towards the Christian faith, we shall similarly want to explore with them what this responsibility means. In particular, we may celebrate the principle upheld by evangelical tradition, that it is a Christian responsibility to show firm allegiance to the truth and not disregard or betray it; and we may then seek to examine together what this means. Evangelical allegiance is, after all, allegiance *to Christ*; the Christian's responsibility is not to show allegiance for its own sake. To put it another way, the Christian responsibility of allegiance entails a responsibility to show critical discernment regarding what commands such allegiance in the first place. Such critical discernment should not be vetoed as contrary to Christian allegiance; rather it is constitutive of allegiance if this allegiance is Christian. Without such discernment, something other than Christian truth may gain our unwitting assent as being Christian. Such discernment will not be a matter of questioning Christ simply "from outside" but rather of entering more deeply and critically *into* Christ in discernment and commitment.

To illustrate this, let us consider the questions raised by the doctrine popularly known as "creationism." This theory of earth's origins conceives the earth as very young by modern scientific standards and supposedly allows the possibility that the opening chapters of the Book of Genesis are chronologically accurate accounts of historical events. In recent decades some evangelical Christians (particularly in the United States) have come to adopt this doctrine. Such Christians have seen it as a matter of their Christian allegiance that they should uphold this doctrine against its critics. Arguments have ensued between these Christians and other people, especially about whether this doctrine should be taught as a theory alongside the theory of evolution in schools.

Now fundamentalism, as we have understood it, is characterized by a stance of allegiance without due discrimination. Is creationism a case in point? Firstly we might note that it is a scientific hypothesis: it is a geological theory. It was formulated originally by a man without geological training who was a Seventh-Day Adventist. The founder of this group, Ellen White, had reported visions in which she witnessed the act of creation in seven days.[5] The geological theory of creationism's founder

---

5. On the provenance of creationism see Numbers, *Creationists*. For a chapter on the rise of this doctrine among evangelical Christians, see Noll, *Scandal of the Evangelical Mind*.

sought to provide scientific legitimation for her visions. Although evangelical Christians do not accept the authority of Ellen White's visions, some do see this creationist geological theory as defending Christian belief against its attackers.

How has this happened? It would seem that creationism has been seized upon by evangelicals as offering scientific legitimation for resisting the excessive claims of "evolutionists." According to the latter, the theory of evolution provides a sufficient account of the appearance of all life and that this account explains all there is to know about life. Now are these claims within the scope of science or are they the claims of a materialist ideology—one inconsistent with Christian revelation? Creationism, for its part, takes them to be based on scientific claims and inconsistent with Christian revelation. It therefore opposes them with an alternative scientific theory.

As Christians we shall undoubtedly want to resist the claims of ideological "evolutionists." One possibility is that the science upon which evolutionist claims build is mistaken. In this case, Christians will be glad of any alternative scientific theory that exposes this (not that this will necessarily be immune to ideological extrapolation in turn). Another possibility is that the science upon which evolutionist claims are built appears to us as itself sound, but that evolutionists build a false ideology upon it. In this case, we shall see no reason to turn to "creationism" to resist this science. Rather, our primary task will be to discern the true nature and scope of science within a Christian worldview. As for creationism, its historical origins suggest (although they do not *prove*) that the evangelical adoption of this theory rests upon disregard for, rather than the exercise of, such discernment.

Now there is a risk that I may be misunderstood at this point. My account of Spong's position and of creationism may seem a simple, detached, second-order explanation of these, showing that each rests upon blind assumption or allegiance rather than lively discernment. However, it is no such thing. Were it so, I could be accused myself of blindly writing off each position. To be valid, my account must rather be itself a matter of lively discernment. It is only with discernment that can we distinguish between discernment and blindness themselves.

More needs to be said about this. First, the discernment with which we distinguish between discernment and blindness themselves is itself an exercise of that latter, primary discernment. It is, in the first instance, a matter of attention to the truth of God. It is only when this reveals the positions of Spong and creationism as seemingly beyond justification that the question of their underlying blindness presents itself to us. This means that, second, although the operation of blind, relativist liberal or fundamentalist presuppositions explains simply these problems, the discernment whether this explanation is *right* entails all that is involved in discerning the truth of God in the first place. In other words, the conclusion of blindness may appear simple but if it is indeed a discerning conclusion it by no means represents an oversimplification of the problem. Third, while such discernment is directed explicitly toward the truth of God, it is also directed implicitly towards communion with dialogue partners, in the truth of God: it is oriented towards consensual exploration. Thus my conclusion that Spong and creationists are each committed to blind assumptions or allegiances leaves an unresolved issue for me before God: can we not agree together upon where there has been blindness?

POLARIZATION AND ITS RESOLUTION: ADDRESSING PERSONAL IDENTITY

Insofar as the polarization between relativist liberals and fundamentalists is a consequence of false assumptions by each regarding the responsibilities of faith—assumptions that those involved can hopefully be persuaded to examine in the light of faith—then the above argument offers a way of healing their respective distortions of faith and of healing the polarization between them. However, more than argument may be required for, typically, the two positions have attracted the personal commitment of their adherents in a way that blocks any such self-examination or acknowledgement of their false assumptions.

What is the nature of this attraction? Briefly, each position may be described as proffering a conscious sense of personal identity upon its adherents. Those who adopt either of these two positions acquire an identity in their own eyes: they see themselves as standing for something that is unquestionably worth standing for. In effect, they see themselves as belonging to a band of crusaders. In the case of relativist liberalism, a sense is acquired of having the personal identity of one who is independent-minded and not subservient to other people's ideas or to human conventions, who is "knowing" and not captive to illusions, and who is bravely skeptical and not reliant on comfortable self-deceptions.

In the case of fundamentalism, a sense is acquired of having the personal identity of one who belongs among those who are unassailably in the right rather than among those who do not know or do not do what is right, and as one who is faithful to—rather than one who ignores or betrays—what is properly required of one.

How does such a sense of identity differ from that bestowed authentically by the Christian faith that forms us as persons each uniquely known and loved by God as his sons and daughters and called to fulfill the purposes for which he made us? The identity God bestows on us is an identity we find as we love and serve God with our whole being as a "living sacrifice." This is not a self-regarding identity; on the contrary, it is self-forgetful: "Whoever wants to save his life will lose it, but whoever loses his life for my sake and the gospel's sake will save it" (Mark 8:35) The sense of identity proffered to us by relativist liberalism and by fundamentalism is different from this. Here it is the sense of "being someone"—in one's own eyes and in the eyes of others—that is at the centre of our concern. Although this identity is achieved as we entrust ourselves to a certain stance, in reality we adopt this stance merely as a means to attaining this sense of identity: our self-regarding self is our end. In other words, here there is no patient, attentive, self-critical, or self-sacrificial spirit seriously at work, but a narcissistic spirit. We shall consider the role of narcissism in contemporary Western culture further in the chapters following.

The identity that God bestows on us is that of a person made in his own image; we are who we are through gracious participation in his own life in Christ and through God's Holy Spirit. Again, the sense of identity proffered by relativist liberalism and by fundamentalism is different from this. It is constituted negatively, at the expense of other people. It is constituted by our view that we stand in right opposition to certain other groups as eternally, damnably in the wrong. It is also constituted secretly by the envious gaze of those who long impossibly for an identity that they feel they themselves lack. Such identity is an illusion; it depends upon a self-regarding gaze that *itself* secretly arises from, and perpetuates, a felt lack of identity; it is as empty as the identity of that which it demonizes; it is as empty as the spectral idol to which, in the very act of defining itself over against it, it secretly defers.

POLARIZATION BETWEEN RELATIVISTS AND
FUNDAMENTALISTS: A MODERN PHENOMENON

Such polarization within the church comes from a distorted view of commitment and questioning within the act of knowing. It is based on a view of these deriving from Cartesian habits of imagination that, as we saw in Part One, reflects the reality of theoretical knowledge (up to a point); but it does not reflect the reality of our most lively knowledge, enquiry, and action directed in openness towards God. This view sees commitment and questioning as mutually exclusive stances directed towards statements; and it is characteristic of modern thinking.

Accordingly, we might expect to find in wider modern society polarizations parallel to those within the church. Are there non-religious forms of the polarization taken between relativist liberalism and fundamentalism? In pursuit of this question, let us consider (1) "fundamentalist" conservative reactions against the erosion of traditional cultures and those who are party to this erosion, and (2) the fundamentalism of progressive "politically correct" ideology including the ideology associated with the phenomenon of "moral inversion" described by Michael Polanyi.

Culturally Conservative Fundamentalism

Lesslie Newbigin visited Germany in 1932. On his return to England, he reported:

> One of the strongest elements in the thinking of modern Germany is a deep distress of the individualism which is felt to have been dominant in the democratic-capitalist civilization of pre-war (i.e., WW1) Europe, a feeling after authority and authoritative forms of government, and a conviction that a man's worth is not just in himself but finds its expression only in a group. This idea is caught up in the conception of *Volkstum*, the conception of the folk or people as the God-given group in which the individual finds his true worth. This passionate "folk consciousness" is the dominating thing in German thought today—a feeling of the oneness and greatness of the German people, and at the same time a burning sense of the humiliations to which that great people is being subjected. Against this stand all so-called international forces which seem to stand for the leveling down and subjugation of the rich distinctiveness of national life.

> Linked with this rejection of individualism is the growth of
> the desire for planning and control in industry and commerce, as
> against the anarchy of present-day capitalism, and it has been the
> triumph of Hitler to wed together these two forces—nationalism
> and socialism—into the movement which he leads.[6]

Thus in Naziism was forged an ideology of absolute, "religious" allegiance to German culture. The purity of the Aryan race was elevated as a sacred cause whose claims relativized all others; the forces that intolerably subverted it were demonized as an enemy against which any means of attack were justified.

Now the fundamentalist racism of the Nazi regime appears a *conservative reaction* against global liberal capitalism and its humiliation of Germany. However, the truth is more ambiguous. Nazi ideology reformulated German cultural self-understanding and the nature of German cultural responsibility. It did not simply conserve German culture; it redefined it. In this regard, Nazi totalitarianism was distinctively modern rather than traditional: it constructed a novel, ideological German identity. The result was an outlook quite different from anything found in traditional culture itself. Nazi ideology was as much a subversion of traditional culture as was liberal capitalism, although perhaps in a less obvious way.

Parallels are evident between the Nazi reaction against liberal capitalism and the contemporary reaction of fundamentalist Islamists against Western-led global capitalism. Here again there is a reaction fed by a sense of the subversion and humiliation of a culture and tradition by anarchic capitalism and individualism. Here again is a reaction, claiming a religious mandate, that demonizes its enemies and sanctions all means in service to its cause. And here again, despite the explicitly conservative intent of fundamentalist Islamists, their allegiance is to a distinctively modern ideology that redefines Islam and its responsibilities, and not to any traditional Islamic culture (on this see further below).

Progressive Fundamentalism

While liberalism commends openness over against prejudice and questioning over against dogmatism, in practice it can become fundamentalist. Once openness and questioning acquire a rigid, distorted meaning

6. Newbigin, "German Outlook Today," 31–32.

in modern thinking, their actual pursuit can reduce to an enactment of ideological allegiance that precisely subverts authentic openness and questioning. A "progressive" program can become, in effect, deeply prejudiced and dogmatic in its handling of reality.

Thus David Bromwich was provoked to begin his book *Politics by Other Means: Higher Education and Group Thinking* (1992) with a chapter titled "The New Fundamentalists." He documented how, in U.S. academia, a person's group identity (as conferred by ethnicity, gender, culture, etc.) had come to be seen as defining their thinking and thus, implicitly, their allegiance; as we might say, "group thinking" had been ascribed absolute or religious status. Accordingly, any attempt that others might make to open up such thinking to "cross-cultural" examination had come to be demonized as an outrage—a blasphemous imposition by imperial Western liberal thinking, inviting unqualified censure.

Such "progressive" fundamentalism extends today more widely through what is often called "politically correct" ideological thinking and management. Its excesses have attracted, in come cases, popular derision as it flies in the face of "common sense" in matters of moral judgment. Thus a proper moral concern for equality of employment opportunity has led sometimes to protocols for processing job applications that are overrationalized ideologically and effectively veto (and demonize) the kind of complex, comprehensive moral judgment involved in any responsible decision-making. We shall discuss such matters further in chapter 8.

The growth of a fundamentalist "political correctness" may be seen as a contemporary expression of a development in moral thinking that arose in association with Marxist ideology and that was characterized by Michael Polanyi as "moral inversion."[7] Here, traditions of moral judgment are dismissed as mere expressions of class interest. Their moral imperative may be dismissed and overridden by the imperative of revolution against the oppressive classes. The *exercise of* moral judgment is now scorned. This scorn does not, however, express a morally relativistic, laissez-faire stance, but rather a passionate "moral perfectionism." Here, what Polanyi calls our "moral passions" are cut loose from the exercise of moral judgment, to which they belong, and invested in a "final" cause to

---

7. Michael Polanyi's account of moral inversion is scattered through his writings. A helpful introduction to it is provided in chapter 7 of Scott, *Everyman Revived*. For a more detailed scholarly treatment see Yeager, "Confronting the Minotaur."

be pursued by all means. Indeed, in an act of inversion, traditional moral judgment is now itself made the enemy to be targeted with an unqualified passion that defines the "moral" by reference to itself. This passion may with equanimity sanction violence. Of course, the fundamentalist "political correctness" we see within Western institutions today does not normally sanction violence, but within the bounds of law it routinely prompts strident initiatives that indiscriminately violate the fabric of moral community without discrimination.

Such "moral inversion" may be understood, I suggest, as an aspect of that logical inversion of primary and secondary that we considered in chapter 3. Whereas moral reaction against any particular practice arises originally in the wider context of the positive exercise of moral judgment, here such a reaction is taken as *itself defining* a moral stance by reference to which all moral questions are to be judged.

In summary then, upon analysis we find that "conservative" fundamentalism actually involves a "progressive" reconstruction of what it claims to conserve, while "progressive" fundamentalism actually involves a "conservative" allegiance to certain abstract ideas and principles rather than being open to progress towards truth and goodness through responsiveness to the real world under God in all its concrete complexity.

DEMONIZATION

Fundamentalism, religious and otherwise, thus conceals a profound irony. On the one hand, its resistance to the enemy that dominates it is an absolute or religious resistance; it effectively demonizes this enemy. However, in so doing *it defines itself in a hidden way by reference to this enemy.* It calls its adherents to unqualified allegiance; but *it defines that to which allegiance is to be shown negatively by reference to that which it resists. In so doing, it fails* authentically to uphold what it intends to uphold; instead it incorporates into what it upholds, the very presuppositions of that which it opposes as its absolute enemy. The opposition between them is conceived within a frame adopted from the enemy. Fundamentalism is thus, on the other hand—precisely in its stance of absolute opposition—domesticated to that which it opposes.

Let me illustrate this irony. Popular culture in New Zealand is dominated by rugby, a sport played and followed predominantly by men. This domination is reflected in television programming. In the 1990s a prominent feminist professor spoke out against this. She argued that television should broadcast more women's sport. However, other women then responded to her by pointing out that they were actually not much interested in sport in the first place; what most women wanted was not the broadcasting of more women's sport in the place of men's sport, but the broadcasting of less sport. The feminist professor, inspired by female opposition to male domination, had framed the issue too narrowly in terms of an opposition itself based on male presuppositions. She had seen the *maleness* of sport broadcasting as the thing to resist; but in so doing she had precisely adopted, by way of unthinking presupposition, the distinctively male interest in sport in the first place. She thereby failed to speak authentically for women, but only for a "masculinized" version of womanhood.

The same irony marks many instances of so-called radical opposition to Western global capitalism by cultural groups. Again, we may take an example from New Zealand. Among the pre-colonial residents of New Zealand—the Maori—efforts to uphold traditional cultural insights in face of their erosion by Western capitalism has taken two forms. In the first, such issues are engaged in a traditional Maori way, through public debate by the local community gathered on the *marae* (the formal village space used for such occasions), in the presence of village elders, who search together for a communal consensus. This traditional method of making decisions offers scope for a variety of nuanced outcomes ranging from extensive accommodation to Western culture to firm resistance by means of one strategy or another. In the second, "radical" form of response, activists adopt postures of opposition through confrontation and protest. They draw a sharp contrast between Western and Maori ways, and their whole interest lies in charging the former with oppressing the latter. They knock the heads off statues honoring colonial figures and so on to express their protest. In truth, however, despite the fact that such activists think of themselves as *radical* representatives of their culture, they have turned away from traditional Maori approaches to the corporate exercise of judgment; they have adopted a viewpoint and self-understanding deeply imbibed from the Western culture they oppose and from Western Marxist ideology. In other words, they are less radically Maori in their practice than those who respond in the other way.

A parallel irony is evident in contemporary radical Islamism. In his article "The Western Mind of Radical Islam," Daniel Pipes notes that Muslim "radicals" have personally experienced and been influenced by the Western world to a great degree. Islamists, he writes, see ideology as the engine driving Western technological prowess, which they greatly admire. This prompts them, in the words of Olivier Roy, "to develop a modern political ideology based on Islam, which they see as the only way to come to terms with the modern world and the best means of confronting foreign imperialism." Their familiarity with Western ways corresponds to a relative ignorance of traditional Islamic societies. Pipes sees Islamist goals as "an Islamic-flavored version of western reality," and examines this with regard to religion, daily life, politics, and the law. "Even in rejecting the West," he concludes, "they accept it. However reactionary in intent, Islamism imports not just modern but Western ideas and institutions."

Of course, our *evaluation* of this state of affairs will depend on our evaluation of "Western reality" and Islam. More generally, our evaluation of such irony in any particular situation will depend on our view of the "combatants" in question. For example, when we encounter Christians who see themselves as countercultural, when actually they incorporate the presuppositions of the dominant culture they claim to counter, we may see this negatively as a matter of hidden betrayal and syncretism; whereas when adherents of other religions define themselves over against Christian religion in terms that are *borrowed from* Christianity and that precisely presuppose Christian values, as Christians we will tend to rejoice in this as involving an (unacknowledged) openness to the truth embraced in Christianity.

ENLIGHTENMENT ORIGINS

I have examined the polarization between relativism and fundamentalism as a distinctively *modern* phenomenon rather than a specifically religious one and have illustrated this by reference to wider aspects of modern culture than religion. In particular, the shift in attitude behind this polarization towards defining a right attitude by reference antithetically to the "enemy" (now demonized) is a distinctively modern phenomenon. I have suggested that this may be understood in terms of the logical inversion described in the previous chapter. However, it has origins that may be detected already in elements of Enlightenment thinking apparent in the philosophy of John Locke, as follows.

On the one hand, when fundamentalist Christians maintain the *truth* of Christian revelation they are indebted to an understanding of truth that was framed by Locke. For Locke, paradigmatic truth was found in truths accessible to reason in the form of timeless propositions, universally valid. The Bible contained, for him, nothing but truths of this sort, resolvable into clear, simple, and distinct ideas the truth of which could be known infallibly. The fundamentalist understanding of revelation is indebted to such a rationalist idea of truth. As Peter Schouls has written in a carefully nuanced paper, "ironic though this may be ... [Locke's] particular approach to what he took to be revelation ... appears to me to cover considerable distance on the road which has led to fundamentalism."[8]

On the other hand, when fundamentalist Christians affirm *allegiance to* the truth of Christian revelation, they are indebted to Locke's understanding of truth in the act precisely of conceding that Locke's methodology precludes any adequate account of this truth. Revelation "beyond the bounds of reason" was, for Locke, a matter of belief and not of certain knowledge; Locke's understanding of truth, when it is adopted by Christians, requires them also to assume that Christian revelation can be upheld only in an act of allegiance and not by discourse that seeks persuasively to bring recognition of the truth.

It is, of course, contradictory at once to hold that the truth of Christian revelation accords with Locke's idea of truth, and to take a stand of allegiance towards the truth of Christian revelation in defiance of the fact that it does not. This is, nevertheless, the character of fundamentalism. Liberal relativism, for its part, is similarly contradictory in denying that the question arises of religious truth, while tacitly upholding this denial itself as a religious truth.

THE NEED FOR DISCERNMENT

Returning to the tendency of polarization in contemporary Christianity and in wider Western culture, we see how inescapable is the need for discernment regarding where Christian responsibility lies. Not only is discernment vital for us when we are caught up on one side or other of a tendency of polarization among Christians if we are to judge where the responsibilities of faith rightly lie; it is also vital for us when we look on at polarizations in which we are not personally involved.

8. Schouls, "Locke and the Rise of Western Fundamentalism."

When we review major developments in the history of Jewish and Christian faith, we repeatedly find ourselves confronted with this need for discernment. Only so can we judge between, on the one hand, occasions when we are faced with the proper contextualization of the gospel in antithetical mode and, on the other hand, occasions when we are faced with a concealed domestication of the gospel to that which it has demonized. Let us recall a few such instances where the question of such discernment arises, without pursuing what might be the outcome of such discernment.

(a) In the Hebrew Scriptures there is sustained polemic against other gods including Baal and, at a later stage in history, Babylonian deities. This polemic often takes the form of ascribing to Yahweh, and to him alone, the attributes ascribed to these other gods. However, insofar as such polemic of opposition simply adopts and reallocates to Yahweh the attributes of divinity assumed by other religions, on the one hand, the danger arises that it may allow these assumptions wrongly to define God by a process of hidden, negative syncretism. On the other hand, such polemic may work more truly and radically to claim, break open, and transform the *meaning* of divinity and of these attributes. Which of these do we see happening in each case when we examine the text of the Bible?

(b) Turning to Christian theology, a question arises importantly regarding the theology of Saint Thomas Aquinas and its relation to Aristotelian philosophy. Aquinas sought to incorporate the philosophy of Aristotle into a Christian framework alternative to that offered by those Islamic scholars who also drew on this philosophy. However, the question is raised by his work: does Aquinas, in the process, allow Aristotelian assumptions wrongly to define God in a process of hidden, negative syncretism? Or does his theology work more radically to claim, break open, and transform the *meaning* of Aristotle's philosophy?

(c) A similar question arises more recently with regard to antithetical Christian responses to modern thinking. It arises, for example, regarding the "worldview" theology of Abraham Kuyper. Kuyper, rightly seeing that modern secular thought conceived a world alternative to that of Christian faith, and not simply divergent in its view of certain matters within that world, formulated a distinctively

Christian worldview. But the question how arises: in so doing, did he precisely adopt the assumptions of those he opposed, that human life may be understood and directed by reference to a theoretical framework or ideology? Or does his theology work more radically to claim, break open, and transform the very *meaning* of "worldview," through its adoption to refer to Christian faith?

In each of the above examples, I have referred explicitly to a context engaged in antithesis by a theological stance. However, discernment is often required to discern any such context in the first place because it may be tacit. Our interpretation of a theological stance will hinge upon this discernment. Take, for example, the use of the *Christus Victor* image in the early centuries of the church. It uses the familiar Roman imperial figure of a king to portray Christ on the cross. Now it might seem that that the use of this image in the early church reflected a refusal to face squarely the brute reality of his crucifixion. However, the early Christians knew perfectly well the reality of crucifixion. The *Christus Victor* image was surely an extraordinary and paradoxical statement of the truth of Christ in the face of, and essentially in antithesis to, the grim reality of crucifixion that is the tacit presupposition of this image. It is we who do not live with this grim reality who are most in danger of "reading" this image without seeing it in polemical engagement with its context.

A similar question of discernment arises regarding "pagan" philosophies, including the philosophy of Plato. Platonic philosophy speaks of universal and timeless forms and might seem itself to reach for a timeless metaphysical position apart from the contingencies of human history. However, his philosophy needs to be seen in the context of Plato's own concrete situation and concerns. Plato, in circumstances where the threat of civil war was pressing, sought to formulate a rational justification for the rational ordering of political life by showing such life to be an integral part of the ordering of all things. His intention was to commend civil unity, as appropriate to wise action.[9] When we consider the use made of Platonic philosophy, and the use of the Platonic tradition by Christian theologians, the question arises: have Christians understood faithfully Plato's intention in its original context? Or have they not taken

---

9. I owe this to Lund, "Platonism, Pragmatism and the History of Philosophy."

this context into account, but made of it (and hence of Christian theology) a metaphysic detached from history?[10]

A further element in the task of discernment is introduced when our access to a theological stance is mediated through an established tradition of interpretation and use. Here the further question arises whether this tradition of interpretation represents the faithful preservation of a true insight, enriched perhaps by application to new contexts. Another possibility is that this tradition of interpretation has failed to grasp the original context of a theological stance and has distorted this stance in the process (the Constantinian conception of Christ in Roman imperial terms is surely a distortion of the *Christus Victor* image in this way). Yet other possibilities are that the original theological stance in question itself presented a distorted gospel, ironically captive to what it opposed, and that this was later recognized as such by a tradition of interpretation and corrected (e.g., Arianism, Pelagianism?)—or again, that this distortion was carried forward without discernment for Christian posterity.

Discernment is needed, then, when interpreting historical statements of the gospel: are we faced here with a proper contextualization of the gospel or with the hidden, ironic capture and negative definition of the gospel by that to which it has been set in opposition? Such discernment is inseparably discernment *in the light of* the gospel and discernment *of* the gospel. In the setting of living dialogue today, the Christian responsibility of discernment *towards the other in the light of the gospel* is always most deeply of discernment *of the gospel shared with the other*, and incorporates openness to greater self-discernment in the process. Where there is no such possibility of living dialogue, but only of examining historical texts, the Christian responsibility is to simulate the same movement of dialogue, for all that the achievement and content of consensus in truth with our imagined dialogue partner will retain a

---

10. Colin Gunton describes well the wider context of Platonism: "The history of thought shows how one emphasis in philosophy tends by a kind of reflex attempt at correction to give rise to trends that stress what is lacking in previous enterprises. It is a process of affirmation and negation, although because only parts of a thesis are negated while others continue as often unrecognized assumptions, the relation of earlier and later is complex, and always particular. Thus there is a complex dialectical pattern, which is illuminating for us as we seek to understand our own era, to be discerned in the movement of Greek thought from the Presocratics, through the Sophists, to Socrates and Plato." Gunton, *The One, the Three and the Many*, 113.

degree of indeterminacy beyond that found in living dialogue. This is the nature of living tradition.

IN CONCLUSION

Enlightenment thinkers trusted that social peace and order could be secured by building society in future on the foundations of universal human nature rather than by looking to religion for guidance. It is ironic, therefore, that the modern period has spawned its own deep polarizations in the form both of "progressive" revolutions and of conservative reactions to "progress." The path from conflict to peace has hardly shown itself to be identical with the path from Christian society to secularist society. Modern thinking has generated its own polarizations—polarizations that today sadly afflict the church in turn.

In summary: Christians today are called by God to live converted to bearings from God. They are called to witness to such bearings and to seek the conversion of others to this through their own Christian practice and reflective thinking. They are called also to acknowledge, and repent of, their own complicity with Western cultural habits of thought and action that subvert this. The Christian calling here is to uncover the dynamics of polarization, both those driven by the ideology of the "hermeneutic of suspicion" or of fundamentalist allegiance and those driven by a more personal pursuit of (false) self-identity and belonging. It is to foster deeper self-awareness and an openness to learn from the other without forsaking the requirements of responsibility before God. This presents distinctive challenges to both liberal and evangelical thinking. The church will then be in a better position persuasively to speak to the polarizations thrown up by modern thinking in wider society, and—in a blessed reinversion of the Enlightenment turn from religious to secular foundations for harmony—host the renewal of public space under God (we shall return to this last theme in chapter 10).

Conversion to bearings from God involves a readiness to entrust ourselves and our understanding of the world to God in radical responsiveness. God calls humankind, in all its diversity, to find its true unity in Jesus Christ, bound to God and to each other in the new covenant inaugurated in Christ.

5   THE NEEDY CONSUMER

Conversion to the Abundance of God

W HAVE SOUGHT TO understand the phenomenon of modern culture in the context of Christian faith. Conceiving it as a cultural *trajectory*, we have asked how this compares with the trajectory of openness to the in-breaking kingdom of God? We have seen that a central role in shaping the modern trajectory has been played by principles adopted by Enlightenment thinkers as a guide for constructing a new society. We have noted that the choice of these principles was strongly influenced by Christianity, and that they were for Enlightenment thinkers tacitly imbued with Christian meaning. In the Enlightenment, however, these principles were severed from their roots in Christian revelation both theoretically (from the start) and practically (as, with the passage of time, faith became less formative for the public imagination). Consequently, Enlightenment principles have led modern culture in a direction ambiguously related to that of openness to the kingdom of God and in some ways increasingly divergent from it. Modern habits of thought have typically misrepresented and marginalized faith itself and (as we shall explore further below and in the chapters ahead) practically subverted faith by promoting narrow rationalizations of public life and breeding private sentiment.

In the previous chapter we considered the contemporary tendency of polarization between relativist liberals and fundamentalists. We saw that although this is driven most obviously by the modern, false *theoretical* dichotomy between questioning, on the one hand, and allegiance or commitment, on the other, other factors are at work within it. We saw that the *practical* stances legitimated by this dichotomy hold appeal as a way of securing a self-conscious personal identity. Thus in relativist liberalism, a person constructs their identity as an honest, intrepid questioner, standing boldly in a world void of objective truth; while in fundamentalism, a person constructs their identity as a faithful upholder of truth and member of "the faithful."

In what follows we shall explore such practical, personal aspects of the modern cultural trajectory. We shall consider the effect of modern culture upon personal formation: Seen in the light of faith, what *kind* of personal identity does modern culture foster?

Let us first recall in summary fashion how the formation of personal character and identity is viewed in Christian faith. Christian faith stands for the promise of personal life in all its fullness, in eternal life with God. Indeed the very concept of the "person" has theological roots in the doctrine of the Trinity. Faith nurtures personal formation in the image of Christ; it directs us towards "mature manhood, measured by nothing less than the stature of Christ" (Eph 4:13). Such formation incorporates diverse genres of human talents and gifts. It includes the diversity of the gifts enumerated by Paul in 1 Corinthians 12; the diversity of individual temperaments explored today by enneagrams and their like; and by the diversity of national temperaments that lie behind stereotypes of, for instance, the English, Scottish, German, and the French characters!

Does the modern vision foster personal formation? Certainly it declares this intention. There is a long-established modern tradition of exalting and pursuing "autonomous individual life." Today, a widely prevalent rhetoric commends that we "choose who we want to be" and thereby seek personal fulfillment. Nevertheless, as we have seen, in practice modernity works deeply against any such thing by distorting theoretically and subverting practically the lively, responsible enquiry into the world that is integral to our personal formation, and the possibility of which is constitutive within our personhood. When in Christian faith we open ourselves to God by giving ourselves radically to seeking and knowing God in lively, attentive love and obedience, we know our calling as persons. In reaching out to God and knowing God, we are his sons and daughters (Rom 8:15–16); in knowing God, we have life from him (John 17:3).

Correspondingly, insofar as we instead construct for ourselves a sense of identity—a sense *that* we exist as a person and a sense of *who* we are—from a stance that is actually evasive of the demands of that lively personal enquiry that constitutes faith, then the identity we entertain for ourselves is a distortion of who we truly are. And it entails self-deception on our part.

How far, then, does modernity nurture and support the formation of persons according to God's purposes and how far does it foster the distortion of personhood and personal identity? In order to probe this further, I want to consider briefly the analysis provided in two books of cultural criticism: David Riesman's *The Lonely Crowd* and Richard Sennett's *The Fall of Public Man*. Although both books are concerned primarily with U.S. culture, they are relevant to modern societies in general. My intention is to reach beyond their cultural or sociological analyses in order to understand and weigh their material in the light of that personal formation that God wills for his people.

Let us begin with the account of character formation formulated by David Riesman and his colleagues in their classic, *The Lonely Crowd* (1950). Riesman was influenced by Eric Fromm, with whom he had worked, in the project of classifying character types. Riesman explored the idea that broadly different historical and cultural settings are associated with differences in character formation. He began by studying changes within Western culture and the changes in character type that appeared to be associated with them. He distinguished three basic types of character. The first—the "tradition-directed" person (the suffix "-directed" means in each case "directed by")—is found in traditional societies that change relatively little and where the individual is required to conform closely to an established culture and social order; in this setting a person "hardly thinks of himself as an individual." The second character type—the "inner-directed" person—has emerged in the West since the Renaissance. Such a person has, at an early stage of life, internalized (from elders) certain beliefs and values that then guide his exercise of personal freedom—a freedom far greater than that found in traditional societies—towards basically unchanging goals. Riesman suggests an analogy between the way that an "inner-directed" character stays on course towards these goals and the way a gyroscope maintains a consistent orientation despite receiving knocks and dislocations. The third character type—the "other-directed" person—has come to the fore in the United States increasingly during the twentieth century and takes a lead from peers, watching for and following with some anxiety patterns of change among them. The concern of the "other-directed" person involves more than a concern to conform or a concern to be liked; he seeks "an assurance of being emotionally in tune with others." This orientation, like that of inner-direction, can be implanted in early life, but whereas the latter remains focused upon received goals the former watches out for the changing preferences and practices of contemporary peers.

Another author familiar with Riesman's work, Richard Sennett, describes in *The Fall of Public Man* (1974) the loss to individuals of any public domain in which to contribute or find a role. He describes the contemporary individual as like an actor without a stage. This has come about through a "psychological imagination of life." Modern psychology invited people to identify and understand their emotions in order to be "liberated to participate more fully and rationally in a life outside the boundaries of their own desires." However, this concern has proved a trap, rather than a liberation, as people have come inappropriately to expect psychological rewards from public and social life. Public space has been invaded by an obsessive desire for intimacy. Thus "we have come to care about institutions and events only when we can discern personalities at work in them and embodying them." When one of these prominent personalities speaks, "instead of judging him, his listeners want to be moved by him, to experience him."

Sennett calls this "the intimate society," and identifies two basic features. The first—*narcissism*—we shall explore further below. Briefly, narcissism is a character disorder in which, in Sennett's words, "self-absorption ... prevents one from understanding what belongs within the domain of the self and self-gratification and what lies outside it. Thus narcissism is an obsession with 'what this person, that event means to me.'" The second feature of the intimate society is a fantasy of being a community "by sharing a *collective personality*." This fantasy of emotional closeness takes the place of real community that involves practical attention, action, and responsiveness to other people with their varying situations, needs, and wants. The reign of intimacy in today's society today is, as Sennett describes it, traumatic for its members.

CHANGING SOCIAL CHARACTER
SEEN IN CHRISTIAN CONTEXT

Riesman and Sennett each depict changes in social character arising in Western culture in the course of the twentieth century. How do these changes appear to us in a Christian, theological context? I suggest that the changes described by each author involve a loss of authentic practical and personal orientation towards God, the world, and (tacitly) towards personal formation itself. I want to explore this loss by reflecting on and evaluating the accounts of Riesman and Sennett.

Many readers of *The Lonely Crowd* interpreted the shift from inner-directed to other-directed character as an unequivocal loss. They saw it as signaling the loss of rugged individualism that they highly prized. Sennett interpreted this shift, similarly, as an unequivocal loss. For him it is about the loss of an impersonal public domain in which individuals may act and its replacement by "the intimate society" involving narcissistic character distortion and the fantasy of participating in a "collective personality."

Riesman himself does not see it like this. Indeed he says he never sought to make such claims about the "inwardness" of individuals in the first place. He and his colleagues had set out rather to trace a correlation between broad cultural and demographic patterns, on the one hand, and the prevalence of broad character types, on the other. In the course of this they described the changing social or occupational roles of individuals; their interest did not extend to personal "inwardness."

Insofar as these changes do have an "inward" side, Riesman suggests that they by no means represent an unequivocal loss. He reminds his readers that his view of nineteenth-century moralism is unflattering towards the inner-directed character and that he sees the contemporary desire to feel in touch with wider circles of people—whether in conformity or non-compliance—as a welcome aspect of the other-directed character. "No lover of toughness and invulnerability should forget the gains made possible," he writes, "by the considerateness, sensitivity and tolerance that are among the positive qualities of other-direction."

How shall we evaluate more deeply the shift in character formation in question, in the light of Christian faith? We may do so by weighing it relative to the Christian vision of personal formation. The latter vision can only be described paradoxically as at once other-directed and inner-directed. It is rooted in the paradox we have acknowledged as fundamental to Christian faith: the paradox of grace.

For Christian faith, personal formation is other-directed in the sense that it is directed by God. It is rooted in openness to God and is led by responsiveness to God's action and self-revelation in Christ through creation. It is not about the autonomous individual life, in disregard for God. Nor is it about the habitual life of thought and action unawake to the deeper transcendent horizons of God.

On the other hand, personal formation is for Christian faith inner-directed in the sense that it is about dwelling in Christ and participating in the life of the Spirit. It is not about mere conformity to culture or ideology, neglectful of the responsibility of personal judgment and exercise of conscience. Nor is it credulous or impulsive. Relative to these it is autonomous, but it is not autonomous *fundamentally*, i.e., in relation to God. Paradoxically, personal freedom belongs to that life which is found by those willing to lose it; this is part of the paradox of grace. God does indeed will our personal formation as free individuals; but this is most fundamentally about our personal formation through self-giving participation in a life of relationship to God and to other human beings— a life with public and social dimensions—in the historical setting of our life in creation.

Accordingly, insofar as the shift from inner-directed to other-directed character represents a personal opening up in which learned rigid assumptions about the goal and meaning of life are revised within a more lively personal exploration of such meaning, it is to be viewed positively. It is consistent with the Christian understanding of personal formation. Here the other-directed character is of a sort that is directed *towards* such meaning and that continues to exercise the responsibility of inner personal judgment in recognizing and serving such meaning.

On the other hand, insofar as the shift from inner-directed to other-directed character represents a *collapse* of that personal formation that is at once oriented towards the transcendent horizons of God and participates personally in the freedom of the Spirit, it is to be viewed negatively. Here the inner-directed character in view but now lost is most deeply of the sort that, rather than being autonomous, is rooted in responsiveness to the demands of loving God and ones fellow human beings.

How, then, shall we evaluate the shift in question as we have actually experienced it in twentieth-century Western cultural developments? I believe that both of the above elements may be seen within it, but that *the latter predominates*. The shift in character-formation is for the greater part to be interpreted, in terms of personal formation, as a loss.

The Christian understanding of this loss differs, however, from that of those readers of *The Lonely Crowd* who interpreted it as the loss of rugged individualism and saw this as an unequivocal loss. Whereas the shift *does* represent an unequivocal loss, this is not to be understood as most fundamentally about loss of autonomy, as in the view of those readers. It is rather about the loss of personal formation as understood by Christians, which is directed towards God. Riesman, for his own part, effectively lends support to this account when he repudiates the equation of inner-direction with autonomy: he points out that insofar as the inner-directed character showed a rugged independence in variable circumstances, this was rooted in principles and values instilled early in life and remaining operative throughout life.

The mistaken equation of inner-directedness with autonomy, and of loss of autonomy with unequivocal loss, reflects the high value that those readers themselves attributed to autonomy within the modern liberal tradition. It reflects the modern liberal misunderstanding of the personal, including precisely its own sources of personal vitality. Modern secular liberalism sees itself as having shed dependence on God; however, the tacit influence of faith upon it has continued, giving it strength in an unacknowledged way, although this strength has been slowly eroding. This erosion has stretched back through the modern centuries. Indeed the liberal rhetoric of rugged individualism has arguably long involved denial of the actual powerlessness of individuals to "create" themselves.

Insofar as the shift to other-directed character does indeed represent a loss of the vision of autonomy, Michael Paul Gallagher suggests that it can be seen as a shift *within* the tradition of liberal individualism and in the tone of culture.[1] He describes this as a shift from the vision of "Prometheus" (in which humanity exults in its adventurous freedom) to that of "Narcissus" (in which the individual is self-absorbed with the mirage of unattainable intimacy). The latter, however, is not entirely new, he says; it has roots way back in modernity. He cites the work of Roberto Mangabeira Unger, who claims that "the 'narcissism' of the self has close links with, among other things, 'the deification of mankind in the Hegelian-Marxist religion of immanence.'" The liberal vision effectively produces a "secularization of transcendence" in which receptivity to love gets distorted in the longing of "romantic love." Gallagher identifies this as "a case of the myth of intimacy ousting any vision of social and faith-based hope." He notes that this myth, which presents an "evasive and sentimental image of human reality," was already an evident feature of novel writing in the nineteenth century.

There are clear resonances here with Sennett's discernment of "the intimate society." However, there are also differences. Sennett, we have

---

1. Gallagher, "Tone of Culture."

seen, describes the shift in social character as the loss of the public domain as a stage for individual action. However, he tends to equate the
former with the impersonal and the latter with the personal. Thus he
writes "confusion has arisen between public and intimate life; people
are working out in terms of personal feelings public matters that properly can be dealt with only through codes of impersonal meaning."
His account is of the improper merging of two spheres of life—the
personal and the impersonal—through the diffusion of the former
through the latter.

Gallagher's article reminds us that in Christian understanding,
firstly there is no such distinction at the most fundamental level. Rather,
the world in which public life is pursued is the creation of *a personal
God*, whose purposes God intends to be reflected in it. Public life is a
dimension of personal life in relation to God and other human beings,
hosted ultimately by God; it arises from the place of corporate belief,
practice, and decision-making within the family of humankind. The
realm of intimate relations is also a dimension of personal life but it is
not a fundamentally different life. It is in participation in the multidi-
mensional life of God's human family that the true meaning of personhood is found. Narcissistic self-absorption with feelings and intimacy
(at the expense of a wider world bleakly empty of personal meaning) is a
distortion of personhood. Admittedly Sennett acknowledges this, but for
him the restoration of personal life is a matter of restoring the distinction between personal desires and an impersonal world, and honoring
the limits imposed upon the former by the latter. This tends to equate
personhood with the pursuit of one's desires and to frame participation
in public life as the pursuit of contracts between self-interested parties
to their own ends. It does not do justice to the Christian understanding of personal formation through participation in a world directed and
responsive towards the purposes of its personal creator.

This critique of Sennett's account may also be framed by reference
to his response to Riesman's use of the terms "inner-directed" and "other-
directed." Sennett sees himself as "turning around the argument David
Riesman made in *The Lonely Crowd*." He suggests, rather, that "Western
societies are moving from something like an other-directed condition
to an inner-directed condition." Now at one level this is a reasonable
statement of what Gallagher has described. At a deeper level, however,
it is not. It fails to acknowledge that what has been lost is precisely a

proper understanding of personal life as informed and inner-directed by orientation towards the transcendent God of creation. And it fails to acknowledge that what has taken the place of this may be seen as directed by the human "other" as readily as by the "inner" self. Narcissism leaves us at the whim of impulse and circumstance and the deliberate influence of what Riesman calls "such institutions as the personality market," which are seen by Christian faith as impacting upon us rather than grounding our deepest inner personal identity. Later in this chapter we shall consider how this dependence has been exploited within contemporary consumerism.

In conclusion, then, for all its seeming exaltation of the individual, modern liberalism has, from the start, worked ambiguously in practice to subvert the personal strength and autonomy of the individual. Severing the roots of personal life in relation to God and to other people, it has chased an illusion of autonomy dismissive of human relatedness and interdependence, which has in practice disoriented and disintegrated the person, "dividing" the "in-dividual." The habits of thought that guide modern life have endorsed the evasion of the demands of lively enquiry into God and God's world, and contributed practically to a disorientation of the person. This distortion is at once a loss of true intimacy and, in self-contradictory fashion, of a public world in which the person is called to affirm and participate in the purposes of its transcendent, personal creator.

We shall now explore more deeply the contradictions within personal life as it is conceived and formed today. The most penetrating account of changes in character formation in recent generations, and of associated cultural change, is that which traces the growing cultural prevalence of narcissism. We shall now examine this at greater length.

CLINICAL NARCISSISM

By the 1970s, psychiatrists in the United States were finding that the personality disorders presented to them by patients had changed from those presented to Freud and described by him during the 1930s. No longer common were the hysterical symptoms and feelings of guilt and inhibition of the sort associated with a morally strict society. In their place, by contrast, was self-absorption and the distress of uncontrolled and unfulfilled longing for meaning and intimacy. This clinical condition, classed as a "borderline personality disorder," was labeled by psychiatrists as *narcissism*.

The clinical indictors of narcissism have been listed as including "a grandiose sense of self-importance or uniqueness; preoccupation with fantasies of unlimited success, power, brilliance, beauty, or ideal love; exhibitionistic need for constant attention and admiration; feelings of rage, inferiority, or emptiness in response to criticism or defeat; lack of empathy; sense of entitlement without assuming reciprocal responsibilities."[2]

It has been said that the illnesses prevalent in a society tell us much about that society. Accordingly, the rise of clinical narcissism tells us something about life in Western culture, particularly, but not only, in the United States. It also suggests that milder, sub-clinical forms of narcissistic personality disorder may be more widely prevalent in Western culture. In *The Culture of Narcissism* (1979), Christopher Lasch shows that many features of Western culture today can be understood in terms of the cultural prominence of narcissism.

Casually observed, narcissism might seem to be a form recently taken by the self-possessed search for personal fulfillment. However, it is nothing of the sort. It is most deeply an expression not of personal self-confidence but of its opposite: a defense against the threat of personal disintegration. Christopher Lasch underscored this in his sequel to *The Culture of Narcissism*, entitled, *The Minimal Self: Psychic Survival in Trouble Times* (1984). Culturally prevalent narcissism is not the "primary narcissism" of the human infant whose needs are the centre of her own life. Rather it is a pathological "secondary narcissism" that is a defense against feelings of helpless dependency, an evasion of what are seen as unfaceable demands of hope and trust. It is in such terms that we can explore the meaning of narcissism in a Christian, theological context.

NARCISSISM SEEN IN CHRISTIAN CONTEXT

The classical myth[3] of Narcissus tells of a young man who is exceptionally beautiful in appearance. His beauty makes Narcissus the object of intense longing by others, whom he scorns. In particular he is desired by a young nymph called Echo who, when rebuffed, pines away to a shadow. One of the gods is indignant with Narcissus and decides to punish him

---

2. Moore, *Disarming the Secular Gods*, 82.

3. Ovid, *Metamorphoses*, Book 3.

by causing him to suffer in the same way as he causes others to suffer. The god causes him to see his own image in a pool and to be captivated by his own beauty. His desire for intimate union with his image is overwhelming and insatiable but such union is unattainable. As his image mocks him from the pool, he suffers for himself the anguish of unrequited longing that Echo and others had towards him, until finally he himself is lost.

Ovid's story of Narcissus is about hopeless longing. It begins with those who are captivated with desire by the seeming possibility of an impossible intimacy with Narcissus. For his part, however, he is regardless of other people and quite unreceptive to their attention. He is dismissive of their desire. But the same desire is destined to overwhelm his own life. He becomes spellbound by an image of himself—an image in which he invests his "self" and yet which renders this self unattainable. In his self-absorption, he forsakes any understanding of the world as distinct from himself; instead he sees it only in relation to his reflected image upon which he gazes. The world he has dismissed mocks him with a self that is unattainable. The end of it all is his destruction.

Seen in a Christian theological context, the story of Narcissus can be read as the story of one who is unreceptive to God, to fellow human beings, and ultimately to the conditions of created life under God. It is about one who evades the demands of loving the transcendent God and of living in the real world in which God has set human beings as creatures. It is about one who has turned away from the demands of trusting in a God beyond ones control and yet upon whom one depends, and the demands of living within creaturely limits of contingency. Narcissus cannot receive and cannot trust and will not find himself in being affirmed and incorporated in the loving purposes of God. He is a figure of isolation and desolation. Disoriented and defeated by the demands of hope, he has come under the spell of irresolvable lack and futile longing; he is a living contradiction of hope in God.

His lack of hope is hidden, concealed behind his pursuit of an imagined "self" that alone matters; the whole world becomes, in effect, merely an extension of this self, existing only to serve it. Narcissus sees other people and the world only through his own image. He does not affirm other people and the world in their own right but sees them only as part of himself, to be manipulated according to his needs. He does not even truly affirm himself; he does not reach out personally into the world so as to discover himself through other people and the world. Instead he is absorbed totally in gazing, in his reflected image, upon a self that he essentially lacks. Everything is devoured and mutated in pursuit of this self but never with satisfaction. Ironically this perpetuates his lack, subverts discovery of his true self, and finally enacts his destruction.

Seen in this way, the story of Narcissus is about the formation of a character shaped by evasion of the demands of responsiveness to God and his hospitality. Evasion takes here the despairing form of being personally overwhelmed and disoriented, shaped by a radical sense of loss. As we have seen in Part 1 of this book, there is a hidden collusion with this loss—a self-deceiving evasion of hope. From this comes the world of narcissism with its inner contradictions, its self-displacing mirages (and specters), and its inner paralysis. Narcissus may seem at first sight to be too full of himself, to the exclusion of all others, but the deeper story is of personal lack and of futile longing.

THE CULTURE OF NARCISSISM:
PARENTS AND CHILDREN

The distortion of personal formation and of worldview represented by narcissism is given impetus and sustained in momentum by modern culture. The reason for this lies in the character of modern culture as I have described it in previous chapters. Fundamentally it lies in the way this culture marginalizes and subverts the lively enquiry of faith and effectively sanctions its evasion. The modern fostering of narcissism can be traced in the effect of the modern vision on the one hand upon family life (and especially upon parenting) and on the other upon life in the mass society it has produced. Let us consider each in turn.

Narcissism and its traits have been extensively described by Heinz Kohut.[4] He identifies the origins of narcissism in early childhood, in the experience of not having one's needs met for personal attention and affirmation. The young child who does not find herself "mirrored" well enough by her mother or other significant figures withdraws from primary, personal, trusting, exploratory engagement with the world. She no longer trusts herself to the outside world for fear that she will be let down again. Concealed within her there forms a deep rage and a passionate refusal to forgive. She may become grandiose and contemptuous, deny-

---

4. Kohut, *Analysis of the Self.*

ing her vulnerability by maintaining the illusion of being in control. Or she may become depressed, submissive, and inclined to aimless, vagrant, promiscuous behavior. Feeling abandoned, violated, or worthless, she herself abandons responsible and creative engagement with the world around her. In each case, within herself she conceals feelings of shame and false dependence. While she may seem totally absorbed in self-love, her deeper attitude towards herself is akin rather to self-hatred.

It will be apparent that such a pattern can replicate itself readily from one generation to another in a family: when the narcissistic child becomes herself a mother, she will tend not to "see" her child but only use her mothering relationship to feed her own narcissistic hunger—with the effect of reproducing her own emptiness in her child in turn.

Why has this distortion in parent-child relations become more prevalent in recent generations? Christopher Lasch says that he was prompted to write *The Culture of Narcissism* by studies "which had led me to the conclusion that the family's importance in our society had been steadily declining over a period of more than a hundred years. Schools, peer groups, mass media, and the 'helping professions' had challenged parental authority and taken over many of the family's child-rearing functions."[5] This invasion has "created an ideal of perfect parent-hood while destroying parents' confidence in their ability to perform the most elementary functions of childrearing."[6] Ironically it has sponsored a measure of self-withdrawal from parental roles and subverted the quality of parent-child interaction, fostering narcissistic depletion in the children.

This loss takes the form partly of sheer loss of time spent participating in family life, as time is spent more watching television and attending school (the former typically occupies more time than the latter for children today). Also, most importantly, there has been a movement of young mothers into the workforce that has often involved placing children too early and too long in crèches. Penelope Leach pointed out in 1994 that in Western societies the total amount of time parents and children spent together had dropped by 40 percent in a single generation.[7] Western culture makes it plausible that economic demands upon a mother's time should override parenting demands upon her time.

5. Lasch, *Culture of Narcissism*, Afterword, 238.
6. Ibid.,170.
7. Penelope Leach, interviewed by Val Aldridge, *The Dominion* (Wellington, New

In such terms, we may link narcissism to the modern failure in general to honor "the primacy of the practitioner," which we explored earlier. In the case of the family, it is cultural regard for the parent as practitioner that has been lost.

THE CULTURE OF NARCISSISM: MASS SOCIETY

Failure to honor the primacy of the practitioner is, we saw earlier, a systematic failure throughout modern society and not just a failure with regard to the practice of parenting. This wider failure can be seen also as a contributor to narcissism, as follows.

Modern thinking fails, we have seen, to honor lively personal enquiry and, as a consequence, fails to honor "the primacy of the practitioner" in matters of lively personal enquiry. This has affected the course of "modernization" in its sponsorship of central cultivation by the state on the one hand and defense of the rights of the individual on the other. So long as the vision of the state and the individual remained embedded within the transcendent horizons of Christian faith, modernization could be consistent with the trajectory of openness towards God's kingdom: it could be in service to God's good purposes and state cultivation could raise individuals to participate in these purposes. However, once these transcendent horizons fade and the state and the individual (abstractly conceived) are seen as absolutes, the path of modernization gets distorted and the "mediating structures" of society through which individuals participate together in transcendent horizons are indiscriminately subverted.

The polarization of individual and state or system gives rise, on the one hand, to conflicting ideologies of corporate and individual life. We shall examine these further in chapters 8 and 9. On the other hand, it gives rise to a personal inner conflict involving the distortion both of personal formation and of practical worldview. It subverts in a practical, personal way our lively enquiry into a world that, under God, welcomes and hosts us as responsible and creative personal participants. This is my theme in this present chapter. Thus in recent decades, those of us living in Western culture have experienced a range of developments directing our attention away from a world in which we are personal, creative par-

---

Zealand), February 27th, 1995, 9. The interview was occasioned by the publication of Penelope Leach's book *Children First*.

ticipants. In place of this, our attention is directed towards a world "out there" in which—for all the public rhetoric we hear to the contrary—we are personally unknown and redundant. We are merely the constructs of marketing and management techniques guided by surveillance and statistical analysis and "addressed" by mass-produced messages. Here is another contemporary (and growing) "lack of mirroring" of the sort that provokes narcissism in infants—which will, of course, resonate within us with any personal experience we may have suffered of the latter.

Let me recall four of these developments on a range of fronts now, sketching complex issues with a broad brush. I shall spend some time on these since they are developments very concrete and familiar to us all in Western culture today. They are "close to home" for us. My concern is, in the usual way, to draw attention to their basic Christian, theological significance, which is often not sufficiently recognized. Some aspects of these developments are a matter of celebration for they belong to a proper modernization of society in openness to the kingdom of God; other aspects of them, however, are associated with the distortion of personal formation and worldview represented by narcissism.

1. From Producer of Homemade Food to Consumer of the Mass-Produced Food

A generation or two ago, it was common for women to make their own home preserves (jams, pickles, etc.) and do their own home baking (cakes, bread, etc.), although many such goods could also be purchased in the shops. Today this is much less common; people tend instead to buy what has been mass-produced. Perhaps the most recent development of this kind is the purchase of prepared meals in place of home cooking.

Associated with this has been a shift in outlook. A generation or two ago it was commonly held that homemade (and home-grown) food was "the best." By comparison with mass-produced food for sale in the shops it was "the real thing," personally made properly using the proper ingredients; one knew "what had gone into it." The mass-produced equivalent was a substitute for this: generally of lesser quality, it was there on the shelves for those who lacked, or preferred not to use, time or skill or opportunity to make their own. As such its availability was undoubtedly welcome; and, of course, in the case of some (e.g., dairy) products it had long been a welcome convenience to buy them rather than produce them for oneself.

Today, by contrast, the view has become common that mass-produced food is "the real thing" and that homemade food is a doubtful substitute for this. Confidence is placed in ingredients selected according to a manufacturer's high standards and processed under controlled, hygienic conditions; sometimes it is the established "brand" that evokes confidence. This confidence holds up generally despite the issues that surface from time to time regarding "what goes into" mass-produced food-generating public scares (e.g., that over the threat of BSE and wariness towards additives, GM crops, etc.). By contrast, the effort of homemaking produce can seem a fumbling, inadequate, even presumptuous enterprise. In an inversion of earlier views, now it is the homemade produce at the school fete, rather than the product on the supermarket shelf, that is more likely to raises doubts in the mind of the potential customer. The doubtfulness of the "homemade" has been reinforced recently by the introduction of legislation requiring that the source be declared of food sold to the public and by a fear of litigation associated with this.

Now, in part, this development may be seen as the continuation of a proper modernization in service to human flourishing consistent with the trajectory of openness to the coming kingdom of God. It represents a further development in the differentiation of labor that has been under way ever since subsistence farming was displaced by a wage economy. People have long bought food from the village butcher, baker, grocer, and dairy. And while home baking was more common a generation ago, most women bought the ingredients for this from the shops. The scale, scope, and refinement of mass production have simply made new advances. The associated change in outlook reflects the recognition that today, more so than in the past, we are best able to secure provision of food by means of specialist corporate enterprises. Thus far, the shift in outlook in question leaves intact the underlying worldview of Christian modernization.

However, in other respects this development may be seen as carrying forward a modern distortion of human life. It reflects a social formation that drives indiscriminately a distortion and inversion of worldview that has personal and cosmic significance, as follows. The "real" world of trustworthy goodness is held no longer to be found in a world to which we belong as inalienable guests, in which we participate personally, and to which we may contribute by our own action whether creative or routine, skilful, or casual. Rather it is a world from which we are essentially displaced and alienated and yet by which we are inescapably haunted: a world that promises to us a belonging, a status, an identity we experience as lacking for us. Effectively it haunts us, in narcissistic fashion, with the image of a "self" we can never attain. Our connection with this world is through the spell upon us of this "self," which is promised to us through buying, owning, using, or otherwise identifying ourselves with what has been mass-produced.

This distortion of worldview is mediated through current conventions for the procurement of food among many other goods. In particular, it is mediated through products by the consumption or ownership of which status is socially endowed and which are purchased partly for this reason. Obvious examples of this are "label" clothing and certain brands and styles of vehicle, but the "purchase" of status extends into many fields beyond these. Through these, mass consumption mediates and reinforces the distorted, hopeless worldview that we have identified in narcissism.

2. From Home Maintenance to Dependence on Professionals

A parallel development has occurred in such matters as maintenance and repair (e.g., of cars, machinery, and household property) and the manufacture and repair of clothes (e.g., knitting and darning, dressmaking, patching, and sewing). A generation or two ago it was much more common for people to service and repair their own cars, bicycles, and other machinery, and to tackle a wide range of household jobs including painting and decorating, electrical, and plumbing repairs. By comparison today it is much more common for people to place such tasks in the hands of professionals. In some cases, advances in technology and changes in design have made it very difficult to do otherwise; in other cases legislation increasingly stipulates that tasks be undertaken by a qualified and licensed operator. Again, it was common for women to make and mend clothes for the family, whereas today it is typically by buying and discarding mass-produced clothes that one "stays in fashion."

Once again there has been associated with this development a change in outlook. In the past it was generally held that if you did a job for yourself, you would know that it had been done well. While it was true that a tradesman might be found and paid to do the same job, the fact that they might only be "doing it for the money," without a personal interest in the result, meant that the question arose whether they could "be trusted to do a good job." In general the "amateur" (literally, the one whose work is driven by love) was taken to be trustworthy, unlike the "professional" who was merely making a living. Today, by contrast, "a professional job" is taken to mean "a job done properly by experts" or "a job done by those qualified to do it," while an "amateur job" has come to mean "a botched job done by someone without the proper skills or resources." Here too there has been an inversion of outlook.

Again, in part this development may be seen as a proper further professionalization and specialization of the sort that makes possible a society in which technology is increasingly complex and in which this serves human flourishing. However, once again it may also be seen in part as carrying forward a modern distortion of human life and world-view. The real, trustworthy world is held no longer to be one in which we inherently participate and to which we make our own contribution through the work of construction, maintenance, and repair. Rather it is to be found in a world constructed by other people than ourselves, who alone have the expertise or authority to do so and to do any work maintaining or changing this world. Our only gate of entry into this world is through the purchase of professional services—a "participation" that secures nothing inalienably, but has always to be renewed by further purchases.

3. From Family Business to Corporate Chain

England has been described in the past as a "nation of shopkeepers." Retailing and the pursuit of trades were conducted in the main by small, independent, local businesses. The role of the one who sold and the one who bought belonged in such circumstances within a community of personal relationships. Relative to our situation today, those who sold goods and services had scope for making judgments and adopting policies responsive to their community and sought to establish a reputation for personal trustworthiness that would attract and maintain custom. Among the latter there was scope to influence and possibly bargain with the former and to make choices between diverse products. Similarly within business itself, the relationship between employer and employee could contain genuine personal elements of loyalty and trust, etc.

Today, it is said, England has turned from a nation of shopkeepers into a nation of checkout operators. In many high streets retail chain stores dominate; the "independent retailer" has become the exception.

This brings a new degree of separation between the owners of retail chains, on the one hand, and their employees and customers on the other. Among the former, policy decisions regarding employment, product sourcing, range, and pricing are made at a national or international level; among the latter, power of personal influence has been lost and freedom of choice between authentically different products has—despite contemporary rhetoric about increasing choice—been in many respects lessened, even though it has been increased in other ways. In general, scope for mutual personal relationship between employers and employees, sellers, and buyers has been much diminished.

Once again, in an associated change of outlook, the "real and trustworthy" has been displaced away from that in which one participates locally, to the "branded" retail chain with its disjunction from customers and employees. Wherever people travel, they can look for a local Tesco or McDonald's knowing what to expect; wherever people live, they are likely to find the same chain shops as they would find if they were living anywhere else.

And once again, this development can be seen in part as a further development of modernization for the good but it can also be seen in part as carrying forward a modern distortion in life and in worldview. Today that which is "real and trustworthy" as the ultimate source of products and of employment is held to lie apart from, and prior to, any world to which humankind in general inherently belongs. It is no longer seen as arising from a shared world, as differentiations arise within this between forms of participation in this world (e.g., between sellers and buyers, employers and employees). Instead, the "real" lies forever beyond the employee and the customer, who identify with it only in a contingent way.

This centralization of power and control in the fields of retailing and trade is paralleled in other fields including those of the press and of political organization. This brings us to the dominance of the mass media in modern life, which, being such a powerful mediator of worldview, invites special further consideration.

4. From Communal Participation to Media Consumption

At the beginning of the twentieth century the mass media were limited to books and journals, magazines, and newspapers. Since then—through the impact successively of radio, cinema, television, and internet—the mass media have come to occupy a far greater proportion of the time and attention of the population than ever in the past. As is familiar, individuals commonly spend more than twenty hours each week watching television.

Before media consumption acquired the prominence in people's lives that it has in our culture today, personal time and attention were given mainly to a world in which one was practically involved and personally known. Today, by comparison, a large proportion of people's time and attention is given through the media to a world over which they have minimal power of influence and in which they are quite unknown.

This development has a variety of elements. Where once people were involved in a community in which stories were followed of people among whom they lived and moved (which might include their own story), today the stories followed are those presented in the soap operas of television and radio. Where once people were personally told (and personally passed on) news of events in the community in which they lived, today the news to which they attend is that presented in the media of events and debates in which typically they play no significant part and to which they typically need make no response. Where once people had need of certain provisions or needed to undertake a certain particular task and so looked for suitable ways and means, today they are presented by mass advertising with invitations to buy goods and services they had not entertained until that moment. Where once people were involved in a community in which certain individuals might gain recognition and win admiration from those around us, today they are presented by the media with celebrities inviting adulation of a kind quite disconnected from any serious personal exercise of judgment.

Once again, this broad development can be seen in part as a further development of modernization for the good but it can also be seen in part as carrying forward a distortion in this and in worldview. The world of real people, real relationships, real actions, events, and debates can come to lie for us comprehensively beyond any world to which we ourselves belong, in a realm with which we identify only through consumption of the media.

The place of the individual person in this world is revealingly intimated, it seems to me, in a 1990s television cartoon about a baseball player whose sporting performance turns him into a television star. The commentator declares: "from being *nobody* in the hearts of *anyone, any-*

where, he became *somebody* in the eyes of *everyone, everywhere.*" This "from zero to hero" storyline is dear to popular sentiment. It is not about heroic action, however, but about winning attention as a celebrity.

We may acknowledge in passing here that more recently television and radio have acknowledged and responded to a desire for participation by offering television programs that invite the casting of votes by telephone and radio programs that run competitions or that invite contributions and requests by telephone, letter, and e-mail. However, the underlying narcissistic distortion of worldview remains largely unaffected by this: it is the media themselves that hold the key to participation and personal visibility in the "real" world that they present to viewers and listeners, and it is the media who define the terms of such participation and visibility, however superficial these may be by normal measures.

THE CULTURE OF NARCISSISM:
CONSUMERISM, MARKETING, AND PERSONAL NEEDINESS

Let me repeat that these developments are ambiguously related to a Christian modern trajectory that is open to the coming of God's kingdom in ordinary ways. Positively, they have contributed to higher standards of living and freed up time spent on routine chores, enabling new kinds of individual participation in wide social circles and horizons of knowledge and skill. Few people would want to return to an older way of life that required giving up these benefits.

Precisely because of these positive aspects, however, it is vital that we discern and eschew such developments wherever they carry forward a distorted modern worldview and foster personal narcissism and neediness rather than human flourishing. This happens when massification becomes indiscriminate, a process driven blindly by ideological assumptions or by vested interests; when it echoes and reinforces practically, such a distortion in personal formation and worldview; and above all when it is used deliberately to manufacture such distortion for political or commercial ends. Let us now brings these concerns to bear on consumerism.

"Consumer society" is a sociological concept. However, sociological studies of consumer society almost inevitably invite, explicitly or implicitly, an evaluation of such society: how does consumer society measure up by reference to the goal of human flourishing? Such evaluation is implicit in, for example, the valuable essays collected together in *The Authority of the Consumer*,[8] and in the range of approaches to consumer society documented by Yiannis Gabriel and Tim Lang in *The Unmanageable Consumer*.

In wider popular discourse, the term "consumerism" refers to a tendency in contemporary Western society to frame wide-ranging aspects of human life in terms of consumption. Patients become customers, students become clients, and so on. This tendency invites appraisal by reference to the goal of human flourishing. Often in this setting the term "consumerism" has come often to be used pejoratively of a tendency in which commercialization distorts a proper understanding and pursuit of human wellbeing.

The pathological character of "consumerism" has been conceived in a variety of ways. Marcuse[9] described it as a fundamentally alienating form of society in which consumers merely echo the choices of those with power. David Collis, in a rambling essay,[10] has explored the concept of consumerism as abuse. This is an extreme viewpoint; however, insofar as consumerism fosters or amplifies the distortion of personal formation and worldview represented by narcissism, it rightly draws attention to a serious issue.

The distortion of personal and social character by consumerism can be seen as operating on three levels. Firstly, consumerism draws upon a fundamental belief that the blueprint for the advancement of human wellbeing is to be found in certain explicit principles of social organization and their systematic application. This allows the idea that the further development of mass production, standardization, and professionalization in general are an unequivocal good. However, as we have seen, when the program of massification is pursued indiscriminately— without regard for the distinctiveness of lively personal enquiry or the primacy of the practitioner and of the community of practice in such matters—this involves losses as well as gains. These losses diminish personal life in community but they tend to be overlooked or shrugged off because of a commitment to this fundamental belief.

Secondly, because private advantage and profit may be made by some from forms of massification such as mass production, mass mediation of communication, professionalization and enforced standardiza-

---

8. Keat et al., *Authority of the Consumer*.

9. Marcuse, *One-Dimensional Man*.

10. Collis, "Abuse of Consumerism."

tion, people may set about providing such things out of private interest without regard for whether they serve the public good. The goal of service gets replaced by that of private profit. Those involved in massification may, of course, argue that success in making a profit is legitimized because it demonstrates that "there is a market for this," and that they are therefore "providing a service." However, this claim diminishes the meaning of "service"; for example, it limits it to provision conditional upon ability to pay a set price and to a range of choices determined by the provider. Indeed the charge is common today that providers deliberately manufacture a desire for products where this desire did not previously exist and where such products do not contribute in any significant way to human flourishing. As a "service" this has dubious status.

Thirdly, and most seriously, in the marketing of good and services for profit, advertisers may exploit the incorrigible neediness of the narcissistic personality. They may deliberately cultivate an immediate association between a product and the "unattainable self" towards which such neediness is directed. This is reflected in the adage within marketing circles that "If you want to sell a product, you need to know what the prospective customer feels is wrong about themselves." Instead of having to convince prospective customers of the usefulness or attractive properties of a product, it is necessary only to associate the purchase of a product with being "someone" in the eyes of others and of themselves.

Narcissism among prospective customers thus provides a special opportunity for those wishing to sell products. Indeed it is the advertiser's dream: it offers the means to unlimited market creation. It turns people from hardheaded, discerning purchasers into malleable, fashion-conscious, impulse-driven consumers with insatiable needs. No product ever meets these needs, of course; yet this is of little consequence to the producer because it does not lessen the effect of a new appeal to these needs when the next new product is advertised. The narcissist within us never learns; its dynamic is precisely that of addiction. In this way advertising practices resonate with, and reinforce, the narcissistic distortion of character. Indeed because narcissism is so useful to marketing, we have reason to fear that those who believe in the inevitable benefits of consumerization, or who stand to gain personally from it, may be only too ready to collude with the deepening of narcissistic tendencies in culture.

By these means, modern consumer society tends today to provide what might be called the "plausibility structure" for narcissistic character formation and the worldview associated with it. The agents of this deformation are ultimately a "religious" allegiance to the modern ideas that legitimize this in a basic way, and the people who shape such a society indiscriminately in pursuit of their private interests. These today constitute the "other" that directs Riesman's other-directed character, insofar as this character is narcissistic; they are the agents who construct and communicate the "collective personality" that Sennett identifies as a feature of the intimate society and with which the consumer is invited to identify.

In summary, (1) Enlightenment thinking and its ideological assumptions is an ambiguous good that has, in practice, sponsored both the pursuit and the subversion of human flourishing; (2) this distortion can be fed by the pursuit of vested interests by "mass" managers and producers of one kind and another; and (3) this extends to a knowing complicity in the theological distortion I have indicated.

IN CONCLUSION: RECOGNIZING IDOLATRY

I began Part 2 of this book by discussing the familiar view that "modern secular society" represents a historical development in which religion is destined to decline and eventually disappear from a world in which "nothing is sacred." I pointed out that, rather, the secular domain has arisen precisely in the setting of Christian faith through the desacralization of the world sponsored by Christianity. The dismissal of Christianity or its relegation to a "private" sphere in the modern world is driven rather by a secularism that turns out to be itself religious in character and to create a "secular" society that actually has its own hidden forms of the sacred. Whereas secularism sees itself as sponsoring human freedom from religion, in reality it rejects the religion that is the ultimate ground of human freedom. And in so doing, it sponsors bondage to hidden idols.

It would seem that we can distinguish now between two aspects of the idolatry concealed within, and contradicting, the modern secularist celebration of human autonomy and freedom.

The first aspect is found in connection with the principles that were identified by Enlightenment thinkers as trustworthy foundations for building modern society. Cut adrift from their tacit meaning in Christian faith, in secularism their character is denied as signs arising from and pointing to the mystery of God who is the ultimate source of all human guidance. Rather, they are held, in themselves, to provide such guidance and are therefore seen as reliable tools available to human social engineers. Having acquired this status, however, they now acquire power to shape the conception of human ends. They attract religious commitment as that which can be trusted as the source of all human wellbeing. At this point they becomes idols, rival to God. They therefore attract the biblical charge against idols that they must not be trusted religiously: they "know nothing," and can offer no sure guidance.

Recalling the account offered by Michael Paul Gallagher, we might say that this first aspect of modern idolatry is the hidden side of the "Promethean" self-conception of modern secularist humanism. Whereas this declares itself as the exaltation of the human being in place of God as the autonomous source of all meaning and action, in reality it conceals a religious allegiance to ideas falsely imbued with religions status.

However, in this present chapter we have seen another side to this. Precisely as humanity celebrates self-sufficient identity in a "freedom" that it conceives as freedom from God the creator, it become vulnerable to a captivity from which God alone raises to freedom. Precisely as humanity turns away from trusting God within the limitations of creaturely life and entertains unlimited possibilities, it falls under the personal spell of narcissism—of hopeless longing for "the unattainable."

Here is the second aspect of modern idolatry. It is found in the practical and personal effects of Enlightenment thinking and of the social structures it has sponsored. On the one hand, it is expressed in *distorted personal character formation*. It invites the biblical warning that those who worship idols will become like them. They will become hollow. On the other hand, this idolatry finds expression in *a consumer culture* that fosters and reinforces this distortion. Gallagher refers to John Francis Kavanaugh's perception of the "enthronement of the commodity as the center of our lives." In North America, Kavanaugh writes, "our problem is idolatry." [**AQ: citations?**] This idolatry entails "a systematic rejection of human freedom." It brings bondage.

The Christian call to the "Promethean" secularist involves a challenge to shun pretentious claims for self-creation and to acknowledge the limitations of created human life and possibility. What, however, is the Christian call to the modern Narcissus who lives secretly burdened by a sense of personal neediness, alienated from the supposedly "real" world

and from an unattainable "self"? Addressing the underlying decision of
the Narcissus against trust, it involves a call to trust in the abundance
of God who has gracefully hosted us and endowed us with life—life
as a creature of God oriented towards life with God, and participating
already in this promised reality to come. Conversion is a matter here
of breaking the spell of personal deformation through the influence of
family life in infancy and through the illusions peddled by consumer
society; it is a matter of liberation for creative, participatory personal life
under God.

Both sides of the contradiction within secularist individualism—
its Promethean deification and its Narcissistic dissolution—need to be
recognized, and recognized as idolatrous distortions of God's purposes
for humanity. The former of these has often attracted attention. In this
chapter, however, we have paid attention to Narcissistic individualism,
and we shall continue to explore matters related to this in the next. When
we have done so, we shall turn in chapters 7 and 8 to the pretensions of
Promethean individualism.

To summarize: Christians are called by God today to live converted
to the abundance of God. They are called to witness to this abundance
and to seek the conversion of others to this by manifesting it in their own
Christian practice and faithfully understanding it upon reflection. They
are called also to acknowledge, and repent of, their own complicity with
Western cultural habits of thought and action that subvert conversion to
the abundance of God, notably the dissolution of character formation
and its replacement by the needy consumer.

To be converted to the abundance of God is to embrace the One
who has given himself to us in an unqualified and unconditional way in
Jesus Christ—and calls us to give to others as he has given to us. When
we do so, says Jesus, we shall receive from God "good measure, pressed
and shaken down and running over," poured into our lap (Luke 6:38).

6   The Tragic Sense of Life

Conversion to the Gospel of Hope

I<small>N</small> P<small>ART</small> T<small>WO</small> <small>OF</small> this book we have been exploring modern culture's characteristic failure to honor, in its thinking, the radical enquiry that constitutes openness to God. In the previous chapter we went on to explore the practical, personal aspect of modern culture's failure to honor such enquiry. We saw that this has inflamed narcissistic tendencies and personal neediness rooted in an abandonment of the hope enacted in radical responsiveness to God. According to the analysis in Part One of this book, this loss of hope involves an element of collusion or choice: it is a self-concealed evasion of the demands of hope.

Now this abandonment is no merely private affair; it is not, so to speak, a statement of personal feelings about the world. Rather it is a statement about *the world itself*. It posits the world as a world that offers no hope. Let us explore further what kind of world is posited here.

THE TRAGIC SENSE OF LIFE

This way of seeing the world is informed and defined by what George Steiner calls a "tragic sense of life."[1] It is evoked with unique power in classical Greek tragedy. The words "tragedy" and "tragic" have a more radical and intense meaning here than they often have when they are used to refer to misfortunes of one kind and another. Something of this more intense meaning is intimated in references to a "tragic figure" or a "tragic story."

Paradigmatically, the "tragic sense of life" is ignited by encounter with a traumatic event in which life and its value are violated without qualification. Such violation is taken as the last word upon human life. It is taken to present the world, and moreover to present the world as *most*

---

1. Steiner, *Death of Tragedy*.

deeply, a place in which humankind suffers catastrophic and irreversible loss, mocking without end the meaning and hope that tacitly ground all human life. This encountered contradiction of life and value is internalized, where it becomes a practical, inner contradiction of meaning and hope that is forever unresolved.

In the history of stage drama during the past two millennia a "tragic sense of life" has been, according to George Steiner, eclipsed by "Judaeo-Christian optimism." However, signs of its re-emergence in popular Western culture have been noted by researchers in contemporary spirituality. David Hay and Kate Hunt, in their report *Understanding the Spirituality of People Who Don't Go to Church*, write:

> We are wondering whether, forty years on from Steiner's analysis, after Auschwitz and after the many other atrocities of the 20th century, we see in post-Christian society the return of a tragic sense of life . . . If at the deepest level there is a conviction that life at depth is pitiless and utterly meaningless, then the optimism of Christianity becomes incredible. The people we spoke to were well aware of this, and it is an issue that church people need to face much more directly in their dialogue with secular culture.[2]

Signs of the return of a tragic sense of life may be discerned in many features of modern Western culture. They present themselves in a most striking form when events happen of an extreme sort. Such events have power to evoke a certain "sense of the sacred" even in a very "secular" society, as Grace Davie notes. She describes these as occasions when in a society "normal" ways of living are, for one reason or another, suspended and "something far more instinctive comes to the fore." A certain sense of the sacred shows itself here in what I shall call "tragic spirituality," and in intense victim sensibility. These are striking expressions of a tragic sense of life. Let us consider each in turn.

TRAGIC SPIRITUALITY

One such occasion, Grace Davie recalls, "occurred in Sweden in 1994, following the sinking of the Baltic ferry, Estonia, with the loss of some 900 lives. The shock for Swedish people, a safety-conscious nation if ever there was one, was colossal; with no exaggeration the unthinkable had happened." Almost without hesitation, Grace Davie notes, the people

2. Hay and Hunt, *Spirituality of People Who Don't Go to Church*.

of this most "secular" society went to their churches to gather, to light candles, and privately to mourn.[3]

This popular response shows some continuity with traditional Christian spirituality, including the use of candles and recourse to a church building. However, there are very significant discontinuities in meaning since the mass of mourners lacked a background of Christian understanding or hope in their grief. Diverging further from traditional Christian practice have been the been mass outpourings of feeling and spontaneous "religious" ritual arising in response to high profile, iconic victims. Famously, the death of the Princess of Wales brought a flood of candles and flowers and impromptu monuments in Britain. A few years later, in 2002, a similar massive outpouring of emotion followed the murder of two young English schoolgirls: over 15,000 candles were lit by visitors to Soham Parish Church, a similar number of letters were sent and flowers placed in the churchyard, and around 2,000 teddy bears were given.

Such events have arisen spontaneously in the sense that they have not been organized by authorized leaders or institutions or in conformity to long established custom. There are also formal events organized from time to time marking loss or victimhood in new ways. These include memorial services, candlelight marches in memory of AIDS victims, government-funded events marking the anniversary of the Jewish Holocaust, and—in 2007—public and media events marking the Abolition of the Slave Trade Act.

At a more local level, the placing of memorials at the site of road traffic accidents is now not uncommon. Here, once again, elements of continuity with traditional Christian mourning are found in such things as flowers and candles but there are highly significant discontinuities in meaning. On the one hand, these gestures assert the worth of what has been lost. On the other hand, they defer to the tragic event as the brute setting of this assertion rather than any traditional religious memorial setting. Lying in sharp disjunction from their bleak public setting, roadside tributes at the scene of accidents speak of tragic violence done to a "private" life. Unlike the traditional grave clustered among others around the building where a faithful God is worshipped, such tokens tend to intimate—in a certain gesture of impossible defiance—that *violation has had the last word.* Where memorabilia are made into a permanent shrine,

3. Davie, "From Obligation to Consumption."

they linger as marks of a tragedy never to be forgotten, rather than of a life lived and now remembered as a gift from God. Gifts of teddy bears in memory of a lost child are enactments of futile giving, intimating unresolved feelings of powerlessness in face of tragedy. The gestures over the death of the Princess of Wales testified to a tragedy claiming the last word upon one already seen as a tragic victim.

VICTIM SENSIBILITY

Closely related to tragic spirituality is a heightened sensitivity towards victims. In contemporary Western culture victimhood is the focus of intense feeling among those who see themselves as victims and those who identify with others whom they see as victims.

Victim sensibility finds expression in indignation, rage, and sometimes violence. In extreme cases it has led to the bombing of abortion clinics and attacks upon those involved in animal vivisection and experimentation. Young Muslims are deliberately radicalized by being shown videos of the victimization of Muslims. The philosophy of Sayid Qut'b, which inspired the Muslim Brotherhood and Al Qaeda, burns with a sense of the victimhood of Muslims at the hands of Jews and Christians.

More generally, victim sensibility has shaped the formulation of legislation on human rights and on rights in general. It has also helped to inflame a litigious turn in culture. We shall consider rights further in chapter 9; for the moment, let us simply note that victim sensibility has fueled the perception that certain groups who suffer victimization habitually (such as black people and women) should be protected from discrimination by law. Through this, "racism" and "sexism" have acquired a special status among the sins publicly acclaimed as such in Western culture.

Victimization is registered here with all the intensity of outrage traditionally directed towards a violation of the sacred. As the violation of victims is registered with passion, they are exalted to sacred status. Precisely as victims, they are endowed with a religious identity. Accordingly, those groups that win recognition as victims sometimes respond by claiming victimhood as a mark of their identity as a group, thus claiming for themselves a certain sacred status.

We might note that this heightened sensibility towards victims does not extend to a heightened discernment regarding where victimhood is to be found (or not to be found). It tends to "run with" stereotypes of victims who have been identified as such in mass culture, such as the groups mentioned above. This points to further issues regarding the nature of victim sensibility and of tragic spirituality. Let us turn to these now.

REAL AND FAKE FEELING

Tragic spirituality and victim sensibility have been criticized by Patrick West as "fake." In *Conspicuous Compassion*,[4] he writes "We live in a post-emotional age, one characterized by crocodile tears and manufactured emotion." He sees extravagant public displays of grief for people one has never met as "recreational" grief, "undertaken as an enjoyable event, much like going to a football match or the last night at the proms." He dubs this "mourning sickness." The phony character of these displays leads, according to West, to "compassion inflation": recalling the practice of keeping a two-minute silence on Remembrance Day, he writes: "When a group called Hedgeline calls for a two-minute silence to remember all the 'victims' whose neighbors have grown towering hedges, we truly have reached the stage where this gesture has been emptied of meaning."

Patrick West finds theoretical resources for his analysis in Stjepan Meštrović's book *Postemotional Society*.[5] Meštrović offers "a sociology of emotion" complementary to existing sociologies of knowledge. He claims that contemporary Western society is marked by a "mechanization of emotions" in which processes of mechanization (an aspect of rationalization, we might note) deriving from the Enlightenment extend today to a neo-Orwellian manipulation of feelings. "Western societies," he writes, "are entering a new phase of development in which synthetic, quasi-emotions become the basis for widespread manipulation by self, others, and the culture industry as a whole." In a "McDonaldization of emotions," bite-size, pre-packaged emotions such as indignation and the apprehension of "niceness" are mass manufactured and cued.

Meštrović draws upon the insights of a number of sociologists including David Riesman. He sees the dominance of Riesman's other-directed character, shaped by a desire for emotional resonance with others, as opening the way for such mass manipulation. But in the process these

4. West, *Conspicuous Compassion*.
5. Meštrović, *Postemotional Society*.

emotions themselves are transformed: "postemotionalism involves the use of 'dead' emotions from a nostalgicized tradition and inner-directed past that are almost always *vicarious* and *conspicuous* and are treated as objects to be *consumed*." In postemotional society, emotions have not disappeared, he writes, but have become distorted into synthetic, quasi-emotions severed from thought and yielding no action.

Meštrović's account of these "quasi-emotions" corresponds in interesting ways with John Macmurray's account, in the 1930s, of "unreal feeling."[6] "Feeling, when it is real feeling, is that in us which enables us to grasp the worth of things," he writes. Unreal feeling, by contrast, is divorced from the world outside and turned in upon itself; attention is upon the feelings aroused themselves, and not, in an act of discernment, upon that which arouses them. It is mere sentiment. It is divorced from experience of the world, divorced from thinking, and does not issue in action. And it is demoralizing.

Meštrović, for his part, is concerned above all to describe a process of mass manipulation in society today that heralds a new loss of freedom—a bondage of the population to those who direct their manipulation. Macmurray, too, was concerned with freedom: his remarks on "unreal feeling" come in his book *Freedom in the Modern World*. He also acknowledges implicitly the risk of manipulation that arises from unreal feeling and unreal thinking: since these do not arise from personal attentiveness towards the real world, he says, we are dependent upon their generation by others on our behalf. Macmurray's concern, however, is with the inner, personal aspects of freedom and their loss, rather than with the mass manipulation that exploits this loss. It is this loss that lies behind unreal feeling and unreal thinking; through it a person becomes "unreal," that is, not who they really are. Turned in upon themselves, their thinking and feeling alike are divorced from the real world and divorced each from the other; the unreal person is interested in the world and in other people only as a source of support, esteem, and stimulation. Macmurray's account of the "unreal person" shows clear similarities with an account of the narcissistic personality.

The link between postemotionalism and narcissism can also be traced via the fantasy of "corporate personality" that Richard Sennett describes, together with narcissism, as marking the "intimate society." This fantasy is the vehicle through which manipulation is able to ex-

6. Macmurray, *Freedom in the Modern World*, chapters 4 and 5.

ploit narcissistic neediness. It accounts for the "fakeness" of these quasi-emotions in terms of narcissistic desire: the real orientation of these quasi-emotions lies not so much towards their declared object of feeling as towards an imagined "self" pursued through a self-conscious display of identification with the declared object of feeling and with all people who similarly identify.

SOURCES OF CONTEMPORARY PAIN

Accordingly "conspicuous compassion," together with the wider phenomenon of narcissism, echoes the pain of unresolved and unfaceable loss of hope. Now, this loss is real; narcissism, as the subtitle of Lasch's book *The Minimal Self* has it, is about "psychic survival in troubled times." But this loss of hope is evasive: it evades the demands of hope through personal disorientation and disintegration, in a self-deceiving collusion with personal overwhelming. It is this which attracts to it the label "fake." In other words "fakeness" here lies not so much in the fact that feelings have been manufactured on a mass scale disconnected from individual thought and action; it lies more in the personal evasion that freely permits such disconnection and opens the way for such manipulation in the first place.

But the loss and pain are nonetheless real. Indeed, as Melvyn Matthews writes, "it is the pain, the actual deadening, horrifying pain of living in the modern world which is at the heart of things."[7] Where does the pain of unfaceable loss come from? After all, the modern period has brought widely throughout Western society huge increases in standards of living, health, safety and education, and new opportunities for social advancement.

At a most general level we have linked this loss of hope with a widening divergence between the trajectory of modern culture and that of openness to the kingdom of God. We have described this in terms of the modern subversion, both in theoretical thought and personal practice, of openness to God and of the lively enquiry that this sponsors. The trajectory of modern culture has brought material advances in wellbeing but also—by scorning the ultimate resources of guidance and empowerment for a lived trajectory open to God—it has brought dislocation and disorientation. As we have seen, the nineteenth cen-

---

7. Matthews, *Delighting in God*, 99.

tury was already marked by a personal loss of hope reflected in the sentimentality of novels.

Beginning with the First World War, the twentieth century brought conflicts and atrocities that ravaged Europe and much of the world. Prior to this, Christian Europe had seen itself as the bearer of civilization to the whole world. The First World War broke upon this as a civil war, radically undermining Europe's confident self-understanding, sense of self-worth, and hope. But this was only the start. The century opened with what Oliver O'Donovan calls a "massive cultural certainty in united natural science, democratic politics, technology, and colonialism." "The four great facts of the twentieth century that broke the certainty to pieces," he writes, "were two World Wars, the reversal of European colonization, the threat of the nuclear destruction of the human race, and, most recently, the evidence of long-term ecological crisis."[8] Today we have a widely felt legacy of guilt over Western exploitation of peoples and resources, an uneasy conscience about the West's current global economic and military hegemony, and apprehension over future prospects for our planet.

Loss of confidence extends today beyond disappointment at setbacks in human progress towards ends that themselves still inspire confidence; it extends to disorientation regarding any such ends themselves. O'Donovan writes, "Western society finds itself the heir of political institutions and traditions which it values without having any clear idea why, or to what extent, it values them. Faced with decisions about their future development it has no way of telling what counts as improvement and what as subversion. It cannot tell where 'straight ahead' lies, let alone whether it ought to keep on going there."

Nevertheless, says O'Donovan, two parts of the old "civilizational ice-shelf"—natural science and technology—drift on like huge icebergs "as though nothing had happened—they are not joined together any more, nor joined to the land." This needs qualification. The older confidence was that science and technology would bring sure progress towards a bright and harmonious future. This confidence was tacitly imbued with Christian faith: it grasped the pursuit of knowledge and skill as good in themselves, and entailed in the God-ordained stewardship of a good world that God had created for his good purposes; and it saw human beings as endowed by God with the goodness and powers of reason

8. O'Donovan, *Ways of Judgment*, xii.

to carry forward these purposes. Scientific and technological advance were noble pursuits, to be pursued altruistically for the good of all.

This outlook has changed. More recently science and technology have been viewed with more ambivalence. To be sure, they still attract much rhetorical confidence in public, as politicians present the confident hope that with their help all problems can be solved; nothing is intractable before them. And technological advances continue to inspire wonder and wide appreciation, especially in the personal use of the information and communication technology available through the internet, mobile phones, etc. But technology has also brought new anxieties in relation to environmental damage, terrorism, surveillance, GM crops, and so on. Today scientific and technological research are pursued less for the good of all than for profit and private advantage; their "goods" are the private ones defined by intellectual property rights, patents, and licenses.

Meanwhile, implicit faith has gone that the goodness and rationality of humankind will ensure that the right advances in science and technology are pursued and that they will be put to good use. Totalitarian regimes, including that of Nazi Germany, have demonstrated that national leaders can be outrageously other than good or reasonable, that the common humanity of those at war with each other provides no adequate safeguards against inhumanity, and that human beings are not even safe in the hands of the states that governs them. Indeed technology, once seen as a blessing in the hands of good and rational people, is now relied upon increasingly in their place—unrealistically, of course—as the mainstay protection against human mischief, through surveillance and other security procedures.

There have been other sources of personal disorientation and demoralization. Recent decades have seen Western governments widely adopting policies prompted by the vision of "free-market" global capitalism. We shall consider this at greater length in chapter 9. Governments and business have between them sponsored an ongoing social revolution: the norms of capitalism have been applied in a more thoroughgoing way and extended to social institutions as wide-ranging as the mass media and public services, including health care, education, transport, energy, and water supplies. Capital and labor have become more fluid and more globally sourced; work has changed, and job security has declined. The resulting social changes have widely undermined people's sense of purpose and security, values, and worth. The visions of wellbeing offered by consumerist marketing have tended to exploit rather than lift people out of the resulting disorientation and demoralization.

In the sphere of personal life and relationships, there has been a significant breakdown in family life following changes in lifestyle and values in the 1960s. A large proportion of children born since then have lived through the separation of their parents. Parents have widely lost confidence in their role instilling good values and behavior in their children; mothers commonly resume employment while their children are still toddlers; at home television presents children with a bewildering range of alternative values in a way unknown to previous generations of children. Together these changes have brought new and widespread sources of insecurity for children in their upbringing.

In the background of all this, as I have said, lies the trajectory of the modern vision as such. This has been associated with a decline in Christian faith and more widely with the erosion of tacit Christian values. It has colluded with evasion of God in theoretical thought, in social environment, and in personal disposition. In place of the Christian integration of hope in a good God with a realistic appraisal of human limitations, there have arisen proud aspirations of unqualified mastery on the one hand and despairing narcissism and neediness on the other.

No amount of rhetoric by today's politicians about modernization, or by businessmen about wealth creation, can overcome this loss of hope.

CONTEMPORARY CULTURAL EXPRESSIONS OF THE ABANDONMENT OF HOPE

Among the features of contemporary Western culture informed by unresolved pain and loss of hope are four related phenomena:

1. Narcissism and Needy Consumerism

We have already described this distortion of character in which a person turns away from the world in despair and constructs a "self" which becomes the focus of their lives and reduces other people and the world to a mere extension of this self. In *The Culture of Narcissism* Christopher Lasch has shown how many features of modern Western culture are illuminated by reference to the prevalence of narcissism. We have also noted how consumerism gains impetus from the needy face of narcissism:

a sense of personal emptiness fuels pursuit of self-displacing mirages of fulfillment and flight from paralyzing specters of personal disaster. The consumerist marketing of goods and services regularly exploits and reinforces this.

2. Credulity and Promiscuity

When the demands of lively enquiry into the world are evaded, enquiry takes distorted forms reflecting what Macmurray calls "unreal" thinking and feeling. In particular, enquiry today widely takes the form of a restless tasting of possibilities without the self-engaging commitment of real exploration. It takes the form of casual self-entertainment. We have recalled the laments of P. T. Forsyth and G. K. Chesterton, early in the twentieth century, over the loss of lively, serious engagement with the world and the rise of distraction. "Unreal" enquiry is about casting around for hope in what is in reality a superficial and indeed *hopeless* way. This can take the form of promiscuous relationships and of an aimless life of anomie that lacks either responsible, personal giving or receiving in any depth. It also shows itself in credulity towards the claims of consumer advertising and towards excessive promises made by, for example, novel therapies, new technologies, and personal consultants. Such credulity masks a radical incredulity: it is an enactment of futile hoping.

3. Escapism through Addictive Pleasures and Fantasies of Control

Pleasure is, of course, to be experienced in the good gifts of God; however, pleasure may itself also be used to provide a temporary escape from the stress of a life deformed by hopelessness. Used in this way, pleasure acquires an addictive quality. This has attracted comment as a feature of contemporary Western culture. Some pleasures serve the desire for escape better than others. Thus alcohol and drugs blank out stress temporarily; sex and violence can be used to override feelings of emptiness with excitement. Gambling is a distinctive vehicle of escapism: it enacts a sense of powerlessness to attain desirable goals while enjoying being at the mercy of fortune. The addictive power of escapist pleasure helps today to fuel a culture of debt, generating a vicious circle of despair and escape.

Oppressed by a sense of powerlessness, escapism may also take the form of fantasies of control; oppressed by anonymity, it may take the form of fantasies of personal impact or celebrity. Computer games may provide for these kinds of escapism through immersion in virtual worlds; in the real world, politicians and the directors of mass media commonly massage, to their own ends, the fantasy that mastery is always promised through use of the right techniques and tools. This explains partly the disjunction noted by Carver T. Yu between the West's technological optimism and its literary despair.[9]

4. Sentiment

Loss of personal hope lies behind the popularity of stories in which sentimental, private solutions present themselves to characters inhabiting a heartless world. Hollywood feeds filmgoers with a diet of stories featuring needy figures for whom there is an unrealistic, gratuitous, and contrived happy ending. From *The Wizard of Oz* to *The Matrix* trilogy, Hollywood preaches an unattainable salvation to the needy soul: the victorious power of positive thinking and of self-originating choice in the face of bleak determinism, perhaps with an inexplicable dose of fated good fortune. Such sentiment simply reinforces personal anomie and demoralization; there is nothing here that nourishes the recovery of personal orientation towards, and responsible, hopeful engagement with, the real world.

A WORLD THAT MOCKS HOPE?

We have noted some features of Western culture that are informed by a loss of personal hope; and we have noted some factors contributing historically to it. Can we now say more about this loss of hope itself? What is its deep character? What perception of the world does it constitute?

The loss of hope in question lies concealed, we have seen, behind narcissistic tendencies and personal neediness. It is radical, personal loss of hope with which we are here concerned. It comes into focus in a special way in a tragic sense of life informing contemporary tragic spirituality and victim sensibility. This tragic sense of life apprehends the world as a place in which human worth and meaning are fundamentally mocked, and this mockery sears the human soul.

9. Yu, *Truth and Authentic Humanity*.

This apprehension of the world arises classically in the encounter with tragic victimhood, either our own or that of other people. At its heart lies a radical dissonance. On the one hand, we are presented with a person whose unqualified worth as such is evident to us; on the other, with an occurrence that overtakes that person as if they were simply not there or were of no worth whatsoever. This dissonance inflames in us a deep moral and spiritual pain.

To have a tragic sense of life is to be overwhelmed by this dissonance. It becomes the last word upon the world and upon ourselves. It thus becomes a matter at once of ultimate cosmic and personal or existential import. We feel that the world should be such that "someone" was there to affirm the victim's presence and worth by saving them in the same way as we would have wanted to do were we able. The fact that the world stands in radical contradiction of what it should be is the last word upon it and upon all human meaning and hope.

There is more to this contradiction. Overwhelmed by a tragic sense of life, we feel that the absence of this "someone" is a mocking *choice* (contradictory as it is to ascribe choice to a non-existent agent). In a strange but passionately felt way, through this mocking absence of a personal agent, the absent "agent" mocks the *victim* as absent—precisely through the victim's presence to the agent *as* a victim. And ultimately all humankind, ourselves included, is the victim in question. This mocking, cosmic "present absence" now penetrates into our very soul: we secretly assent to its negation and mockery of the human victim. We treat the human victim (ourselves included) as "deserving the undeserved"; we become our own victim. In this way we collude with the tragic as for ever the last word upon ourselves.

It is this internalized contradiction—a personally mocking absence—that informs narcissism and personal neediness as an evasion in which a person enacts the abandonment of personal hope. When (according to Kohut's account) the narcissistic person treats the world as an empty vessel to be filled with the narcissistic self, it is because they have secretly constructed their own self as unreal and empty in response to the parental "absence" towards them as a child that led them to experience their own "presence" as unreal because contradicted. As for the world (represented initially by the parents of the child), having betrayed the child as the child's source of self and self-affirmation, this world now appears to the child as empty; it promises nothing. This contradiction of the child's reality is now carried into the false "self" upon which the narcissistic person gazes: like the image in the pool of water into which Narcissus gazes in the Greek myth, it mocks by its refusal to present itself in the realm of what is real, accessible, and trustworthy. At this point the tragic sense of life adds a recognition that this mocking absence is not just a mockery of an individual's longing desire (as in the Greek myth) but a mockery of all human, personal, moral, and spiritual concern.

How does this world, as apprehended by a tragic sense of life, relate to the world as it is conceived in secularism? Secularism sees the world as having no meaning or purpose as the creation of a personal God whose wishes it to be the medium of his blessing. Instead, meaning and value are seen as ultimately things that human beings themselves create and through that they determine how to behave in the world. Belief in God is seen as the vehicle through which, in the past, religious authorities have wrongly imposed upon individuals their own meanings and values. The modern secularist vision is one of liberation for the innately good, rational individual who is enlightened enough to see that the world is impersonal and empty of such authority and to live freely by the light their own goodness and rationality.

We have seen that this secularist distortion of the Christian world-view is born partly of a proper reaction against a "sacral" worldview, but that it diverges from the Christian desacralization of the world in that it conceives a world in which "nothing is sacred" rather than a world through which the sacred reveals itself by signs, and that in reality secularism breeds its own distorted forms of the sacred. Now since the truly sacred is found in a personal God, we may express this alternatively by replacing the "sacred" here with "divine personhood." We may describe secularism as born partly of a proper reaction against a wrong kind of "personalizing" of the world which, in sacral religion, endows direct, personal, divine warrant upon features of the world. However, secularism diverges from a Christian worldview in at once conceiving the world as *impersonal*—rather than as a world hosted ultimately by a personal God and through which the personal reveals itself in signs—and also breeding its own distorted concepts and forms of the personal.

As we have seen, secularization has been associated often with "Promethean" concepts of the person. This conception can be seen as involving dismissiveness towards the demands of radical responsiveness to a personal God in a desacralized world. The demands of seeking a

personal God in an impersonal world, seeking his presence in his seeming absence, are simply dismissed as not arising. However this stance can
be also interpreted, we have seen, as a defense against a felt loss of hope
in the face of the absence of God. It can also be seen as reinforcing this
loss of hope: because radical responsiveness is towards a personal God,
the declaration that God does not exist is overwhelming to the human
soul. For us the world cannot be *simply* impersonal; if it is impersonal
it is cruelly, mockingly so. In this way a dismissive secularist view of the
world actively breeds, as its foil, an overwhelmed, tragic sense of life.

CHRISTIAN ENGAGEMENT WITH THE "TRAGIC SENSE OF LIFE"

Christian critiques of secularism have generally overlooked this side of
the matter. Typically, Christian critiques of secularism focus upon its
proud claims for human rationality, autonomy, and self-sufficiency in
general. However, modern life, like life in any age, is in reality tempted
not only by proud dismissiveness but also by a despairing disposition,
overwhelming, and disorientation. How does the gospel speak into this
setting? Alister McFadyen, in *Bound by Sin*, recognizes that sin has been
identified too routinely with pride. He associates despairing disorientation by victimhood with the sin of "sloth."[10] David Ford, in *The Shape
of Living*, confronts the threat of being *overwhelmed by despair* with a
gospel that speaks of being *overwhelmed by a God who blesses*.

The empty space presented by the secular world gets filled, then,
precisely with personal presence in the form of absence—a mocking
negation. The Christian gospel addresses this with the decisive faith that
in some utterly hidden way, behind this mocking absence, there remains
the mystery of a personal God who calls us to rise to responsible participation in his good purposes and who hosts and upholds us faithfully
in them.

The foundations of this gospel message lie in the death and resurrection of Jesus Christ. We explored how this event addresses the human evasions of dismissal and disorientation in Part One of this book.
Jesus lived among those who hoped for a future Messiah who would
inaugurate once and for all the rule of a righteous God. When he began proclaiming the coming of God's kingdom, and restored hope to

10. McFadyen, *Bound to Sin*, 139f.

many victims he met, these expectations began to focus on himself. In the context of such hope, Jesus' rejection and barbaric execution realized the worst scenario. The Messiah, instead of being upheld by God and his fellow human beings, was deserted by both. God's good purposes, far from being fulfilled, were contradicted in a final way. Here was the ultimate denial of hope, the final mockery of meaning. Tragedy claimed the last word upon human life.

Jesus, however, embraced this extremity open to God. He allowed the unthinkable possibility that even this could be a vocation from God—that against seemingly impossible odds, God's good purposes would have the last word. In so doing he carried the dignity of hope— hope for God and for humankind—into the fathomless depths of tragic victimhood.

For us, accordingly, to stand before Jesus' crucifixion is to be confronted by the ultimate denial of meaning and hope for humanity in a tragic world. However, it is also to be addressed by Jesus who accepted this "impossible" vocation from God, trusting that somehow the last word *would be spoken by God*. Not overcome by despair or rage, he faced God in the unfaceable. In so doing he confronted the spellbinding power of tragedy to overwhelm and capture the human spirit. In so doing he restored to victims their dignity, liberating them to embrace both the hope of their ultimate vindication and forgiveness for their complicity (so intimidating to acknowledge), and empowered them in turn to forbear and to forgive.

This passion of Jesus always remains a mystery bigger than we can fathom; the grief of his victimhood and the joy of his victory together stretch and enlarge our souls. As I have already quoted, Austin Farrer wrote, "The cross defeats our hope; the resurrection terrifies our despair." And so it always remains.

To summarize: Christians are called by God today to live converted to the gospel of hope. They are called to witness to this hope, and to seek the conversion of others to this by manifesting it in their own Christian practice and faithfully understanding it as a matter of reflection. They are called also to acknowledge, and repent of, their own complicity with Western cultural habits of thought and action that subvert hope: a tragic sense of life (including its expression in what I have called "tragic spirituality"); narcissism, and the needy, credulous consumerism that peddles false hopes; escapism and sentiment; an overwhelmed, enraged, victim sensibility; managed "fake feeling"; and fantasies of (in reality non-existent) personal control.

To be converted to the gospel of hope is to entrust ourselves to God and to the promised gift of resurrection to eternal life in Jesus Christ, now and forever. It is to embrace real hope, hope that is to be maintained with fortitude, come what may. It is to entrust ourselves to the God whom Paul invokes in these words: " May God, who is the ground of all hope, fill you with all joy and peace as you lead the life of faith until, by the power of the Holy Spirit, you overflow with hope" (Rom 15:13).

7 PERSONAL FULFILLMENT AND CONTEMPORARY SPIRITUALITY

Conversion to Eternal Life

THERE HAS BEEN A loss of personal hope in contemporary society. We have considered some of the factors contributing to this. We have also seen that diverse features of cultural life today are driven by this loss of personal hope, although this driving force may be hidden. Among these are cultural practices that may be described as expressing illusions of hope or distorted forms of hopefulness. They embody hope of a sort that is in reality a false substitute for the authentic act of hope to which God inspires us. In some instances this illusory hope appears specific to the individual, although its cultural availability to the individual in the first place may nevertheless derive in some measure from its mass manufacture. Examples of this are the hope of winning that impels the compulsive gambler and the hope of becoming a celebrity that impels the narcissist. In other instances, illusory hope finds expression in the form of public "creeds" promulgated on behalf of all: it comes with a kind of official endorsement as "something we all hope for, something we all pin our hopes on." The next three chapters will be given to examining three major examples of such culturally mandated hope.

In this present chapter we shall focus on the creed of "life": the hope of fulfilling one's personal potential for "life." This is "what we all hope for" for ourselves as individuals in contemporary western culture today. It is what we reasonably and naturally want. It is supposedly the underlying orientation and purpose of our lives.

Now the hope of "life" is, in a defining sense, fundamental to Christian faith: the promise of God to us is precisely eternal life, in and through Jesus Christ.[1] And the contemporary desire to fulfill our poten-

---

1. For a thoughtful reflection on life, and on the will of life *for* life, which is God and

tial for life has roots partly in this Christian hope. However, there are also marked divergences between these two hopes. We need therefore to reflect carefully on the nature of the contemporary hope of "life" in order properly to compare this with Christian faith.

What is the nature, then, of the contemporary hope of fulfilling one's personal potential for "life"? This hope conceals two initial assumptions about "life" that stand somewhat in tension with each other. Firstly, "life" is a private *possession* of the individual, by inalienable right, and may therefore be used as the individual sees fit (or disposed of, for that matter, in suicide). Secondly, it comes in the form of an *opportunity* that is to be taken. It is something we have to "make happen" for ourselves. Thus, we at once *have* life, but *must do something in order to* have a life. In both respects—as a possession at our disposal and an opportunity to be seized—life is quite the most important thing there is for us, and therefore has first claim upon our attention and energy as individuals.

The contemporary vision of fulfilling our potential for "life" also involves two other, related ideas in similar tension with each other. On the one hand, "life" is something we at once live and construct for ourselves *in the act of making choices*. It is through our decision-making that we define what it will mean for each of us as a unique individual to realize our potential for "life." On the other hand, we tend to follow common views of what an attained "life" will look like and what ingredients will be involved. Prominent among these is the goal of "health"—health incorporating the concerns of "health and beauty," "health and fitness," and "health and wholeness." Each of these is the subject of promotion by commercial interests offering goods and services in pursuit of these ingredients of "life."

The cultivation of *health and beauty* involves the pursuit of physical beauty as conceived and promoted in contemporary society. This includes, for example, youthful physical characteristics and a slim figure. The cultivation of beauty tends to be seen—especially for women—as a matter of tending one's body with love and respect, through the use of suitable skin and hair products, etc., and the service of beauticians. It also widely involves the pursuit of weight loss and sometimes extends to cosmetic surgery. The cultivation of *health and fitness* involves the pursuit of physical fitness through exercise including the use of sports clubs and gyms. It overlaps with the pursuit of beauty. Regular atten-

---

then God's gift to humankind, see MacDonald, "Life."

dance at a gym can fulfill a certain "religious" role as a ritual display of inclusion among those committed to "life." The cultivation of *health and wholeness* is wider in scope. Beyond the profiles of physical beauty and physical fitness lies a penumbra of other visions of "wellbeing" of a personal, emotional, and spiritual kind. The pursuit of such wellbeing involves a wide range of practices and therapies incorporating many theories about the way the human body works that originate elsewhere than in Western experimental science. Among them one meets theories about, for example, achieving inner harmony through balancing figurative elements within the person and about eliminating what is "unclean" in the body by "detoxing" it. Pleasurable experiences such as massage hold a key place as "feel-good" indicators of wellbeing.

In arenas such as these, the task of fulfilling one's potential for "life" and maintaining one's "wellbeing" typically includes the following four visions.

1. *Self-valuing*: it is held that we must tell ourselves and remind ourselves that, as individuals, we are of great worth. It is uniquely our responsibility that we do so and that we affirm our worth by suitable self-affirming actions. This especially involves "positive thinking," which extends to entertaining the belief that our possibilities are limitless if we will but dream dreams and follow them. In such matters our natural inclinations may be followed as a true indication of what we should seek.

2. *Self-care*: our self-valuing is seen as implying self-care: we are to nurture lovingly our "selves" in all their aspects. This is a foremost obligation imposed upon us—"because we deserve it." As illustrated by the retailing slogan "Be good to yourself," this responsibility of care is typically presented as a matter of treating ourselves to whatever we want. As when we are encouraged to "dream dreams," the message is that *limits* are to be scorned as the enemy of wellbeing. "Feel-good" experiences are privileged as messages of care.

3. *Mastery*: effective self-care is furthered by discovering, mastering, and applying techniques. These techniques are diverse and include the use of health foods and supplements, beauty treatments, exercise regimes, meditation, dietary management, and alternative therapeutic regimes.

4. *Faith in "nature"*: in tension with the pursuit of mastery stands the desire to feel that one belongs in an intimate personal way to "the natural world," and can trust this for nurture in a comprehensive way. In this context herbs and natural essences have appeal both in food and in medicine. Trust in "the natural" may extend to confidence that our body "knows what is best for itself," and to the faith that our "natural" intuition tells us what is good for us, or tells us what we ought to do, and that we should therefore "listen to ourselves."

How does such contemporary pursuit of "life" compare with the Christian hope of life from God—of new and eternal life through Jesus Christ and "in Christ"? Is it pursuit of the same thing, albeit without explicit reference to Christ? Or is the "life" that it pursues quite different in nature from true life and its pursuit a distortion of the hope of true life?

Health, beauty, and fitness are not, of course, exalted in Christian faith as an end in themselves in the same way as in the contemporary pursuit of "life." Certainly a good measure of each is in general something we may enjoy as a good gift from God; we may show God's love towards other people by seeking this gift where it is lacking; and we may accept it as a matter of responsible stewardship to seek this for ourselves especially where it offers to enhance our opportunities to serve God and other people. But sometimes we may be called precisely to sacrifice a measure of such "health" in our service to God and to other people. Again, sometimes it is precisely through our *lack* of "health" that we become the occasion of God's grace, as God makes of us a special gift to others among whom we live. The same considerations distinguish some contemporary visions of "wholeness" from the Christian vision of, and hope for, the fullness of eternal life.

Turning to the contemporary dispositions of self-valuing, self-care, pursuit of mastery, and faith in "nature," we again find differences between these and the dispositions fostered by Christian faith.

1. In Christian faith, we do not so much *value ourselves* as honor God who is beyond all value, is the source of all value, and who *values us*. We know that although we are made of the dust of the earth, God counts us little lower than the angels (Ps 8). And although our sin and our creaturely limitations mean that we are not what God intends us to be, we know that he remains radically committed to our value, forgiving and transforming us. Our being of value is thus an unshakable *fact* reflecting

the will and purpose of God who is the creator of all and the source of all value. It is our responsibility to honor this, in an act of positive faith (rather than "positive thinking"). Entrusting our worth into God's hands, we are freed to act without pursuing what will feed our self-esteem. We are free even to suffer humiliation, confident that he values us even though our humiliation suggests otherwise; paradoxically we may even discover God's esteem for us through this at a new and deeper level.

2. This has implications for the Christian understanding of *self-care*. In Christian faith our care is for what honors and furthers the purposes of God. This awakens us to care for others and to show a certain duty of care for ourselves, assisting us to serve both God and neighbor well. Such care needs only to be "good enough"; we need not conceive or strive for "perfection" in wellbeing. Indeed we need to be open to self-sacrifice. Jesus says those who are willing to lose their life will gain it; and this has implications for self-care. This is the very opposite of the spirit of narcissism that informs much contemporary self-care. Eugene Peterson expresses Jesus' message thus: "Now that you've got a life, I'm going to show you how to give it up."[2]

3. Turning to the contemporary pursuit of *mastery* in self-care and such matters, we find the underlying premise of contemporary self-valuing and self-care is to the fore: we have control (potentially, at least) of our "self" as a possession at our disposal in the same way that a mechanic has control over a machine or a chemist over a chemical process in a laboratory. In Christian faith, however, mastery belongs first to God; it belongs to his kingdom or sovereignty. For our part, mastery is always a vocation arising from the requirement of obedience to God; we are called to be *responsive* to God's will and to the cultivation of skills that will enable us to further this. Life itself is not something we are required to attain through our mastery of skills and techniques; God himself, in his mastery, will bring us to eternal life. Our task is to seek first the kingdom (i.e., mastery) of God.

4. The contemporary faith in "nature" expresses longing for a world to which one belongs in an intimate personal way and that one can trust for motherly guidance and nourishment of a comprehensive kind. Whereas the contemporary desire for mastery is about tapping

2. Peterson, "What's Wrong with Spirituality?" 54–55.

and managing the resources for personal wellbeing, faith in nature is about the desire for dependence without responsibility. In Christian faith, however, belonging is of a different kind: belonging is a matter of personal relationship with God through the gift of the Holy Spirit. Personal unity with God and with other people is through this Spirit; personal gifts are the gifts and fruit of this Spirit; and personal guidance is to be found through the Spirit.

Christian faith thus differs from the contemporary exaltation of "life" in key ways. Briefly, for Christian faith the way of eternal life is characterized by responsible stewardship (rather than mastery) and by personal relationship (rather than self-abandonment), and these are both shaped by the worship of One who, himself of unqualified value, faithfully entrusts all that is of value into our hands as creatures who are ourselves of unqualified value in his sight.

How may we analyze further the contemporary pursuit of "life"? In what follows we shall explore these questions by reference primarily to two authors: W. Visser 't Hooft, and Linda Woodhead.

THE "WORSHIP OF LIFE": NEO-PAGANISM?

The pursuit of "life" has gained prominence in recent decades. However, it has been in evidence much longer. In 1937 W. Visser 't Hooft observed that "the worship of life" had "captured the realm of literature and art, so that it is hard to find a modern novel, play or film that does not preach the primacy of life. It has revolutionized our moral conceptions, so that self-expression has become the cardinal virtue . . . In a short time life has been promoted . . . to the position of the ultimate criterion of truth, goodness and beauty, which is sacred and worthy of devotion."

W. Visser 't Hooft then asked: "But what is meant by 'life' in this connection? . . . The most important [recognizable traits] may be characterized as: the protest against the subordination of life to reason and rational civilization; the search for intensity of experience; and the desire for communion with the natural forces."[3] It will be apparent that these traits have developed further in the contemporary exaltation of "life."

Forty years later, in 1977, Visser 't Hooft returned to this theme in the article "Evangelism among Europe's Neo-pagans." By labeling as "neopagan" a type of person widely represented in the European population

3. Visser 't Hooft, *None Other Gods*, 140.

he located them within "the (unwritten) history of paganism." Were this history ever to be written, he said, it would explore the incomplete medieval conversion to Christianity, the syncretism of the Renaissance, romanticism, and Nietzsche.[4]

Visser 't Hooft described the traits of "life" exalted by neo-paganism as being monism, pluralism, naturism, vitalism, *eros* without *agape*, and absence of hope. He compared and contrasted each of these with what is found in Christian faith. Neo-pagan *monism* offers humankind the prospect of absorption into an impersonal universe (meaning that the depersonalizing forces of the modern world have the last say); Christian faith, by contrast, trusts in a personal God and creator of the world who calls human beings to respond in the interpersonal relation of prayer. Neo-pagan *pluralism* looks for revelation of its "god" everywhere without discrimination—it is relativistic, accepting no norms or criteria originating in any defining revelation; Christian faith, by contrast, finds God revealed in the particular and definitive events of Jesus' life, death, and resurrection. Neo-pagan *naturism* assimilates God and nature, endorsing the longing for communion with nature; Christian faith, by contrast, honors nature as the creation of God and the vehicle of his purposes. Neo-pagan *vitalism* seeks the intensification of life, taking whatever shows itself with unbridled vitality to be self-validating as life; Christian

4. There are glimpses of this historical backdrop in Angela Tilby's description of her encounter with paganism while working in television. She writes of TV executives:

Now I have come to believe that those faces are the faces of gods. They stare, critically and selectively. They choose the world they make. They are Western gods, Greek gods, manifestations of Apollo, the great God of the sun, the healer, the communicator, the averter of evil ... Working in television I quickly discovered that the detached faces could also become wrathful, deeply engaged, and emotional. Some pictures of television executives pick up the exact moment when Apollo departs and his great opposite appears: Dionysus, the intoxicating god, the eater of flesh, and tearer apart of men.

I introduce Apollo and Dionysus as a way in to my main theme, which is that the television world is a world alive to paganism. I don't mean the benign, liberal-minded paganism of so-called ecofeminists and post-Christians, who want to save the world by invoking the Great Goddess, but the paganism that resides in Western ways of seeing, in our visual culture, from Greek sculpture to Madonna. This paganism is part of our history. It is deeply intertwined with Christianity, and cannot be separated from it. But whereas book culture and middle-ground speech radio are comfortable with Christian ideas and ethics, television culture is the culture of the theatre and the hippodrome. Television is where we play out our most potent fantasies of power, sex and violence." Tilby, "Like the Appearance," 324.

faith, by contrast, celebrates the transformation and orientation of life by God's gift of new and eternal life. Neo-pagan exaltation of *eros* is but one expression of such vitalism; like it, however, it is blind without the orientation of *agape* that it finds in Christian faith.

Finally, neo-paganism "is a religion without a definite, well-grounded hope. Where there is only the concept of infinity, but no meeting with God, only an abstract omnipotence, but not the omnipotence of the qualities of this one God, there is no centre of time, there is no beginning and no end and we live in an unlimited freedom without orientation and in immeasurable loneliness." Infinity, omnipotence, freedom for present choice—these are the idols of "life." They are even more so today.

And yet they bring contradictions; as Visser 't Hooft remarks, they run counter to deep and widespread concerns voiced today:

> It is strange that in a generation in which the sense of social jus-
> tice and of the solidarity of mankind is strongly developed, we
> find so much naïve faith in the goodness and reliability of uncon-
> trolled and unbridled life force. For such a faith can only produce
> a society in which the most vital will dominate and which will
> oscillate between explosions of vitalism from the right such as
> fascism, and those from the left such as anarchism. When the
> neo-pagans attack Christianity as a life-denying faith and preach
> their gospel of the affirmation of life, we must admit that in many
> expressions of Christianity the negation has been more audible
> than the affirmation. But we must go on to make it clear that the
> new life in Christ is truly abundant and does not destroy, but
> transforms and orients the original life force in us.

The accusation that Christianity is "life-denying" is relevant to some more recent studies on contemporary spirituality. Let us turn to one of these now.

CONTEMPORARY SPIRITUALITY

Our attention so far has been upon a contemporary exaltation of "life" that, although religious in character, is not conscious of itself in these terms. We now turn our attention to a version of this that is more explicitly religious.

Linked clearly with the desire to fulfill one's potential for "life" is to the contemporary growth of interest in "spirituality." The forms taken by such spirituality have been shaped strongly by this desire. Let us examine how this link is portrayed in research by Linda Woodhead and her colleagues who studied contemporary forms of religion and spirituality among the people of Kendal during the 1990s. In an article published to coincide with her ensuing book coauthored with Paul Heelas, *The Spiritual Revolution*,[5] she acclaims "a momentous shift in the sacred landscape."[6] Today, she says, "Those forms of 'religion' that locate authority outside of the self, in a God, priests, scriptures, and sacraments are waning, whereas those forms of 'spirituality' that empower people to trust their own sensibilities are waxing."

Woodhead sees this as reflecting, in wider society, "a massive cultural turn to inner life": "Rather than heeding the old voices of authority, rather than abiding by the roles and duties prescribed for our particular 'station in life,' rather than doing what we are told, many people now *find the value of life in life itself*, and wisdom in 'the song you realize in your own heart,'" she writes (italics mine).

Woodhead depicts a change in the focus of value, setting the new focus in contrast with the old. In the context of spirituality she depicts this also as a contrast between belief in a God "out there" and discovering the sacred at the heart of life, and between "discovering one's own path" and reliance on "clear truths and objective realities." This change of outlook involves turning deliberately from the old focus of value in favor of the new. In fact, Woodhead sees her research as suggesting that the old is, for those pursuing the new spirituality, the very enemy and rival of what is rightly to be valued. It seems to her that her research ultimately suggests a deep incompatibility between inner holistic spirituality and traditional congregational Christianity.

"SPIRITUAL REVOLUTION"? A CHRISTIAN APPRAISAL

How shall we appraise this "spiritual revolution"—and Woodhead's account of it? The foregoing pages offer some leads. Among them is Visser 't Hooft's account of the "worship of life." His identification of this in 1937 reminds us that the spiritual (and wider cultural) change in the focus of value that Woodhead describes is by no means a feature only of recent decades, although it has developed further during this time. Indeed, already in 1919 a writer had noted that following the blow delivered by the

5. Woodhead and Heelas, *The Spiritual Revolution*.
6. Linda Woodhead, "Should Churches Look Outward, Not Inward?"

First World War to the confidence that reason would continue bringing progress, the new criterion was that of "life," the truth of which was to be discovered by intuition, instinct, and experience.[7]

Our appraisal of the "spiritual revolution" will depend upon our judgment, on the one hand, of the "life" that has now become the focus of value and, on the other hand, of the notion of a "God out there" from which people have turned as the focus of value, as each of these is understood (a) by the respondents taking part in the research and (b) by the researchers themselves.

Briefly, Linda Woodhead and her colleagues claim a change in the focus of value from *God* to *life*. Viewed in the context of Christian faith, however, such a change is, of course, a self-contradiction. God is the true focus of all value and the source of life; there can be no turning *from* God *to* life. John V. Taylor expresses the matter boldly: God is "not hugely concerned as to whether we are religious or not. What matters to God, and matters supremely, is whether we are alive or not. If your religion brings you more fully to life, God will be in it; but if your religion inhibits your capacity for life or makes you run away from it, you may be sure God is against it, as Jesus was."[8]

So what is the reality of this perceived change "from God to life"? Two broad eventualities invite consideration:

1. There is indeed a turn to life—life, which is the gift and promise of God. However, this turn involves no consciousness of being a turn to God. Indeed according to researchers, it involves a conscious turn from God. God is seen as a challenge to such life, making rival claims upon us that block life.

Now this may indeed be the self-understanding of the respondents themselves. It may be that modern prejudices against religious belief have prevented these respondents and their researchers alike from attending properly to the God presented to them by Christianity. Or it may be that their personal experience of Christianity has itself hidden this God from them, giving them reason to see it as opposed to life. On the other hand, it may be that the respondents are less conscious of "turning from God"

---

7. de Bunsen, "The War and Men's Minds," quoted by Wickham in *Church and People*, 205.

8. Taylor, *A Matter of Life and Death*, 18, quoted in Yates, "Reading John V. Taylor," 153.

than their researchers claim, and that this claim reflects the researchers' own beliefs. It may be that the God of Christianity has simply never "come alive" for respondents and that Christianity therefore appears to them as irrelevant to life. In this case, of course, there would seem hope that the turn to life may yet show itself open to the discovery that life has its deepest source and promise in God.

2. There is a turn to "life," but this is a turn not to real life but to a (neo-pagan) illusion. In truth it is, albeit unrecognized, a turn *away from* real life—and from God the source and path of such life. This turn to "life" may again involve either a conscious rejection of belief in God as standing in opposition to such "life," or an assumption that Christianity is irrelevant to it. Either way, here conversion will be involved in any turn to real life and to God, from the illusions of neo-paganism.

Each of these eventualities shows the influence of cultural distortions of the truth. The first reflects the false idea that belief in God is opposed to the pursuit of life, and the second reflects the personal impulse towards a neo-pagan exaltation of "life" as being life itself. Each of these can be seen, drawing on the analysis offered in our previous chapters, as distortions characteristic of modern culture.

Let us take first the false idea that belief in God is opposed to the pursuit of life (whether this idea is prevalent among those embracing the new spirituality or whether it has been introduced by researchers into their account of this). We may note the similarity between the means by which life is defined here and the means by which the Enlightenment defined itself. Each defines itself *by opposition to* certain things—indeed opposition to *similar* things. Each rejects, as the paramount enemy, unthinking conformity to tradition and domination by unquestioned authority. Correspondingly, like Enlightenment thinking, the contemporary pursuit of life generates the one-sided distortions described earlier in Conversion 4. Scorning false subservience to dogma and authority, it fails to distinguish this from a proper, attentive regard towards the truth that may be mediated by dogma and authority. Scorning thoughtless cultural conformity, it fails to distinguish this from living community. Exalting a proper celebration of life, personal judgment, and choice, it fails to distinguish this from subjective, impulsive, or narcissistic inner bondage. Exalting a proper individuality, it fails to distinguish this from disregard for committed relationship with other people.

At root the modern pursuit of "life" reflects, as does Enlightenment thinking, the theoretical and practical failure to honor that radical enquiry in which, giving our lives to seeking and serving God, we receive and live life most fully. Rather than receiving the mystery of life defined by God alone, it imagines wrongly to define life as something we can secure for ourselves by sustained opposition to an identified enemy. And it imagines to locate and critique belief in God—and in the promise of life in Christ—within the horizons of this "life." In reality, however, this constitutes a logical inversion: the "life" here exalted is rather to be located and critiqued within the horizons of God and of real life. The adoption of such "life" as our ultimate horizon distorts the meaning both of God and of life, and turns us away from both.

Understood in this way, in the context of Christian faith and of the Enlightenment cultural heritage, we can understand better two dominant tendencies in contemporary spirituality that, although they reflect (as above) the modern reaction against the "premodern," are equally responses *to* the modern and therefore might be called "postmodern." On the one hand, there has been a turn away from trust in the personal promise of science; on the other hand, there has been a tendency to reconstruct "science" in a form that offers after all to fulfill the hopes people wish to place in it. These two seemingly contradictory responses reflect a radical disappointment. In the course of the modern period, faith has declined and people have turned increasingly for personal hope to the fruits of science and technology, in which much confidence had been placed from its start. As they have been increasingly disappointed, their loss of hope has been personal and profound.

Thus on the one hand within contemporary spirituality we find a skepticism regarding the personal promise of science. An illustration of this is the quip that "medicine is the art of entertaining the patient while the body heals itself." The fruits of experimental science are held (when applied to the person) to be ineffective, dubious, or even oppressive. On the other hand, contemporary new spirituality continues typically to place much hope in "science" and technology and in their promise of unqualified mastery. This is apparent in two ways. Firstly, those who adopt the "new spirituality" tend, like those around them, to live thoroughly modern lives dependent upon the fruits of science. Secondly, they often see spirituality as a matter of fulfilling their potential for "life" through their mastery of techniques grounded in scientific-sounding theories.

Let us consider these two seemingly contradictory faces of contemporary spirituality in turn.

LIFE, NATURE, AND NARCISSISM

Consider first the skepticism towards the personal benefits of science. In 1937 Visser 't Hooft had described the "worship of life" as in part a "protest against the subordination of life to reason and rational civilization." How shall we evaluate this in a Christian context? Is there perhaps a resonance with Christian faith here?

For its part, Christian faith certainly insists that personal life cannot be adequately guided and nourished by reference to scientific knowledge. It acknowledges the primacy of a realm of knowledge and of enquiry wider than science marked by lively, tacit, personal engagement with the world. It rejects the narrowness of Enlightenment rationality and the rationalizations of human life that that has sponsored. For example, Christian faith sees the practice of medicine as fundamentally concerned with "the whole person" and not just with clinical diagnosis and biochemical treatment of disease. Hospitals are places of hospitality. A striking demonstration of this today is the hospice movement, inspired by the Christian faith of Dame Cicely Saunders, in which a multidisciplinary team seeks to serve comprehensively the personal needs of those whose death from disease cannot be prevented.

Does this Christian relativization of the potential of science undermine science? By no means. The mastery we achieve through explicit scientific knowledge is an integral part of Christian stewardship of creation. But so too is a necessary acceptance of the limitations of such mastery. This belongs within the purposes of a loving creator, for love of whom we love creation and who himself accepted the limitations of creaturely life in the incarnation of the Son.

How does the skepticism shown in contemporary spirituality towards science compare with this outlook? It is very different. It is informed by a deep disappointment in science—a disappointment of what was in reality a quite excessive expectation that science would provide, like religion, personal guidance and means to personal wellbeing. Science is now seen to have elicited radical trust only then to betray it. This leads to despair of the world itself (as revealed, supposedly, by science) and of ourselves as its scientist masters, in a narcissistic turn inwards for private solace. There is no recognition here of the world known by Christian faith, in which science can play its part in loving service to a good creator; instead there is only a bleak world "out there" contrasting with a private, intimate, and ultimately illusory world.

This worldview, split between bleak impersonality and intimacy, can already be seen in William James's commendation, in 1909, of pantheism over theism. He sees only the alternatives of separation and fusion, alienation and intimacy: "[T]he place of the divine in the world must be more organic and intimate. An external creator and his institutions may still be verbally confessed at church in formulas that linger by their mere inertia, but the life is out of them, we avoid dwelling in them, the sincere heart of us is elsewhere."[9]

James's pantheism anticipates the belief, found in contemporary spirituality, in semi-divine powers of self-creation belonging to a semi-divine, mythical world of nature and realized by abandoning oneself to feeling and instinct. On the other hand, it conceals a gnostic tendency: it seeks escape from the actual, created world in favor of this mythical world with its illusion of escape from the painful experiences of separation and responsibility. P. T. Forsyth, writing in the same period, observes:

> The old gnosis has never since risen in such critical and yet plausible antagonism to the gospel till its recrudescence in our own time . . . even apostles of that Word . . . are more drawn to the gnosis of speculation, the occultism of science, the romance of the heart, the mysticism of imagination, than to the historic and ethical spirituality of the evangelical Christ the crucified. Now there will be no doubt of your popularity if you take that Gnostic course with due eloquence, taste, and confidence. For it expresses the formless longings and the dim cravings of the subjectivity of the day. But it has not the future, because it misses the genuine note of the gospel[10]

In place of "formless longings and dim cravings" there belongs to the "genuine note of the gospel" (as Visser 't Hooft says) a "clear hope"; in place of an "immeasurable loneliness" there is relationship with God. The hopelessness and isolation concealed in contemporary spirituality are remarked by Ann de Roo:

> I am not subject to claustrophobia except in New Age bookshops, where the bookshelves seem to close on me with their weight of

9. James, *Pluralistic Universe*, 30.

10. Forsyth, *Positive Preaching*, 74.

"Me, me, me." Nothing on the shelves points me towards any other person, except perhaps a small group of like-minded friends,
huddling together as they search for self-fulfillment within the
blankness of a universe that ends with the death of the one being
that matters in it, me, me, me. But worse than the claustrophobia
is the smell of despair. This is a new age, not the first of its kind,
but an age so caught up in hopelessness that it can find no better
answer than, "I can't change anything. It's all written in the stars."
Or an age that looks at the world and can find no response but a
retreat into self and self-fulfillment.[11]

This retreat from God's created world and from other people is very different from the movement of Christianity. Personal experience of God
draws people together and to a shared hope for the world. John V. Taylor
writes: "It is not true, as the saying has it, that religion is what people do
with their solitude. Religion is very much more how people relate to each
other and to God in the light of certain corporately remembered solitary
experiences—their own or, more often, other people's in the past. We are
not meant to think of our individual selves as local shrines of the Holy
Spirit. In Old Testament times local shrines fostered idiosyncrasy and
idolatry, and they do so still."[12] Again, the pursuit of a fulfilling "life" by
following one's instincts and feelings contradicts the sacrificial demands
of patient love, committed service, and the pursuit of justice and reconciliation, and is on these counts very different from Christian faith.
Eugene Peterson writes: "There is always a strong ascetic element in true
spiritual theology. Following Jesus means not following your impulses
and appetites and whims and dreams, all of which are sufficiently dam-
aged by sin to make them unreliable guides for getting anyplace worth
going . . . Ascetic practice sweeps out the clutter of the god-pretentious
self, making ample space for the Father, Son, and Holy Spirit; it embraces
and prepares for a kind of death that the culture knows nothing about,
making room for the dance of resurrection."[13]

LIFE, SCIENCE, AND MAGIC

The other face displayed by contemporary spirituality, which at first
seems contradictory to the one just described, is that of renewed com-

11. de Roo, *Becoming Fully Human*, 28.
12. Taylor, *Uncancelled Mandate*, 28.
13. Peterson, "Spirituality for All the Wrong Reasons," 44.

mitment to (new formulations of) "science" as the source of hope. How does this development appear in a Christian context?

For its own part, Christian faith sponsors the hope that there is progress to be made in science for the good of humanity. It honors the place of science in the human stewardship of creation including our human creaturely life. And it celebrates a world that, while not compliant with our narcissistic desires, has been created by God as good and can be made the occasion for celebration of, and a vehicle for, God's good purposes.

Does this Christian celebration of science see science as offering personal guidance and securing our wellbeing in an ultimate, religious way? By no means.[14] Science is to be pursued and used in the context of Christian faith. This does not limit its potential; rather, it releases it.

How does the renewed commitment to "science" in contemporary spirituality compare with this outlook? Again it is very different. It belongs, like the gnostic turn we have noted above, to a wider cultural disappointment of excessive expectations from science; here, however, the excessive expectations are credulously retained and directed towards new forms of "science."

This response in wider culture can be seen already in the rise of "surrogate" sciences, described by Alan Storkey. The human sciences, expected especially to resource the pursuit of human wellbeing, first found their epistemological foundations increasingly questioned and then their effectiveness. Storkey writes: "Many came to see theory in the human sciences as other-worldly and out of touch with reality. Despite their claims to know, these disciplines did not help people to live in a world subject to a dynamic process of change.

Because this failure was so immediate and important, it was necessary to create a range of praxis disciplines which would have as their agenda telling people what to do. Thus, business studies ranged alongside economics, counseling alongside psychology and environmental studies alongside geography."[15]

These pragmatic new "surrogate" sciences conceal within themselves the interests and intentions of those wanting to employ them, without bringing these interests and intention within the scope of appraisal. And these interests are, in general, those of industry and government, from

---

14. On false pretensions on behalf of science, see Midgley, *Science as Salvation*.

15. Storkey, "The Surrogate Sciences."

whom funding can be secured and who are in a position to sell what can now become "private" knowledge. This shift to "surrogate" sciences and their hidden frameworks of interest is spread widely through information technology and education today.

The desire for "sciences" that will in this way serve our expressed purposes brings with it the danger of wishful thinking. We may be too ready to believe in them. Richard Stivers describes the result in *Technology as Magic:*[16] techniques and the consultants who claim mastery of them can be little more than shamanism dressed up as "science," while providing a good living for their purveyors.

At first sight it may seem puzzling that the skepticism associated popularly with science is now supplemented by credulity. However, as Lawrence Osborn explains: "Skepticism is recast in an optimistic mode: if nothing is certain, then anything is possible. It is no less rational and certainly far more comforting to believe anything than it is to believe nothing. The close relationship between skepticism and credulity is highlighted by the way both extremes may be found in the same individuals."[17]

In contemporary spirituality, "psychologies," and "alternative" therapies, surrogate science is taken a step further. *Simulacrae* of science are employed to provide new accounts of the workings of body and spirit, and to offer knowledge and tools at our service that guide us to sources of nurture and equip us for the pursuit of personal wellbeing.[18]

Stivers' warnings apply especially here in the realm of goods and services offered in pursuit of "life" and of spiritual fulfillment: credulity serves well the interests of those who have seen a "market opportunity." Accordingly, Kenneth Leech warns that in contemporary spirituality, "There is a dangerous concern with spiritual technology, with method and technique, the carrying over into the spiritual realm of the corrupting effect of consumer capitalism."[19]

16. Stivers, *Technology as Magic*.

17. Osborn, *Angels of Light*, 106–7.

18. On pseudo-science, including that promulgated in some alternative therapies, see Goldacre, *Bad Science*. On "psychologies" such as Myers-Briggs, see Long, "Myers-Briggs."

19. Leech, *The Sky Is Red*, 122.

IN CONCLUSION

The pursuit of "life" that is culturally prevalent today and which is reflected in contemporary spirituality is, as Visser 't Hooft has said, in part a "protest against the subordination of life to reason and rational civilization." However, it differs from Christian protest. Instead of recovering hope in the deeper sources of life in God, within which reason and civilization have their place, it turns away in despair from radical enquiry into and responsibility towards God and God's world. As it does so, it turns in two apparently contradictory directions: an exaltation of life accompanied by defiant skepticism towards science and reason, and an exaltation of life promised by new speculative forms of "science" and its techniques.

These two attitudes towards life echo in some measure those of the two classical Greek pagan gods, Dionysius and Apollos. The former exults in impulse, pleasure, and abandonment to nature; the latter in the power of control over nature. However, as we have noted, the contemporary forms of these are by no means expressions of vitality. Rather, both are directed inwards in longing towards a missing life, while precisely abandoning the true hope of life found through engagement with God and God's world. They are expressions of narcissism and gnostic escapism and of the loss of hope that marks these.

It is this loss of hope that Christians must address if they would address the contemporary pursuit of "life." It would be misguided to see the "exaltation of life" as being implicitly directed towards the eternal life that is offered in Christ, and simply to affirm it. There is rather a need for conversion from despair to hope: from despair of science as promising personal salvation, to hope in God who gives science to use for the good within the limitations and ambiguities of created life; from despair of ourselves as trustworthy masters of the world through science, to God who calls us to use it well in his service.

To summarize: Christians are called by God today to be converted to eternal life, the gift of God. They are called to witness to this life, and to seek the conversion of others to this by manifesting it in their own Christian practice and faithfully understanding it as a matter of reflection. They are called also to acknowledge, and repent of, their own complicity with Western cultural habits of thought and action that subvert the conversion to eternal life by luring them into the pursuit of (in reality illusory) "life."

To be converted to eternal life is to embrace God's gift to us of his own life in Jesus Christ. That life was in the Word of God, the "light of mankind" (John 1:4). Jesus came that we might have it "in all its fullness" (John 10:10)—Jesus who is "the resurrection and the life" (John 11:25). That life finds its fulfillment in the kingdom of God. Paul writes, "Were you not raised to life in Christ? Then aspire to the realm above, where Christ is, seated at God's right hand, and fix your thoughts on that higher realm, not on this earthly life. You died; and now your life lies hidden with Christ in God. When Christ, who is our life, is revealed, then you too will be revealed with him in glory" (Col 3:1–4).

8   THE IDEOLOGY OF RIGHTS
AND POLITICAL CORRECTNESS

Conversion to God-given Dignity

IN THE LAST THREE chapters we have reflected on some of the more personal ways in which modern culture has affected people, forming their characters and shaping their desires. In this present chapter and the next, we shall turn back to the political and public modern project of crafting society by reference to certain ideas and principles—the Enlightenment vision which, as we saw earlier, Ernst Gellner depicts as cultivating or "gardening" culture. We shall explore this further, considering in turn two particular public ideologies influential within this project today.

The influence of public ideology is exercised first and foremost through the formulation of ideological frameworks for understanding—and programs for shaping—society and the adoption of these by people managing public life. Such people include those who see their work as communicating with, influencing, directing, or coercing the public in respect of basic public ideas, goals, and practices. They include those who work in politics, the mass media, public services, marketing, and spokespersons for various businesses and professions. They are the people—the elite group—who mediate professionally what has been called "secondary culture" as distinct from the primary culture of informal family and community life.

Although the influence of ideologies is exercised most obviously upon such "secondary culture," it does also have an effect—sometimes a great effect—on primary culture. It does so both directly, by shaping the way people think and act personally, and indirectly, by shaping the public world to which they are required to conform in order to participate in it.

Turning now to examine ideologies influential in our culture today, we resume investigating the self-conscious trajectory of modern culture and the relation of this to the trajectory of openness to the in-breaking kingdom of God. As we noted earlier, the modern trajectory has historical roots in such openness towards the kingdom of God and early in the modern period the application of modern principles was often—despite their lack of reference to, or even claims of rivalry against, Christian doctrine—deeply informed tacitly by the Christian imagination. With the passage of time, however, this tacit influence has weakened and Enlightenment principles, cut loose from their Christian moorings, have tended to acquire what is, in effect, an absolute or religious status in the shaping of society. When this happens, they lead society away from the path of openness to the in-breaking kingdom of God and into what is effectively the enslaving power of idols.

This danger, which is the danger posed in a general way by deliberate social "cultivation" and planning itself, has been remarked on by various Christian writers. Let us recall two examples of this. The first can be found on the letters and papers of Dietrich Bonhoeffer from his Nazi prison cell. Sketching an idea for a future book, he anticipates a coming age of humanity in which the immediate environment of human life is no longer nature but technical organization, through which immunity is sought from nature. "But this immunity," he notes, "produces a new crop of dangers, i.e., the very organization. Consequently there is a need for spiritual vitality. What protection is there against the danger of organization? Man is once more faced with the problem of himself. He can cope with every danger except the danger of human nature itself. In the last resort it all turns upon man."[1] A second, more recent, example can be found in Oliver O'Donovan's call for self-awareness regarding the danger posed by our own visions of progress: "The disciplines we need are those that good modernity-critics display: to see the marks of our time as the products of our past; to notice the danger civilization poses to itself, not only the danger of barbarian reaction; to attend specially not to those features which strike our contemporaries as controversial, but to those which would have astonished an onlooker from the past but which seem to us too obvious to question."[2]

---

1. Bonhoeffer, *Letters and Papers,* 164.
2. Oliver O'Donovan, *Desire of the Nations,* 273.

In this and the next chapter, we shall examine briefly two ideologies having great influence today. We shall assess them in the light of Christian faith and consider how we might point from them towards greater openness to the approach of God in sovereignty.

THE IDEOLOGY OF RIGHTS

In this present chapter we shall examine the ideology that seeks to shape society in conformity with certain rights ascribed to individuals or to groups of people. This ideology is very influential in public vision and policy formulation today.

The ideology of rights has grown in prominence and influence in recent generations. A key point of reference is the Universal Declaration of Human Rights, issued by the United Nations in 1948. In Britain, human rights issues have come to a particular kind of prominence through her membership in the European Union, which has formulated its own Convention on Human Rights. On the basis of this Convention, the EU produces directives that the governments of member countries are required to apply in their own circumstances. More widely than human rights legislation as such, various pieces of legislation have been introduced prohibiting discrimination against various groups of people on grounds such as gender, race, sexual orientation, and most recently, age. Such legislation is premised on the basic right of every individual to fair and equal treatment.

Now at one level, the ideology of rights converges with the concern that individuals fulfill their personal potential for life, which was the theme of the previous chapter. However, whereas the latter sponsors a seemingly endless pursuit, the former seeks rather to safeguard certain identified prerequisites for a full life. It seeks—in the first instance, at least—to redress the lack of that freedom that is proper to persons and especially to defend this freedom against its removal by other people.

Thus far, the ideology of rights may commend itself as sharing a Christian concern for persons. It may be understood as seeking to conform the world and human society more consistently with the demands of human persons and their flourishing. However, issues now arise regarding how these demands are to be understood. In order to explore these issues, let us first consider briefly the setting of some historical initiatives to defend and uphold rights.

THE PROMULGATION OF RIGHTS
IN HISTORICAL SETTING

In the Hebrew Scriptures, the concept of individual rights arises in the context of a concern for justice. Justice, in turn, is among the consequences of divine blessing as God calls his people to seek and uphold his good purposes. The concern for justice arises in the course of a concern to seek and uphold what is right in God's eyes. It reflects the righteousness of God, to which he also calls his people. To seek and uphold "the right" (sometimes called "objective right," as distinct from "subjective rights" adhering to the individual) is to honor a righteous God and this righteousness as he wills it among humankind by his grace.

Within this scheme of things, certain kinds of human action present themselves as violating what is proper to individuals. Such violation is an injustice condemned by God. Thus, for example, we find the prohibition—in the Ten Commandments—of murder, theft, and adultery. It would consistent with biblical witness to call these violations of subjective rights—the right under God to life, to property, and to one's spouse. In such terms the prophets castigate those who rob the poor of their rights (e.g., Isa 10:2; Jer 5:28). In brief, in the Bible the language of rights gets used when checking violation of the demands of justice, which, in turn, belong within the further blessings willed by a good God.

In Christian tradition up until the fourteenth century, objective right remained dominant in Christian thinking about justice, legitimizing law and the political authority of those who enforced it. As Joan Lockwood O'Donovan writes, "justice (*iustitia*) was synonymous with objective right (*ius*)—i.e., the objectively right action in any situation—and objective right was accorded to law, to legal right (*lex, ius*). Political authority or government was primarily a matter of divine institution, appointment and authorization; and the central moral-political act on the part of ruler and ruled alike was to consent to the obligations inhering in communal life according to divine intention and rationally articulated as laws." [3]

"In the fourteenth century," she continues, "there was a turn to the moral subject and his capacity for right action, and, from the start, this subjective capacity (i.e., subjective right) was associated with man's created freedom and lordship over the rest of creation. In this newer

---

3. O'Donovan, "Rights, Law and Political Community," 31–32.

orientation to natural right, the active individual will occupied a central position, the emphasis being on the subject's control and ownership of his own acts, and increasingly, on his control over his moral and physical environment. Nevertheless, the late medieval development of subjective rights took place on the basis of 'objective right,' of natural and divine law."

The issue of subjective rights (rights pertaining to the human subject) was put in a quite new context with the emergence of modern society. In the modern reconstitution of society—compared by Gellner with a change in the role of rulers from that of "gamekeeper" to that of "gardener"—the moral fabric of feudal society was dissolved. With its dissolution was lost the web of rights and responsibilities binding people together in local communities and having ultimate appeal to God. As people were expelled from their common or ancestral lands and forced to sell their labor in order to survive and move home as this required, what protection had they to check the new power over them of landowners, employers, and state? The promulgation of individual rights associated with such spokesmen as John Locke and Thomas Paine provided such a check. Individual rights constitute an integral part of that modern framework, comprising the claims of the state, on the one hand, and of the individual, on the other, which, as we saw in Conversion 2, has deeply shaped the course of modern society.

Insofar as such individual rights then continued to be understood (at least tacitly) by reference to pursuit of what was right under God and in the context of human mutual responsibilities, their role could remain basically a derivative, protective one. They were there to be invoked when, despite social moral imperatives, individuals found themselves deprived of what was justly theirs. However, from the beginning of modern society, individual rights were also endowed with a more constructive role than this. In continental European political thought, they came to be incorporated into the modern project of constructing society in a thoroughgoing way on the basis of explicit "secular" principles. In England, John Locke's account of the rights of the Englishman, which granted to the individual absolute rights over the acquisition and use of private property, opened the way for a society formed deeply by such acquisition and use of property. As Joan Lockwood O'Donovan points out, the connections are close between human rights (understood, in the modern tradition of liberal natural rights, as the rights of self-proprietors), on the one hand, and liberal economics and free-market capitalism, on the other.

More recently, in the twentieth century, a further key development in the role of human rights thinking followed the Second World War. Nazi atrocities had demonstrated that civilized human beings can behave without moral constraint towards each other even at the level of official state policy. As Hannah Arendt wrote, "The world found nothing sacred in the abstract nakedness of being human ... The survivors of the extermination camps, the inmates of concentration and internment camps, and even the comparatively hapless stateless people could see ... that the abstract nakedness of being nothing but human was their greatest danger."[4]

Spurred by this, the United Nations came together in 1948 to promulgate the Universal Declaration of Human Rights. This was an attempt to frame, in the language of rights, the requirements of human dignity to which all nations might subscribe. Although it eschewed an explicit basis in Christian faith or the justice of God, Christians played a formative part in this initiative. John Nurser describes their thinking:

> [A] remarkable mutation of the old territorial concept of "Christendom" was floated by J. H. Oldham and Jacques Maritain, and then developed by others. Within secular states, an organically related bundle of principles might be established and given statutory constitutional expression, and there should be no limit to their rapid extension to include the whole world. Christians and others—society's "best minds"—could probably agree upon and define whatever is required to protect human social well-being. The UN's Universal Declaration of Human Rights of 1948 was seen as such a bundle of *desiderata*. Once these had been established in a regime worldwide, Christian communities would be liberated to live out every aspect of their lives. They would neither expect nor desire any privileges not equally available to other faiths, and there would be no question of coercing "the other," or of self-consciously "Christian" territories. Such an outcome would be the triumph of the public half of Oldham's missionary vision for "Christendom." What would remain would be the churches' task of education, persuasion, and exemplification of "the Christian way" ... the Protestant, Anglican, and, to an extent, Orthodox ecumenical movement

---

4. Arendt, *Origins of Totalitarianism*.

contributed enormously to the events that led up to the United
Nations General Assembly [in 1948].[5]

In the last couple of decades, Britain has introduced much new legislation aimed at securing compliance with human rights. A number of
factors have been at work in this. Most obviously, Britain's membership in the European Union has required it. A succession of directives
have been issued by the European Union, to which member countries
are required to defer by acts of national legislation, embracing many
aspects of society including employment law, product quality-control/
definition, and health and safety standards. In this way, continental
European pretensions of constructing society comprehensively on
Enlightenment principles are having a new impact today upon the
government of British society.

In some cases the older, protective function of rights has been more
to the fore, in response to social change bringing new vulnerabilities for
the individual. An example of this is the introduction of new privacy
laws. These are intended to provide some protection for individuals
against potential injustices associated with huge advances in information technology. These advances present new opportunities for corporate
bodies to gather information about individuals that the former might
use unjustly against the latter.

In other cases, the promulgation of individual rights can be seen as
serving in a more active way the program of intensifying capitalism—
that is, the further rationalization of society in conformity with capitalist
ideology. Just as the promulgation of absolute private property rights
served the formation of a market economy at the beginning of the modern period, so the extension of such rights serves its intensification today. An example is the extension of rights in matters such as patent and
copyright, now incorporating within the scope of "intellectual property
rights" novel aspects of creation not previously conceived as "private
property." Prominent among the claimants of such rights are, of course,

5. Nurser, *For All Peoples and All Nations,* 173. Note that by "Christendom" Oldham
referred not only to medieval Europe but also more widely to the continuing Christian
heritage of Europe. Thus in 1916 he could write that the First World War had "shown
Christendom to be in a sorry state" (Oldham, *World and the Gospel,* 54), and in
1939—more ambiguously—that "the present century has witnessed within what was
once known as Christendom the vehement repudiation of the Christian tradition and
a deliberate attempt to establish a post-Christian world" (Oldham, "Christian News-
Letter," 1).

economic institutions having the status of a "corporate person"—an arrangement long employed in the modern economic world—and such corporations have recently secured a place within the scope of certain newly legislated "human rights."

Another aspect of human rights legislation—anti-discrimination legislation—has served in a protective role for individuals or groups enabling them to participate freely in the movement of labor required by intensifying capitalism. Because the multicultural society created by such movement of labor is not one in which traditional shared cultural values survive so easily, legislation gets used to promote the values it is thought to require. In particular, legislation is used to address the risk in multicultural society that parochial prejudices will hinder individuals' freedom of economic endeavor. The rights enshrined in legislation outlawing discrimination of the basis of race or sex seek to facilitate the participation of immigrants and women in the workforce.

RIGHTS AND THE LOSS OF THEIR CHRISTIAN CONTEXT

How does the contemporary ideology of rights and its legislative enforcement appear in the light of Christian faith? Like other aspects of modern secular society, it must be understood by reference to a modern vision that has long claimed for itself explicit, secular foundations and that has been slowly losing the resources of Christian imagination that nevertheless tacitly inform this. Severed increasingly from its roots in Christian faith, the language of rights is increasingly ambiguous as a guide to the purposes of God. As part of what we have called the trajectory of modern culture, the ideology of rights belongs to developments increasingly divergent from the trajectory of openness to the in-breaking kingdom of God. It has brought indisputable blessings but also, increasingly, some more destructive effects. Let us explore these now.

As generally conceived today, rights are prior endowments natural to the individual and without religious or social grounding of any kind. These rights are taken as determining the requirements of right action by people in general towards any individual. Accordingly, their claims are absolute; they may not be overridden. In a sense, therefore, they are sacred and signify the standing of the individual as sacred.

The rights-bearing individual, conceived in abstraction, now comes to provide a normative framework for human society. The promulgation of individual rights today represents a program of shaping or rationalizing the world in greater conformity with this framework.

This abstraction and exaltation of the rights-bearing individual, no longer seen in a Christian context, is having a number of effects that are morally ambiguous when seen in that context, as follows.

1. A Diminished Scope of the Moral

In truth, to do what God requires of us extends far beyond upholding justice by not violating rights pertaining to persons as such, as these have been specified formally within a theoretical framework. In Christ God wills unqualified, abundant blessing for persons and our fulfillment of such rights of others is but a minimal indication of what such blessing entails. In rights ideology, however, rights are conceived in abstraction from the unqualified blessing that is God's purpose for persons and are put in its place as themselves *determining what constitutes right action* towards persons. This, however, diminishes God's purposes for a person, and therefore arguably diminishes *what it means to be* a person. And it limits the scope of the imperative to "do right," leaving us free beyond this scope to do as we please. It divides life between that in which we are constrained by the requirement to uphold the rights of others and that in which we are free to act without reference to God or "the right." Although such a division is a recognizable feature of much human religion, including that which Jesus criticized among some of his contemporaries, it does not reflect the comprehensive gift and scope of God's blessing in Christ or his calling that we serve this as "a living sacrifice."

George MacDonald wrote well:

> It is hard enough to be just to our friends; how then shall our enemies fare with us? . . . Man is not made for justice from his fellow, but for love, which is greater than justice. By including it, love supersedes justice. Mere justice is an impossibility, a fiction of analysis . . . Justice to be truly justice must be more than justice. Love is the law of our condition, without which we can no more render justice than a man can keep a straight line walking in the dark.[6]

---

6. MacDonald, "Love Thine Enemies."

2. The Distortion of Moral Wisdom

If the ideology of rights today *limits* the scope of the imperative to "do right," it also *distorts* this imperative precisely by constructing it entirely by reference to explicitly formulated rights with which all individuals are naturally and equally endowed. But this is not how we fundamentally discern the right thing to do. The aphorism I quoted earlier—"true measure, when it is made a target, is no longer a true measure"—applies to rights as a measure of the right. Rights ideology operates with a reductionist account of the right. This can play havoc when imposed by directives upon activity requiring "official" license, which is an expanding proportion of all activity. It has led to the conduct of job interviews in which each candidate is asked identical questions with no scope for discretionary follow-up and references may not be consulted until after a job has been offered. Justice is held to be secured when such procedures are followed. This eliminates the primary role of moral wisdom and devalues the role of personal, tacit judgment and experience in seeking the right, replacing it with reliance upon abstract concepts of equality and fairness. Correspondingly, "discrimination" is understood only in the negative sense of unwarranted prejudice and not as the exercise of positive powers of discernment and wisdom. It is this suppression of personal judgment that has led to the excesses of "political correctness" that are today a blunt instrument of oppression and an object of common mockery.[7]

3. Subversion of Moral Motivation

A grave consequence of this devaluation of the role of personal judgment in doing what is right is its subversion of moral motivation. For the recognition of, and desire to honor, rights is most deeply rooted in, and nourished by, lively responsiveness and radical enquiry into what is right in God's eyes. Without this deeper motivation to do right (which is ultimately worship of God), the concern to honor rights loses its deepest impetus. It is severed from the roots that nourish it. We shall be inclined to honor rights only once it is absolutely plain that they arise before us and that they have a claim upon us. We need acknowledge no requirement actively to seek out such claims. This makes way for us to adopt the

7. For a theological essay on the ideology of political correctness by one who has experienced its strictures, see Torrance, "Theology and Political Correctness."

philosophy that "if its legal its OK" in matters of our personal behavior, and for companies to do the same in matters of practice and standards (so that "we have done nothing illegal" gets offered as an implicit claim to have fulfilled moral obligations, as in the practice of tax avoidance). It even makes way, ironically, for declarations to uphold rights that are more rhetorical than real. John de Witte writes, "human rights norms need a human rights culture to be effective." "Declarations are not deed," John Noonan reminds us. "A form of words by itself secures nothing; words pregnant with meaning in one culture may be entirely barren in another . . . As we have moved from the first generation of human rights declarations following World War II to the current generation of human rights implementation, this need for a human rights culture has become all the more pressing."[8] The problem of "barren" words about rights extends to every culture insofar as these words are no longer nourished by a godly desire to do right.

A widespread response to the attenuation of moral impetus in Western cultures has been to expand legislation and its enforcement through forms of surveillance. Now this has its place; with good reason Martin Luther King Jr. urged, "Let us never succumb to the temptation of believing that legislation and judicial decrees play a minimal role . . . The habits, if not the hearts, of people have been and are being altered each day by legislative acts, judicial decisions, and executive orders." Yet in the long run, without a change of *heart* much good cannot come about; and this drives us back to the roots of moral concern.

Where there is no godly concern to do right, legislation and surveillance can produce only a minimal, grudging compliance or one fuelled by self-interest. Although not concerned directly with rights, the effect of the growth in speed cameras in Britain today offers a parable. Not only do many motorists respond to these with the minimal compliance demanded by coercion; this very coercion—by too indiscriminate use— overrules and devalues the personal, responsible, judgment that is the surest foundation of safe motoring. Their coercive operation addresses an irresponsible minority at the expense of subverting the responsible exercise of judgment by the majority.

The vision of renewed cultivation of personal responsibility is sometimes seen today as a promising corrective to the ideology of rights. And this may certainly restore the recognition that just as when

8. de Witte, "The Spirit of the Laws, the Laws of the Spirit."

we insist upon our rights we call upon others to take responsibility for upholding these, we too are called to take responsibility for the rights of others. However, this does not go so far as recognizing that we are *called to see what it will be right to do towards others whether or not they claim this as their right*, or even when they could never conceive of making any such claim. God's call upon us to see and do what is right is a call not only to act responsibly, but in worship of God, to share in God's self-giving to others.

4. Irreconcilable Rights

The inadequacy of individual rights to provide a coherent moral framework shows itself also when conflicting demands arise between one right and another, or between the rights of one person and another. Since rights are conceived as each absolute and distinct and as endowed upon individuals each absolute and distinct, no moral framework exists beyond them, within which their respective demands may be weighed in pursuit of right action. Such a framework would have to possess moral authority equal to the claims of any right. Whereas this was available when rights were understood within the Christian tradition of justice, it is no longer so.

5. Incommensurable Moral Frameworks

The problem of irreconcilable claims arises not only within rights ideology—between the claims of one right and another—but also between the ideology of individual rights as such and the ideology of management and utility. Typically today we are subject to both ideologies and their claims. On the one hand, we prize our own absolute value as an individual endowed with absolute rights; on the other hand, as individuals acting in society we are typically caught up in corporate activities that aim to manage and control others in service to our own goals. The individualism to which rights ideology belongs can provide no coherent moral framework for integrating these two aspects of life. Alasdair MacIntyre frames the contradiction well:

> Seeking to protect the autonomy that we have learned to prize, we aspire ourselves not to be manipulated by others; seeking to incarnate our own principles and standpoint in the world of practice, we find no way open to us to do so except by directing

towards others those very manipulative modes of relationship that each of us aspires to resist in our own case. The incoherence of our attitudes arises from the incoherent conceptual scheme which we have inherited.

Once we have understood this it is possible to understand also the key place that [the concept of rights has] in the distinctively modern moral scheme ... the culture of bureaucratic individualism results in their characteristic overt political debates being between individualism which makes its claims in terms of rights and forms of bureaucratic organization which make their claims in terms of utility. But if the concept of rights and that of utility are a matching pair of incommensurable fictions, it will be the case that the moral idiom employed can at best provide a semblance of rationality for the modern political process, but not its reality. The mock rationality of the debate conceals the arbitrariness of the will and power at work in its resolution.[9]

Here again we are presented with irreconcilable moral claims consequent upon the loss of a Christian context in the pursuit of what is right.

6. The Endowment of Rights

The loss of coherent moral horizons for the pursuit of justice reflects the abstraction of rights from any such horizons. Oliver O'Donovan writes:

What effect does this ... have upon the conception of justice? It dissolves its unity and coherence by replacing it with a plurality of "rights." The language of subjective rights (i.e., rights which adhere to a particular subject) has, of course, a perfectly appropriate and necessary place within a discourse founded on law ... What is distinctive about the modern conception of rights, however, is that subjective rights are taken to be original, not derived. The fundamental reality is a plurality of competing, unreconciled rights, and the task of law is to harmonize them ... The right is a primitive endowment of power with which the subject first engages in society, not an enhancement which accrues to the subject from an ordered and politically formed society.[10]

If, as O'Donovan implies here, rights are properly derived "from an ordered and politically formed society," does this not reduce their moral

---

9. MacIntyre, *After Virtue*, 66.

10. Oliver O'Donovan, *Desire of the Nations*, 247–48.

force or render their claims provisional upon "external" authority? Not if such a society formulates such rights without claiming any absolute kind of authority of its own, but rather in recognition of the demands of justice under God. This locates both individual rights, and the civil obligation to uphold them, within the fuller purposes of God—purposes that ground the formation of civil society in the first place. Accordingly, the fact that rights are socially endowed therefore still permits Robert Evans to claim:

> Human dignity is the foundation for nurturing and protecting human rights. It is rooted in the vision of the "fullness of life" promised in the incarnation of Jesus Christ and his identification with all humankind. We must be reminded that human dignity is something persons have, not something they must earn or be granted. Dignity is not a quality bestowed on others by the family, by society, or by a government. Rather, dignity is a reality as a consequence of God's good creation and never-ending love. This reality requires acknowledgement and respect.[11]

7. Choice as a Right

Among individual rights, the right of (unspecified) choice is distinctive. Originally, within the context of Christian faith, the right of choice concerned that liberty that is granted by God to individuals to judge and pursue the right in the light of conscience and of his good purposes. Such choice is a matter of lively personal enquiry and responsiveness to the truth.

In rights ideology, however, individual choice is abstracted from any such context and is taken itself to define the good as it pertains to the choosing individual. Indeed, since every claim to rights by the individual can be seen as a choice to claim these rights, the right of choice acquires logical supremacy over rights in general. It becomes the defining and self-defining expressive act of the individual, conceived as absolute and underived. Such performance of choice is sometimes assigned conceptually to a private "space" proper to each individual.

Choice is misrepresented here precisely as it inheres personally creative and personally responsible action. This may be illustrated equally from the fields of art and ethics. By way of an illustration from art, we

---

11. Evans, "Human Rights in a Global Context."

might consider the invitation once seen by the author to a "creativity workshop." The invitation flyer carried the headline, "Let your creativity ooze." However in reality, creativity—as every serious creative artist knows—is hard work requiring the most demanding attentiveness to reality, with regard both to any subject of the art work and to the materials and tools to be used. It is emphatically not a matter of something "oozing" from within the artist. Creativity cannot be reduced to expression; it is born, in travail, of engagement with and demanding responsiveness to reality.

By way of an illustration from ethics, the expressive view of choice shows itself most dramatically in the claim that the individual has the "right to die"—by which is usually meant today, the right to terminate one's own life. Now this claim stands in the starkest contradiction with the upholding of individual rights as such, rooted as they are in the responsibility to which God calls us to seek and do right. For of all such rights, the search to do right entails most fundamentally upholding the right to life. But the "right to die" pre-empts the search to do right by making the latter conditional upon the individual's choice to live rather than to die. It reduces "doing what is right" towards an individual to upholding whatever may be their underived choice. And in so doing it subverts the motivation to uphold this or any other right, which lies in the godly desire precisely to seek and do what is right. The "right to die," if legally endowed, will subvert all rights—including this "right" itself.

This is ironic, of course, given that the tradition of individual, natural rights has historical origins in a medieval turn to the moral, judging subject; for this tradition has today served precisely to subvert the personal formation of any such subject by severing these rights from the religious and social context that forms such judgment. As Joan Lockwood O'Donovan remarks, "The secular liberal-democratic rights culture of today . . . is in danger of collapsing into legal and political incoherence. It is largely the remnants of Christian political thought and practice in advanced western polities, in their legal and public traditions, and in the social and moral sentiments of at least some of the population and politicians, that keeps collapse at bay."[12]

It is similarly ironic when rights are propounded as the ultimate basis of human dignity. In truth human dignity is God-given. It is the

---

12. O'Donovan, "Rights, Law and Political Community," 38.

Christian vocation today to be converted to the dignity that is bestowed upon us by God.

Christians are called by God today to live converted to this dignity. They are called to witness to this dignity, and to seek the conversion of others to it by manifesting it in their own Christian practice and understanding it faithfully in reflection. They are called also to acknowledge, and repent of, their own complicity with Western cultural habits of thought and action that deny the God-given dignity of all.

This dignity reflects the regard for human beings that is God's own affirmation of his creation, dignified by the incarnate Christ. While legally formulated and enforced rights most certainly have their place defending individuals and groups against exploitation by others, theirs must always remain a subsidiary place. They can never replace the dignity bestowed by God upon his people, or replace our free and responsible participation in God's affirmation of his creation. To such dignity God graciously raises us by the Holy Spirit; it is our dignity as the sons and daughters of God.

9 Neoliberal Capitalist Ideology

Conversion to the "Commonweal" of God

W E TURN NOW TO the ideology most influential in the public life of
Western societies today. The ideology of rights just considered has
not been the strongest driver of social change in recent decades. Another
ideology has been stronger. Indeed it has guided the program for such
change throughout modernity. This is the vision of progress towards
greater mastery of the world by humankind, for the good. This vision
was, in its origins, deeply informed by the Christian vision of openness
to the in-breaking kingdom of God. The *means* of such progress (which
also tends to shape the *meaning and goal* of "progress" as such) was until
recent generations seen broadly in the advance of scientific knowledge
and technical skills hand in hand with rational enquiry, in a population
endowed with an innate human goodness and rationality and civilized by
education. Under state management, society was to be conformed more
closely to the requirements of, and by the fruits of, such "progress."

Throughout modernity, a significant element within this vision of
progress has been the vision of greater material wellbeing. A framework
and program for the pursuit of wealth took form in the developing
theory and practice of capitalism.

The explicit rationality framed by capitalist economic thinking has
been very formative for the vision of, and in the management of, social
change. This is a narrower rationality, however, than that in which traditional forms of society are embedded and has therefore had the effect of
constraining society in certain directions. Famously, Max Weber saw the
program of rationalization sponsored by capitalism as locking society
into an "iron cage."[1]

Although capitalist thinking has influenced Western economic life
throughout the modern period, in recent decades it has been applied

1. On economic rationalization, see Gay, "An Ironic Cage."

with new rigor to frame a comprehensive vision for society and an ambitious program of economic rationalization for the restructuring society in conformity with this vision. This intensified application of *neoliberal capitalist ideology* has been made possible through technological advances in such areas as transport, information, and communications technology. These have provided the means both for new developments in international trade and its management through a global capitalist infrastructure and also for the restructuring of society in general.

Already early in the twentieth century, Christian thinker J. H. Oldham had expressed concern over the negative aspects of burgeoning economic expansion within Western countries and reaching across the world from the West: "Will western governments have sufficient strength of mind and purpose to protect the peoples of Asia and Africa from the commercial greed and the domination of selfish private interests which in the West itself seriously threaten to deprive men of their real liberties and to drive the weak to the wall? It seems vain to hope that without some large increase in their spiritual capital the Christian nations can grapple successfully with these prodigious tasks."[2]

Nearly a century later, Oldham's fears seem sadly to have been realized. To take one example, John Hodges writes: "The use of gene transfer in the food species has, I fear, been used only for the financial benefit of a minority in the rich West. Meanwhile the evident global strategy to take ownership of the world's seed resources threatens the three billion rural poor who have only their land and their labour and who need empowerment, not further burdens on their only economic activity—farming."[3]

Central to more recent developments since the 1980s has been a more focused, ideological program of economic rationalization. Building upon the program of economic reconstruction initiated following the Second World War by the United States and Britain, this has been pursued, on the one hand, globally through the creation of such structures as the World Trade Organization, the World Bank, and the International Monetary Fund and its structural adjustment programs. This program has been pursued, on the other hand, through the new penetration of society in general by social reforms under the banner of "modernization"—reforms that in reality amount to nothing less than an unmandated program for social revolution.

2. Oldham, *World and Gospel*, 57.
3. Hodges, "Given for Food," 3.

It is important to distinguish between capitalism as such (which can take a variety of forms, and is not in itself in fundamental conflict with Christian belief) and neoliberal capitalist ideology with its program of economic rationalization (which does conflict with Christian belief in ways we shall explore below). It is common for those who propound neoliberal ideology to obscure this distinction by presenting arguments for "capitalism" that by no means provide warrant for the neoliberal program they actually espouse.[4]

The thinking behind this new program originated in the years following the Second World War when think-tanks and their funders, drawing on the philosophy of Friedrich von Hayek, began formulating neoliberal capitalist ideology.[5] Since then the further development, promotion, and implementation of their program has been a matter of progressive policy among political leaders and corporate business managers. It is reported that Margaret Thatcher, in the 1970s before becoming Prime Minister in Britain, told a Conservative political think tank, "We must have an ideology. The others [i.e., Labour] have one; we must have one too." This process of formulation, promotion, and implementation of neoliberal ideology can be seen as a development out of Enlightenment thinking in the eighteenth century, when the ideas basic to the modern revolution were framed, legitimized, strategically promoted, and implemented by those who espoused them.

"Enlightenment" was the rhetorical term used among these eighteenth century thinkers to promote their program for the pursuit of sure knowledge in place of traditional custom and ignorant prejudice. This program had a precursor in Francis Bacon's attempt to study society on the basis of observation, no longer obscured by what he called the idols of tribe, cave, marketplace, and theatre.

The term "ideology" has related origins. David McLellan writes that this term "is the product of the social, political and intellectual upheavals that accompanied the Industrial Revolution," which included "the idea that, since we have made the world, we can also remake it." He quotes Jürgen Habermas, who writes that such ideologies "replace traditional legitimations of power by appearing in the mantle of modern science and by deriving their justification from the critique of ideology." McLellan continues, "Whereas traditional religion concentrated on the interaction

---

4. A classic example of this is Novak, *Spirit of Democratic Capitalism*.

5. See Harvey, *A Brief History of Neoliberalism*.

between the everyday life of individuals and the sacredness of an other-worldly dimension, the secularized universe of ideology concerned itself with public projects of this-worldly transformation to be legitimized by apparently self-justifying appeals to science and to reason."[6]

The link with Enlightenment thinkers is clear. As McLellan writes, these "were the intellectual precursors of the French Revolution of 1789; and it was in the immediate aftermath of the French Revolution that the term ideology was first coined. Its originator, in 1797, was Antoinne Destutte de Tracy . . . de Tracy proposed a new science of ideas, an idea-logy, which would be the ground of all other sciences."[7]

Now today there are those who today espouse "the triumph of global capitalism" in similar terms. They exalt this as self-justifying and as critiquing and moving beyond all ideology—specially beyond Marxism. The most well-known example of this is Francis Fukayama's work.[8] Seen in its historical context, of course, this self-promotional rhetoric by defenders of capitalist ideology has an ironic aspect, and indeed Karl Marx used the term "ideology" *for capitalism* as a comprehensive theory and program for governing society and social change, before the term was ever used of Marx's own thinking.

Christian concerns about capitalist ideology are directed most fundamentally towards its absolute claims for the normative status of its program for economic rationalization severed from a Christian context, whether these claims are explicit or implicit. Whatever is consistent with economic rationalization tends, by default, to secure legitimation, while whatever is inconsistent with it tends to be resisted. As the autonomous, absolute dictates of economic rationalization are followed for the management of society and social change, modern culture is set on a trajectory increasingly divergent from that of openness to the in-breaking kingdom of God.

Seen in this way, capitalist ideology, like rights ideology, represents a program of rationalization that seeks to conform the human world more closely to an explicit, normative framework that has been abstracted from, and stands in ambiguous relation to, the purposes of God among humankind. Whereas rights ideology seeks to conform the human world more closely to the individual human subject conceived in abstraction

---

6. McLellan, *Ideology*, 2–3.

7. Ibid., 5.

8. See especially Fukayama, *End of History*.

from and dissociation from God and from human community hosted by God, capitalist ideology seeks to conform the human world more closely to an economic model for the world conceived in abstraction from and dissociation from God and from human life hosted by him. Whereas rights ideology defines the good by reference to the autonomous individual, capitalist ideology defines the good by reference to the "economic realities" of capitalist society and the vision guiding it.

Central to contemporary neoliberal global capitalist ideology is the claim that this is an appropriate response to "reality." Whatever is dictated by this ideology is supposedly dictated by reality; whatever harm follows from it is supposedly an unavoidable, regrettable aspect of the real world. "There is no other way," it is declared.

A Christian critique of capitalist ideology challenges this by arguing that what is here invested with normative reality is only part of the richer reality of creation and that when it is abstracted from this rich reality and made absolute it is a human fiction and idol.

The ascription of absolute, normative status to capitalist ideology may, of course, represent a rhetorical promotion and legitimation of particular vested interests. This may in turn be a matter of deliberate, conscious strategy or a broader tendency of the sort that Michel Foucault discerned in post-Enlightenment social institutions whose appeals to truth and goodness could function to legitimize the interests of those in power. On the other hand, allegiance to capitalist ideology may represent the capture of our imaginations by a worldview severed from and at odds with a Christian imagination. In particular, it may reflect the philosophical inclinations of Hayek. He showed the Romantic idealist inclination to trust in biological metaphors. In circular fashion he assumed and trusted in the existence of something ("the market") analogous to a human mind or a self-regulatory organism with a coherent, immanent purposiveness of its own. This turns capitalism into a kind of fertility cult that entrusts itself to capital as defining, self-propagating, and breeding wealth in the form of credit. The Christian vision of economic activity as service is lost; the destiny is forgotten—as portrayed in Dante's *Inferno*—of those who love as fertile that which is not so. We shall return to this point later in chapter 9.

Let us explore further, some elements in the dislocation of capitalist economics from the trajectory of Christian openness towards the kingdom of God.

ECONOMICS SEVERED FROM A CHRISTIAN CONTEXT

Christian and biblical tradition allow, and offer guidance for, owning, buying, and selling private property and for employment, i.e., buying and selling labor. Economic activity has its place within the *oiko-nomia* of God, which originally signifies "the ordered life of those living to-gether in a household." It is a matter for responsible stewardship of God's creation and the maximization of God's blessing of human wellbeing.

In a Christian context, economic activity finds its place within a society open to the in-breaking kingdom of God, and is called itself to embody this openness and contribute to the formation of society and inform change within it. In so doing, it is called to incorporate the wider demands of Christian righteousness. Critically, these include taking responsibility for long-term social wellbeing and not merely pursuing short-term gain.

Neglect of this responsibility in capitalist enterprise today—as seen in, for example, practices harmful to the future of the environment—often attracts criticism. Most recently, of course, the banking institutions have displayed a horrific disregard for the responsibilities of steward-ship—they have played false prophets of sustainable economic growth by peddling false profits and relying upon governments and taxpayers to bail them out. Such neglect violates the demands of the Christian vision of stewardship. It also violates the moral demands made upon commerce in traditional forms of society. The engine driving such neglect has been described by Parry and Bloch as follows. They find in traditional cultures a broad pattern whereby "short-term transactions concerned with the arena of individual competition" are subservient to "the reproduction of the long-term social or cosmic order."[9] Today, they argue, there has been a revolution: "By a remarkable conceptual revolution what has uniquely happened in capitalist ideology, the argument would run, is that the val-ues of the short-term order have become elaborated into a theory of long-term reproduction. What our culture (like others) had previously made room for in a separate and subordinate domain has, in some quar-ters at least, been turned into a theory of the encompassing order."[10]

Now the Christian vision is not, of course, to be equated with that of traditional or sacral society. Its vision of openness to the in-breaking

9. Parry and Bloch, "Money and the Morality of Exchange," 24. See also 24-28 in general.

10. Ibid., 29.

kingdom of God allows change in the social order and allows economic activity to play a part in shaping these changes; it does not locate economic activity within any kind of enduring, sacral, social order. What is does *not* allow, however, is for economic activity (or a theoretical blueprint for economic activity) to become absolute and independent of the trajectory of openness to God's kingdom, or to extend its scope so as to provide a framework for all aspects of human life shaping them according to principles abstracted from this openness. It does not even allow economic activity to have full autonomy within "external" constraints imposed by Christian principles; rather, economic activity finds its authentic meaning and purpose when it in woven integrally into the wider Christian context of God's *oiko-nomia*.

Much has been written by Christian authors on contemporary economic thinking and policy, seeking to critique these in a Christian context.[11] Let us consider four tendencies in neoliberal capitalism today linked with the severance of economic activity from its proper Christian context.

1. The Capitalist Market Tends to Win Acceptance Tacitly as the Presupposed Setting of All Possible Moral Values, Issues, and Choices

The intention of market activity has moral aspects. Today, however, "the market" tends itself towards the defining context for all possible moral concerns, judgments, and values in the first place. Robert Wuthnow lists some of the elements of market activity that are today ascribed moral character. First, participation in the market as a producer or consumer is viewed as a direct form of participation in public life, analogous to

---

11. Let me commend a small handful of writers on economics. Among those concerned to set economic enterprise is a biblical context, notable are Bob Goudzwaard's writings and lectures. These include *Globalization and the Kingdom of God*, and *Hope in Troubled Times* (co-authored). For a discussion of economic life in the Old Testament, see for example Wright, *Old Testament Ethics*. For a theological critique of three prominent U.S. neoliberal capitalist Roman Catholic writers—Michael Novak, Richard Neuhaus, and George Weigel—see David Schindler, "Neoconservative Economics." Looking beyond explicitly Christian writing, among those who propose constructive practical alternatives to neoliberal ideology are Porritt, *Capitalism as If the World Matters*, and Goudzwaard and de Lange, *Beyond Poverty and Affluence*. Trenchant critiques of aspects of neoliberal ideology and its recent outworking include James, *Affluenza*; Hamilton, *Growth Fetish*; and Palmer, *Toxic Childhood*. As a contemporary global myth, neoliberal ideology is integral to the critique offered from a non-Western perspective in Ramachandra, *Subverting Global Myths*.

voting; second, the market provides individuals with a sense of freedom and dignity and helps to shape moral character, as a testing ground for the development of talent; third, the moral character of the market is evident in that it is frequently the focus of moral crusades (e.g., campaigns on behalf of fair trade and of the environment); fourthly, "there is a comparison and implicit corollary between market freedoms and other freedoms. This places the idea of the free market on the same moral plane as freedom of speech, freedom of religion, and freedom of thought."[12]

Now Christian faith will endorse such moral aspects of market transactions. However, it will reject the distortion that arises once the market becomes *our defining context*, in effect defining the scope and character of morality itself. For at this point the very meaning of "moral," which derives from religious roots, gets distorted. The meaning of "wealth" as a blessing also gets distorted.[13] And the meaning of "religion" itself gets distorted now, being viewed within the absolute frame of "the market" as a matter merely of private choice. This denies religion the authority to morally critique the market itself. The market is now seen as the context of all possibility for moral good and bad alike, while the market itself, as such, escapes moral appraisal.

2. The Capitalist Market Tends to Enlarge Indefinitely in Its Scope

While private ownership of property has its place in Christian and biblical tradition, it does not reflect the primary relation between human beings and the world. Rather, human beings primarily find themselves born into a natural world that sustains them in life and from which they may draw resources for their own ends.

This world has been created by a good God who has given humankind dominion over it as stewards of God's good purposes. Whereas in sacral societies (as we are reminded by the essay collection edited by

12. Wuthnow, "The Moral Crisis in American Capitalism."

13. Thus greater economic wealth among the Western nations in recent decades has not translated into greater wealth of happiness for their populations in general; see for example James, *Affluenza*. Again, the extensive work of Richard Wilkinson has demonstrated that the "commonweal" of lower morbidity (across many parameters) does not correlate with greater economic wealth in a given society. Rather, in a global setting, such low morbidity correlates with a high degree of relative social equality within a given society, not with its absolute measure of material wealth. See for example Wilkinson and Pickett, *The Spirit Level*.

Parry and Bloch, *Money and the Morality of Exchange*) human use of the natural world is typically subject to a range of taboos in deference to gods, for Christian faith human beings have the right and the responsibility to enrich and manage the natural world in ways that will sustainably promote human flourishing in this setting.

While private ownership of property is one important way in which such stewardship may be exercised, there are others. Another is through public ownership, with property held in trust as a public good and managed with funding from public taxation. Another—retaining a certain given primacy—is through informal personal participation in the natural world given to all: participation in what has traditionally been called "commons" (referring not only to certain areas of land but also to other naturally occurring resources such as air, rain, daylight, and other elements of the environment living and inanimate). Such informal participation in, and enjoyment of, the gifts of creation has, and retains, a given primacy over private ownership of property. The latter may not be taken as the defining human relation to the world; rather it is a relative way of ordering the stewardship of creation formally within this informal setting. Accordingly, it is always wrong for humans beings to understand themselves born into a world that is fundamentally the private property of someone else, from which they are barred right of access or use; and it is equally wrong for human beings ever to understand themselves born into the world with property over which they themselves have absolute private rights. This is to violate the truth that ultimately we and all creation are hosted by God.

Turning to the modern period, private ownership of property has had an important place in the modern vision of society from its beginnings. When, in medieval land enclosure, people were forced off the common land from which they drew subsistence and were compelled to sell their labor in order to survive, a new market for buying and selling private goods was created. Such privatization of "common" land continues around the world today as traditional lands are taken and used to produce goods for the global market. Meanwhile in Western countries, services provided by the state on behalf of the public good have been widely privatized including energy supplies, water, and public transport. New private property rights have been conceived in, for example, "plant breeders' rights" and "emissions trading." In another major development, principles such as copyright and patent have been broadened into the formulation of "intellectual property rights," bringing wider areas of knowledge (even, in at least one attempt, knowledge concerning the human genome) within the scope of private property rights.

Capitalist ideology distorts the Christian vision of shared participation in, and responsible stewardship of, creation whenever it pursues the extension of private property markets without regard for the proper place of commons, of property held in public trust, and of public services as ways of fulfilling this vision. It promotes the assumption that everything is properly owned privately by someone and that nobody else has any claim upon this except by purchase. This radically distorts the Christian truth of the gift of our own personal creation and of the creation as our inheritance and our responsibility as its stewards before God who ultimately hosts us.

3. Capitalist Ideology Tends to Promote Itself as Offering the Normative Description of Human Society as a Whole

Just as the capitalist market extends in scope into new areas of human society, so capitalist ideology tends also to frame social institutions systematically in terms of market transactions as it conceives them. It envisions, on the one hand, the production of goods and services for profit, and, on the other hand, individuals who purchase these for their own private good. It applies this model for private property transaction indiscriminately to organized corporate human endeavor of any kind and, where it can, it implements with revolutionary rigor its program of economic rationalization. More widely, beyond the realm of formal social institutions, market metaphors get projected on to other more informal areas of society, capturing the popular imagination in service to neoliberal ideology. For example, pupils and patients alike become "customers" purchasing private goods.

Market transactions do indeed have their place in a Christian context. However, as a model for human endeavor in general they are quite inadequate and when allowed to *define* this they seriously distort it. This distortion is perhaps most obvious where the aim of certain corporate human endeavor is originally to serve the good of each as the public good and private fortune requires. Take, for example, the Christian vision for education and health care. This vision is distorted when capitalist ideology frames education and health as fundamentally private goods for sale and purchase. Here the primary goal of education is no longer envisaged as helping individuals to contribute their full potential as citizens serving the public good but as providing them with the knowledge and skills to adapt to the requirements of the employment market and achieve personal profit from doing so. It is this stance that, for example, provides the warrant for the current student loan scheme in England and subsequent indebtedness, and for the high fees for university education in the United States. Higher education now turns itself into a market in which courses get offered if there is a market for them among prospective students even though, as courses, their educational or employment value may be small. In a similar way, private healthcare (including that provided by "alternative medicine" therapists) tends to be led by market demand and profitability; it is no longer led fundamentally by the vision of good health and wellbeing for its customers, free as far as possible from medical interventions.

4. Capitalist Ideology Tends to Orient Social Institutions towards Maximizing Profit for Shareholders

As capitalist ideology is applied with ever widening scope and it frames its areas of operation increasingly in its own terms, it directs institutional endeavor towards one particular goal above all other: the maximization of financial profit for shareholders. Social institutions have, of course, originated historically in service to other goals than this. Today, however, wherever tension arises between maximizing the achievement of these goals and the maximizing of profit, capitalist ideology tends to promote the latter as fundamental and to reduce the former to the status of formal constraints imposed upon this. That is to say, it is required that the maximization of profit be constrained only by certain other quantified goals and targets. Fundamentally, the greater the profit that can be secured for shareholders who have invested capital in the institution, the more "successful" the institution is deemed to be.

Here once again it is with respect to corporate endeavor whose purpose is to serve the public good and alleviate private misfortune that capitalist ideology most obviously has its distorting effect. For example, the provision of healthcare and of education originated historically in pursuit of a vision held to be more fundamental than that of increasing the capital held by investors. The pursuit of this older vision may be perfectly consistent with the aims of a "non-profit" organization.

In summary, we may describe the distortion at the heart of capitalist ideology as follows. Firstly, it distorts our social orientation towards the good (which is ultimately formed with reference to, and bestowed by, God). It does so by falsely exalting financial capital as the unqualified and unambiguous good, to be sought and multiplied above all else. Secondly, it distorts the agency or means of securing the good (which is ultimately found in human service to God and humankind, empowered by God's grace). It does so by constructing a society in which financial capital is the basic means by which good may be secured, by which good is ultimately defined, and therefore to which all pursuit of good must ultimately defer. The role assigned here to humankind is to provide human resources maximally at the disposal of this capital.

Here, capital is effectively conceived as the living subject and agent of historical progress or advance. The responsibility of humankind is to identify with, and serve, capital as this living subject and agent of good. In place of the biblical injunction upon humankind to "go forth and multiply," here it is *capital* that is to be multiplied. Indeed capital becomes the very symbol of fertility, interest repayments for loans being the purest expression of such fertility. In such terms, capitalist ideology might even be described as having a religious meaning akin to that found in a fertility cult such as biblical Baalism—in other words, an idol.

There is a contradiction at the heart of all such idolatry: the worshippers of an idol maintain that it calls for servitude and yet it has no life at all; its life has been invested in it entirely by those who worship it. An idol is a puppet on strings; having a semblance of life, it is parasitic upon the life of those who worship it. These two contradictory faces of idolatry—human servitude to an idol and the hidden construction of an idol by human beings in the first place—together displace and distort the creativity, service, and freedom of human life oriented towards God. An idol saps the life of those who idolize it, drawing them into its own emptiness (Ps 115:8).[14]

In capitalist ideology, the maintenance of this contradiction has a peculiarly knowing character. On the one hand, the idea of capital is presented for public consumption as that of a kind of living subject or agent deserving subservience. Indeed in its embodiment in the business

14. On idolatry, as it is understood in the Bible, see Beale, *We Become What We Worship*. On idolatry in contemporary Western society, see for example Goudzwaard, *Idols of Our Time*, and Guinness et al., *No God but God*.

corporation, capital has been granted the legal status of a fictional "person" with absolute private property rights (and even, as I noted earlier, recently with certain "human rights"). The corporation and those who share in it as investors thus play together the role in capitalist markets of a free personal agent. On the other hand, as we have seen, neoliberal capitalism is a human construct. It has been crafted knowingly in recent decades as a tool in the hands of those who seek and expect to profit from it. Its semblance of life fertile for the human good has only the life breathed into it by its creators; its dominating, autonomous power lies, in truth, rather with its constructors who have crafted it in the first place and now maintain it as a tool for their profit.

This contradiction is deliberately concealed, however, by carefully crafted rhetoric that portrays subservience as rather an exercise of freedom and conceals the human construction of the capitalist framework by depicting it as, rather, a matter of natural forces at work in the world. Let us examine some elements of this rhetoric now.

THE RHETORIC OF NEOLIBERAL IDEOLOGY

The neoliberal program of economic rationalization has been presented to a popular audience by means of certain key concepts. These have been used as rhetorical tools to win assent to this program, portraying as free and natural that which is in reality a deliberately constructed and constraining program. Some of these rhetorical tools are as follows:

1. "Wealth Creation" and "Trickle-Down"

The term "wealth creation" presents business investment as bringing into existence (where previously it has not existed) the blessing of wealth. This rhetoric serves to pre-empt attention to such questions as:

(a) Has the wealth in question rather been *transferred* from other ownership (formal or informal), rather than created "out of nothing"? In this case, should not those who previously participated informally in its ownership and responsible stewardship have continuing claims upon it? This question arises, for example, when the imposition of structural adjustment programs on nations by the World Bank and of trade rules by the World Trade Organization deprives people of their livelihood.

(b) Has the wealth in question rather been created *jointly* by the corporate activities of owners, workers, customers, and shareholders, and not by capital investment alone? In this case, should not its "distribution" be a matter of shared responsibility and consensus between them? We might recall that the purchase price of goods and services, for example, used often to be a matter of negotiated, mutual agreement between buyer and seller. This was, of course, the old meaning of a "bargain." Today disparities of power between buyer and seller often leave little room for negotiation of respective advantage.

(c) Has the wealth in question relied greatly for its generation upon a heritage of existing social "wealth," in a wider than monetary sense? In this case, should not this wealth be required reasonably to sustain and enhance this heritage through the taxation of profits and by self-limitation as necessary? To take a very basic example, mass marketing and consumption rely very much upon a social heritage of trustworthiness and trust in relatively anonymous public practices with reference to moral responsibilities as well as to explicit legal compliance. What responsibilities should business enterprise accept towards sustaining and enhancing this social heritage, rather than simple exploiting it parasitically?

Other elements in neoliberal rhetoric work in a similar way. The rhetoric of "trickle down"—which depicts capitalist profit as like a vital spring and source from which wealth trickles down to the poorer in society—occludes the same questions. So too does the rhetoric of "windfall" profits, which presents the wealth in question as floating out of the sky into the hands of business, deflecting attention to from the question of what responsibilities arise from such wealth in the light of its actual sources.

2. "Free Market"/ "Deregulation"/ "Competition"/ "Level Playing-Field"

Here is a set of terms that portrays business enterprise as an activity of competing agents in a domain of freedom. The picture is of a natural world free of artificial constraints, in which something comparable to a virtuous "survival of the fittest" operates with the assurance of an ultimately beneficial outcome. The term "level playing field" presents this natural world as a fair and morally justified world.

In the real world, adoption of this model for business corporations and social institutions has profoundly ambivalent moral consequences including the following:

(a) The various dimensions of human social freedom are constrained by the imposition of a program for economic freedom of a certain kind. Far from being "naturally" free, the "free market" is an artifice constructed and maintained at the price of undermining other dimensions of freedom, including some that are equally economic. Policies may secure economic freedom for one at the expense of taking economic freedom from another. Thus when "free market" policies work indiscriminately against tariffs and quotas, they may indeed stop some injustices but they may also destroy some important local social and economic freedoms, especially at the level of regional and local communities.

(b) While rules prohibiting monopoly are common enough, large corporations are often able in practice to acquire unreasonable power to eliminate smaller competitors and control supply prices. Their power enables them to adopt a range of morally dubious strategies to further increase their power while remaining within the law as they do so. An example of this was the successful pursuit by large companies of legislation that would legalize trading on Sundays in the UK.

(c) While the rules of competition get portrayed as guaranteeing fairness, they are not sufficient to do so. For example, although rules prohibit price fixing between competitors, the pursuit of common self-interests among large corporations generally protects them against "price wars" among themselves. Again, the older vision of fairness embraced fair prices and fair profit, whereas moral justification is now found in "what the market will sustain," and in a price determined by the "scarcity" of goods. Similarly the vision of a fair wage has given way to the payment of the lowest wages that the labor market will sustain. In each case "the market"—despite its apparently autonomous agency—serves the interests of capital investors.

(d) Such goals as "survival," "growth," "fitness," and "success" belong in the first place to the vision of human life; their attribution to business corporations or social institutions is derivative and is appropriate *only insofar* as these participate in and serve the same vision of human life.

However, in neoliberal ideology these goals get applied to capitalist enterprise *in its own right* and indeed at the expense of their human meaning. For example, in business circles today the term "efficiency" is used in the first instance of that which serves capital growth rather than the human good: where "efficiency" once referred to the reliably effective provision of good service to the customer, today in business circles it tends to be used to refer to efficiency in maximizing profit.

(e) Competition towards superior "economic efficiency" is accordingly indiscriminate in its effect upon efficiency in the wider sense of "efficient service of the human good." Pursuit of the most economically profitable may be at the cost of undermining a wider but less profitable service towards human wellbeing. When business remains guided by the vision of service, it may bear with equanimity the provision of relatively less profitable goods and services alongside the more profitable in the name of good service. Today, however, it is not uncommon for a business enterprise to move in and "cream off" the most profitable part of a service, cutting adrift from this the rest and leaving it unable to survive without these more profitable parts. Of course, neoliberal economics will typically criticize the former vision of service as entailing that the more profitable trading artificially subsidies the less profitable. The explanation, however, is that the former vision honored an integrated vision of service to the public good more highly than maximizing profit. The guiding vision of service is of serving need, whatever this may happen to be, rather than providing whatever happens to be most profitable to provide.

3. "User Pays"

The rhetoric of the "free market" and of competition commends the business corporation, on the one hand, as an individual, autonomous agent. On the other hand, in unresolved tension with this it presents the "customer" in similar terms as an individual engaged through acts of purchase in acts of autonomous choice. A key element in neoliberal rhetoric here is the "user pays" principle.

In the real world, unqualified application of this principle creates various distortions including the following:

(a) It wrongly validates the distortion described in 2(e) above by reducing service to its component elements and attacking what it depicts as the unwarranted "subsidizing" of less profitable by more profitable services.

(b) It misrepresents and betrays human actions that are oriented towards offering service by depicting these as the private use of resources for private profit. It takes the principle that individuals should pay for what will be only to their private advantage and applies this indiscriminately: it treats *all* human initiative as in pursuit of private advantage and counts private advantage the *only* consequence of such pursuit. Perhaps the most obvious illustration of this distortion is the contemporary political treatment of education as a private good.

(c) It unjustly insists that individuals pay for the relief of personal misfortune (even of a serious nature) where this misfortune is beyond their control. In the real world, however, the brute fact of human need morally invites consideration of a corporate response and corporate planning for such eventualities. The proper form of such corporate provision varies: sometimes it may be through public taxation (as with the National Health Service in Britain); sometimes it may be through institutional or private insurance (as when institutional or private activity exposes an individual to its own distinctive risks).

Each of the above distortions arises from the policy of treating our basic human relation to the created world as that of individuals purchasing resources and using them for our private advantage. Here the truth—that human beings are called to be united in love and service to God and to each other—is distorted. In place of this, social unity and coherence are expected sustain themselves in the context of the pursuit of capital investment and growth.

4. "Consumer Choice"

A key element in the rhetoric of neoliberal ideology is the promotion of individual "choice" as a good provided by the free market. When all attention is directed towards this good, however, attention is distracted from other goods at their expense; the wider good is distorted. This is apparent in the following ways:

(a) The offer of choice to consumers diverts the attention of consumers away from their search for what accords with their view of the substantive good; it invites them to lay aside such views and begin from the requirement to choose from between possible purchases available. Some choices are not worth having, such as poor schools or dirty hospitals.

Nobody wants these. The exaltation of choice conceals this by imposing "market scarcity" upon that which everyone wants.

(b) Consumer choice is about individual choice of purchase. It is therefore limited in various ways, most obviously by the limitations of financial resources: the wealthy have more choices than the poor. This is concealed, however, in the rhetoric of choice.

(c) Consumer choice is limited to the range of choices available from those offering them, which often reflects prior choices made by the latter regarding what they will offer. The choices presented to consumers will tend to be limited to those selected beforehand by sellers as providing the most profit. Such profitability will often reflect, among other things, the size of the market for them: the most popular choices tend to be most profitable to sell and so are made most readily available. The creation of such mass markets is achieved often through the mass promotion of changing fashions in widening areas of consumption.[15] Here again, the rhetoric of consumer choice diverts the attention of consumers from the fact that they are typically offered a limited, constructed set of possibilities.

(d) Because mass production, distribution, and retail tends to be more economically profitable for those involved, they tend to take over the market. As a result, a single mass-produced product tends to take the place of the richly varied local provision of many types of good, producing a "homogenization" of products available. This has been compared metaphorically with a loss of "biodiversity" or of "gene pool"; towns with high streets full or retail chain stores selling the same products (sometimes under different brand names) as can be bought anywhere in the country have appropriately been called "clone towns." Once again, the rhetoric of consumer choice conceals actual losses of choice.

IN CONCLUSION

The program of social reform pursued by neoliberal capitalism presents itself as oriented towards the creation of wealth. However, it does not point in the direction of that "commonweal" that is represented by the abundant blessing of God in his coming sovereignty. Both by suppress-

15. Three books early in identifying and critiquing this development are Tawney, *Acquisitive Society*; Packard, *Hidden Persuaders*; and Walter, *All You Love Is Need*.

ing the non-economic aspects of human wealth intended by God and by distorting the proper working of economic wealth in the context of God's purposes, neoliberal ideology distorts society away from openness to the in-breaking of God's kingdom.

Perhaps this suppression and distortion may be likened to the way that a practical maxim misleads when it gets applied indiscriminately. It is like treating as an infallible guide the saying that "too many cooks spoil the broth": one will be led to invoke it in circumstances when one should rather be pointing for guidance from the saying that "many hands make light work." In the same way, while the principles extolled by neoliberal ideology and framed in its rhetoric may be precisely those that need to be invoked in certain circumstances, when they are invoked *indiscriminately* they offer false guidance.

Seen in the context of previous chapters of this book, the distorting effect of neoliberal capitalist ideology reflects its character as an inadequate *rationalization* of human society—a form of revolutionary or "from scratch" cultivation of society in accordance with a limited ideological vision. This vision is an abstraction from the vision of openness to social transformation under God in radical attentiveness to God and his purposes; cut adrift from these roots, it rests in autonomous principles defined and upheld by theorists and by those who seek to benefit from it.

Equally, however, as our reflections in this chapter have reminded us, the distorting neoliberal ideology can be thought of as a matter of ascribing to capital and to the holders of investment capital the status of the defining, autonomous and good "personal" agent who bestrides the world, with whom human beings are called to identify themselves implicitly as guaranteeing—indeed as defining—their own wellbeing. It is this face of ideology that intimates most forcefully its idolatrous character. It is associated with romantic idealist philosophies such as that upon which neoliberal ideology is built: the philosophy of Friedrich von Hayek, with its faith that the workings of the market have the coherence and purposiveness found in a living organism.[16]

This dual face of idolatrous ideology—as at once a program of comprehensive rationalization and a commanding of personal identification with, and subservience to, a constructed "agent" of all good—marks both neoliberal capitalist ideology and the ideology of individual rights that

16. See Mirowski, "Economics, Science, and Knowledge: Polanyi vs. Hayek," 36.

we considered in the previous chapter. Together these ideologies strongly influence public thinking and the shaping of public space in Western societies today. It is to this public domain that we shall turn our attention in our last chapter. What is the vision of a public domain as understood in the context of Christian faith? To what vocation are Christians called today by this vision?

To summarize this chapter, meanwhile: Christians are called by God today to live converted to the "commonweal" of God. They are called to witness to the great wealth with which God has blessed them in Jesus Christ, which is compared by Jesus and New Testament authors often with treasure. They are called to seek the conversion of others to this wealth by manifesting it in their own Christian way of life and thought. They are called also to acknowledge, and repent of, their own complicity with Western ideological commitments that effectively deny this by defining wealth in another, idolatrous way: in terms of financial capital and economic growth.

Conversion to the "commonweal" of God involves finding our treasure in God and investing our lives in this. Jesus warned: "Do not store up for yourselves treasure on earth, where moth and rust destroy, and thieves break in and steal; but store up treasure in heaven, where neither moth nor rust will destroy, nor thieves break in and steal. For where your treasure is, there will your heart be also" (Matt 6:19–21). This is not a call to be "other-worldly"; it does, however, call us to define the wealth in which we should rejoice by reference to God's good purposes for human flourishing. Human wealth, when it is defined in this way (and also, importantly, when we are willing to sacrifice it in the name of God's good purposes), then becomes a sign in creation of the treasure we have in God and to which we should attend. As Jesus said, "Set your mind on God's kingdom and his justice before everything else, and all the rest will come to you as well" (Matt 6:33).

10 PUBLIC FACTS AND PRIVATE VALUES

Conversion to the Sovereignty of God

MANY SEE THEMSELVES AS contributing to the management of Western society today. They include politicians and professionals working in business, education, and the mass media. How do they view Christian belief in relation to this task? Do they see this belief as a potential source of guidance? When they direct their efforts towards the social "good," do they look to the Christian conviction that such "good" is to be understood by reference to Christian faith? How do they view attempts by Christians to influence public life in these terms?

In reply, many such people hold the doctrine that Christian faith is a matter of "private" religious beliefs and values that may shape the life of Christian individuals but should not be allowed to shape public life in which (supposedly in contrast to Christian life) reason, and liberty of enquiry and action reign unconstrained by religious commitments.

In this concluding chapter we shall draw upon previous chapters to critique this secularist doctrine and to frame a more faithful vision and understanding of public life as it appears when seen in the context of Christian faith.

At root the secularist doctrine above misunderstands both Christian faith and the secular realm itself. In particular, as we saw in chapter 3, it relies theoretically upon Cartesian habits of imagination that misrepresent Christian faith and its character as radical enquiry and that collude with evasion of the demands of such enquiry. This misrepresentation finds expression in two forms that have appeared successively and now appear sometimes in odd conjunction. In the first form, religious belief is seen as a commitment to unproven truth-claims—as a kind of presupposition, prejudgment, or prejudice regarding what is the truth. In the second form, religious belief is seen as imbuing the world with certain personal values held by religious people. In chapter 3 I illustrated this from a primary school religious assembly on the meaning of "God"—an example of the secularist misrepresentation of both Christian faith and the secular realm, translated into educational practice. This misrepresentation has been similarly translated into other areas of managed public life through state legislation and policy formulation. To explore this further we need to turn our attention to the concepts of "public" and "private," as these have been understood explicitly or implicitly in the course of the modern period.

Let us begin by acknowledging that the term "public" is commonly used with three emphases. Each of these can be understood as reflecting an aspect of human life in community under God and open to enrichment in this context. When, on the other hand, any one of them is taken to *define* the "public," and Christian faith is fitted (supposedly) within the framework proved by this definition, then the reality of human life in community is misrepresented and distorted practically.

1. It is sometimes used to refer to *people in general*, and hence to what characterizes them, or what may properly be asked of them, or what is properly due to them, etc., simply *by virtue of their being persons*. There is an implied contrast here with that which may be said, asked, etc., of some particular individual or group by virtue of considerations that apply to them in a distinct way. This the most basic meaning of "public," as when we refer to "members of the public."

2. It is sometimes used more particularly for *a space to which people in general have access by right and in which they may exercise a liberty which is rightfully theirs*. This space may take the form of amenities or services provided by the state or public benefactors. In this space, limits may be imposed upon civil behavior in order to protect these facilities, protect their accessibility to any given member of the public, and protect the public themselves. After all, if people in general are to dare use public amenities, they need some assurance that they will not encounter certain kinds of "lawless" behavior from other members of the public. The vision of public life is here of a benefit to be protected, enriched, and extended for the good of all; accordingly, "public spiritedness" and "public service" are virtuous.

3. It is sometimes used to refer to the statutory *authorization and control* of practices. It is about the terms under which people are formally per-

mitted to exercise a role among and towards "the public"—terms that are a matter of formulation, legislation, education, and enforcement by the state—as too are the terms under which people may participate in public space. Here "public" means "licensed" and operating in conformity with state-directed norms. Typically behind the formulation of such norms lies one or another ideological vision.

Now the first, basic understanding of "public" above may be relatively full or empty; in principle open towards the deeper meaning of "a member of the public" as a person created in the image of God and called to love God and neighbor.

The second understanding of "public" above has links with Plato and Aristotle, as interpreted by Hannah Arendt. In her book *The Human Condition*, writes Reinhard Hütter, these philosophers understood "a public" as "a human space that is constituted by its defining walls. A totally 'open' space . . . is not a human space and cannot create a coming-together for humans to speak, act, and co-operate."[1] This understanding of "public" too is open in principle to deeper Christian meaning: here the public realm is a space for which all take responsibility together as an act of Christian stewardship under God, in which members of a nation contract together formally to make general provision for the population (e.g., through taxation) and participate informally in the fabric of public and civil life. However, this understanding has been eroded, especially in recent decades. The call to show "public spirit" and give "public service" no longer has normative power in the population. Indeed public space often gets seen not so much as a matter of shared participation in, and exercise of, common values, as a space where "I can do what I like within the law and nobody has the right to stop me because I have as much right to this space as they do." This vacation of public space has a longer history, we have seen in chapter 5, in the social developments since Victorian times described by Richard Sennett, in *The Fall of Public Man*, as an emergent narcissistic personality turns away from the demands of participation in public life, and the latter gets replaced by the fantasy of belonging to a corporate personality.

It is, however, the third understanding of "public" above that gives rise to particular concerns for Christians today. This is because, firstly, Christians find themselves under increasing pressure from such autho-

1. Hütter, "Church as Public," 347.

rizing and controlling public ideology in matters of Christian belief and practice. Distorted views of Christian faith are taken increasingly to authorize the coercion of Christians through the enlarged formulation and application of state legislation and the increasing management of public life. In particular, these relegate Christian faith from the realm of (authorized) "public" life to that of "private" life.[2] Secondly, the Christian vision for a world open to the in-breaking sovereignty of God is increasingly subverted both theoretically and practically for people in general, with the result that they are hindered strongly from finding the liberation God wills for them.

IDEOLOGICAL INTENSIFICATION

In recent decades, ideological doctrines have been applied with new penetration throughout the fabric of society. Accordingly their distorting effects have become more pronounced.

Recent decades have seen a huge growth in the formulation of public norms through legislation and mass social "programming" enabled by new information and communication technology. They have included, in the UK, reform of the curriculum and the practice of teaching in schools, medical practice, repeated Criminal Record Bureau checks,[3] and health and safety regulation. We note the advance of such legislation on norms in chapter 2. These norms have been implemented by a variety of people who see their professional task as communicating with and influencing the public *en mass* in respect of public ideas and goals. These "managers of the public" include people who work in politics and the civil service, the mass media, education, marketing, and spokespersons for businesses and professions. They are the gatekeepers today of more

2. At the time of writing, a recent example of this is the dismissal of Dr. Sheila Matthews as a medical adviser on Northamptonshire County Council's adoption panel. She had asked to abstain from voting on cases where it was proposed to place children for adoption with same-sex couples, believing this was wrong. She argued that her dismissal meant that "people of faith are not permitted to sit on government bodies unless they are prepared to silence their beliefs." Her appeal was turned down by Regional Employment Judge John MacMillan, who said that the issue "transcended the boundaries of all religions."

3. The Criminal Records Bureau is an executive agency of the British Home Office set up to help organizations make recruitment decisions by checking the criminal records of job applicants. The number of "jobs" in the UK that have required CRB checks has grown considerably in the past few years as has the number of times the same individuals must be checked. This has raised various concerns.

formal, public, "secondary" culture as distinguished from the relatively informal, primary culture of family and local community.

The training given to those professionally employed in this secondary culture today tends towards the teaching of strategies based on ideological presuppositions and goals rather than the older approach of apprenticeship in a tradition of practical wisdom. The same is true of the regimes of accountability within which those trained go on professionally to operate. In recent years central government has sought to shape public practice according to its own ideological doctrines more directly, explicitly, and in a more thoroughgoing way. It has pursued this by such means as legislation, directives and protocols, targets, and the requirement of repeated re-accreditation.

Concurrently with this, the state has taken steps to "professionalize" a range of well established activities (paid and voluntary, formal and informal) by requiring or promoting "official accreditation" for those involved. This has brought ideological doctrines to bear upon new areas within what has previously been primary culture.

In order to engage such ideologically formed political programs from within a Christian context, we must move beyond our earlier consideration of secularism as an act of logical inversion, personal evasion of God, and erosion of tacit Christian imagination. We must address it as an exercise of power and of statutory authority that bears upon the Christian life and its vision for the public good.

PUBLIC AND PRIVATE LIFE, AND
THE SOVEREIGNTY OF GOD

The Christian gospel proclaims the sovereignty of God. It calls the world to be open towards God's in-breaking kingdom. And it therefore challenges anything that effectively claims to be sovereign over, or rival to, God himself. Such claims are made notably in sacral societies where divine status is attributed to a particular cultural order and its rulers. Early Christians challenged Roman imperial ideology for its veneration of the Roman emperor as divine; Christians claimed divinity rather for Christ and Christ alone.

In modern secular society, of course, no explicit claim to divinity would be entertained (whether by a ruler, institution, or whatever) as a matter of public doctrine. However, such a claim may be made implicitly. In particular, it may be implicit in a certain definition of "public," by reference to which human life in community under God is (falsely) framed. This not a distinctively modern phenomenon, however; as is well known, it was integral to the witness of the early church that it conceived of itself as *ekklesia* (a public gathering), rather than as one of those many privately hosted religious associations of the sort routinely licensed by Roman authorities.

Reinhard Hütter argues that "it is essential for the church to be a public." The gift of the Holy Spirit at Pentecost, he says, inaugurated the church as a new polis. This is "not just another instantiation of the overarching genus '*polis*'" but rather "a public in its own right" defined by its own very particular and concrete designation. Distinctively, it is similar both to a *polis* and to an *oikos* or household (Eph 2:19), while not the same as either. "The *ekklesia*," he concludes, "explodes the framework of antique politics which is precisely built on the strict dichotomy between *polis* and *oikos*."[4]

Accordingly, today "when it is not characterized by those aspects that constitute it as a public in its own right, the church is a church in crisis. It is not God's crisis but self-inflicted by the church's accommodation to modernity's norm for the organization of a 'public' that is shaped by the liberal nation-state and the free market." He continues: "As a political project, modernity is constituted by a particular way of organizing the 'private' and the 'public' that entails the dichotomizing—and thereby the effective taming—of religion. On the one hand is a 'civil' religion destined to justify and stabilize the project of a liberal society. On the other hand are those idiosyncratic opinions which particular individuals and traditions might hold on their own. These latter are strictly relegated to the realm of privacy."[5]

More particularly, the "goods" presented publicly as right and proper goals for all in secular society may be presented, explicitly or implicitly, as demanding unqualified deference. As we saw in chapter 1, although in secular society "nothing is sacred"—at least not explicitly—beliefs and practices may be endowed implicitly with features of the sacred. We went on to see that sacred status may be endowed upon consumer products (chapter 5), "life" (chapter 7), and public ideologies (chapters 8 and 9).

---

4. Hütter, "Church as Public," 352. For further discussion see O'Donovan, *Ways of Judgement*, chapter 15: Household and City.

5. Hütter, "Church as Public," 336.

In such "secular" guises, resistance to God's sovereignty takes a distinctively modern form. In particular, it finds expression not in explicit claims to divine authority or doctrine rival to those of God, but in rival claims to sponsor *liberation*. Modern resistance to God's sovereignty typically presents itself as the pursuit of liberation and protection of liberty. Of course, this misrepresents both God and liberty owing to its commitment to unacknowledged, false assumptions.

In order to engage this issue further, we must reflect on how liberty is understood in a Christian context and how this understanding differs in Enlightenment thinking. In a Christian context, human beings are endowed with a created liberty by the grace of God. This is the liberty of free, responsible participation in a life that reflects the good purposes of God. Accordingly it does not license people to "do what they like." Law now has its place preserving this liberty: briefly, it challenges individual behavior that fails to honor the gift of such responsible participation by imposing constraints upon the offending individual. In this way the law has a role in "limiting" endowed freedom in order precisely to preserve it in general. The law has moral status serving the liberating purposes of God. The freedom it upholds has, since the rise of Christendom, been embedded in the complex intermediate social structures of family, community, professional institution, and voluntary association.

The distinctively modern, Enlightenment understanding of freedom is different from this, and it lies—together with the commitment to pursue freedom thus understood—at the heart of the modern vision. The modern vision, we have seen, effectively defines freedom by reference to its (defining) enemy, which it holds to lie in ignorant prejudice and unquestioning submission to tradition and authority. Religious tradition in particular is seen as making unwarranted claims for the truth and for right practice, unreasonably constraining the individual. The secular state addresses this by taking on responsibility for the freedom of its citizens. It does so by affirming only that which is self-evidently true and by upholding publicly only that which preserves the domain of public freedom. In the course of this it implements the Enlightenment's *negative* definition of freedom of enquiry as freedom from deference to traditional dogma (including religious dogma) and freedom of action as freedom from submission to coercive, conventional authority (including that of religion). Religious deference and submission have no place in public; they are tolerable only where they do not bear upon the public realm as such, in a "private" realm of belief and action.

This vision of the secular state and its task has been depicted, we have seen, by Ernst Gellner as a shift of vision "from gamekeeper to gardener." In pre-modern society, a self-reliant communal way of life is passed on "naturally" from generation to generation, with the ruling aristocracy taking their share of "bounty"; in modern society, the state takes over control of the ordering of civil society and the civil-izing of its inhabitants through education, legislation, and policing through either its own institutions or accreditation of other licensing agencies. In so doing it sees itself as pursuing liberty for its members through the sponsorship of individual autonomy, rationality and equality, and absolute private property rights. Critically, the modern state now sees itself as *defining* the possibilities for action: it aspires to prescribe and legislate for such possibilities. It no longer sees its task as that of protecting a given, created liberty (to which it is subservient) by placing certain limits on behavior. Rather it sees itself as *creating and defining* liberties in the first place, by means of state legislation.

This, of course, gives a novel meaning also to law and its functions. It also gives a novel meaning to the concepts of "public" and "private." The public domain now becomes a project constructed on explicit principles and licensed by state legislation with absolute authority. Indeed such legislation implies a legal prohibition of activity in public that has not been explicitly licensed. However, as we have seen, such absolute claims by the state have provoked opposing claims to counterbalance them. They have, since the beginning of the modern period, precipitated an ideology of subjective rights ascribed to the individual as proprietor. These rights include among them absolute private property rights. The modern realms of "public" and "private" have thus come to be grounded each in opposed rights claiming their own absolute authority. They are mutually exclusive, autonomous realms, each severed practically from their common origin in personal life in community under God.

We have seen that in practice these modern tendencies have been qualified tacitly by the Christian imaginative world that gave birth to and nourished them. At the same time, since the beginning of modern period they have been drifting away from this anchorage, prompted by the Enlightenment claim that such concepts as reason, autonomy, justice, and equality (upon which the modern world was to be built) need not be understood by reference to a Christian context. But the drift has been gradual. It was not until the mid-nineteenth century that a self-consciously autonomous secularism began to gain political influence. Then the trauma of the First World War brought a new and profound loss of cultural self-confidence. In his analysis of this development,[6] Michael Polanyi describes the Enlightenment as having injected liberal humanism into science as science picked up the mantle of responsibility from medieval Christianity. (For our part we have discussed this rather in terms of the continuing tacit nourishment of secular moral imagination by humanistic Christian faith.) Such humanism worked in partnership with science, qualifying its skeptical tendency in a partnership that held popular confidence until the First World War. After this, however, a more radical skepticism gained ground, feeding the pathological "moral perfectionism" of revolutionary secular ideology described by Polanyi and evident in both communism and Naziism.

FALSE PROGRAMS OF LIBERATION

We have ourselves described in previous chapters the slow severance of modern culture from the Christian trajectory of openness towards the in-breaking sovereignty of God. We have described this as comprising a theoretical distortion and practical subversion of lively personal enquiry as sponsored radically by Christian faith. We are now led to consider it as a *theoretical distortion* and *practical subversion* of the liberation inaugurated by God in Christ.

The former, *theoretical distortion*, has given rise to the domination of social organization by distorting ideologies and their narrow programs of social rationalization and supposedly of liberation. Such secularist programs of liberation have taken various forms. As we have seen, Enlightenment thinkers envisioned a society in which individuals might freely pursue the truth for themselves by questioning beliefs in the light of reason rather than unquestioningly accept tradition and authority. In this Enlightenment vision, freedom of rational enquiry and autonomy of choice are the dominant, even defining, features of freedom. We discussed in chapter 2 the exaltation in these terms of the cultivating state on the one hand and the individual (abstractly conceived) on the other; the tendency of polarization between them; and the ensuing erosion

6. Polanyi, "Why Did We Destroy Europe?"

of the intermediate social structures of family, community, and professional or voluntary association, and of the participation in liberty that
these mediate.

In more recent decades the dominant poles shaping the norms for
public life have shifted; they have become the ideology of subjective rights
and neoliberal economic ideology as described in chapters 8 and 9. Each
of these have been promoted as a program of liberation. The ideology of
subjective rights has been promoted as a program of liberation enabling
individuals to take their rightful place in the public domain; similarly
the neoliberal program of economic reform has been promoted as pursuing freedom through the construction of a free market in the purchase
and sale of goods and services. In each of these visions, the proper role
of the secular state is to secure and guard the conditions of freedom thus
conceived, and to enhance them. Once again, there has appeared between these two ideological poles a tendency of polarization—between
the global capitalist system, on the one hand, and the individual bearer
of rights (especially of consumer rights), on the other.

Such ideological programs, which are based on a distorted theoretical understanding of lively personal enquiry and liberation, give rise to
illiberal forms of liberalism and promote *intolerant* forms of tolerance.
Ultimately they sponsor a *dismissive* evasion of the demands of lively,
personal enquiry. They drive the totalitarian tendency of modern society, which is founded on the misguided attempt of modern thinkers to
construct the domain of public freedom by their own lights.

In recent decades, as this distortion has intensified it has caught
the attention of, and met with protest from, a widening range of people
and cultural institutions tacitly upheld by a Christian heritage. Thus
today neoliberal ideology's "free market" has been widely recognized
as coercively destructive of the rich local ecology of retail business and
community life; while "politically correct" doctrines have, despite their
avowed pursuit of liberation, been widely experienced as repressive of
actual richly endowed communal structures. Indeed, as we have noted,
David Bromwich calls those who implement such doctrines in higher
education today "the new fundamentalists."

Bromwich's book reminds us that what is at issue here is not only
the distortion and suppression of *truth* but also of *liberty*. Ideological
programs of rationalization that claim to sponsor "liberation" may in reality represent a struggle for power in which scant attention is paid to the

authentic demands of justice and compassion. Under their implementation, people may be coerced away from paying due attention to these by the imposition of "carrots" and "sticks" in service to political goals. Thus neoliberal ideology commands uncritical submission to its policies of economic rationalization, while the ideology of subjective rights commands uncritical submission to its own directives and rationales. Both of these together command submission (by means of legislation, targets, and strategies such as the requirement of formal registration and repeated re-accreditation among e.g., general medical practitioners) to the authorizing state that implements these ideologies. This is most serious because they command such submission *in place of* attentiveness to guiding traditions of wisdom.

Turning from modern ideology and its theoretical distortion of lively personal enquiry and liberation, let us consider the *practical subversion* of lively enquiry in modern culture. While ideologies construct norms for public life they leave empty of norms the "private" realm. Here liberalism takes rather a relativistic form. It sponsors a tolerance indifferent to questions of truth. In so doing it ultimately sponsors evasive personal *disorientation* of the sort that represents personal defeat by the demands of lively enquiry. It sponsors a despairing, narcissistic, dissolute, and escapist personal culture. This represents the nihilistic tendency of modern society with its sponsorship of a deepening personally and morally vacuous space.

Again in recent decades this nihilistic tendency has grown. Whereas lively personal enquiry is directed towards what is good and true, the ideology of individual rights sponsors a space in which one has the right to do what one likes provided this does not infringe the same right of others. In parallel fashion, neoliberal capitalist ideology sponsors the right to buy and sell what one likes within the law. These ideological distortions of liberty discard the pursuit of moral truth in favor of the exercise of subjective choice within a domain of choice constructed by the ideology in question. Of course, some might dispute this by arguing that there is no reason why such liberty and exercise of choice should not be morally informed. Ultimately, however, ideological rule precludes or rejects any moral critique *of this ruling ideology itself* by its claim to *define in itself* what is good; and in so doing it logically denies the responsibility of moral judgment as such because this responsibility is inherently unqualified in its scope and includes responsibility to judge this ideology. The resulting liberty thus slips towards a dissolute subjectivity. Once again, the liberation promised by ideological programs turn out to be a deception.

LIBERATION, CHURCH, AND STATE

In all this secularist resistance to the sovereignty of God, framed as a program of liberation, God is displaced and explicitly contradicted as the source of liberation. Belief in God—belief, that is, that God's defining action in Christ is real and to be recognized and honored as the way of liberation as such by every member of the general public—is contradicted for what it is. Belief in God gets associated rather with the defining *enemy* of liberation: with unquestioning conformity to custom, prejudice, and coercive traditional authority.

In the implementation of this secularist program room may be made however for a certain distorted version of faith framed within secularist presuppositions. "Faith" may be permitted as something operative within, and in its consequences limited to, a conceived private domain. Such faith may be seen as a matter of private commitment to unproven truth-claims, or a subjective personal choice, or an expression of personal values or personal identity. It is not seen for what faith authentically is, however: our most lively personal enquiry in radical responsiveness toward the real.

Christians are encouraged in public thinking today to accommodate to this secularist definition of faith. They are prompted to think of their faith as a *private choice*, to be understood as such by reference to the ultimate enemy, which is identified by secularism as "coercion." Once the *church* is now interpreted in these terms, it becomes a voluntary association of the converted, an institution that finds its defining enemy in coercive Christian religion of the sort associated here with "Constantinianism" or with "Christendom" in general. When the *Christian contribution to public life* is now interpreted in these terms, it becomes a "stakeholder" contribution; it is limited to a defense of Christian "vested interests"—the interests of one party among others in a plural society. No doubt in the course of making such a contribution, Christians may take the opportunity to present in public arguments based on explicit Christian principles; however, let us be clear that this does not amount to a witness directly to the reality of God's action in Christ. Rather, because the acceptance of these principles is presented as a matter of personal conversion to Christian faith, it is a testimony only to a private choice, and not as recognition of a truth demanding serious enquiry by all.

Now, of course, the coercive imposition of ideas and practices in public life is improper of the church. However, when coercion is made a *defining enemy* of free enquiry and action, as Enlightenment thinking makes it, intended opposition to coercion also condemns indiscriminately much else, including *that which is integral precisely to free enquiry and action themselves.* This happens once free enquiry gets wrongly equated (as described in chapters 3 and 4) with doubt, and set in contrast to receptivity or readiness, in the act of enquiry, to entrust oneself to, and rely upon, belief. Similarly, free action gets wrongly defined by a supposed mutual exclusion between this and readiness to entrust oneself to, participate in, and rely upon, any tradition of practice. In reality, however, free enquiry and action involve openness and receptivity. Commendation of such receptivity is by no means to be equated with coercion.

When the commendation of such receptivity is wrongly taken *a priori* as an act of coercion it attracts secularist condemnation in the name precisely of free action and enquiry. However, in reality it is rather this condemnation itself that is coercive: it is the attempted imposition, in public, of false beliefs about the nature of free enquiry and action. Thus we find ourselves confronted today with secularist condemnations of dogmatism that are completely misplaced and are themselves unwarranted dogmatic pronouncements; and we find secularist condemnations of intolerance that are themselves completely misplaced and are themselves intolerant.

Christian faith resists such secularist condemnations. It challenges secularism to address the possibility that the secularist identification of free enquiry and dogmatism, tolerance and intolerance, free action and coercion is based upon assumptions that are themselves dogmatic, intolerant, and coercive insofar as they have rejected, explicitly or implicitly, the true source of free enquiry, tolerance, and liberation that is the gracious initiative of God in Christ towards humankind.

The "public truth" of the gospel (as Lesslie Newbigin wrote of it[7]) is not at all about coercion. It is about the fact that the very meaning

---

7. For two good accounts of Lesslie Newbigin's vision of the public truth of the gospel, see Barns, "Christianity in a Pluralist Society," and Barns, "Contesting Secular Public-ness."

of "public" and "private" are most richly defined and nourished in a Christian context, in which the distinction between them is relativized. Public and private life constitute aspects of a personal life in community with other people under God, in which human liberty as a gift of creation imbued with moral purpose is directed and open towards the inbreaking sovereignty of God. It is secularism that distorts and coerces such life. It distorts the public domain when it turns it into a domain over which those claiming statutory authority hold proprietorial rights to define what constitutes free action, and to license it; and distorts the private domain when it turns it into a domain of "private" or "intimate" life impelled by the dynamics of needy narcissism.

We see these distortions of the public and private domains impacting in a new and distinctive way in Britain at the beginning of the twenty-first century, in the context of its particular historical background, as follows.

BRITAIN AND THREE PATHS OF SECULARITY

Secularist ideology is today shaping Britain's "public" and "private" domains in a distinctive and dramatic way. This may be fruitfully explored this using Martin Marty's account of the paths taken by secularity in Britain, the United States, and continental Europe. The drama taking place in Britain today is bound up with the recent impact upon Britain of the second and third of these.

In Britain, the United States, and continental Europe secularization has followed three somewhat different paths, described by Marty in is 1969 book *The Modern Schism: Three Paths to the Secular*.[8] In continental Europe, originating chiefly from the nineteenth-century and earlier European Enlightenment thinking, there is what Marty calls "utter secularity." This involves "a formal and unrelenting attack on gods and churches and a studied striving to replace them." In the United States, by comparison, there is a contractual, negotiated, and controlled relation (albeit one contested in its application) between state and religion that he labels "controlled secularity." Finally, in Britain the path of secularization has been different again: it has been formed more by a practical tendency simply to *ignore* Christian religion. Marty labels this "mere secularity."

8. Marty, *Modern Schism*, 10.

Britain's "mere secularity" is reflected clearly in Edward Wickham's account of the early twentieth-century English church. He observes the "neglect to adhere" by many, and the "looser membership of many within" the who were "accordingly more easily detachable by all the immediate causes, excuses, and rationalizations that human beings can discover."[9]

This "mere secularity" represents a different path from that of either "utter secularity" or "controlled secularity." As a social phenomenon it is connected with the fact that, as Wickham writes, "England has been singularly unfavorable ground for dogmatic atheism, and also perhaps for dogmatic religion." As a result, despite the fact that the secular mode of thought—"that almost total preoccupation with immediate and temporal affairs"—has grown in dominance in the course of the twentieth century, "sharp lines between fidelity and infidelity cannot be drawn in English society." "One way of stating this," he writes, "is to say that the secular-minded outside the churches have a Christian coloration, and that practicing Christian inside the church have marked secular characteristics." It still persists," writes Wickham in 1957, "a baffling feature of English life."[10]

BRITAIN'S "MERE SECULARITY" AND HER CHRISTIAN HERITAGE

Looking back beyond the nineteenth and twentieth centuries, there appears a connection between the social phenomenon of "mere secularity" and the English reluctance to adopt Enlightenment ideology with its vision for the revolutionary construction of society on the basis of dogmatic principles, however virtuous these principles might be. Now this reluctance had an important effect that has been pointed out by Nicholas Boyle: "because Britain could treat the path of reform rather than revolution as it adapted to an industrialized economy, it took with it into the new age many of the medieval institutions that elsewhere perished as new nations were born."[11] In particular, medieval institutional and practical embodiments of Christian faith could persist in, rather than be expelled from, public life. Correspondingly, faith could continue to inform the understanding of public space as such.

9. Wickham, *Church and People*, 180.

10. Ibid., 88.

11. Boyle, "Understanding Thatcherism," 23.

In particular, the older Christian presumption of human liberty as a gift of creation could retain much of its vitality. The function of laws (which were few) was to set limits upon a public space rooted in endowed human liberty and informed with moral judgment: their function was not the more defining, comprehensive, "Enlightenment" one of explicating possibilities for action in a newly constructed public domain. Human liberty endowed by God was embodied, as earlier in Christendom, in complex participation in a variety of informal, mediating structures and associations.

The continuing vitality of this older Christian-informed vision of social participation in England may perhaps be discerned in the nineteenth-century movement to provide facilities and services that were designated "public." The provision of public amenities (public baths, public parks, public libraries, public schools, public roads, etc.) was at one level, of course, an attempt to provide the rising social classes with opportunity to share in liberties already enjoyed privately by the aristocracy. At a deeper level, however, they may reasonably be understood as attempts to embody new ways of exercising a morally informed liberty endowed ultimately by a Christian country within the hospitality of God.

The continuing formative power of Christian faith upon English public life also reflects the historical origins of Western democratic freedom itself. This freedom, far from deriving from the marginalization of religious authority, is deeply indebted to the principle of religious freedom hammered out in England in the seventeenth century. Michael Polanyi notes that whereas in continental Europe social progress was associated with anti-clericalism and Enlightenment, in Britain it was prompted on the whole more by religious sentiment and the influence of Puritanism. He writes: "It is true that tolerance was eventually achieved on the continent as the outcome of growing indifference to religion. But the English doctrine of tolerance was established in the 17th century by a kind of people who would abandon their homes for the wilderness overseas rather than agree that the communion table in the village church should be moved to the eastern window. Tolerance in England was a religious doctrine."[12]

In religious tolerance can also be found the main origins of modern British democracy; the insistence, writes Tawney in *Religion and the Rise of Capitalism*, "on the right of every church to organize itself, and on

12. Polanyi, "The English and the Continent."

the freedom of the Churches from the interference from the State, was to leave, alike in the Old World and in the New, an imperishable legacy of civil and religious liberty ... it is probable," he says, "that democracy owes more to Nonconformity than any other single movement."[13]

Britain's distinctive Christian-informed heritage is however under particular pressure today from secularist ideology. This due, to a considerable extent, to the recent impact upon Britain of other traditions of secularity that have appeared in the United States and in continental Europe, as follows.

BRITAIN'S CHANGING SECULARITY

The impact of secularism is felt to a new degree today for two reasons, as we have seen: first, the principles guiding its program of modernization/rationalization have become severed increasingly from the Christian roots that once nourished them, and become increasingly distorted; second, advances in technology (especially information and communications technology) have allowed more systematic penetration by ideological programs into the fabric of society.

Britain, like other nations, has felt this impact. However, in her case additional factors are at work heightening this impact. These factors arise from Britain's engagement with other paths of secularity than her own through her strengthening links with the United States and with continental Europe.

First, secularism presses upon Britain in her "public" and "private" life in a new way through her contemporary ties with United States culture. Thus the combative relations found in the U.S. between some Christians and a secularist elite—disputes associated with the negotiations of "managed secularity"—are becoming more familiar in the British mass media. Indeed strident U.S. religious fundamentalist spokespersons get drafted in by the media to provide live targets for vocal secularists such a Richard Dawkins and spokespersons for the Secularist Society. The rise of fundamentalist Islam has also, as we have noted, provided vocal secularists with a new stick publicly to beat religion in general. The prominence given today to religious and anti-religious polemicists is new in a country where dogmatic religious beliefs and dogmatic atheism have alike been largely alien.

13. Tawney, *Religion and the Rise of Capitalism*, 272.

A more serious influence upon the institutions of British society is U.S. neoliberal capitalist ideology (which has in recent decades intensified also in the U.S. itself), shaping British social policy and gradually revolutionizing her business practices. Such ideology has a more dominant position in the U.S. than in Britain, reflecting a greater readiness in the U.S. to implement without compromise dogmatic public strategies without regard to religious concerns that are relegated to the realm of private life and voluntary association. Britain feels the impact of this ideology today to a greater degree than continental Europe, through trade and investment links with the U.S. and through the global economic power of the U.S.

Neoliberal ideology has introduced to Britain a program of financial discipline by which central government has sought to bring all the agencies of society into line with what it wants. This program—begun in Britain by Margaret Thatcher while Prime Minister and followed up by New Labour—has clear links with U.S. politics, though it has roots further back in Enlightenment ideology and especially in eighteenth-century German political ideology. Nicholas Boyle has noted the impact of such ideology today upon Britain, that has until recent decades been relatively sheltered from its influence. Neoliberal ideology sponsors today a "sustained assault" on her heritage of mediating structures and their embodiment of liberty. This ideology, Boyle notes,

> has no theory of the public social world as a medium in which people exist and which shapes their lives: it has no theory of the constitution, or institutions, or of social, as distinct from economic behavior. The possibility of . . . wishing to work for the common good, rather than for individual reward, is no more (a neoliberal concept) than "public service," "public duty," or "public responsibility." It is the evacuation of terms such as these, rather than simply poor pay, which has brought about what is often called a "loss of morale" in professions such as teaching or nursing.[14]

Boyle concludes: "British society is thus at once polarized and homogenized. The great institutions that gave it depth and complexity fade away. Instead we have on the one hand the undifferentiated mass of individual 'consumers,' and on the other hand the legislative and executive power of central government organizing those same masses, but as workers,

14. Boyle, "Understanding Thatcherism," 20.

into employment and unemployment and enforcing its will, in the last analysis, by the power of the police."[15]

Second, secularism presses upon Britain's "public" and "private" life through her membership of the European Union. This membership puts Britain under new pressure from the vision of "utter secularity" (as Marty calls it) of continental Europe, notably through European Union Rights legislation and its anti-discriminatory directives today.

The impact of "utter secularity" is heightened by its unfamiliarity in Britain, in an ironic way. Continental Europe, for its part, has lived with this vision in a way that mitigates its implications as follows. Since in practice no state authority could ever fulfill the vision of utter secularity and explicate adequately what may properly be done in civil society among a given population, in many respects life in such societies "goes on as usual." State legislation is interpreted popularly so as to accommodate this: in modern Latin countries at least, legislation tends not be taken "literally," but is interpreted as a tool of the state for influencing public life. Law carries no moral force beyond the will of the secular state; it is not an attempt seriously to declare what is right and wrong.

Britain, by contrast, has a Christian-informed tradition in which laws—relatively few in number—protect an endowed liberty and have corresponding moral status. The clash of traditions that now ensues through Britain's membership of the E.U. is responsible for the dramatic impact on Britain of continental secularism. For when the British are subject to E.U. directives, they tend to take these with a seriousness not found in continental Europe itself. As a result, the implementation of E.U. directives in Britain is often all the more destructive towards her rich heritage of informal mediating social structures and their practices informed tacitly by a Christian worldview.

This is, of course, a very simplified sketch of the pressure of secularism upon Britain herself. In reality, secularism is intensifying not only in Britain but also in the U.S. and in continental Europe themselves. Again, while neoliberal ideology hold a particularly dominant place in U.S. society, its effects are also felt increasingly in continental Europe; and conversely, while the ideology of subjective rights is particularly favored in the E.U., it is also influential in the U.S. Meanwhile the "controlled secularity" of the U.S. is accompanied in practice, on the one hand, by religious influence upon her public sphere and, on the other, by the in-

15. Ibid., 21.

fluence of public ideology upon her religious belief; and the "utter secularity" of continental Europe continues to be mitigated (as we have seen)
by the pursuit of traditional ways of life regardless of state legislation.

DESECULARIZATION AND THE VISION
OF MULTIFAITH SOCIETY

It may be protested that this account of contemporary trends in secularity ignores a significant development in Western societies: in recent
decades there has been a resurgence in religion as a social and political
force. This development is so evident that it has prompted sociologists in
general to abandon their classical "secularization thesis" that in modern
societies religion will eventually wither away and die.

This development is part of a wider global phenomenon. Within
Western societies themselves it has come about partly through the
policies of global capitalism that have introduced to Western secular
societies new populations of religiously committed people. Open im-
migration policies to secure labor where this is in short supply have
brought to Britain, for example, an influx of people traditionally
Muslim, Hindu, or Buddhist in religion. The political management of
this new population has given rise, especially in Britain, to the vision
of a "multicultural" and "multifaith" society. The extent to which this
has recently influenced policy decisions by local politicians has been
documented by Jenny Taylor.[16]

In *The Desecularization of the World*, sociologist Peter Berger
has considered possible reasons for the global resurgence in religion.
One possible explanation, he suggests, is that where modernity under-
mines the taken-for-granted certainties by which people live, religious
movements claiming to give such certainty have great appeal. Another
explanation is that secularist thinking is located primarily among the
elite who "control the institutions that provide the 'official' definitions
of reality" (the mass media, education, the legal system) and that these
are resented by many people for undermining and attacking their own
beliefs and values. These people accordingly find appeal in "anti-secular"
religious movements. However, Berger concludes by remarking that in
one sense desecularization needs no explaining: it simply demonstrates
"continuity in the place of religion in human experience."[17]

16. Taylor, *After Secularism*.
17. Berger, *The Desecularization of the World*, 11–12.

How does Berger's account appear in the light of the analysis in this book? The answer depends, first, upon whether there is indeed a resurgence of attention to religion in the core Christian sense of that which sponsors a deeper and more lively personal enquiry into the real world than does secular thinking. If this is the case, then we are bound to remark that Berger's account largely fails to address this resurgence for what it is. No doubt he recognizes that Christian faith is not going to wither away and die. But he hardly acknowledges the possibility that a resurgent Christian faith might represent a *deeper exploration of questions* than secularism, and offer a *more adequate account of public reality* than that offered by a secularist elite. Regrettably he seems only to perceive a desecularization of a kind such that the leaders of secular society will have to learn to *manage* Christian religion and other religions because they refuse to go away; he does not see (or perhaps even conceive of) a desecularization in which secular leaders might be called to converse with, and listen to, and learn from, religion.

He may well be right, of course, in perceiving only this indifferent kind of "desecularization" today. There may be no resurgence today in radical enquiry of the sort sponsored by Christian religion. There may be a resurgence only of what may be called human religion, of a sort at best ambiguously related to responsiveness to God.

Let me characterize briefly this ambiguity. It may be approached in two ways from the fact that Christian faith sponsors a radical desacralization of the world. If, on the one hand, "religion" is taken to denote one sacral worldview or another, Christian faith is tangential to the genre of religion; it does not belong univocally to it. Accordingly, state provisions that may be appropriate for managing "religions" may not be appropriate in the case of Christianity. Indeed it may be important that the state defer to the role of Christianity in exposing tacitly "sacral" tendencies within the state itself. If, on the other hand, Christianity is taken as *defining* "religion" (and often it is implicitly taken to do so when interpreting the belief and practices of other religions, for example, when calling them "faiths"), then other religions stand in ambiguous relation to "religion." The vocation of Christians may now be understood as that of hosting conversation in which other religions explore their religious meaning through transforming engagement with the gospel and in conversation with Christians regarding the Western "way of life" and its history of engagement with Christian faith.

This portrayal of Christian faith vis-à-vis "religion" may well be rejected by those who manage public life, who may continue to insist that Christianity is but one among many religions. In reply, however, Christians may argue that "religion" as conceived here is not a coherent genre but is generated by the secularist illusion of religion as a phenomenon belonging to a sphere of private belief or choice. Seen from this viewpoint, of course, the prospect of an unending multiplicity of religions raises no contradictions. This viewpoint would find contradictory, however, multiple religious allegiances by a given individual, since each religion is taken to be its own final authority; and also find contradictory the possibility that one religion might transcend another or that conversion between religions is genuinely reasonable. However, this viewpoint finds no contradictions presented to public reason itself by religion— provided that religion stays in its private place and does not try to affect public life or its principles.

Secularists view this way of managing religion as securing maximum freedom of enquiry and liberty among a population. However, as we have seen, it is *secularists* who make an unquestioned assumption— the assumption that they sponsor reasonable enquiry and liberty more adequately than does Christian faith. In truth, however, it is Christian faith that more truly sponsors enquiry and liberty. Secularism tends rather towards illiberalism, on the one hand, and nihilistic relativism, on the other.

Similarly secularists of a more "postmodern" variety would view this way of managing religion as best allowing people to preserve their subjective values and identity expressed through religion. However, such secularism simply *assumes* an idea of personal identity that ultimately consigns personal life to the realm of narcissism. By contrast, much in this book has argued that it is not secularism but Christian faith that sponsors openness to our deepest personal identity, in relationship with God and with others.

What now becomes of the secularist perception that the differences between people of differing religious allegiance are greater than those between people of the same religion, since the former have differing ultimate commitments or presuppositions among themselves? It is dispelled. If the reality is that Christian faith sponsors radical enquiry, then we have reason to expect that this will give rise within the body of Christians to the richest expressions of diversity—as well as the richest expressions of agreement and unity. And indeed in the local church at its best we find gathered together in common worship and service people of diverse backgrounds and cultures, class and education, age and experience, temperament and interests, such as can hardly be found elsewhere in Western society today. We also have reason to expect here the most pressing issues of discernment to arise, between responsiveness to the demands of radical enquiry (which after all constitutes the vocation of the body of Christians) and evasion of these demands. The demands of receptivity and responsibility towards the truth, and the demands of tolerance and of integrity, among a country's citizens are most richly acknowledged and addressed when they are encountered in the light of the gospel.

THE CHURCH AS PUBLIC HOST

As the vision of secular society is severed increasingly from its roots in a Christian worldview and the tacit influence of Christian imagination upon it fades, the public and private worlds sponsored by this vision are alike impoverished and distorted

The public world tends to become understood as a private domain, the property of those who give statutory authorization for its use; those who use it are "members of the public" only by license; fundamentally they are aliens in a domain not their own. As public regimes of this sort penetrate more deeply into "primary" culture, they tend towards totalitarianism. This is the tendency of secularist programs of social rationalization including those generated by the ideologies of neoliberalism and of subjective rights explored in chapters 8 and 9, for all that they blandish the rhetoric of liberation.

The private world tends meanwhile to become understood as a space private to the individual conceived in abstraction from relationship to community, God, and world. In this space there are only subjective choices, beliefs, and values; there are no matters of truth and goodness inviting attention and regard. Here in what Richard Sennett has characterized as "the fall of public man," there is only a life of personal disorientation marked by narcissism, escapism, and a consumerist search for lost identity, purpose, and belonging (chapters 5 and 6).

Faced with these distortions of public and private, Christians are called to do more than defend a private niche of their own in society. They are called to host richer, more lively expressions of public life and public service than those hosted by the secular state, rooted in the vision of public worship of God in his sovereignty. They are called to host private life open to the demands of relationship to God and other people, rooted in the vision of persons deeply loved and upheld by God.

Here the vocation of hospitality is key. At the beginning of this book I noted some Christian authors who have drawn attention to this theme. Fundamentally, the domains of public and private life are hosted by God their creator, who hosts both lively enquiry and knowledge of trustworthy truth, personal liberation and dedicated service. And the church is called to be a steward of God's hospitality. It is called to promote a vision of public and private life that enhances the opportunity for people to enjoy the liberating hospitality of God their creator, and itself to model such hospitality.

To contextualize this discussion in my own context: the vocation of challenging distorted visions of public and private life lies before the church in Britain today. The church is faced with, and indeed participates in, the traditional British lack of enthusiasm for applying dogmatic frameworks to grand matters of religion and society. Yet she cannot responsibly ignore the grand ideologies of neoliberalism and of subjective rights that are in process of revolutionizing British society today with their powerful programs of social rationalization. The church is called inescapably to explicate faithfully the practical, tacit wisdom of Christian faith—which is her own and which itself imbues these ideologies with such truth as they have—while embedding them faithfully within God's fundamental purposes for humankind.

Such engagement with contemporary ideologies and with the vision of consumerism requires both a firm grasp of the essential role of tacit knowing and persistence in identifying and challenging ideological presuppositions. It is an engagement to which Michael Polanyi's work, inexcusably neglected, has much yet to provide. At root it demands theological attentiveness towards the themes of this book: fundamentally, a more faithful account of the sovereign approach of God who comes to us as our ultimate context enlivening our most radical personal enquiry.

In conclusion, then: Christians are called by God today to live converted to the sovereignty of God as a matter of public enquiry, truth, and obedience. They are called to witness to this sovereignty and to seek the conversion of others to this by manifesting it in their own Christian public hospitality, in the vision they bring with their contribution to public life, and their public reasoning in defence of faith. They are called also to acknowledge, and repent of, their own complicity with the Western cultural assumption of a fundamental dichotomy between "public" and "private," and between "facts" and "values," and the assignation of Christian faith to the latter.

To be converted to the sovereignty of God is to discover, and to commend, unqualified liberation for humankind through participation in God's good purposes for all.

CONCLUSION

Concluding Remarks on the Mission Agenda

THIS BOOK HAS BEEN about the gospel through which God opens our eyes to his approach in liberating sovereignty. God, our creator and redeemer, is sovereign over us as persons, sovereign over our whole life, sovereign over our whole world. It is the vocation of the church to bear witness to this. However, in modern Western culture this vocation has been widely betrayed. The churches today, in their understanding of the gospel, are not uncommonly domesticated to modern cultural assumptions and personal attachments that evacuate the gospel of its liberating power over the whole of human life. In particular, too often the churches have accepted the modern relegation of Christian faith to the realm of subjective beliefs and values.

This is a betrayal. By its nature, the gospel engages all the cultural assumptions and personal attachments that form the context of our lives, breaking them open to bring us knowledge of God, now embraced as our deepest context. As God thus brings us to know him, we indwell him in the most lively, self-giving, personal way, and see with new eyes, in God's light, the (largely unrecognized) assumptions and commitments by which we live. This was the subject of Part One of this book.

In Part Two of this book, I held up to the light of faith ten assumptions widely prevalent in modern culture. I have proposed that the gospel calls us to conversion with regard to each of them. The gospel transforms each of them, giving them new, defining meaning by reference to itself. In so doing it reveals itself and liberates us from captivity to these limiting and distorting assumptions. It does so as it confronts our habitual assumptions and commitments—often in a paradoxical way—reorienting us by reference to new bearings disclosed in their new, paradigmatic gospel meaning.

342

Many of the insights I have incorporated into this account of Western culture in the context of the gospel are not new but have been drawn from authors stretching from the present back through the twentieth century and beyond. However, they have not been taken up with due recognition by the churches in all aspects of their life. This is, it seems to me, a matter inviting serious concern and reflection. It makes the question urgent: how might neglect of these insights and their practical implications be overcome? How might their recognition and application give new direction and impetus to Christian mission today?

I do not see any one single locus where this might begin, nor any one single obvious Christian institution or body or leadership with whom it might begin. "Begin" is too strong a word in some cases: there are settings where there is insight and where it is being applied and I shall mention below a few of these with which I happen to be familiar. I am sure there are many more. It is vital that Christians recognize where such leads are to be found and that vision and practical guidance be drawn from them.

In many other settings within the churches, however, the necessary vision remains lacking. Without such vision no new or reformed bodies or strategies will succeed in equipping the church for more faithful witness in and to Western culture.

One significant factor in the failure of the churches to recognize and act upon the insights I have passed on in this book is as follows: these insights invite response from a wide, indeed imponderable, range of readers. They extend to formally trained church leaders; those who train them and resource their continuing ministry; lay Christians working in the secular professions; Christian organizations that aspire to equip lay Christians to fulfill their professional work in a Christian way; academic theologians and missiologists; and those who offer Christian hospitality of one kind and another to Christians and to the public in general. Positively, this invites the diffusion of the insights in this book widely through the culture of the church in all its facets and beyond. However, this very fact can mean that no one in particular may see it as their brief to take an initiative in these matters. The difficulty is compounded where there is a poverty of networking, cross-fertilization, and joined-up thinking between the different constituencies within the church necessary for such diffusion and application.

What practical conclusions, then, are to be drawn from this book? Let me offer some suggestions of my own, for what they are worth. I do so with the caveat that my own involvement in church strategic planning has been very limited and that I have never held any academic post in theology or missiology or pursued systematic study of a particular field within academic theology. My involvement in church planning has been primarily restricted to my six-and-a-half year ministry in New Zealand in the 1990s as an Anglican tertiary education chaplain and minister of an Anglican/Methodist/Presbyterian cooperative venture. My theological reading and writing has been throughout a matter of reflective practice during parish ministry in England, while completing an MLitt in Theology and writing a wider text for publication, while ministering in New Zealand, and while working as coordinator of The Gospel and Our Culture Network in Great Britain these past twelve years.

E. R. WICKHAM RECALLED

Let me begin by returning to insights offered half a century ago by E. R. Wickham in his book *Church and People in an Industrial City*, which I believe still deserve quoting at length. Having envisaged the church in the situation where it is "acutely conscious of belonging to the world, subject to the conditions of the world, yet a catalyst within the world which is its only sphere of obedience"—that is, the situation I have characterized in this book as that of a church bearing an essentially transcendent, inculturated gospel—Wickham writes:

> No doubt this is a concept that gains the assent of many intelligent Christians, suggesting as it does the role of the laity dispersed into the world, the secular obedience of a Christian man, the notion of the "Christian frontier" ... Yet in fact these ideas are not widely actualised in the life of the church. Where they are brought to birth, the premature death rate is high, and the few that remain are exceptional prodigies.
>
> The reasons are several—the catalytic action of the church through a dispersed laity presupposes an understanding of the secular implications of the Christian faith and a clear understanding of the role of the church in the world that are both comparatively rare. And the structure of the church is inimical to the required clarity of understanding—there is no organizational expression of the church deployed into the secular "frontier" positions; and the idea is completely secondary, if it has any place at

all, to the highly exclusive understanding of the church as the visible congregation of faithful men, in which the pure word of God is preached, and the sacraments be duly administered—a concept adequate enough in a conformist society, but wholly inadequate in the missionary situation.[1]

Later, having identified concerns to be addressed by the church, Wickham writes:

All of this is to insist that there is a huge intellectual task requiring the best minds of the church and indeed of many who may be outside it: the co-operation of theologians who understand the secular problems, laymen with their appropriate expert and technical knowledge who live with the problems, "lay theologians," men of wisdom and good counsel who know the social temperature and have a finger on the social pulse. A church seeking to help her own members, let alone a church seeking engagement and dialogue with the world, would require more effective machinery for thinking, good minds corporately focused on the hardest issues of our time, some planned use of brains at the service of the Christian mission in the contemporary world. Tawney's devastating word that the church has ceased to count because it has ceased to think is not without point. Its implications would be even more urgent if the church were more closely geared into this problem-beset world.[2]

The need for such theological thinking in service to Christian mission is more pressing than ever today. It remains vital, of course, to recognize the challenge of mission in the first place and to respond to this in an organized way (as Wickham himself urges), but more is needed than this. In particular, the insights in this book highlight two tasks that have become more prominent since Wickham wrote. The first task is that mission be integrally related to theological engagement with, and critique of, those Western secular ideologies that have today come to the fore providing answers (or rationalizations and legitimations for answers which have won political and public allegiance) in "this problem-beset world." Such ideological engagement has been pursued particularly in chapters 4, 7, 8, and 9 of this book. The second task is that mission be integrally related to personal, spiritual formation. This second theme has been pursued particularly in chapters 3, 5, and 6.

1. Wickham, *Church and People*, 230–31.
2. Ibid., 261.

Unless the integral relation is maintained between mission, theological reflection upon the world, and personal and spiritual formation, those Christians who are most intentional about mission tend today to take a lead—quite unreliably—from managerial, marketing, consumerist ideology and its strategies. Meanwhile theology and spirituality, for their part, tend to drift from their proper relation to mission and to each other. The need for their reconnection has been urged by Rowan Williams as follows: "to say, then, that mission is not intelligible apart from some grasp of what holiness is—the radically other-directed life of God lived in finite and vulnerable subjects—means that we do indeed have to turn to reflecting on 'spirituality' in theologising about mission . . . If mission can't be understood apart from holiness, the search for holiness and the disciplines of the spirit can themselves only make sense in the context of mission—God's mission, God's sharing of the communion that is the divine life."[3]

The integral relation between mission and theological engagement with secular ideologies, on the one hand, and with spiritual formation, on the other, is described as follows by Carver T. Yu. Of the former relation he writes, "If the Christian faith is to have a vital impact on culture, then the proclamation of faith needs a sharp cutting edge in its confrontation with hostile ideologies of the world. Theological reflection and research is the labour for the sharpening of that cutting edge. It is unfortunate that theologians are often perceived to be working in the ivory tower, far away from the frontier. As a matter of fact, theologians are in the forefront of the frontier of ideological conflicts. Many church leaders and laymen see the significance of serious theological research, and they champion for the strongest support of it."[4] Of the latter relation he writes:

> The cultivation of inwardness, the restoration of personhood, the renewal of the sense of community and thus the sense of responsibility to others, and the reclaiming of the objective realm of reality, is what our world needs most desperately. The world does not need counselling to soothe its restless soul, nor creative ideas for fixing socio-economic problems, nor strategies to cope with their hectic life. The world needs the message of truth and life. The problem for man in the present age is ontological and spiritual.

3. Williams, "Doing the Works of God," 265.
4. Yu, "Sabbath with a Mission."

The world needs genuine spiritual leaders setting life examples before them. The world needs a life-sustaining community.

The temptation of relevance is hard to resist. However, to be truly relevant, theological educators should not be afraid to stand against the stream. Instead of swirling around with the world, we have to stick covetously to the basic. The world needs the unadulterated message of the Word, and thus we have to train future leaders to be faithful interpreters of the Word. The world needs spiritual-emotional sustenance in its struggle with the loss of inwardness. We have to train leaders with strong inner-directedness and deep spiritual resources that the world can draw from.[5]

Yu's reference to the need for "life-sustaining community" reminds us that a society polarized into an ideologically framed public life and the private life of individuals is a false one. For Christians there is an integral relation between thinking (through the renewal of minds in theological formation) and spirituality (through the renewal of hearts in personal formation), and they are embedded together in community. Correspondingly, the restoration of this integral relation—a restoration of the older Christian tradition of pursuing what Ellen Charry calls "sapiental" truth—requires the nurture of community in the face of its modern erosion (chapter 2) and of individuals formed for participation in it (chapter 5).

With these considerations in mind, let me identify some areas for strategic action. In passing I shall quote from various writers who have identified these areas as such.

THEOLOGICAL FORMATION

It is vital that theological vision inform the work of mission. But it is essential that the theology in question be visionary. Vinoth Ramachandra points to the kind of theology needed:

> In our technology- and market-driven environment, the real theological challenges are being faced by our children and by Christians who are at the cutting edge of scientific and medical research, or who are engaging with new artistic media thrown up by the communications revolution, or who are caught up in the complex arenas of economic modelling and social policy, are asking questions of a profound theological character that

5. Yu, "Teaching the Faith," 3–4. For brief popular proposals regarding the agenda for spiritual formation in the decades ahead, see Foster, "Spiritual Formation Agenda."

professional theologians need to address. It is they who should
be setting the agenda for our theological schools. Is it too late
to envision a theological fraternity in every nation, indeed every
city, that encompasses such folk and their work? If the church
is to be true to its calling, theology needs to be taken out of our
seminary classrooms, even our church buildings, and into the
boardrooms, urban council meetings, research laboratories and
national newspapers.[6]

Lesslie Newbigin insists that such strategic theological thinking
must inform ministerial as well as lay training. He calls for

a Christian community equipped for vigorous controversy . . . the
development of a spirituality for combat, training for skill and
courage in the use of those spiritual weapons which alone are
appropriate for Christian warfare . . . I have spoken of the need
for a lay theology, but it is equally important to develop a type of
spiritual and intellectual formation for priests and pastors and
bishops which will enable them in turn to equip the members of
the body of Christ in each place for this spiritual warfare. I do not
think that this is now a feature of most ministerial formation.[7]

Often in practice the provision of such theological training rests upon
the commitment of, and availability of material support for, a visionary
and gifted leader who is able to bring together a team of collabora-
tors who can work faithfully and creatively together. Significant also,
however, are the spiritual and theological resources that inspire and
guide the vision of Christians in such work. Some of these resources
are associated in a special way with individual luminaries, including
the twentieth-century prophets I have mentioned in this book, such
as C. S. Lewis, G. K. Chesterton, P. T. Forsyth, Henri de Lubac, Gabriel
Marcel, Dorothy Sayers, J. H. Oldham, Harry Blamires, and Lesslie
Newbigin. More recently, there have also arisen valuable opportunities
to listen attentively to non-Western Christians and their critique of the
West: people such as Carver T. Yu (China) and Vinoth Ramachandra
(Sri Lanka), quoted above.

Theological resources for engaging secular culture and ideology are
found in many traditions of Christian scholarship. These resources have

6. Ramachandra, "Learning from Modern European Secularism," 47.

7. Newbigin, "Can a Modern Society Be Christian?" 6. On Newbigin's acclamation
of the mission vocation of lay Christians, see Goheen, "Missional Calling of Believers."

informed the thinking of some luminaries mentioned in this book and some of the organizational initiatives I refer to below. They include:

1. The Neo-Calvinist Tradition

The neo-Calvinist "worldview" tradition is associated with Abraham Kuyper and those who have taken a lead from him, especially Herman Dooyeweerd. In recent decades "worldview" perspectives have nourished the work of influential figures such as Elaine and Alan Storkey and authors such as James Sire (*The Universe Next Door*, 2004) and Brian J. Walsh and J. Richard Middleton (*The Transforming Vision: Shaping a Christian World View*, 1984), and organizations such as the Christian Academic Network, the Institute for Christian Studies in Toronto, Canada, and the West Yorkshire School of Christian Studies in England. This tradition has shown the potential to lead Christians into fuller consideration of the comprehensive, coherent implications of a Christian understanding of creation in all its aspects relative to alternative worldviews. It has been especially influential among evangelical Christian groups around the world. In recent years, two books co-authored by Craig Bartholomew and Michael W. Goheen have introduced a "worldview" approach to a potentially wider readership: *The Drama of Scripture: Finding Our Place in the Biblical Story* (2006) and *Living at the Crossroads: An Introduction to Christian Worldview* (2008). No doubt sometimes this tradition has shown a tendency towards a rationalist understanding of Christian faith, indicating the potential fruitfulness of further dialogue with authors who highlight the transcendent freedom of God, such as Jacques Ellul, Henri de Lubac, and authors in the Pentecostal tradition. Also, more reflection is needed on the uniqueness of Christian faith. Depending how the term "worldview" is to be used, this uniqueness extends to placing Christian faith in special, paradoxical relation to the genre of "worldviews" in general, or makes it the ultimate paradigm for "worldview" as such. David Naugle's book *Worldview: The History of a Concept*, useful as it is, fails to address this fundamental issue.

2. The Anabaptist Tradition

The Anabaptist tradition has a long history of emphasis upon Christian distinctives, calling the church to maintain these over against wider society in a way that the mainstream churches of Christendom are seen as failing to do. Although this can involve such things as an over-negative reading of Christendom, a somewhat sectarian (and ironically more modern than Christian) self-understanding of the church, and a reduction of Christian faith towards conformity in moral practices and principles, its call for allegiance to Christian distinctives and to membership of a gathered Christian community based on these is an important message for the churches today. Noteworthy, among others, in this tradition have been Wilbert Shenk, John Howard Yoder (whose critique of Richard Neibuhr's influential *Christ and Culture*—or rather, of how it has been understood—warrants attention), Paul Fiddes, Alan Kreider, Alan Roxburgh, Douglas John Hall, and Stuart Murray Williams.

3. The Ressourcement Tradition

The *ressourcement* tradition in Roman Catholicism has its origins in mid-twentieth century reflection by theologians including Hans Urs von Balthasar, Henri de Lubac, Louis Bouyer, Jean Danielou, and Yves Congar, with earlier figures such as Henry Newman and Charles Peguy in the background. Faced with cultural crises and something of a fortress mentality in the Roman Catholic church itself, *ressourcement* thinkers saw that the church was called to engage with the modern secular world but that to do so faithfully required a "return to the sources" of Christian faith in matters both of spiritual formation and theology. Their influence was considerable upon the documents of the Second Vatican Council, and upon the thinking of Pope John Paul II, Pope Benedict XVI, and David Schindler.

4. The Anglican Tradition

The Anglican tradition locates theology in worship of God, understood as the offering of the whole of life to the glory of God.[8] This insight holds theology in integral relation to practical attentiveness to the eschatological mystery of God—while seeking a rich rationality for faith. This has the potential to interact creatively with the first two traditions mentioned above, especially if Anglicans will learn from them to rise above a certain English reluctance to think about and articulate matters

---

8. This comprehensive understanding of worship is expressed in Anglican hymns such as "Teach me, my God and King" (Herbert), "Fill Thou my life" (Bonar), "Forth in thy name" (Wesley), "Take my life" (Havergal), and "Awake, my soul" (Ken).

of Christian doctrine. Of special note here are two recent examples of attention to worship by scholars in the Baptist and neo-Calvinist traditions. The first is a book by Elizabeth Newman, who lectures at the Baptist Theological Seminary in Richmond, Canada. In her *Untamed Hospitality: Welcoming God and Other Strangers* (2007), she reflects upon the "strange hospitality" of God offered in worship. By reference to this, she examines the distorted hospitality offered by the contemporary projects of science and economics, the culture of choice, and politics. She also notes that the hospitality of worship itself can distort into mere niceness and sentiment, mere consumer satisfaction of needs, or mere inclusivity. Accordingly the vocation of offering God's own hospitality— both public and ecclesial—requires vigilance.

The second book comes from the neo-Calvinist tradition: James K. A. Smith, *Desiring the Kingdom: Worship, Worldview and Cultural Formation* (2009). This is the first, key volume in a planned trilogy that seeks to offer a vision of authentic, integral Christian learning in its relation to worship. The author points behind "worldviews" to the formation of hearts and their desires and to the indwelling of a "social imaginary" (Charles Taylor's expression) that is embedded in the practice of Christian worship. In these terms the author compares Christian and secular "liturgies." His shift in focus from "worldview" to a tacit "social imaginary" resonates to some measure with the insights of Michael Polanyi, although—unlike Elizabeth Newman—he does not draw from Polanyi's work. However, his understanding of worship stands in need still—in the manner characteristic of much neo-Calvinist theology—of further development in dialogue with those who emphasize the transcendent freedom of God.

To mention these diverse traditions of scholarship is to be reminded that formal church bodies tend to draw exclusively upon their own confessional or denominational traditions of scholarship. This is a limitation today when the task of Christian witness to Western culture needs fresh theological reflection, and when diverse Christian traditions of scholarship have much to teach to, and learn from, each other. Whether this problem suggests the formation of new bodies with formal ecumenical status and funding, or a greater openness within each denomination to wider ecumenical resources, or voluntary Christian associations independent of any formal status among the churches, I cannot say.

SPIRITUAL FORMATION: AN ENHANCED VISION
OF CHRISTIAN HOSPITALITY

1. Hospitality among Christians

Residential Christian communities, and residential and other special events, can provide hospitality in which people experience a daily pattern of life that is framed explicitly, and nourished implicitly, by Christian faith through participation in worship, study, and common activity. The underlying vision here is to be stewards of the hospitality of God himself.

For a significant minority of Christians today, such hospitality is experienced through association with a religious order involving, for example, a rule of life and participation in organized events. In recent years there has been a widening interest in this. From the United States, John Michael Talbot reports, "People who express the spirit of monastic orders while living in the world are multiplying like loaves and fishes . . . I am reminded of Saint Bonaventure's prophecy in the fourteenth century of a contemplative church of the future . . . Most monastic communities are finding that growth among associates is matching the numbers of the celibate monastic community by ten or twenty to one."[9]

Theological reflection of the sort that engages with our culture relies upon the wisdom and discernment that come with spiritual formation. These are fostered by "retreat" hospitality at its best. As Gabriel Marcel writes, the refusal to believe today takes the form commonly of inattention or distraction—something that he believes is encouraged, indeed almost enforced, by modern life. He continues: "the inattentive man may be awakened just by meeting someone who radiates genuine faith—which, like a light, transfigures the creature in whom it dwells. I am," he writes, "one of those who attach an inestimable value to personal encounters. They are a spiritual fact of the highest importance, though unrecognised by traditional philosophy."[10] Immersion in Christian "retreat" hospitality is an important way in which Christians can learn to give God space, time, and opportunity to shed light upon the whole of our lives and open the eyes of others to the light of God.

Well established examples of Christian hospitality are offered by places of pilgrimage such as Taize and Iona; the *Cursillo* movement;

9. Talbot, *World Is My Cloister*, 11–12.
10. Marcel, "Some Thoughts on Faith," 212.

large Christian festivals such as the British Greenbelt, Spring Harvest, Soul Survivor, and the New Zealand Parachute festival; and the rather different German Kirchentag (in which participants are given accommodation by local Christians).

Lay association with religious communities and their traditions may be either with a monastic order or with communities such as the Iona Community. However, there may be no residential community of affiliation involved; a significant ecumenical example of this in Britain is the Lay Community of Saint Benedict, since its links were untied with the Benedictine monastery at Worth Abbey.[11]

Britain also has a rich heritage of retreat centers. While these are first and foremost places where people find personal and spiritual formation and enrichment, there is, I think, the potential to combine this with prayerful theological reflection upon the opportunities and demands of living and thinking Christianly in contemporary Western culture, as explored in this book.

How explicit does such engagement need to be with Western culture and with the features of it addressed in this book? Some traditional Christian voices would suggest that if we attend in a deep spiritual way to God, discernment will generally follow, with little effort, regarding the mundane concerns of life.[12] Contrast our close attention today to our personal appearance, health, and nutrition. However, we need to remember that mundane life involved relatively few choices for them compared to those largely manufactured for us today and which we are urged to preoccupy ourselves. We are increasingly "gardened" as consumers *en masse* by those seeking intrusively to direct our personal choices, and these choices may be bad, such as eating a diet dominated by "junk" food. This situation calls sometimes for countercultural stances that

11. Austin Milner, OP, having made his acquaintance with LCSB in 2010, wrote: "It is very difficult to survive in the present secular atmosphere without the support of a community and the parishes seldom provide such a community. But this you seem to have and even the children benefit because they have made many friends of their own age who believe. In this way they have some protection from the onslaught of the secular world in their schools and from the media." Milner, "Reflections," 20.

12. Thus the anonymous author of the medieval *Cloud of Unknowing*: "If I am able to give a vital and wholehearted attention to this spiritual activity in my soul, I can then view my eating and drinking, my sleep and conversation and so on with comparative indifference. I would rather acquire a right discretion in these matters by such indifference, than by giving them my close attention, and weighing carefully all their pros and cons" (ibid., 102).

speak with prophetic power—and raise the question of conversion. In my own experience, I have found that decisions made by my wife and me to raise our four children without a television at home and to own no more than one car scandalized some in our community. It challenged their own choices in a way that made them uncomfortable, tempting them to be dismissive of us and our powers of reason![13]

Also, the saturation of Western culture by mass-communicated cultural artifacts (music, film, literature, and internet materials) asks for deliberate, strategic, Christian engagement with popular culture. This especially shapes the imaginative world of many younger people. Christian reading groups are an example of such strategic engagement; music and film invite other approaches. Such engagement may involve much appreciation of culture. At other times, there is need to identify and critique stereotypical modern myths about God, the nature of faith, Christian history, and the purpose of human life, which are rehearsed endlessly in film and literature.[14]

2. Christian Public Hospitality

Christians are also called to offer public hospitality. This is the calling to offer public space that enacts and embodies God's own hospitality to all: public space that is open to all and is rooted in, and nourished by, God. For example, God's people are called to host events and provide settings that intimate hope, belonging, and freedom in a culture where hopelessness, alienation, and captivity of spirit are prevalent. Such hospitality

13. Although the shaping power of mass culture upon human life today can seem insurmountable, it can show itself surprisingly brittle. It does, after all, rely upon mass messages constantly reinforced, and if these are halted, other possibilities open up. Retreats can serve precisely this function. See also Maushart, *The Winter of Our Disconnect,* in which the author describes the unexpectedly fruitful results of an experiment in disconnecting her "wired up" teenage family for six months.

14. See, for example, Sampson, *Six Modern Myths.* Engagement with contemporary popular culture is too often limited to celebrating parallels between its storyline and the Christian message, but without proper discrimination. Thus, too often a storyline of neo-pagan self-deification with its "power of positive thinking" is falsely equated with "faith." For an example of good, discriminating engagement with popular culture, see May, *Stardust and Ashes.* Stephen May also writes with discernment of historic cultural transformation following the arrival of Christianity—another story too often subsumed indiscriminately under Hollywood stereotypes or ideological narratives of oppression. For a brief example see May, "Beowulf." On the cultural dominance of narratives of oppression, see Finkielkraut, *Undoing of Thought,* and Girard, *Satan.*

speaks of Christian hope and belonging with special eloquence when it is extended to those who are "homeless" in one way or another: those who need nursing care, the dying, the unborn child, the child unsafe at home, the refugee, and the scapegoat.

Such public hospitality finds expression in many forms of Christian service. Prominent among these historically are Christian schools and hospitals (the fortunes of these in Western secular society today are a reminder of the need for vision and vigilance if these are faithfully to fulfill their vocation of witness). The L'Arche communities founded by Jean Vanier are a fine example of Christian hospitality today.

Gatherings for worship are an obvious occasion of explicit Christian hospitality, including baptisms, weddings, and funerals. There is room for much creative, discerning development of these today beyond their traditional forms and some of this is already happening. The churches also have a vocation today, I believe, to offer new occasions of ritual where groups of Christians may gather to mark significant "life events" for a person such as moving into a new home, retiring, starting a new job, falling ill and recovering health, and suffering victimhood or loss. The provision of such occasions calls, of course, for spiritual wisdom and creativity if they are to be personally meaningful and not be mere formalities.[15]

"Softer" examples (no less important for this) of Christian hospitality range from those with explicit Christian sponsorship that make no explicit reference to Christian faith in the service they offer, to those that make no explicit claim to Christian sponsorship but which are nourished by the Christian-informed vision of their pioneers. They include such things as the public events held by Christian surfers in New Zealand, that witness to the hospitality of God in their own way simply by providing well-organized occasions marked by an ethos of goodwill and service. The same "soft" witness is offered by many enterprises, both profit- and non-profit making, that consistently display and defer to the Christian virtues and values of service and integrity rather than deferring ultimately to the maximization of profit or other private vested interests. "Soft" examples of Christian public hospitality include the publication of "freebie" magazines, etc. informed by Christian values. Again, two examples from New Zealand come to mind: the *Clipboard*

---

15. Some interesting examples of such "creative liturgy" can be found in Ward and Wild, *Human Rites*.

leaflet, distributed by Dick Hubbard in the cereal packets of his compa-
ny, and the *Grapevine* magazine (founded and edited since 1981 by John
Cooney, of Auckland). Rather different are imaginative, one-off acts of
generous public hospitality by Christians (no strings attached), which
can surprise recipients and speak to them with prophetic power of a gracious God. Again, to provide opportunity for reflection and prayer in a
church building kept open to the public for this purpose can embody the
hospitality of God. Another area of "soft" witness, lamentably neglected
in my view, is the retail of greetings cards informed by Christian values,
and—in the case of cards for occasions such as personal bereavement,
Christmas (over and above the "charity card" scene), and Easter—cards
that make explicit reference to the Christian faith and hope.

INSTITUTIONAL-BASED FORMATION AND CONTINUED
RESOURCING FOR MINISTRY

1. Licensed Ministry

I suggest that the theological training and personal formation provided
for licensed ministry should be integrally informed by the insights shared
in this book. This applies, for example, to the study of the Bible, doctrine,
spirituality, and church history. I suggest the same with regard to ministerial in-service training (clergy study days and conferences, continuing
ministerial training, etc.) concerned with the practices of preaching,
pastoral care, and the preparation and direction of baptisms, weddings,
and funerals. This will not be a case, in the first instance, of adding new
subjects to the curriculum of theological education and development
but rather of integrating mission and spirituality into the fundamental
self-understanding of the curriculum and its purpose, in all its aspects.

Such formation should be integral not only to theological training
for clergy, but also to continuing development of the clergy through formal training days and through the work of voluntary associations with
similar aims, such as those associated with "missional church" training
in the United States. Leander E. Keck makes the apposite point: "Where
does one begin? Where pastors already are and with what they are already doing—in the study and the pulpit, where one wrestles with the
truth about God who is praised in worship. Academic theologians can
renew theology *for* the churches, but it is preachers grappling with the

meaning of the faith for today who will renew it *in* the churches."[16] The distinction between the two may be too sharply drawn here but the point is to be taken. Examples of organizations that seek to enrich preaching are the evangelical Langham Partnership International, and the Church of England organization Praxis (http://www.praxisworship.org.uk), with its wider brief towards worship in general.

2. Informal Lay Ministry: Resourcing Christians in Secular Professions through Both Sector and Inter-Disciplinary Education

Normally each of the secular professions develops, with time, its own tradition of reflective, practical wisdom. Among the older professions in Western culture such as law, education, and health care, such traditions have been informed historically by a Christian imagination and a Christian spirit of service. Today the secular professions have largely lost contact (at least in their formal management, training, and policymaking) with these imaginative resources. Also, they are not uncommonly subject to pressures from government to pursue a program of economic rationalization framed by neoliberal ideology, on the one hand, and to defer uncritically to ideologically framed "rights" legislation, on the other. In this setting, Christians working in the secular professions are called to witness to the truth of Christ, bringing to their work a rich Christian rationality and the rich discernment and passion that come with mature spiritual formation.

The inculcation of this vision among lay Christians and the theological and spiritual formation that it requires to be operative, have been largely neglected by the churches. And where Christian groups have been formed they have tended to slip either towards private, personal, devotional, prayer/social support groups, or towards justice-oriented advocacy groups, each of which unknowingly reflect, in their limited vision and scope, secular habits of thought.

The inculcation of more faithful Christian vision and practice can be pursued in a variety of ways. It can be organized for each profession in a specific way, as was attempted by the "professions" arm of the Whitefield Institute of the Universities and College Christian Fellowship (the British equivalent of the InterVarsity Christian Fellowship) for a number of years. Another interesting recent example is Making Connections:

16. Keck, *Church Confident*, 67.

Reflecting on Christian Discipleship in Professional Practice, a project directed by Ian Barns in Perth, Australia.

Another approach brings together Christians from disparate professions. Here something is lost by way of focus on the issues specific to any given profession. Positively, however, this brings the advantage of a "synoptic" vision exposing basic ideological and secularist worldview assumptions common to a variety of professions today. For example, for six years I convened a Gospel and Cultures discussion group in Palmerston North, New Zealand, that was hosted by the local Anglican bishop, Brian Carrell, and comprised an ecumenical group of clergy, academics, and Christians working in non-academic lay professions.

Such informal groups of Christians need, like prayer groups, a core of people who have a certain spiritual and personal maturity and an openness to grow further in knowledge and obedience to God. Richard Foster calls such groups the *ecclesiola in ecclesia*—"the little church within the church." Such a group is, he writes, "deeply committed to the life of the people of God and is not sectarian in any way. No separation. No splitting off. No setting up a new denomination or church. We stay within the given church structures and develop little centers of light within those structures. And then we let our light shine!"[17]

Turning from informal groups to voluntary mission agencies, these face the challenge of integrating theological and spiritual formation more closely into their understanding of mission. I believe there is much yet to be learned if agencies will attend to this challenge together, interacting among themselves as they do so. In my British context such agencies include, amongst others, the Church Mission Society, the Bible Society, CARE, Damaris, Maranatha, The West Yorkshire School of Christian Studies, The Church Army, Faithworks, and The London Institute for Contemporary Christianity.

Such agencies bring their own vision and experience into conversation with each other. The same applies to networks that provide a forum for reflection among Christian practitioners who share a concern for engaging Western culture but follow the Christian way as "off-roaders" rather than working formally within any particular established church institution. Noteworthy examples of such "off-roaders" are Philip Sampson, Ian Barns, Douglas Knight, David Lyon, Stephen May, and Alan Storkey. The Gospel and Our Culture Network aspires to be one

17. Foster, "Spiritual Formation Agenda."

such loose network, enriching theologically reflective practice among individual Christians scattered in diverse circumstances.

Christian magazines offer another way of enriching theological reflection and spiritual formation among Christians immersed in a secularist world. Current examples of this are *Third Way* (Britain), *Stimulus* (New Zealand), *Zadok Perspectives* (Australia), and *First Things* (United States).

We might also note the more tacit contribution offered by the presence among us in the West of Christian immigrants from other cultures. These Christians not uncommonly recognize in contemporary Western culture that which is largely unrecognized by us ourselves: on the one hand, the continuing influence of Christianity on Western culture, and on the other, the ways in which our modern cultural assumptions diverge increasingly from Christian faith and capture and distort this faith itself. Christians need to listen and learn from these international arrivals through informal conversation and by more formal occasions such as presentations and interviews in the setting of local church events including worship.

Finally, it is vital that lay Christians be strengthened to embrace, in their professional life, suffering and victimhood in the name and spirit of Christ and not turn either to denial or despair. As we noted in chapter 3, Western culture is too often brutal today towards the best of practitioners and towards whistleblowers who are morally committed to think for themselves and to take a stand where appropriate. Michael Goheen quotes Lesslie Newbigin as saying, "The New Testament makes it plain that that Christ's followers must expect suffering as the normal badge of their discipleship, and also as one of the characteristic forms of their witness." He adds that the "encounter with anti-Christian ideological or religious beliefs is especially acute in the public sphere where the believer works."[18]

3. Institutional Christian Engagement with Secular Culture

As well as organizations that equip lay Christians for witness in the secular professions, there is need for Christian organizations that engage policymakers and gatekeepers in the secondary, public culture of politics, media, education, etc. They have a role participating in, and

---

18. Goheen, "Missional Calling of Believers," 49.

promoting, public debate on the fundamental purposes of managed public life and its consequent social organization, seen in the light of a rich Christian rationality. This may take the form of reasoned reports of the kind offered by think-tanks such as Theos in London and the Kirby Laing Institute for Christian Ethics in Cambridge. It may include the pursuit of wise policy decisions and advocacy in the face of injustice towards vulnerable groups and individuals (which sometimes includes Christians themselves today, in a dogmatically secularist society), of the kind offered by the British organization CARE. It may also include public apologetics. And it may include education in Christian literacy, in an age when the general population has grown illiterate in Christian faith and therefore vulnerable to adopting prevalent ideological prejudices against it—prejudices that, voiced by vociferous atheists like Richard Dawkins and Christopher Hitchens, articulate only "vacuous arguments afloat on oceans of historical ignorance, made turbulent by strident storms of self-righteousness."[19] An example of an agency providing such education is Lapido Media, directed by Jenny Taylor, which seeks to foster religious literacy in the mass media. The teaching of Christian literacy extends into teaching self-awareness of our Christian history. This includes understanding the Christian formation of our artistic heritage (literature, music, architecture, etc.), our personal values and judgments (individual dignity, a spirit of service, honesty, charity, marital faithfulness, etc.), modern social provision (health care, education, social welfare provision, and social reform—including abolition of the slave trade and women's rights), secular public life (justice, equality, rights, democracy, tolerance), and the worldview that was a prerequisite for the birth of experimental science. In each of these areas the aim must be not simply to provide information but to invite recognition that we inhabit still to some measure (perhaps largely unawares) a culture of lively regard, exploration, and response to Christian truth and goodness that call for our continuing lively regard, exploration, and response.

4. A Revived Adult Catechumenate

Introducing this topic in 1995, Brian Davis, Anglican archbishop of New Zealand, deserves quoting at length:

19. Hart, *Atheist Delusions*, 4.

The catechumenal process describes the way the early church evangelised, instructed, and incorporated new members into the worshipping and serving fellowship of the church. It involves an enquiry stage, a formation stage of basic instruction, an intensive candidacy stage (immediately prior to baptism, confirmation or renewal), and a reflection and training for ministry stage. Lay people are involved in the educational and formation process as supporters and catechists (or teachers). Learning takes place in a small group as the scriptures are read and discussed, and as the faith story of the people of God is seen to relate to the life journeys of the participants. The small group provides the opportunity for deep interpersonal sharing and reflection. And each of the main stages in the process are liturgically celebrated in the public life of the congregation. The whole congregation is involved in the formation of new Christians and is constantly reminded what it means to be a baptised people of God ... The catechumenate will also help the whole church understand that every baptised person is called to be both a disciple and a minis-ter, and not simply a customer and consumer. It directly involves the laity, as well as the clergy in the all-important task of making new Christians. It will help us to become a church more aware of our overall purpose and more free and obedient in mission ... The catechumenal process deserves wider application and the provision of supporting education and liturgical resources, while clergy and lay leaders need to be more aware of the implications and opportunities the changes have brought.[20]

A revived catechumenate should engage theologically with the secular ideologies that press upon new Christians and their thinking as described in this present book, while Davis's comment that every Christian "is called to be both a disciple and a minister, and not just a customer and consumer" reminds us of the need for a catechumenate that will nurture personal and spiritual formation in face of the cultural tendencies described in this book under the headings of narcissism, needy consumerism, and a tragic sense of life. James Packer has summa-rized this personal, spiritual formation aspect of adult catechesis under the headings of doxology, humility, generosity, honesty, intensity, bravery and solidarity, and realism about death.[21] There has been valuable con-sideration of catechism today by a number of writers, church bodies,

20. Davis, *Way Ahead,* 63–65.
21. Packer, "Reflection and Response," 6.

and conferences—not least within the Roman Catholic Church—all of which is a useful resource for further reflection and action in this area.

EMERGING CHURCH

"Emerging church" is a catch-all phrase for quite diverse explorations currently in process. There is great need here to sift wheat from chaff. Some of the positive potential in these explorations—at least as they are found in North America—has been identified, it seems to me, by Leander S. Harding. On his internet blog, in June 2009, he reflects on a conference on the relation between the emerging church and "the Great Tradition." [22] Let me quote him at some length:

> The Emergent Church is a term that characterizes a wide spectrum of Christians and churches often composed of young adults that are seeking an "ancient-future" way of being the church. These young Christians often come out of Evangelical and Pentecostal circles, though there are refugees from the Mainline churches as well, and they are looking for something more significant than the trendy consumerist relevance that has characterized many of the approaches to reaching a secularized society in the 20th century. It is a very disparate movement and includes examples that resonate deeply with the orthodoxy of the ages and other examples that seem, as one of the conference presenters George Sumner said, the latest instalment in the long book of Gnosticism.
>
> As I listened to the themes that were attracting these young Christians: a more narrative understanding of the message of the Bible, an interest in ancient practices of prayer and spiritual discipline, a turn toward the writings of the earliest Christian centuries of the Patristic period, an interest by formerly free church types in sacramental theology and in the theology of the church, I was struck by the way in which this movement is revamping much of what was good about the story of the church and theology in the 20th century.

Leander Harding believes we are in a moment when there is "a fresh wind of the Holy Spirit moving to renew the ecumenical church." He recalls movements of the Spirit in the course of the twentieth century: the impetus of the Edinburgh 1910 World Mission Conference, the rise of the biblical theology movement, the liturgical movement, the new em-

22. Harding, "Emergent Church." By "the Great Tradition" Harding means classical, orthodox Christianity as encapsulated in the creeds.

brace by churches of the poor and the marginalized, and the charismatic renewal. "All of these movements," he writes, "in some way brought with them a painful consciousness of the brokenness of the body of Christ as it faced the challenge of an increasingly hostile and secularized world. Out of the renewal in theology, liturgy and mission came a new desire for ecumenical healing and partnership."

What has happened to this heritage in the churches? Leander Harding is critical: "During the 20th century God gave to the broken and fractured global church a gift of the Holy Spirit, an ecumenical moment of mission and renewal. It was for the most part squandered and has been allowed to fall to the ground." Against this background, today is:

> a moment for repentance for those of us in the historic churches which have stewarded the Great Tradition but have lost touch with the life which generates the tradition and which carries it forward. It is also a moment of testing for that which is emerging. Will they marginalize doctrine and the labour of seeking a consensus in faith and order? Will they succumb to the motto that deeds unite and doctrine divides and then find themselves in the midst of church-dividing controversy with no deep doctrinal consensus to guide? Will they be lured into trivial and faddish relevancy and all too worldly politics at the expense of a more profound service of peace and justice? Will the established churches who are in a panic about their declining influence in the culture repent of quick fixes and pandering to culture and engage with a new generation in a deep renewal of the roots of Christian wisdom and practice? Will we all catch this new wind of the Spirit or let it pass us by?

Harding's closing comments bring us back to the issue highlighted at the beginning of this chapter: insights into modern Western culture, seen in the context of the gospel, have been presented by many writers in the course of the twentieth century. The challenge before the churches in the twenty-first century is to recognize these insights for what they are, and find liberation from a faith that is culturally domesticated and thereby betrays the gospel. The challenge is to draw upon these liberating insights in the practice of theologically informed, spiritually mature mission that desires nothing less than "the conversion of the West."

Bibliography

Abraham, William J. *The Logic of Evangelism*. London: Hodder & Stoughton, 1989.

Allchin, A. M. *The World Is a Wedding: Explorations in Christian Spirituality*. London: Darton, Longman & Todd, 1978.

Alston, William P. *Philosophy of Language*. Englewood Cliffs, NJ: Prentice-Hall, 1964.

Anonymous. *The Cloud of Unknowing*. Translated by Clifton Wolters. Harmondsworth, UK: Penguin, 1961.

Arendt, Hannah. *The Origins of Totalitarianism*. Rev. ed. London: Allen & Unwin, 1967.

Baillie, Donald. *God Was in Christ: An Essay on Incarnation and Atonement*. London: Faber & Faber, 1948.

Baillie, John. *Our Knowledge of God*. London: Oxford University Press, 1939.

———. *The Sense and the Presence of God: Gifford Lectures 1961–62*. London: Oxford University Press, 1962.

Barns, Ian. "Christianity in a Pluralist Society: A Dialogue with Lesslie Newbigin." *St Mark's Review* 158 (1994) 27–37.

———. "Contesting Secular Public-ness." In *God Down Under: Theology in the Antipodes*, edited by Winifred Lamb and Ian Barns, 241–60. Adelaide: ATF.

Barth, Karl. *Church Dogmatics*. Vol. IV/2: *The Doctrine of Reconciliation*. Translated by G. T. Thomson. Edinburgh: T. & T. Clark, 1958.

Bartholomew, Craig, and Michael W. Goheen. *The Drama of Scripture: Finding Our Place in the Biblical Story*. London: SPCK, 2006.

———. *Living at the Crossroads: An Introduction to Christian Worldview*. London: SPCK, 2008.

Bauman, Zygmunt. *Legislators and Interpreters: On Modernity, Postmodernity and Intellectuals*. Cambridge: Polity, 1987.

———. *Liquid Modernity*. Cambridge: Polity, 2000.

Beale, Gregory K. *We Become What We Worship*. Nottingham: InterVarsity, 2008.

Bellow, Saul. "The Distracted Public." In *It All Adds Up: From the Dim Past to the Uncertain Future: A Non-Fiction Collection*, 153–69. London: Viking, 1994.

Berger, Peter L. "In Praise of Particularity: The Concept of Mediating Structures." In *Facing Up to Modernity: Excursions in Society, Politics and Religion*, 167–80. New York: Basic, 1977.

———. *The Desecularization of the World: Resurgent Religion and World Politics*, edited by Peter L. Berger, 1–18. Grand Rapids: Eerdmans, 1999.

———. *The Heretical Imperative: Contemporary Possibilities of Religious Affirmation*. London: Collins, 1980.

Bevans, Stephen. *Models of Contextual Theology*. Maryknoll: Orbis, 1992.

Blamires, Harry. *Meat Not Milk*. Bromley: Marc Europe, 1988.

Blond, Phillip. *Red Tory: How Left and Right Have Broken Britain and How We Can Fix It.* London: Faber & Faber, 2010.

Bloom, Allan. *The Closing of the American Mind: How Higher Education Has Failed Democracy and Impoverished the Souls of Today's Students.* New York: Viking, 1988.

Bonhoeffer, Dietrich. *Christ the Center.* Translated by John Bowden. New York: Harper & Row, 1966.

———. *Letters and Papers from Prison.* Translated by Reginald H. Fuller. London: SCM, 1953.

Bosch, David J. *Believing in the Future: Toward a Missiology of Western Culture.* Valley Forge, PA: Trinity, 1995.

Boyle, Nicholas. "Understanding Thatcherism." In *Who Are We Now?*, 13–34. Edinburgh: T. & T. Clark, 1998.

Bretherton, Luke. *Hospitality as Holiness: Christian Witness amid Moral Diversity.* Aldershot, UK: Ashgate, 2006.

Bromwich, David. *Politics by Other Means: Higher Education and Group Thinking.* New Haven, CT: Yale University Press, 1992.

Caird, George B. *The Language and Imagery of the Bible.* London: Duckworth, 1980.

Cash, W. Wilson. *The Responsibility of Success.* London: CMS, 1934.

Charry, Ellen. *By the Renewing of Your Minds: The Pastoral Function of Christian Doctrine.* New York: Oxford University Press, 1997.

Chesterton, Gilbert K. *Tremendous Trifles.* London: Methuen, 1909.

———. *Orthodoxy.* London: John Lane, The Bodley Head, 1909.

Collis, David. "The Abuse of Consumerism." *Zadok Paper S101* (1999). Online: http://www.zadok.org.au/papers/collis/colliss10103.shtml.

Conway, Ruth. *Choices at the Heart of Technology: A Christian Perspective.* Harrisburg, PA: Trinity, 1999.

Cowling, Maurice. *Religion and Public Doctrine in Modern England*, vol. 3: *Accommodations.* Cambridge: Cambridge University Press, 2001.

Crossan, John Dominic. *The Dark Interval: Towards a Theology of Story.* Niles, IL: Argus, 1975.

Cupitt, Don. "Our Dual Agenda." *Sea of Faith* 23 (1995) 3–7.

Dalferth, Ingolf. "The Historical Roots of Theism." In *Traditional Theism and its Modern Alternatives*, edited by Svend Andersen, 15–43. Aarhus: Aarhus University Press, 1994.

———. *Theology and Philosophy.* Oxford: Blackwell, 1988.

Davie, Grace. "From Obligation to Consumption: Patterns of Religion in Northern Europe at the Start of the 21st Century." Online: http://www.eauk.org/_commission/commission/evidence/1%20From%20Obligation%20to%20Consumption.pdf.

Davis, Brian. *The Way Ahead: Anglican Change and Prospect in New Zealand.* Christchurch: Caxton, 1995.

Dawson, Christopher. *Religion and the Rise of Western Culture.* London: Sheed & Ward, 1950.

Donaldson, Terrance L. *Paul and the Gentiles.* Minneapolis: Fortress, 1997.

Donovan, Peter. "The Intolerance of Religious Pluralism." *Religious Studies* 29 (1993) 217–29.

Dooyeweerd, Herman. *A New Critique of Theoretical Thought*. Translated by David H. Freeman, Wiliam S. Young, and H. De Jongste. 4 vols. Jordan Station, Ontario: Paidea, 1984.

Drane, John. *Do Christians Know How to Be Spiritual?* London: DLT, 2005.

Dupré, Louis (interviewed). "Seeking Christian Interiority." *Christian Century*, July 16–23, 1997, 654–60.

Eagleton, Terry. *The Illusions of Postmodernism*. Oxford: Blackwell, 1996.

Ebeling, Gerhard. *Introduction to a Theological Theory of Language*. Translated by R. A. Wilson. London: Collins, 1973

———. *Word and Faith*. Translated by James W. Leach. London: SCM, 1963.

Elliot, T. S. "Notes Towards the Definition of Culture" (broadcast talk, 1948). In *Christianity and Culture: The Idea of a Christian Society and Notes towards the Definition of Culture*. New York: Harcourt Brace, 1968.

Ellul, Jacques. *The New Demons*. Translated by C. Edward Hopkin. New York: Seabury, 1975.

Evans, Robert A. "Human Rights in a Global Context." In *Human Rights: A Dialogue between the First and Third Worlds*, by Robert A. Evans and Alice Frazer Evans, 1–13. Maryknoll, NY: Orbis, 1983.

Farrer, Austin. *The Glass of Vision*. London: Dacre, 1948.

Finkielkraut, Alain. *The Undoing of Thought*. Translated by Dennis O'Keeffe. London: Claridge, 1988.

Ford, David. *The Shape of Living*. London: Fount, 1997.

Forsyth, P. T. "A Rallying Ground for the Free Churches: The Reality of Grace." *Hibbert Journal* 4 (1906) 824–44.

———. *Positive Preaching and the Modern Mind*. London: Independent, 1907.

———. "The Cross as the Final Seat of Authority." *The Contemporary Review* 76 (October 1899) 597–98.

———. *The Principle of Authority in Relation to Certainty, Sanctity, and Society: An Essay in the Philosophy of Experimental Religion*. London: Hodder and Stoughton, 1910.

Foster, Michael. "Mystery and the Philosophy of Analysis." In *Mystery and Philosophy*, 13–28. London: SCM, 1957.

———. "The Christian Doctrine of Creation and the Rise of Modern Natural Science." *Mind* 172 (1934) 446–68.

Foster, Richard. "Spiritual Formation Agenda," *Christianity Today* (January 2009). Online: http://www.christianitytoday.com/ct/2009/january/26.29.html.

Fukayama, Francis. *The End of History and the Last Man*. New York: Free, 1992.

Gadamer, Hans-Georg. *Truth and Method*. London: Sheed & Ward, 1975.

Gallagher, Michael Paul. "The Tone of Culture: From Prometheus to Narcissus. In *Struggles of Faith*, 84–93. Dublin: Columba, 1990.

———. *Clashing Symbols: An Introduction to Faith & Culture*. 2nd ed. London: Darton, Longman and Todd, 2003.

Gay, Craig M. "An Ironic Cage: The Rationalization of Modern Economic Life." In *Faith and Modernity*, edited by Philip Sampson, Vinay Samuel, and Chris Sugden, 252–72. Oxford: Regnum Lynx, 1994.

Girard, René. *I Saw Satan Fall like Lightning*. Translated by James G. Williams. Maryknoll, NY: Orbis, 2001.

Goheen, Michael. "The Missional Calling of Believers in the World: Lesslie Newbigin's Contribution." In *A Scandalous Prophet: The Way of Mission after Newbigin*, edited by T. Foust et al., 37–54.Grand Rapids: Eerdmans, 2002.

Goldacre, Ben. *Bad Science*. London: HarperCollins, 2008.

Goudzwaard, Bob. *Globalization and the Kingdom of God*. Grand Rapids: Baker, 1999.

———. *Idols of Our Time*. Translated by Mark Vander Vennen. Downer's Grove, IL: InterVarsity, 1981.

Goudzwaard, Bob, and Harry de Lange. *Beyond Poverty and Affluence: Toward an Economy of Care*. Translated by Mark Vander Vennen. Grand Rapids: Eerdmans, 1995.

Goudzwaard, Bob, Mark Vander Vennen, and David Van Heemst. *Hope in Troubled Times: A New Vision for Confronting Global Crises*. Grand Rapids: Baker, 2007.

Gray, John. "New Statesman Christmas Essay 1: The Myth of Secularism." *The New Statesman*, December 16, 2002. Online: http://www.newstatesman.com/20021216 0045.

Greene, Colin J. D. *Christology in Cultural Perspective: Marking Out the Horizons*. Carlisle: Paternoster, 2003.

Guinness, Os. *The Dust of Death: A Critique of the Establishment and the Counter Culture—and a Proposal for a Third Way*. London: InterVarsity, 1973.

Guinness, Os, and John Seely, editors. *No God but God: Breaking with the Idols of Our Age*. Chicago: Moodey, 1992.

Gunton, Colin. *The One, the Three and the Many*. Cambridge: Cambridge University Press, 1993.

Habermas, Jürgen. *An Awareness of What's Missing: Faith and Reason in a Post-Secular Age*. Cambrdge: Polity, 2010.

Hadley, Elaine. "The Past Is a Foreign Country: The Neo-Conservative Romance with Victorian Liberalism." *Yale Journal of Criticism* 10 (1997) 7–38.

Hamilton, Clive. *Growth Fetish*. Sydney: Allen & Unwin, 2003.

Hancock, Maxine. "Some Reflections on the Use of Language in the Stott-Spong Dialogue." *Crux* 294 (1993) 28–33.

Harding, Leander S. "Reflections on the Emerging Church after the Trinity Ancient Wisdom—Anglican Futures Conference." Online: http://www.leanderharding.com/blog (June 7, 2009).

Hardy, Daniel. "God and the Form of Society." In *The Weight of Glory: A Vision and Practice for Christian Faith: The Future of Liberal Theology: Essays for Peter Baelz*, edited by Daniel W. Hardy and P. H. Sedgwick, 131–44. Edinburgh: T. & T. Clark, 1991.

Hart, David Bentley. *Atheist Delusions: The Christian Revolution and Its Fashionable Enemies*. New Haven: Yale University Press, 2009.

Harvey, David. *A Brief History of Neoliberalism*. Oxford: Oxford University Press, 2005.

Hastings, Adrian. "The Twentieth Century." In *Christianity: Two Thousand Years*, edited by Richard Harries, 218–36. Oxford: Oxford University Press, 2001.

Havel, Václav. "The Power of the Powerless." In *Living in Truth*, 40–50. London: Faber and Faber, 1987.

Hay, David, and Kate Hunt. *Understanding the Spirituality of People Who Don't Go to Church*. Nottingham: Centre for the Study of Human Relations, University of Nottingham, 2000.

Heelas, Paul, Linda Woodhead, et al. *The Spiritual Revolution: Why Religion Is Giving Way to Spirituality.* Oxford: Blackwell, 2004.

Hiebert, Paul H. *Transforming Worldviews: An Anthropological Understanding of How People Change.* Grand Rapids: Baker Academic, 2008.

Himmelfarb, Gertrude. *The De-Moralization of Society: From Victorian Virtues to Modern Values.* New York: Knopf, 1995.

Hodges, John. "Given for Food: Creation and the Limits of Private Ownership." *The Gospel and Our Culture Network Newsletter* 53 (2008) 1–3.

Hodgson, Peter. *Theology and Modern Physics.* Aldershot: Ashgate, 2006.

Hooykaas, R. *Religion and the Rise of Modern Science.* Edinburgh: Scottish Academic, 1972.

Houston, James. *The Hungry Soul: What We Long for and Why It Matters.* Oxford: Lion, 1992.

Hütter, Reinhard. "The Church as Public: Dogma, Practice and the Holy Spirit." *Pro Ecclesia* 3 (1994) 334–61.

Jaki, Stanley. *The Road to Science and the Ways to God.* Edinburgh: Scottish Academic, 1978.

James, Oliver. *Affluenza.* London: Vermilion, 2007.

James, William. *A Pluralistic Universe.* New York: Longmans, Green, & Co., 1909.

Jenkins, Tim. "Sacred Persons." In *The Gestures of God,* edited by Geoffrey Rowell and Christine Hall, 57–72. London: Continuum, 2004.

Julian of Norwich. *Showings.* Translated by Edmund Colledge and James Walsh. New York: Paulist, 1978.

Kavanaugh, John F. *Following Christ in a Consumer Society: The Spirituality of Cultural Resistance.* 2nd ed. Maryknoll: Orbis, 1991.

Keat, Russell, et al., editors. *The Authority of the Consumer.* London: Routledge, 1994.

Keck, Leander E. *The Church Confident.* Nashville: Abingdon, 1993.

Kettle, David. "Bearings on the Sea of Faith." *Leading Light* (1995) 17–19, 26.

———. *Beyond Tragic Spirituality.* Cambridge: Grove, 2005.

———. "Cartesian Habits and the 'Radical Line' of Enquiry." *Tradition and Discovery* 27 (2000–2001) 22–32. Online: http://www.missouriwestern.edu/orgs/polanyi/TAD WEB ARCHIVE/TAD27-1/TAD27-1-pg22-32-pdf.pdf.

———. "Knowledge, Context and Evasion." Online: http://www.davidkettle.org.uk.

———. "Three Actors with Interchangeable Roles?: Christian, Modern, and Postmodern Thinking." Online: www.davidkettle.org.uk.

———. "Truth and Dialogue: Polanyi, Gadamer, and Theological Hermeneutics." In *Michael Polanyi and Christian Theology,* edited by Murray Rae. Forthcoming.

———. "When John Spong Met Don Cupitt." *Stimulus* 5.3 (1997) 17–21.

Kirk, J. Andrew. *The Mission of Theology and the Theology of Mission.* Valley Forge, PA: Trinity, 1997.

Kohut, Heinz. *The Analysis of the Self: A Systematic Approach to the Psychoanalytic Treatment of Narcissistic Personality Disorders.* New York: International Universities Press, 1971.

Lasch, Christopher. *The Culture of Narcissism: American Life in an Age of Diminishing Expectations.* New York: Norton, 1979.

———. *The Minimal Self: Psychic Survival in Troubled Times,* London: Picador, 1985.

Leech, Ken. *The Sky Is Red.* London: Darton, Longman & Todd, 1997.

Leeuwen, Arend Theodoor van. *Christianity in World History: The Meeting of the Faiths of East and West.* London: Edinburgh House, 1964.

Lewis, C. S. "Imagination and Thought in the Middle Ages." In *Studies in Medieval and Renaissance Literature.* Cambridge: Cambridge University Press, 1966.

———. *Poems.* Edited by Walter Hooper. London: Bles, 1964.

———. *The Lion, the Witch and the Wardrobe.* London: Bles, 1950.

———. *The Business of Heaven: Daily Readings.* London: Fount, 1984

Linden, Nico ter. "In the Middle of Winter." Translated by Jan van Royen. In *Candour* Special Supplement, September 1994. New Zealand.

Lubac, Henri de. *The Discovery of God.* Translated by Alexander Dru. Edinburgh: T. & T. Clark, 1996.

Long, Thomas G. "Myers-Briggs and other Modern Astrologies." *Theology Today* 49 (1992) 291–95

Lund, James. "Platonism, Pragmatism and the History of Philosophy." Unpublished.

Lyon, David. *Jesus in Disneyland: Religion in Postmodern Times.* Cambridge: Polity, 2000.

———. *Surveillance Society: Monitoring Everyday Life.* Buckingham: Open University Press, 2001.

MacDonald, George. "Love Thine Enemy." In *Unspoken Sermons, First Series,* 217–31. London: Strahan, 1867.

———. "Life." In *Unspoken Sermons, Second Series.* 138–56. London: Strahan, 1886.

MacIntyre, Alasdair C. *After Virtue: A Study in Moral Theory.* London: Duckworth, 1981.

Macmurray, John. *Freedom in the Modern World.* London: Faber & Faber, 1932.

———. *The Self as Agent: The Gifford Lectures for 1953.* London: Faber & Faber, 1953.

Marcel, Gabriel. "A Metaphysical Diary." In *Being and Having,* translated by Katharine Farrer, 9–13. London: Dacre, 1949.

———. "Some Thoughts on Faith." In *Being and Having.* Translated by Katharine Farrer. 203–16. London: Dacre, 1949.

Marcuse, Herbert. *One-Dimensional Man: Studies in the Ideology of Advanced Industrial Society.* London: Routledge & Kegan Paul, 1964.

Marty, Martin E. *The Modern Schism: Three Paths to the Secular.* London: SCM, 1969.

Matthews, Melvyn. *Delighting in God.* London: Fount, 1987.

Maushart, Susan. *The Winter of Our Disconnect: How Three Totally Wired Teenagers (and a Mother Who Slept with Her iPhone) Pulled the Plug on Their Technology and Lived to Tell the Tale.* New York: Penguin, 2011.

May, Stephen. "Beowulf and Cultural Conflict." *Gospel and Our Culture Network Newsletter* 51 (2008) 5–6. Online: http//www.gospel-culture.org.uk/2008.htm.

May, Stephen. *Stardust and Ashes: Science Fiction in Christian Perspective.* London: SPCK, 1998.

McFadyen, Alister. *Bound to Sin: Abuse, Holocaust and the Christian Doctrine of Sin.* Cambridge: Cambridge University Press, 2000.

McLellan, David. *Ideology.* 2nd ed. Buckingham: Open University Press, 1995.

McMillan, Joyce. "A Christian Evolution Holds Key to Tolerance." *The Scotsman*, March 5, 2005.

Meštrović, Stjepan. *Postemotional Society.* London: Sage, 1997.

Midgley, Mary. *Science as Salvation: A Modern Myth and Its Meaning.* London: Routledge, 1992.

Milbank, John. "On Complex Space." In *The Word Made Strange: Theology, Language, Culture*, 268–92. Oxford: Blackwell, 1997.

Milner, Austin. "Reflections on Easter with the Lay Benedictines." *Listen* (Summer 2010) 20.

Mirowski, Philip. "Economics, Science, and Knowledge: Polanyi vs. Hayek." *Tradition & Discovery* 25 (1998–99) 29–36.

Moltmann, Jürgen. *Theology of Hope: On the Ground and the Implications of a Christian Eschatology*. Translated by James W. Leitch. London: SCM, 1967.

Moore, Peter. *Disarming the Secular Gods: Sharing Your Faith So that People Will Listen*. Leicester: InterVarsity, 1989.

Morris, Colin. *The Discovery of the Individual, 1050–1200*. London: Harper & Row, 1972.

Morris, Kevin L., editor. *The Truest Fairy Tale: An Anthology of the Religious Writings of G. K. Chesterton*. Cambridge: Lutterworth, 2007.

Murphy, Nancy. *Beyond Liberalism and Fundamentalism: How Modern and Postmodern Philosophy Set the Theological Agenda*. Valley Forge, PA: Trinity, 1996.

Naugle, David K. *Worldview: The History of a Concept*. Michigan: Eerdmans, 2002.

Newbigin, Lesslie. "Can a Modern Society Be Christian?" In *Christian Witness in Society: a Tribute to M. M. Thomas*, edited by K. C. Abraham, 95–108. Bangalore: Serampore College, 1998.

———. *Foolishness to the Greeks: The Gospel and Western Culture*. London: SPCK, 1986.

———. *Honest Religion for Secular Man*. London: SCM, 1966.

———. "Human Flourishing in Faith, Fact and Fantasy." *Religion and Medicine* 7 (1988) 400–412.

———. "New Birth into a Living Hope." Keynote address to the European Area Council of the World Alliance of Reformed Churches, Edinburgh, 1995. Online: http://www.newbigin.net/assets/pdf/95nblh.pdf.

———. "The German Outlook Today." *The Student Movement* 35.2 (1932) 31–32.

———. *The Light Has Come: An Exposition of the Fourth Gospel*. Grand Rapids: Eerdmans, 1982.

———. "The Summons to Christian Mission Today." *International Review of Missions* 48 (1959) 177–89.

———. *Truth and Authority in Modernity*. Leominister, UK: Gracewing, 1996.

Newman, Elizabeth. *Untamed Hospitality: Welcoming God and Other Strangers*. Grand Rapids: Brazos, 2007.

Niebuhr, H. Richard. *Christ and Culture*. New York: Harper, 1951.

Noll, Mark A. *The Scandal of the Evangelical Mind*. Grand Rapids: Eerdmans, 1995.

Novak, Michael. *The Spirit of Democratic Capitalism*. New York: Simon & Schuster, 1982.

Numbers, Ronald L. *The Creationists: The Evolution of Scientific Creationism*. Berkeley: University of California Press, 1993.

Nurser, John. *For All Peoples and All Nations: Christian Churches and Human Rights*. Geneva: World Council of Churches, 2005.

O'Donovan, Joan Lockwood. "Rights, Law and Political Community: A Theological and Historical Perspective." *Transformation* 20 (2003) 30–38.

O'Donovan, Oliver. *The Desire of the Nations: Rediscovering the Roots of Political Theology*. Cambridge: Cambridge University Press, 1996.

————. *The Ways of Judgment.* Grand Rapids: Eerdmans, 2005.

Oldham, J. H. *The Christian Newsletter* (Oct 15). London: Council on the Christian Faith and the Common Life, 1939.

————. *The World and the Gospel.* London: United Council for Missionary Education, 1916.

Osborn, Lawrence. *Angels of Light,* London: Darton, Longman & Todd, 1992.

————. *Restoring the Vision: The Gospel and Modern Culture.* London: Mowbray, 1995.

Ovid, *Metamorphoses,* book 3. Bristol, UK: Bristol Classical, 1991.

Packard, Vance. *The Hidden Persuaders.* Harmondsworth, UK: Penguin, 1957.

Packer, James I. "On from Orr: The Cultural Crisis, Rational Realism, and Incarnational Ontology." *Crux* 32.3 (1996) 12–26.

————. "Reflection and Response." *Crux* 43.1 (2007) 2–12.

Palmer, Sue. *Toxic Childhood.* London: Orion, 2006.

Pannenberg, Wolfhart. *Christianity in a Secularized World.* London: SCM, 1988.

————. *What Is Man? Contemporary Anthropology in Theological Perspective.* Translated by Duane A. Priebe. Philadephia: Fortress, 1970.

Parry, J. and Maurice Bloch. "Introduction: Money and the Morality of Exchange." In *Money and the Morality of Exchange,* 1–32. Cambridge: Cambridge University Press, 1989.

Pascal, Blaise. *Pensées.* Translated by Martin Turnbull. London: Harvill, 1962.

Péguy, Charles. *Portal of the Mystery of Hope.* Translated by David Louis Schindler Jr. Edinburgh: T. & T. Clark, 1996.

Pelikan, Jaroslav. *Jesus through the Centuries: His Place in the History of Culture.* New Haven: Yale University Press, 1985.

Peskett, Howard, and Vinoth Ramachandra. *The Message of Mission: The Glory of Christ in All Time and Space.* Leicester: InterVarsity, 2003.

Peterson, Eugene. "Spirituality for All the Wrong Reasons." *Christianity Today,* March 2005, 42–48.

————. "What's Wrong with Spirituality?" *Christianity Today,* July 1998, 54–55.

Pieper, Joseph. *Über die Hoffnung.* Munich: Kosel, 1949.

Pipes, Daniel. "The Western Mind of Radical Islam." *First Things* 58 (1995) 18–23.

Pius XI. *Quadragesimo Anno.* Encyclical promulgated on May 15, 1931.

Pohl, Christine D. *Making Room: Recovering Hospitality as a Christian Tradition.* Grand Rapids: Eerdmans, 1999.

Polanyi, Michael. *Knowing and Being: Essays by Michael Polanyi.* London: Routledge & Kegan Paul, 1969.

————. *Personal Knowledge: Towards a Post-Critical Philosophy.* London: Routledge & Kegan Paul, 1958.

————. "The English and the Continent." *The Political Quarterly,* October–December 1943, 372–81.

————. *The Tacit Dimension.* Garden City, NY: Anchor, 1967.

————. "Why Did We Destroy Europe?" *Studium Generale* 23.20 (1970) 909–16.

Postman, Neil. *Amusing Ourselves to Death: Public Discourse in the Age of Show Business.* London: Methuen, 1985.

————. *Technopoly: The Surrender of Culture to Technology.* New York: Knopf, 1993.

Putnam, Robert. "Bowling Alone: America's Declining Social Capital." *Journal of Democracy* 6 (1995) 65–78.

Ramachandra, Vinoth. "Learning from Modern European Secularism: A View from the Third World Church." *European Journal of Theology* 12 (2003) 35–48.

———. *Subverting Global Myths: Theology and the Public Issues Shaping Our World.* London: SPCK, 2008.

Ramsey, Ian T. *Christian Empiricism.* Studies in Philosophy and Religion 1. London: Sheldon, 1974.

———. *Religious Language: An Empirical Placing of Religious Phrases.* London: SCM, 1957.

Rieff, Philip. *The Triumph of the Therapeutic: Uses of Faith after Freud.* 2nd ed. Chicago: Chicago University Press 1987.

Riesman, David. *The Lonely Crowd.* New Haven: Yale University Press, 1961.

Roo, Anne de. *Becoming Fully Human.* Palmerston North, New Zealand: Church Mouse, 1991.

Sampson, Philip J., et al., editors. *Faith and Modernity.* Oxford: Regnum, 1994.

Sampson, Philip J. *Six Modern Myths about Christianity and Western Civilization.* Leicester: InterVarsity, 2001.

Schindler, David. "Mystery and Mastery: Philosophical Reflections on Biblical Epistemology." In *The Bible and Epistemology*, edited by Mary Healy and Robin Parry, 181–98. Carlisle: Paternoster, 2007.

———. "Neoconservative Economics and the Church's 'Authentic Theology of Integral Human Liberation.'" In *Heart of the World, Center of the Church: Communion Ecclesiology, Liberalism, and Liberation*, 114–42. Grand Rapids: Eerdmans, 1996.

Schouls, Peter. "John Locke and the Rise of Western Fundamentalism: An Hypothesis." *Religious Studies and Theology* 10 (1990) 9–22.

———. "Revolution and Postmodernism." Inaugural professorial lecture, faculty of humanities, Massey University, New Zealand, 1996. Unpublished.

Scott, Drusilla. *Everyman Revived: The Common Sense of Michael Polanyi.* Grand Rapids: Eerdmans, 1995.

Sennett, Richard. *The Fall of Public Man.* London: Faber & Faber, 1977.

Sherrard, Philip. *The Greek East and the Latin West: A Study in the Christian Tradition.* London: Oxford University Press, 1959.

Sire, James. *The Universe Next Door: A Basic Worldview Catalog.* Downer's Grove, IL: InterVarsity, 1976.

Smith, James K. A. *Desiring the Kingdom: Worship, Worldview, and Cultural Formation.* Grand Rapids: Baker, 2009.

Soskice, Janet Martin. *Metaphor and Religious Language.* Oxford: Clarendon, 1985.

Spong, John. "Closing Conference Address." *Sea of Faith* 23 (1995) 18–19.

———. "Religion as a Human Creation." *Sea of Faith* 23 (1995) 7–12.

Squire, Aelred. *Asking the Fathers.* London: SPCK, 1973.

Steiner, George. *The Death of Tragedy.* London: Faber & Faber, 1961.

———. *Real Presences: Is There Anything in What We Say?* London: Faber & Faber, 1989.

Stivers, Richard. *Technology as Magic: The Triumph of the Irrational.* New York: Continuum, 1999.

Storkey, Alan. "The Surrogate Sciences." *Philosophia Reformata* 51 (1986) 110–16.

Talbot, John Michael. *The World Is My Cloister: Living from the Hermit Within.* New York: Orbis, 2010.

Street-Porter, Janet. *Don't Let the B*****ds Get You Down.* London: Quadrille, 2009.

Tarnas, Richard. *The Passion of the Western Mind: Understanding the Ideas that Have Shaped Our World View.* New York: Ballantine, 1993.

Tavener, John. "Notes from the Celestial City." *Third Way* 21.10 (1998) 18–21.

Tawney, R. H. *Religion and the Rise of Capitalism: A Historical Study.* London: Murray, 1928.

———. *The Acquisitive Society.* New York: Brace and Howe, 1920.

Taylor, Charles. *A Secular Age.* London: Belknap, 2007.

Taylor, Jenny. *After Secularism: Inner-City Governance and the New Religious Discourse.* PhD diss., School of Oriental and African Studies, London, 2001.

Taylor, John V. *The Uncancelled Mandate: Four Bible Studies on Christian Mission for the Approaching Millennium.* Board of Mission Occasional Paper 8. London: Church House, 1998.

Tilby, Angela. "Like the Appearance of Lamps . . ." *Theology* 97 (1994) 322–31.

Torrance, Alan. *Persons in Communion: An Essay on Trinitarian Description and Human Participation.* Edinburgh: T. & T. Clark, 1996.

———. "Theology and Political Correctness." In *Harmful Religion*, edited by Lawrence Osborn and Andrew Walker, 99–121. London: SPCK, 1997.

Torrance, Thomas F. "Questioning in Jesus." In *Theology in Reconstruction*, 117–27. London: SCM, 1965.

Traherne, Thomas. *Centuries of Meditations.* London: Dobell, 1908.

Turner, Denys. *The Darkness of God: Negativity in Christian Mysticism.* Cambridge: Cambridge University Press, 1995.

Turner, Harold. *Frames of Mind: A Public Philosophy for Religion & Cultures.* Auckland: DeepSight Trust, 2001.

———. *The Roots of Science: An Investigative Journey through the World's Religions.* Auckland: DeepSight Trust, 1998.

Visser 't Hooft, W. A. "Evangelism among Europe's Neo-Pagans." *International Review of Mission* 66 (1977) 349–60.

———. *None Other Gods.* New York: Harper & Brothers, 1937.

Wainwright, Geoffrey. *Lesslie Newbigin: A Theological Life.* New York: Oxford University Press, 2000.

Walls, Andrew F. "Culture and Coherence in Christian History." In *The Missionary Movement in Christian History: Studies in the Transmission of Faith*, 16–25. Edinburgh: T. & T. Clark, 1996.

———. "'A History of the Expansion of Christianity' Reconsidered: The Legacy of George E. Day." Occasional Publication 8. New Haven: Yale Divinity School Library, 1996.

Walsh, Brian J., and J. Richard Middleton. *The Transforming Vision: Shaping a Christian World View.* Downer's Grove: InterVarsity, 1984.

Walter, Tony. *All You Love Is Need.* London: SPCK, 1985.

Ward, Hannah, and Jennifer Wild, editors. *Human Rites: Worship Resources for an Age of Change.* London: Mowbray, 1995.

Wells, David F. *God in the Wasteland: The Reality of Truth in a World of Fading Dreams.* Leicester: InterVarsity, 1994.

West, Patrick. *Conspicuous Compassion: Why Sometimes It Really Is Cruel to Be Kind.* London: Civitas, 2004.

Weston, Paul. *Lesslie Newbigin: Missionary Theologian—a Reader.* London: SPCK, 2006.

Wickham, E. R. *Church and People in an Industrial City.* London: Lutterworth, 1957.

Wilkinson, Richard, and Kate Pickett. *The Spirit Level: Why More Equal Societies Almost Always Do Better*. London: Allen Lane, 2009.

Williams, Rowan, "Against Anxiety, beyond Triumphalism." In *Open to Judgement*, 267–79. London: Darton, Longman and Todd, 1994.

———. "Archbishop's Address to Faith Leaders in Birmingham." November 16, 2008. Online: http://www.archbishopofcanterbury.org/2035.

———. "Doing the Works of God." In *Open to Judgement*, 253–66. London: Darton, Longman and Todd, 1994.

———. *Lost Icons: Reflections on Cultural Bereavement*. Edinburgh: T. & T. Clark, 2000.

Wilshire, Bruce. *The Moral Collapse of the University: Professionalism, Purity, and Alienation*. Albany, NY: State University of New York Press, 1990.

Witte, John, Jr. "The Spirit of the Laws, the Laws of the Spirit: Religion and Human Rights in a New Global Era." In *God and Globalization*, vol. 2: *The Spirit and the Modern Authorities*, edited by Max L. Stackhouse with Don S. Browning, 76–106. Harrisburg, PA: Trinity, 2001.

Woodhead, Linda. "Should Churches Look Outward, Not Inward?" *Church Times*, December 31, 2004.

Wright, Chris. *Old Testament Ethics for the People of God*. Leicester: InterVarsity, 2004.

Wuthnow, Robert. "The Moral Crisis in American Capitalism." *Harvard Business Review* 60 (1982) 76–84.

Yates, Timothy. "Reading John V. Taylor." *International Bulletin of Missionary Research* 30.3 (July 2006) 153.

Yeager, D. M. "Confronting the Minotaur: Moral Inversion and Michael Polanyi's Moral Philosophy." *Tradition and Discovery* 29 (2002–2003) 22–48.

Yiannis, Gabriel, and Tim Lang. *The Unmanageable Consumer: Contemporary Consumption and Its Fragmentation*. 2nd ed. London: Sage, 2006.

Yu, Carver T. "Sabbath with a Mission: Research for the Cutting Edge of the Christian Faith." Online: http://www.cgst.edu/Publication/Bulletin/English/2001JulSep/1.html.

———. "Teaching the Faith." *Gospel and Our Culture Network Newsletter* 35 (2002) 3–4.

———. "The Concept of Being as Being-in-Itself in the Western Tradition." In *Being and Relation: A Theological Critique of Western Dualism and Individualism*, 64–114. Edinburgh: Scottish Academic, 1987.

———. "Truth and Authentic Humanity." Plenary Address at the Gospel and Our Culture Consultation, Swanwick, 1992. Unpublished.

Zizioulas, John D. *Being as Communion: Studies in Personhood and the Church*. Crestwood, NY: St. Vladimir's Seminary Press, 1985.

Author Index